D1706853

A Few Interested Residents

A Few Interested Residents:

Wyoming Historical Markers & Monuments

written and compiled by
Mike Jording

Copyright © 1992 by Mike Jording

All rights reserved, including the right to reproduce this book or parts thereof, in any
form, except for the inclusion of brief quotations in a review.

Library of Congress Catalog Card Number: 92-70250
ISBN: 1-56044-135-6

Published by Mike Jording, P.O. Box 594,
Newcastle, Wyoming 82701, in cooperation with
SkyHouse Publishers, an imprint of Falcon Press Publishing Co., Inc.,
Helena, Montana.

Design, typesetting, and other prepress work by Falcon Graphics,
Helena, Montana.

Distributed by Falcon Press Publishing Co., Inc., P.O. Box 1718,
Helena, Montana 59624, or call 1-800-582-2665.

Manufactured in the United States of America.

Acknowledgments:

Thanks to "a Few Interested Residents"

When I married my wife in 1983, she had no idea that Wyoming historical markers were so interesting! I gave her a sampling of the roadside signs when we traveled across Wyoming on a honeymoon in January 1983. In the next few years we talked about my "vision" to make a book of the Wyoming markers. With her blessing and encouragement in 1988, I started the project that consumed nearly all of "our" free time and vacation time for three years. For her willingness to help, patience in adversity, and encouragement through the years, I owe her a handful of hugs and thank-yous and a vacation wherever she wants to go!

Joey joined our family in 1984, and Alex came in 1986. I engrained in their minds that historical markers were fun and interesting. For three years they thought we were vacationing while we looked at all of those markers! For their patience and understanding, for their help and interest, I thank them for being the best little boys in the state of Wyoming.

The State of Wyoming employees have been ever so cooperative. I know that there were many who helped me, but some deserve special mention. Sheila Bricher-Wade, Richard Collier, and Mark Junge at the State Historic Preservation Office encouraged and guided me along from the very first days of my research. Even though they were initially skeptical about the project being completed, I thank them for helping me out from day one. Cindy Brown and Paula West Chavoya from the Wyoming State Archives, Museums, and Historical Department directed me to many files of useful marker information and photos. They were able to offer new insights into the history of the marker programs.

Lee Underbrink of the Oregon California Trails Association provided all of the information about OCTA, as well as much useful information about the markers he had visited in all of his travels. I am indebted to him for his cooperation, and I hope that his reservations about publicizing historical markers will not lead to the destruction or loss of any of Wyoming's historical marker treasures.

The Bureau of Land Management cooperated with me by providing information and pictures of many of their signs. Without that help and the BLM's *Oregon/Mormon Pioneer National Historic Trails Management Plan* that outlined the BLM's preservation effort and provided much Oregon Trail history, my work would have been incomplete in many areas.

There were many people who I met as I traveled across Wyoming looking for and researching historical markers. Some were landowners, historians, museum directors, or librarians; some were old, and some were young. Many had genuine interests in markers and historical preservation. For all of their help I owe them all a big thank-you.

TABLE OF CONTENTS

The History of Wyoming's Historical Markers and Monuments

Wyoming Historical Markers and Monuments

The History of Wyoming's Historical Markers and Monuments

Historical Monuments—Why?

The Union Pacific Railroad Company started Wyoming's historical marking efforts in 1875. In honor of the two brothers who developed the transcontinental railroad, company stockholders voted to build Ames Monument. In those days, the whole idea of historical marking must have seemed a bit eccentric. Many people, no doubt, asked "Why?"

Why spend $65,000 to build a stone monument on a windy hill next to Sherman, Wyoming? Why place a bronze plaque of Ezra Meeker on Independence Rock? Why erect an informative sign at Field City? Why mark the corner where Colorado, Nebraska, and Wyoming meet? Why memorialize Bomber Peak? Well, there were answers to those questions in 1875. And those answers have lived on into twentieth-century Wyoming. In fact, because of those first historically-minded people, Wyoming became a leader in historic preservation and historical marking.

Historical markers and monuments expressed the continuity between past and present and reconstructed history in a way the public could appreciate and enjoy. Marking was not a subject of academic study in the 1800s. Even in the early twentieth century, there was no systematic plan for historical marking. There were, however, a few individuals who recognized the need to save the past. Those early leaders were, in all likelihood, a bit out of step with the mainstream. While most folks were just trying to feed their families or survive nature's hardships, the early leaders of marking efforts were recording and preserving history for their children and grandchildren. Not infrequently, those placing historical markers worked alone or in pairs on desolate stretches of the Oregon Trail. Historical marking wasn't a science; it was more an instinct, something that some individuals bore inside themselves. Many had experienced firsthand the harshness of emigration and the hardships of pioneers. From those experiences, the early preservationists developed a desire to pass their memories on to others.

But simple, unschooled, historical instinct wasn't intended to last forever. In 1966, the need to make the process more concrete led to the passage of the National Historic Preservation Act. Acknowledging that the spirit and direction of the nation was reflected in its historic past, the act defined these aims of historical marking and preservation: to preserve our historical and cultural foundations as a living part of our community life and development, and to give a sense of orientation to the American people.

Historical marking in Wyoming took on many forms, but the unifying feature of all marking efforts was that they told a story. Every marker preserved a feature of the state that might otherwise have been lost. Just as historical monuments, collectively, tell the story of Wyoming history, this book tells the story of historical monuments in the state. It chronicles the efforts of many of the major groups that have worked in the preservation of historic sites and in historical marking. Wyoming historical markers are a part of history themselves, and the story of how, why, when, and where is the subject of these pages.

Ezra Meeker, the Oregon Trail Memorial Association, and the American Pioneer Trails Association

Ezra Meeker was born in Huntsville, Ohio, in 1830. He migrated with his wife to the Oregon country in 1852. To him the Oregon Trail was a "symbol of the heroism, the patriotism, the vision, and the sacrifices of the pioneers who had won the West for America," and he pioneered the preservation effort to mark historic spots along the Trail.

When he began his first campaign in March 1906, there were only twenty-two monuments on the entire route. Meeker traveled by covered wagon—pulled by oxen—for fifteen months, from Puget Sound to Independence, Missouri. He later traveled by covered wagon to and from Washington, D.C.—another thirteen months—where he lobbied for a congressional bill appropriating $50,000 to mark the Trail. By 1908 Meeker's efforts had resulted "in the immediate or later erection of over one hundred fifty monuments to the memory of the Oregon pioneers and the trail that they blazed across the continent." He described the construction of the South Pass marker in *Ox-Team Days:*

> On June 22 we were still camped at Pacific Springs. I had searched for a suitable stone for a monument to be placed on the summit of the range, and, after almost despairing of finding one, had come upon exactly what was wanted. The stone lay alone on the mountain side; it is granite, I think, but mixed with quartz, and is a monument hewed by the hand of Nature.
>
> ...With the help of four men we loaded the stone, after having dragged it on the ground and over the rocks a hundred yards or so down the mountain side. We estimated its weight at a thousand pounds.
>
> ...The letters were then cut out with a cold chisel, deep enough to make a permanent inscription. The stone was so hard that it required steady work all day to cut the twenty letters and figures:
>
> THE OREGON TRAIL, 1843-57.

Meeker's early marking efforts succeeded only because of his vision and ambition. He was a national leader in historic preservation and left his impact in every state along the Trail.

2.

1. Ezra Meeker began historical marking and preservation of the Oregon Trail before 1906.

2. Ezra Meeker and his oxen-led covered wagon. In 1906, Meeker traveled the Oregon Trail from Puget Sound in Washington to the Missouri River at Independence, Missouri.

3. Ezra Meeker met Governor Brooks in Cheyenne in 1906.

3.

1. The citizens of Kemmerer and the Oregon Trail Memorial Association erected this handsome marker in 1931 in the city park in downtown Kemmerer.

2. The Oregon Trail Memorial Association bronze plaque portrayed a covered wagon led by an oxen team walking into the setting sun.

Ezra Meeker influenced many Wyoming efforts to mark and memorialize historic trails and sites. He had fond memories of Split Rock, Devil's Gate, and Independence Rock—all of which are now marked with interpretive displays and other plaques. In Cokeville, Meeker and the local citizens erected a marker which still stands as a symbol of the sacrifices of the pioneers. And the people of Casper, Glenrock, and Douglas all built monuments based on his influence.

When he first traveled the Oregon Trail in 1852, Meeker was especially impressed by Fort Laramie. However, he was disillusioned on the return trip in 1906. Again, from Meeker's *Ox-Team Days:*

There is no vestige of the old traders' camp or the first United States fort left. The new fort—not a fort, but an encampment—covers a space of thirty or forty acres, with all sorts of buildings and ruins...The old place is crumbling away, slowly disappearing with the memories of the past.

Ezra Meeker's visions eventually led to the creation of the Oregon Trail Memorial Association. He was elected the first president of the association in his late nineties. Although an aging pioneer with but a few years to live, Meeker visited western cities to rally new support. In Pocatello, Idaho, he met with a local group who planned to mint a memorial coin to finance markers and preservation programs. The Trail Association joined forces with the Idaho group to lead a national movement known as the Memorial Coin Bill. Sponsored by Addison Smith, representative from Idaho, and Wesley Jones, senator from Washington, the bill authorized the coinage and sale of Oregon Trail Memorial Fifty-Cent Pieces

in commemoration of the heroism of the fathers and mothers who traversed the Oregon Trail to the Far West with great hardship, daring, and loss of life, which not only resulted in adding new states to the Union but earned a well-deserved and imperishable fame for the pioneers; to honor the twenty thousand dead that lie buried in unknown graves along two thousand miles of that great highway of history; to rescue the various important points along the old trail from oblivion; and to commemorate by suitable monuments, memorial or otherwise, the tragic events associated with that emigration—erecting them either along the Trail itself or elsewhere, in localities appropriate for the purpose, including the city of Washington.

The bill was approved on May 17, 1926, and "six million silver half-dollar coins were placed at the command of the Oregon Trail Memorial Association to carry on the work of perpetuating the pioneer story."

Ezra Meeker died on December 3, 1928, at the age of ninety-eight. The members of the Trail Association resolved "to carry on the work for which the dauntless old pioneer had struggled." Their efforts were directed towards uniting all groups engaged in historical preservation and memorialization: historical societies, Boy Scouts and Girl Scouts, Sons and Daughters of the Pioneers, and Sons and Daughters of the American Revolution.

First, the leaders of the association spoke in Casper with Robert S. Ellison, ex-governor Bryant B. Brooks, Senator Thomas Cooper, Dan W. Greenburg, and Richard Evans—all of whom had been instrumental in the development of the Wyoming Historical Landmark Commission, procurement of Fort Bridger, and efforts to save Fort Laramie. The Trail Association outlined its plans for a nationwide program to the Wyoming leaders. Later, they met again with representatives from other states along the Trail and finalized plans for a national celebration. What followed was a proclamation by President Hoover, setting aside the period between April 10 and December 29, 1930, as the Covered-Wagon Centennial.

The entire country took part in the event. Wyoming honored the Centennial with an impressive display at Independence Rock on July 4, 1930:

> Friday, the Fourth of July, Scouts representing the nation, pioneers from everywhere, survivors of those heroic days to whom the country is paying tribute, thousands of citizens of Casper and from many states, joined in the greatest celebration in the history of Wyoming—in the annals of the West.

On the same day, plaques memorializing Ezra Meeker and Father P. J. DeSmet—who in 1840 had dubbed Independence Rock "the Register of the Desert"—were unveiled, and a marker placed ten years earlier by the Masons of Casper and Wyoming was rededicated. Two more Oregon Trail memorial plaques and monuments were also unveiled at the Tom Sun Ranch. One was commissioned by the Business and Professional Women's Club of Casper to honor pioneer women; another commemorated some three dozen unknown emigrants whose bodies were buried near the site.

The next day, July 5, eight hundred Boy Scouts dedicated two markers. A plaque and monument provided by scouts from Woodmere, Long Island, honored the old scouts who traveled the Oregon Trail. The other was built with native stone brought by Boy Scout troops from New York, Georgia, Ohio, Missouri, Nebraska, Colorado, Utah, and Wyoming.

On August 15, a second celebration commemorating the Covered Wagon Centennial was held at old Fort Laramie. Planned by the Wyoming Historical Landmark Commission, the great event renewed interest in preservation of the fort. Despite the rainy weather, a substantial crowd attended:

> Fully seventeen thousand persons—old scouts, pioneers, veterans of Indian wars, and other representative Americans, old and young—gathered at this historic old trapper-soldier way station on the Oregon-Mormon-California Trail, to revive the epic story that links so closely with this spot. Out of the celebration came a renewed determination to make old Fort Laramie a national shrine—a memorial to the pioneers. The movement toward securing the site of the old post with its surroundings to be dedicated to that purpose was given new vigor by the stirring commemoration of 1930.

(Private ownership, however, survived condemnation proceedings by the Commission in 1933 and 1934. Governor Leslie Miller finally made arrangements for transfer of the property from private to state ownership in 1937. A more complete discussion appears later.)

The Oregon Trail Memorial Association cooperated with state leaders on many early marker projects. Besides Ellison, Brooks, Cooper, Greenburg, and Evans, several other Wyoming residents were life members of the Association, including Frank Emerson, Grace Raymond Hebard, Frank W. Mondell, John T. Scott, and Clarence B. Richardson. The close relationship between the state and the association helped preservation efforts on both sides. The Trail Association benefited from the realistic and practical leadership of its Wyoming members, while Wyoming received much support and exposure from its affiliation with the association. In addition, Trail Association leaders James A. Shoemaker and Howard R. Driggs provided state marking efforts with immeasurable assistance.

By the late 1930s, the association had expanded its efforts to include several branches of the Oregon Trail, as well as other historic trails, such as the Santa Fe. On December 29, 1939, members formally adopted plans to form a new organization, to be named the American Pioneer Trails Association. But interest in the new group lasted only another fifteen years. In 1954, the American Pioneer Trails Association became history, too.

President Hoover celebrated with Boy Scouts and members of the Oregon Trail Memorial Association when he proclaimed 1930 as the Covered-Wagon Centennial.

The Daughters of the American Revolution and the Oregon Trail Commission

Early in Wyoming's history, the Daughters of the American Revolution (DAR) was responsible for marking and memorializing many historic sites. The organization was guided by its early state regents, including Mrs. H. B. Patten of Cheyenne (1912-14), Miss Grace Raymond Hebard of Laramie (1914-16), Mrs. Edward Gillette of Sheridan (1916-18), and Mrs. Bryant B. Brooks of Casper (1918-22). The DAR began its marking efforts in Wyoming around 1908. In 1909, they dedicated the bronze tablet at the grave of Sacajawea on the Wind River Indian Reservation in Fremont County. (Although later research indicated Sacajawea's grave was actually at Fort Manuel, in South Dakota's Standing Rock Indian Reservation, the tablet has continued to rest in Wyoming.) On July 1, 1911, the Jacques LaRamie Chapter of the DAR marked the Old Overland Trail in Albany County. Two years later, on April 4, 1913, the Sons and Daughters of the American Revolution of Nebraska and Cheyenne

placed an imposing monument on the boundary line between the two states where the old Oregon Trail crossed the States' line...The monument, with a large cement base, is in a field of alfalfa, but can be easily located from the established road by the aid of a stone "finder" about five feet high, which is on the main road.

The Fetterman Monument was also mentioned in Grace Hebard's early records of marking activity by the DAR, but the participation of the organization was not stated. Although constructed several years earlier, it was dedicated on July 3, 1908.

Even more credit should be given to the DAR for its efforts

to introduce a bill to the Twelfth State Legislature in 1913. Grace Hebard advocated marking the old Oregon Trail before the historic highway was obliterated. She suggested markers along the Trail at stated intervals, and monuments at the most noted landmarks, such as Forts Laramie, Fetterman, Casper, Stambaugh, and Bridger. These memorials, Hebard said, would do "honor to those who endured hardships and privations, encountered dangers and peril, who gave up their lives to make possible the civilization of the great west." The Sons of the American Revolution and other interested citizens of Wyoming also assisted in this legislation—which established the Wyoming Oregon Trail Commission. The text of the law (Session Laws, 1913, page 24, Chapter 29) read as follows:

CHAPTER 29.
House Bill No. 39.
MARKING THE OLD OREGON TRAIL
AN ACT entitled, "An act providing for the marking of the Old Oregon Trail and other historic landmarks; making an appropriation therefor; and providing a penalty for the defacement of such monuments or markers."

Be It Enacted by the Legislature of the State of Wyoming:

Marked Under the Supervision of a Commission.

Section 1. The Old Oregon Trail and historic landmarks in the State of Wyoming shall be marked by appropriate markers under the supervision of a commission of three members, the same to serve without compensation, to be appointed by the Governor, provided that no indebtedness shall be contracted or incurred hereunder beyond the actual amount in the hands of the State Treasurer appropriated for the payment thereof.

1.

2.

3.

4.

2. Mrs. Bryant B. Brooks, wife of former Governor B. B. Brooks, guided the historical marking efforts for the DAR while she was state regent, 1918-1922.

3. Mrs. James Mathison, regent of the Jacques LaRamie Chapter of the DAR, unveiled the Overland Trail marker on the Wyoming-Colorado state line on July 4, 1917.

4. The Wyoming Chapter of the Daughters of the American Revolution placed this large historical marker on the Wyoming-Nebraska state line on April 4, 1913.

1. Grace Raymond Hebard personified the historical marking activities of the Daughters of the American Revolution in Wyoming. She was instrumental as secretary of the Wyoming Oregon Trail Commission, 1915-1921.

Expenditures.

Sec. 2. The appropriation provided for herein shall be paid out only on certified vouchers, granted in like form, approved by the said commission, and the State Auditor is hereby authorized to draw warrants on the State Treasurer for the expenses provided by this act upon certified and approved vouchers as herein provided, but no such warrant shall be drawn for any amount in excess of the amount that may be, at the time in the State Treasury, appropriated for this purpose.

Penalty for Defacing Monuments.

Sec. 3. Any person who shall destroy, deface, remove or injure any monument or marker erected as herein provided for, shall be guilty of a misdemeanor, and upon conviction thereof, shall be punished by a fine not exceeding one hundred dollars, or by imprisonment in the county jail for a period not less than thirty days nor more than ninety days, or both by such fine and imprisonment at the discretion of the court.

Appropriation.

Sec. 4. The sum of two thousand five hundred dollars, or so much thereof as may be necessary, is hereby appropriated out of any moneys in the State Treasury, not otherwise appropriated, for the purpose of paying the expenses to be incurred under this act.

Sec. 5. This act shall take effect and be in force from and after its passage.

Approved February 20th, 1913.

A large number of markers were purchased and built with that initial appropriation of $2500. After 1913, subsequent legislatures appropriated $500 at each session.

The first commission was led by its president, Captain H. G. Nickerson, of Lander,

who from 1913 to 1921 has not only assisted locating trails and historic sites and battlefields, but has traveled on foot, by wagon, by horse and automobile into the territory that is located west of Casper to Cokeville and from Fort Washakie in the central part of the State to the Union Pacific railroad to the south. Here and there Captain Nickerson has placed stones, boulders and slabs of native material on which he, in the open, has carved with his chisels and mallet inscriptions and notations. No task has been too difficult for Captain Nickerson to undertake, no distance too long to journey, in order to locate sites off of the Oregon Trail, no weather too disagreeable, no mosquitoes too numerous to make him waver in this service for the State. Not only has Captain Nickerson helped to make the history of Wyoming since the year of 1866, but he has assisted in writing Wyoming's history on these stones and boulders.

The first secretary of the Oregon Trail Commission, Mrs. H. B. Patten from Cheyenne, was probably a close friend of the governor. She began recording descriptions of every marker placed in Wyoming by both the commission and the DAR. Her extensive reporting provided a good record of the state's early historical markers. Her term on the commission ended prematurely, however, when she and her husband moved to Washington, D.C.. In a letter dated August 4, 1914, Governor Joseph M. Carey wrote:

I want to congratulate you on the substantial stones that you procured and the very attractive way in which they were marked by the stone cutter. I was very sorry that you could not be there. You know I have never been reconciled to you all picking up your belongings and abandoning us as we need all the members of your family here. It seems to be Wyoming's luck to lose the people that she can least afford to lose.

Mrs. Patten had also been the state regent of the Wyoming DAR from 1912 to 1914. Her absence must have been felt in several circles of historical activities.

Others who served on the commission included Mrs. J. T. (Elizabeth) Snow of Torrington, vice president from 1918 to 1920, and—once again—Grace Hebard, who was secretary from 1915 to 1921. Her association with the DAR and Wyoming Colonial Dames kept her in the forefront of early historical preservation, and even in the writing of Wyoming history.

A. J. Parshall of Cheyenne, a civil engineer (and the state engineer), was also appointed to the first Oregon Trail Commission. In "Marking The Oregon Trail, The Bozeman Trail, and Historic Places in Wyoming 1908-1920," Hebard noted that Parshall "contributed greatly to the value of the Oregon Trail Commission, a value beyond an expression in words." Hebard also commended the two governors who followed Joseph Carey—John B. Kendrick and Robert D. Carey—for their support in marking historical sites.

The Oregon Trail Commission was quite active in 1913 and 1914. From Hebard's report the commission marked twenty-four sites, all but two or three along the Oregon Trail. Captain Nickerson, accompanied by Hebard, left many markers which stand unchanged today—at Fort Augur, Burnt Ranch, St. Mary's Station, and Independence Rock, among other sites. The commission was busy again from 1915 to 1916, erecting another twenty to twenty-five markers. However, World War I—known at that time as the Great War—interrupted the commission's activities. The commission stopped recording history and started helping the war effort. Practically no markers were placed from July 21, 1917, to July 4, 1920. The money previously appropriated was returned to the Wyoming Treasury. The last monument erected by the Oregon Trail Commission was a granite marker dedicated September 1920 at the site of the Wagon Box Fight. No further legislative appropriations for the commission were made after 1920.

2.

3.

1.

1. Ezra Meeker, on the left, and H. G. Nickerson, on the right, were Oregon Trail pioneers. They led efforts to preserve and mark historic sites along the trail.

2. Captain H. G. Nickerson of Lander was president of the Wyoming Oregon Trail Commission 1913-1921. He traveled the Oregon Trail and chiseled many markers, such as St. Mary's Station and Burnt Ranch.

3. Dr. Grace Raymond Hebard at the dedication of the Mary Homsley grave on May 30, 1926.

4. The Oregon Trail Commission was founded during the term of Governor Joseph M. Carey. He and other early Wyoming governors were supportive of historical marking efforts.

4.

1.   2.

1. Editor of the *Guernsey Gazette*, George Houser, led efforts to preserve Fort Laramie. The Wyoming Historical Landmark Commission probably grew from those initial efforts.

2. Warren Richardson of Cheyenne became the first treasurer of the Wyoming Historical Landmark Commission in February 1927 and was chairman of the Commission 1939-1959.

Historical Landmark Commission of Wyoming

Origin of the Historical Landmark Commission

The seed that grew into the Wyoming Historical Landmark Commission was planted by individuals interested in the preservation of old Fort Laramie. In spite of the efforts of Ezra Meeker and Wyoming leaders of historic preservation, Fort Laramie had continued to deteriorate. After twelve years of public debate, those individuals interested in the preservation of the fort planned a state commission which would have wide-ranging powers to acquire historical properties. Ironically, the powers of the commission were ineffective in dealing with the private owners of the site. Twelve more years elapsed before Fort Laramie was finally acquired.

The idea of preserving Fort Laramie began on June 17, 1915, with James Johnston, editor of the *Torrington Telegram*. In the same issue that reported on the dedication services for a marble plaque at the fort, the *Telegram* made the first documented plea for its preservation. The editorial, entitled "A NOTABLE PLEASURE RESORT," read:

> Few people realize the importance of Fort Laramie as a historic spot in Wyoming, and to think that the site of the first fort in the State lies within the borders of our county ought to arouse the patriotism of the present generation to restore the works and make it into a beautiful summer resort.
>
> There are a dozen or more buildings intact, and can be put in shape for use at very little cost. The hospital commands a beautiful sight of the valley, and the dormitory for the privates is now the beautiful home of Mr. and Mrs. Joe Wilde....
>
> The Oregon Trail marker of 1915 is by far the best one put up on the trail.... Close to this is the old trading post—the very building where the white man obtained his supplies, and the Indian bartered his wares.
>
> The home of Mr. and Mrs. John Hunton is in the row of buildings bordering on the Laramie River front, the end of which now terminates with the Bedlam house made famous by the writings of Captain Charles King.... This is the ideal spot for a summer home, or for a picnicking place during the summer months. It is a convenient distance from Torrington, Guernsey and Wheatland and because of the fame of Old Fort Laramie it would be a popular place for gatherings and chautauquas as well.

In 1925 George Houser, editor of the *Guernsey Gazette*, reported that "a movement is on foot in which a number of Wyoming towns are interested in having a portion of old Fort Laramie set aside as a national monument for future generations." This was the first recorded instance of Fort Laramie being associated with the term national monument— "the official designation of 'objects of historic and scientific interest' set aside by Presidential Proclamation by authority of the Antiquities Act of 1906." Uinta and Goshen County officials urged the House of Representatives to introduce House Joint Memorial No. 4, "Memorializing the Congress of the United States to set aside Old Fort Laramie and Old Fort Bridger and Independence Rock as Historic Reserves." It was approved February 25, 1925.

Public support for restoring the deteriorating fort reached its peak in 1926. And this campaign for Fort Laramie may have been the primary factor in the creation of Wyoming's Historical Landmark Commission the following year. George Houser and L. G. (Pat) Flannery of the *Fort Laramie Scout* served both as mobilizers and reporters during these events. In the July 23 *Gazette,* Houser discussed the novel idea that the state, rather than the federal government, might be the most logical protector of the fort. Then, responding to a question from the *Cheyenne Tribune-Leader* about what the state should do with the "John Higgins Trust," Houser wrote:

1.

1. L. G. (Pat) Flannery and his family in front of the Officer's Quarters "F" taken in the 1920s. Flannery, editor of the *Fort Laramie Scout*, and George Houser, editor of the *Guernsey Gazette*, worked hard to preserve Fort Laramie. From those preservation efforts grew the Historical Landmark Commission.

2. Robert S. Ellison of Casper actively supported Fort Laramie preservation efforts. He became the first chairman of the Wyoming Historical Landmark Commission in February 1927.

3. Joseph S. Weppner of Rock Springs, a member of the Wyoming Historical Landmark Commission from its beginning in 1927 until its dissolution in 1959, was the Commission's first secretary.

2.

3.

One very appropriate way of using the bequest of this fine old man would be to purchase the site of Old Fort Laramie as a state park, restore the old buildings and grounds to something of their former appearance. Fix up one of the buildings for an historical department and move the old records and curios from Cheyenne where they are now seldom noticed, to this beauty spot where these things would become a great attraction.

We talk about the federal government setting aside this old post as a national monument, but the State of Wyoming should not relinquish it and should need no further urging to make a beautiful state park.

The old place is dear to the heart of every Wyoming citizen...it revives in the archives of our memory the trials and tribulations of the early pioneers.... Our citizens, for who else can we lay it to, should be put to shame for any further neglect in preserving this fine old Fort, the most famous outpost of the old West.

Robert S. Ellison—a man dedicated to preserving historic reminders of pioneer virtues—presented a guest editorial in a special edition of the *Guernsey Gazette* on August 27, 1926. Stressing the importance of securing and preserving Old Fort Laramie, he wrote:

Wyoming is fortunate in having two of the three great out-fitting points on the Oregon Trail between the Missouri River and the Pacific Ocean. Of these Fort Laramie in southeastern Wyoming possesses an even greater wealth of historic values than Fort Bridger in southwestern Wyoming, and outranks in the history of the west any other trading or military post...

I realize full well the need for most of us to make a livelihood and not dwell too long upon our past, no matter how heroic and glorious, but I also believe that no people can be truly great and hope to endure without due regard for the knowledge of the worthy deeds and sacrifices of our ancestors....

It is therefore, a matter of no mean importance, in my opinion, that we secure and preserve as best we can the site and ruins of old Fort Laramie...just how this can be done best is not easy to outline, but we must first resolve and want it done.

Quoting Horace Albright, then Superintendent of Yellowstone National Park, and soon to become the second director of the National Park Service, Ellison went on to note that

unless the private ownership of these landmarks can be extinguished the Federal Government would feel that it would be futile to try to handle them as national monuments....It seems to me that the first step would be to get the Legislature to pass an act authorizing condemnation of the properties, and at the same time authorizing the acceptance of private donation for the purchase of historical landmarks. The law ought also to contain authority to transfer such landmarks to the Federal Government.

Senate File No. 34, prepared by Casper attorney G. R. Hagens and introduced to the Nineteenth Wyoming State Legislature by Senator Thomas Cooper of Natrona County, created the Historical Landmark Commission of Wyoming. Approved February 26, 1927, its first members were appointed by Governor Frank C. Emerson. Robert Ellison of Casper became the first chairman; Joseph S. Weppner of Rock Springs became secretary; and Warren Richardson from Cheyenne became treasurer. Mrs. Cyrus Beard from Cheyenne—also a member of the State Historical Society—was appointed assistant secretary, and Dan Greenburg of Casper was appointed publicity director.

The powers and purposes of the act followed the recommendations of Superintendent Albright. The best means for acquiring, marking, and preserving historic sites and monuments in Wyoming was born. From the First Biennial Report of The Historical Landmark Commission of Wyoming:

POWERS AND PURPOSES.—The Act creating the Commission provides that the Commission shall have power to acquire by gift, devise, bequest, donation, purchase, lease, or otherwise, money and property, as well as historical landmarks and lands and sites of historical interest and books, manuscripts and other personal property of historical value, and hold, control and own the same and provide for the restoration, care and preservation of the same.

The Commission also has power to acquire by condemnation and to take therein the fee simple title absolute, any real estate situate in the State of Wyoming, which in the opinion of the Commission is of sufficent historical interest as to require that the same be permanently set aside and preserved for the general public welfare, which power of condemnation shall be exercised in the manner prescribed by law for the condemnation of real estate by railroad companies in the State of Wyoming.

The Commission also has power to arrange by contract or otherwise with the United States Government or its constituted agencies for the preservation and care of sites and places of historical interest in the State of Wyoming.

The Act also provides that any person or persons marking, defacing, removing or tampering in any manner whatsoever with any property acquired by the Commission shall be deemed guilty of a misdemeanor and upon conviction thereof shall be punished by a fine of not less than $25.00 nor more than $100.00.

Nearly all of the historic sites in question were privately owned. Chairman Ellison hoped that acquisition could be financed without state funds. The commission sought the interest and cooperation of local citizens, and hoped "that the necessary funds for furthering the purposes of the Commission could be raised primarily by those locally interested in the acquiring and preservation of their most important historic sites."

The first acquisitions by the Historical Landmark Commission were the Fort Reno Site in Johnson County in

July 1927 and the Connor Battlefield State Park in Sheridan County in December of the same year. Acquisition of Fort Bridger in Uinta County followed in 1928.

Perhaps more significant than these early activities was the commission's attention to the plight of Fort Laramie in Goshen County—the first permanent establishment in what is now Wyoming. Fort Laramie was partially owned by three private parties. Whereas acquisition of Fort Bridger and Fort Reno proved relatively uncomplicated, the acquisition of Fort Laramie presented the commission with one of its longest and most frustrating battles.

The Landmarks Commission had been established by those who wanted to preserve old Fort Laramie, and much effort was expended on its repeated attempts to acquire the fort. Besides the power to evaluate all historic sites in the state and to recommend sites for acquisition, the commission was also charged with appointing an advisory committee in each county. On October 18, 1929, the commission set up the advisory committee representing Goshen and Platte counties. Pat Flannery and George Houser—a member of the State House of Representatives from Platte County in addition to his editorship of the *Gazette*—accepted invitations to serve. They named Charles L. Bruce of Fort Laramie, Fred Burton of Guernsey, Dr. G. O. Hanna of Lingle, the Hon. Thomas G. Powers of Torrington, and the Rev. E. L. Tull of Wheatland to round out the committee.

The acquisition effort made little further progress in 1929 and 1930. At the direction of the advisory committee, an appraisal of the properties was made: $26,000 for just under fifty acres.

In 1931, the Twenty-First Wyoming Legislature appropriated $15,000 for acquiring Fort Laramie. The commission drew up a resolution stating:

> Fort Laramie...has a wide historical significance, not only as regards this State, but as regards the history of the United States as a whole...said site be set aside and preserved for the general public welfare and benefit.
>
> It is appropriate that the said Fort Laramie land site should be acquired by the Historical Landmark Commission of Wyoming as an historical landmark....
>
> The Historical Landmark Commission deems the said site an historical landmark and should be purchased with the legislative appropriation for the same.

In June of that same year, the commission and its Goshen-Platte advisory committee met with the owners of the old Fort Laramie property. Thomas Waters stated that he and his partner Marlin Hartmann "owned 640 acres, of which 25 acres were within the estimated 55 acres of the old Fort proper, and they wanted to sell the whole thing for $22,500." The Landmark Commission explained that its duty was to acquire historical sites, and that it was interested only in the twenty-five acres. Warren Richardson "explained the Commission's right of power of domain under the law to acquire by condemnation." But Waters was not frightened by that threat.

In 1932 the Landmark Commission began condemnation proceedings for Old Fort Laramie. The Board of Appraisers designated by the court of Goshen County stipulated the following prices:

Owners	Acres	Price
Thos. Waters and Marlin S. Hartman	22.5 acres	$6,340.00
James Auld	18.5 acres	3,890.50
George Sandercock	8.75 acres	1,376.00

Condemnation proceedings continued on February 23, 1934, with Attorney General Ray Lee representing the commission. Treasurer Richardson stated that the commission was willing to pay the valuation per acre made by the appointed board of appraisers, approximately $11,500 in all. He also stated that the commission would go no further than the appraisers' valuation. Attorneys for the Auld and Sandercock parties were willing to accept the offer. The attorney for Waters and Hartman, who owned the major part of the property, was dissatisfied and asked for a jury trial. The two-day trial in Torrington resulted in an appraised valuation to the owners of $500 an acre. The jury's decision eliminated the purchase in any form by the state.

That legal defeat quieted efforts to acquire Fort Laramie for the next three years. Finally, Governor Leslie Miller led another fight to purchase the fort from its private owners. Options to buy the site were secured by an appointed committee—excluding the Historical Landmark Commission. It did, however, include D. Shoemaker and Marshall Sandercock of Torrington; George Houser of Guernsey; and James Flenor, Lloyd Glade, and R. J. Rymill of Fort Laramie. The committee was ably chaired by Rymill, and negotiations began in December 1936. In January 1937, Rymill reported to Governor Miller that the property could be purchased for $25,594.75 as follows:

Owners	Acres	Price
Thomas Waters & Martin S. Hartman	58.91 acres	$16,869.00
Molly Sandercock	77.01 acres	3,012.00
Jessica C. Auld	76.80 acres	5,713.75

The 1937 Legislature of Wyoming (Chapter 71, Page 110, Session Laws of 1937) authorized and empowered the Historical Landmark Commission to acquire Old Fort Laramie at a price not to exceed $27,000. On March 31, the commission adopted a resolution to purchase the properties. After obtaining the deeds for Old Fort Laramie, it resolved on July 31 to prepare a deed of conveyance giving title of the site to the United States government (National Park Service). President Franklin D. Roosevelt stated in a proclamation on July 16, 1938:

> WHEREAS The Historical Landmark Commission of Wyoming has donated the United States in trust certain lands with the structures thereon comprising the abandoned Fort Laramie, for the purpose of improving, preserving, and conducting such lands and structures as a public historical site; and
>
> WHEREAS the lands and structures are of great historic

interest and constitute a historic landmark; and

WHEREAS it appears that it would be in the public interest to reserve such lands and structures as a national monument, to be known as the Fort Laramie National Monument:

NOW, THEREFORE, I, FRANKLIN D. ROOSEVELT, President of the United States of America, under and by virtue of the authority vested in me by section 2 of the act of June 8, 1906...do proclaim that the following-described lands in Wyoming are hereby reserved and set apart as the Fort Laramie National Monument....

The Director of the National Park Service, under the direction of the Secretary of the Interior, shall have the supervision, management, and control of this monument as provided in the act of Congress entitled "An act to establish a National Park Service, and for other purposes," approved August 25, 1916.

This turn of events must have been humiliating to the Landmark Commission. After all, the Commission had its origin in efforts to acquire the fort. Following their legal defeat in 1934—ending all negotiations by the commission to acquire the property—an exclusive committee of local folks appointed by Governor Miller accomplished the negotiations with apparent ease. The formalities of acquiring the properties were then handed back to the commission by the legislature.

In retrospect, however, the Historical Landmark Commission—and the principles behind it—laid the groundwork for the eventual acquisition of Old Fort Laramie.

Historical Marking by the Wyoming Historical Landmark Commission

In its first two years, the Wyoming Historical Landmark Commission acquired three important historic sites. As mentioned earlier, the first was Fort Reno, in Johnson County. On July 11, 1927, Mr. and Mrs. Homer L. Payseno of Sussex donated 14.21 acres of land to the commission "for historic site uses and purposes only." The Fort Reno monument—erected by the State of Wyoming and citizens of Johnson County in 1914—had been located near the school house about two miles north of Sussex. On September 5, 1927, the marker was moved to the newly acquired site on the northwest bank of a bend in the Powder River, some twelve miles northwest of Sussex.

The Connor Battlefield State Park in Sheridan County was acquired later in the same year, on December 13. The O-Four-Bar Ranch, Inc., deeded the land to the commission on the condition that the "premises be kept, used, and maintained as a public park."

Fort Bridger in Uinta County was the third acquisition. On June 27, 1928, the Hon. Maurice Groshon sold 30.532 acres—"embracing all of the remaining buildings and most important portions of the old fort site"—to Commissioners Ellison and Richardson who, in turn, "placed in escrow a deed running to the Historical Landmark Commission of Wyoming, pending payment to them of the purchase price of $7100." Through Roy A. Mason of Kemmerer, the citizens of Lincoln County paid $800 on the purchase price. The state legislature appropriated the funds to complete the acquisition on February 1, 1929.

A few months later, on July 29, 1929, Grand Teton National Park was dedicated at a ceremony at String Lake. As part of the ceremonies, the Landmark Commission dedicated a bronze plaque commemorating the first ascent of Grand Teton Peak by the Hon. W. O. Owen on August 11, 1898. Professor F. M. Fryxell, Ranger Phil Smith, and William Gilman carried the plaque to the summit and cemented it into the rock atop the peak.

As reported in the section on Ezra Meeker and the Oregon Trail Memorial Association, the commission cooperated with several organizations on the Fourth of July 1930 celebration at Independence Rock. Besides the memorials for Meeker, Father DeSmet, and the first Masonic Lodge meeting in Wyoming—held on July 4, 1862—a plaque was unveiled honoring all pioneers who had passed the rock, and a section set aside for a tablet honoring Mormon pioneers.

The commission also participated in other celebrations during the Covered Wagon Centennial. Festivities at Fort Laramie commemorated the hundredth anniversary of the Smith-Jackson-Sublette wagon caravan of 1830, the first wheeled vehicles up the Platte River Road. That event was inspired by the Oregon Trail Memorial Association and organized by George Houser and Pat Flannery, who declared it "the largest crowd ever assembled in the North Platte Valley." Attendance figures varied from 7,500 to 16,000.

The Third Biennial Report of the Landmark Commission reported that Robert Ellison regretfully resigned, as he was moving from the state. Former Wyoming governor Bryant Brooks assumed the chairmanship in 1931. Several dedication ceremonies occurred across the state, most centering around the Oregon Trail. On June 21 at Independence Rock, Heber J. Grant, president of the Mormon Church, dedicated a plaque commemorating the more than 80,000 Mormon emigrants who had passed by in the 1840s and 1850s on their way to the Great Salt Lake valley. Elsewhere in the state, the Oregon Trail marker in the small park adjoining the Burlington Railroad Depot in Torrington—along with the one dedicated May 15, 1932, in Lingle—became the first markers to be electrically illuminated. Later in 1932, the Fredericks of Guernsey deeded Register Cliff to the commission; the E. J. Brandley family deeded an acre of land in Granger including the intact Old South Bend Stage Station; and the commission instructed Secretary Weppner to purchase a plaque honoring Esther Hobart Morris, who in 1870 had become the first woman justice of the peace in the nation.

During 1933 and 1934, ceremonies continued to flourish under the direction of Brooks, Weppner, and Richardson. At Fort Bridger, dedications of the Fort Bridger Museum, American Legion Post Home, and a plaque on the Old Mormon Wall were "attended by the largest crowd of people ever assembled in Uinta County for any purpose." Attendance estimates varied from 5,000 to 12,000. The social event

1.

2.

3.

4.

1. Leslie Miller, governor of Wyoming 1933-1939, succeeded in guiding the state's purchase of Fort Laramie from its private owners in 1937. Miller accomplished what the Historical Landmark Commission had been unable to do for ten years.

2. Mr. and Mrs. Homer L. Payseno and children of Sussex, Wyoming. In 1927, they donated the site of Old Fort Reno to the State of Wyoming.

3. During the dedication of Grand Teton National Park in 1929, the Wyoming Historical Landmark Commission participated in the dedication of a marker to be placed at the summit of Grand Teton Peak. On the left is Professor F. M. Fryxell who was one of three who carried and mounted the plaque on the summit. In the middle is William O. Owen, first climber of the Grand Teton.

4. Professor F. M. Fryxell and Ranger Phil Smith unveiling the historical marker on Grand Teton Peak at the end of July 1929. The plaque commemorated the first ascent of the peak by William O. Owen August 11, 1898.

was described in the commision's Fourth Biennial Report:

> After all, the most pleasing feature of the entire affair was the meeting of relatives and old time friends and associates. Picnic lunches were enjoyed by parties in the shade of the trees.
>
> The weather was ideal. Early in the day a breeze came up from the west, which cooled the atmosphere and drove the hungry mosquitoes to cover. It was a day 'made to order.' There was little or no rowdyism, no confusion of a disturbing nature. and so far as we know not a single accident to mar the peace and pleasure of the day.

Also in 1933, the Landmark Commission received a deed from George A. Bible of Rawlins for five acres of land at the Old Platte River Crossing on the Overland Trail. Bible had received the land from Ella Mary Davis, whose name appears on the marker located at the site today.

Brooks, Weppner, and Richardson continued the work of the Landmark Commission during 1935 and 1936. The Samuel Parker plaque in northern Sublette County was dedicated on August 23, 1935, memorializing the first Protestant sermon in Wyoming. The land was deeded to the state by Frank Van Vleck, owner of the V-V Ranch at the entrance to Hoback Canyon. During the same year, the commission participated in the Pony Express Diamond Jubilee Celebration—a commemorative ride sponsored by the Oregon Trail Memorial Association that traversed the nation from California to Missouri. In 1936, near Daniel, the Narcissa Whitman-Eliza Spalding monument was dedicated to the first two white women to enter Wyoming. A ten-scene pageant portraying life at the 1836 Green River Rendezvous was also held.

Perhaps more notable in the Fifth Biennial Report was mention of T. J. (Jim) Gatchell and Elsa Spear Edwards. Jim Gatchell was a pioneer and historian well-versed in the history of the Indian battles of north-central Wyoming. Johnson County paid tribute by naming their museum in Buffalo after him. Elsa Spear Edwards, president of the Sheridan Chapter of the DAR in 1935, guaranteed cooperation in any way she could to mark historical sites in northern Wyoming. Now in her nineties, she has continued to serve as a spokesperson for Sheridan County history.

The major event of the sixth biennium was the acquisition of Old Fort Laramie, discussed earlier. Although the commission's efforts to obtain the fort drained the group's time and energy, it was able to continue other marking efforts during that period.

During 1937 and 1938, work began to acquire the Red Buttes Battlefield and the Old Fort Caspar Graveyard, both in Natrona County. Dan Greenburg represented the Natrona County Historical Society, which offered deeds to the two sites, and the Landmark Commission voted favorably on the proposition to purchase the properties. In February 1938, the commission also began correspondence with Dora McGrath, president of the Thermopolis Pioneer Association, about acquiring and marking the first cabin in the Big Horn Basin,

built by John D. Woodruff on the M Bar ranch on Owl Creek. The deed for the Woodruff cabin was not presented until November 2, 1940. Sarah Frances Torrey, Wallace B. Hodge, and Ethel Langford Hodge donated the one-acre site.

The resignation of Bryant Brooks in 1939 brought change to the membership of the commission, but the same ideals, objectives, and accomplishments continued to flourish. John C. Thompson of Cheyenne was appointed to fill the vacancy. In July 1939, the four-day dedicatory tour marked monuments at Medicine Bow (to Owen Wister), the Continental Divide (to Henry Joy, Sr.), Star Valley (to the Lander Cutoff of the Oregon Trail), Jackson (to John Colter), and South Pass City (to Esther Morris).

In July of the following year, Wyoming and Idaho marked their golden anniversaries. Along with three or four thousand enthusiastic spectators, the Landmark Commission and Idaho officials dedicated a marker on the Wyoming-Idaho state line, twelve miles north of Cokeville on old U.S. Highway 30.

The July 1940 dedicatory tour also included the DeSmet centennial celebration of a pontifical high mass in Sublette County, near the Daniel Cemetery. Five or six thousand people attended this service, performed by the Reverend Bishop P. A. McGovern, and assisted by twenty priests from Wyoming parishes. In that same month, Names Hill Monument in Sublette County and the Big and Little Wind River Rendezvous Monument in Fremont County were dedicated.

In August 1940, markers were dedicated to John "Portugee" Phillips on the front porch of Old Bedlam at Fort Laramie and at Old Fort Kearny. In Lusk, the Texas Trail monument and the Lathrop monument were dedicated. Markers were also dedicated in several other locales: Johnson County (Father DeSmet); Sheridan County (Connor Battlefield); Park County (Buffalo Bill and Dead Indian Hill); Teton County (to the Old Trappers' Trail at Leek's Lodge); Crook County (Custer Expedition); and Weston County (Jenney Stockade).

In 1941 the Landmark Commission purchased nineteen oil paintings of pioneers by Ruth Joy Hopkins of Casper, and displayed them in the lobby of the Capitol Building. These portraits of the men who built the West—Jedediah Strong Smith, Wilson Price Hunt, Robert Stuart, Robert Campbell, Jim Bridger, Jim Baker, Kit Carson, Father DeSmet, John C. Fremont, E. W. Whitcomb, Gen. George Armstrong Custer, John C. Friend, Capt. B. L. E. Bonneville, John D. Woodruff, John "Portugee" Phillips, Hiram "Hi" Kelly, James H. Moore, Jack Hunton, and Lt. Caspar W. Collins—cost the commission fifty dollars apiece. They reside now in the art vault in the Barrett Building in Cheyenne.

The dedicatory tour in September 1941 first traveled to Hot Springs County. Governor Nels H. Smith spoke at the dedication of the Woodruff Cabin site:

> The further we grow away from the pioneer life of the frontier, the greater becomes our appreciation of those things which tie us to the romantic history of the old West.
>
> Mr. Woodruff was a prominent rancher and a foremost resident of the State of Wyoming. He was a valuable

1.

4.

2.

5.

3.

1. Bryant B. Brooks, governor of Wyoming 1905-1911, was chairman of the Wyoming Historical Landmark Commission 1931-1939. The Commission flourished under his leadership.

2. Dedication of the Owen Wister Monument in Medicine Bow, Wyoming, July 2, 1939. From left to right, Warren Richardson, Joseph Weppner, John Charles Thompson, and Bryant Brooks (all members of the Wyoming Historical Landmark Commission).

3. Dedication of the Esther Morris Monument in South Pass, Wyoming, on July 6, 1939.

4. Dedication of the Idaho-Wyoming Monument on July 5, 1940. From left to right, Warren Richardson (chairman of the Historical Landmark Commission), John Charles Thompson (Commission treasurer), Governor C.A. Bottolfsen of Idaho, Governor Nels H. Smith, of Wyoming, and Joseph Weppner (Commission secretary).

5. Dedication of the Texas Trail Monument near Lingle, Wyoming, on August 1, 1948. From left to right, Russell Thorp, Earnest Dahlquist, and Joseph Weppner (all members of the Historical Landmark Commission).

member of the State Legislature. In erecting here a marker we pay tribute to a son of our territorial days, and we make a permanent record of an event which was a fore-runner of the building of homes over our entire State.

The tour then went to Fort Washakie, where more than a thousand people—Indian and white—gathered to pay tribute to Sacajawea, the Shoshone woman who accompanied the Lewis and Clark expedition to the Pacific in 1805. Mystery had engulfed the story of Sacajawea, her death, and her burial site. During the marker dedication, three people who knew Sacajawea well—Pandora Pogue, Quantan Quay, and the Reverend John Roberts—authenticated the site at the Shoshone cemetery at Fort Washakie. Despite the testimony of Roberts, Pogue, and Quay however, the real burial site of Sacajawea would be questioned further in the decades to come. Eventually, this controversy would prove damaging to the Landmark Commission.

By 1943, the commission began to feel the effects of World War II:

Owing to a lack of funds, and also to the more pressing needs of bronze and other materials for the war effort, the Commission has not been as active as in preceding years. However, plans have been discussed for a number of projects which will be carried out just as soon as this is feasible.

However, they were able to participate with the American Pioneer Trails Association (formerly the Oregon Trail Memorial Association) in marking the hundredth anniversary of the Oregon Trail. The Landmark Commission set six granite markers along the Trail from Guernsey to South Pass: at the Wyoming-Nebraska line; south of Guernsey; five miles west of Douglas on the Fetterman Trail Crossing; at Bessemer Bend; at Devil's Gate on the Tom Sun Ranch; and at the Hudson Ranch on the Sweetwater River. Also in 1946, the Union Pacific officially turned over the Sherman Hill Tree-in-a-Rock site to the state.

Over the next three years, 1947 to 1949, the Landmark Commission planned and successfully completed the rehabilitation of the Big Barracks at Fort Bridger into a new museum. The commission also moved to protect Independence Rock from further defacement and mutilation by the public, and began talks to acquire title to the landmark from Tom Sun, partial owner of the site. Several unsuccessful attempts were made to gain state control of DeSmet's "Register of the Desert." With the help of Governor Stan Hathaway's twenty-one member Bicentennial Commission, the state finally received full title to the disputed twenty-five acres in 1977.

The Texas Trail monuments in Pine Bluffs and Lingle—elaborate granite markers with a map of Wyoming engraved—were both dedicated in 1948. Also engraved on the monuments were cowboys, Texas longhorn cattle, and the path of the Texas Trail across eastern Wyoming. Although

dedicated by the Landmark Commission, public-spirited citizens and the Wyoming Stockgrower's Association planned and financed these markers.

The dedication of the Edison Monument at Battle Lake was one of the most unusual moments of 1949. About six hundred people attended the ceremonies, held at the site where Thomas Edison supposedly thought of the idea for a filament for his electric lamp. At an altitude of over 12,000 feet, Battle Lake was a beautiful location, but the whimsical notion to memorialize the spot hardly represented an historic event.

In 1950 the commission obtained the deed for the Charcoal Kilns at Piedmont in Uinta County, and the property was designated historic for preservation. Also, the commission dedicated a plaque to Esther Hobart Morris at her old home in Cheyenne—2114 Warren Avenue. In that same year, eight acres near the old Platte River crossing on the Overland Stage Route, in Carbon County, were donated by Mr. and Mrs. Isadore Bolton. The granite marker there was dedicated in 1954.

One thousand people gathered at Fort Bridger in August 1951 to dedicate the new museum. Chairman Warren Richardson presented the history of the commission's efforts to save and preserve the fort:

He told of the purchase by Mr. Robert Ellison and himself of the Fort Bridger site by them in order to save the historic fort to the State of Wyoming. Two years later, the Legislature appropriated the amount paid out by Mr. Robert Ellison and Mr. Richardson and the State has held it ever since. The property consists of 32 acres and the priceless museum. Mr. Richardson then presented the new museum to Governor Barrett and the people of Wyoming.

During the ensuing years the Historical Landmark Commission erected several new markers. Three markers were placed at Fort Laramie. Plaques memorializing the Old Army Bridge over the Platte River, Fort Platte, and the horse ride of "Portugee" Phillips were dedicated. The Grattan Massacre marker in Goshen County was erected in 1953. The Evanston Pony Express Station and Overland Stage Route marker, the Little Box Elder Massacre marker in Converse County, and the Sibley monument in Sheridan County were dedicated in 1954. The C. H. "Dad" Worland monument was dedicated August 27, 1954.

The Decline of the Wyoming Historical Landmark Commission

The late fifties were restless times for the Landmark Commission. Originally, Wyoming history had grown from the legendary tales of settlers, old-timers, Indians, and pioneers. With the development of a state museum and the appointment of a state historian, Wyoming history became more sophisticated. These two separate camps—legendary history and sophisticated history—were destined to collide and to create conflict.

The commission and its members obviously had their roots in "legendary" history. Critics challenged the inscriptions on many markers, contending that they were either exaggerations, or, in some cases, absolute historical errors. Perhaps two specific examples—Sacajawea's burial site and "Portugee" Phillips's dramatic ride—reveal this story best.

Controversy about Phillips's ride arose when David L. Hieb, superintendent at Fort Laramie National Monument, asked the commission to "correct 'erroneous' statements and 'exaggerated' language in reference to the ride." Although the original letter from Hieb could not be located, the rebuttal from Chairman Richardson showed the commission's sensitivity to challenge. The letter read:

P.O. Box 515,
Cheyenne, Wyoming,
August 10, 1952.

Mr. David L. Hieb,
Superintendent, Fort Laramie National Monument,
Fort Laramie, Wyoming.

Dear Sir:

Since coming back from Fort Laramie I have re-read your letter to Secretary Weppner.

I am surprised that you, a Government employee, should have the temerity to in any way reflect on the man, "Portugee" Phillips. You call upon the Commission to "correct" "erroneous" statements and "exaggerated" language in reference to the ride of Mr. Phillips. Well sir, there are no erroneous statements on the plaque to the noble horse ridden by Phillips. There is no language capable of exaggerating the ride, so long as it sticks to truth. You, being a critique, no doubt having been sent to Fort Laramie for that purpose, are in doubtful business, throwing any kind of trivial doubt upon the honor, stamina or courage of John "Portugee" Phillips, who made the greatest ride in the history of the world.

Old fellows, still living, are very apt to be rather foggy mentally, and are apt to be wrong about dates or events. Mr. Meeker, of ox team fame, who travelled over the Oregon and other trans-continental trails, marked, at his own expense, several important places. His markings should surely be taken as correct; yet, we have letters from Women's and other Organizations demanding that we move monuments he placed. Monuments placed by order of the Legislature of the State of Wyoming are questioned now—fifty or seventy-five years after their erection. We will not move or "correct" the phraseology on any such monuments, most of which are fifty to a hundred years old, because some ambitious would-be historian says they are "erroneous" or "exaggerated".

The plaque on the monument of the horse is correct. It will not be changed. The statement concerning Phillips is correct and will not be changed at your whim or any one else's. Phillips, as you know, left Fort Phil Kearney the night of December 21st, 1866—probably late—perhaps even the early morning of the 22nd. He arrived

at Ft. Laramie the night of December 25th, 1866, during a dance in the old Bedlam Building. The man who was officer of the day, and who received Mr. Phillips, was Herman Haas, a highly respected oldtime citizen of Cheyenne. He took the nearly frozen and exhausted Phillips into the place where the dance was going on and presented him to the Commandant of the fort to whom Phillips gave his message of horror about the Fetterman battle. He was on the road four days, but he rode only at night on account of the Sioux Indians, who were on the war path and infested the surrounding country. In other words, he made the ride in two days—not "four or five", as some jealous oldtimers are reported by you to have said. All such trivial and immaterial points amount to nothing. Phillips did ride 235 miles in two days in weather of intense cold—the worst winter in years.

Don't let us by trivialities deny to the immortal Phillips the honor due him, or put into the minds of posterity doubts or insignificant matters. The fact is he made the ride in the time designated. It was the greatest ride ever made. The literary question of "exaggeration" in describing the ride is a matter of taste. I made the plaque, and I doubt if exaggeration is possible in describing "Portugee" Phillips's ride which will charm the imagination of men, women and children for ages to come.

Yours very truly,
Warren Richardson
Chairman, Historical
Landmark Commission

The same conflict surfaced again at the dedication of the monument at Fort Laramie on June 28, 1953. As Richardson was unable to attend, Joseph Weppner read his address. It spoke of legends, "trivial comments that are made to us [the Landmark Commission]," and the strange fact "that more accuracy had not been shown." Richardson's address mentioned his personal acquaintance with Phillips and Herman Haas—the man who received Phillips at Fort Laramie—and noted that he had consulted them both. Despite those claims however, historians still argued the facts of Phillips's ride.

The other controversy—over Sacajawea's burial site—began earlier in the century. The Daughters of the American Revolution had dedicated a marker in 1909 at a grave in Fremont County. The plaque read:

SACAJAWEA
Died April 9, 1884
A Guide with the
Lewis and Clark Expedition
1805-1806
Identified 1909 by Rev. J. Roberts
Who Officiated at Her Burial

Grace Hebard's efforts to locate the site of the grave were major factors leading to the erection of this marker.

1.

2.

3.

1. Dedication of the DeSmet Monument in Sublette County on July 5, 1940. On the left was the Most Reverend Bishop P. A. McGovern.

2. Mrs. P. J. Quealy of Kemmerer and Governor Nels Smith at the dedication of the Names Hill Monument, July 1940.

3. Dedication of the Father DeSmet Monument in Johnson County in August 1940. Joseph Weppner is second from the left, and John Charles Thompson is on the right.

Father DeSmet Monument in Johnson County, erected in 1940.

Dr. Hebard, professor of political economy at the University of Wyoming, published her research on the subject in 1932. It was entitled "Sacajawea: A guide and interpreter of the Lewis and Clark Expedition, with an account of the travels of Toussaint Charbonneau, and of Jean Baptiste, the expedition papoose." Despite this comprehensive work, doubt remained as to where Sacajawea was really interred.

The Landmark Commission dedicated another marker to Sacajawea on September 26, 1941. According to *Wyoming: A Guide to Its History,* published in the same year, additional controversy arose at that time. The commission's dedication ceremonies attempted to provide "legendary" proof of the burial site:

> Then came that part of the ceremony which gave proof to the reality of Sacajawea. Pandora Pogue, ninety-eight years old, stood straight and proudly as Interpreter Compton repeated the interview that he had with her in which she told of knowing Sacajawea at Fort Bridger in 1868 and later at the Shoshone Agency. Pandora Pogue was present when Sacajawea died and she saw her buried in the cemetery near the Roberts Mission.
>
> Quantan Quay, over one hundred years old, stated that he had known Sacajawea very well, also her sons, Baptiste and Basil. He told of her presence at the council at Fort Bridger when the reservation was given to them. He also told of attending her burial.
>
> The next speaker was the Reverend John Roberts, the Episcopal minister who for more than sixty years has served as the missionary to the Shoshone Indians on the reservation. He cited incidents of the burial ceremony of Sacajawea and stated that he had the privilege and honor of leading the burial services of that great woman. She was buried in what is now called the Shoshone burial grounds in the Shoshone cemetery. Said Rev. Roberts, "For us and future generations to come it indicates that she was buried in the Shoshone cemetery—may the memory of that noted Shoshone woman live forever in the hearts of a grateful people."

The Reverend Roberts was associated with the Indian School at Fort Washakie for over sixty years. He was respected and considered "an authority on the ways and customs of the Indians on the Wind River Reservation." The *Annals of Wyoming,* October 1941, quoted Roberts in essentially the same way:

> I wish to say to you that I did have the privilege and honor of leading the burial services of this great woman. She was buried in what is now called the Shoshoni burial grounds which the monolith indicates, which is dedicated and unveiled today. For us and future generations to come, it indicates that she was buried in the Shoshoni Cemetery.

But the Historical Landmark Commission was challenged by new historians with new facts. Richardson rebuked the doubters:

The Old Sherman Cemetery marker was erected by the Historical Landmark Commission in 1958.

Does any man call this "legendary?" Or, is Reverend Roberts to be considered lacking in "schools of thought!" The so-called "de-bunkers" of history are like the writers of history hundreds of years afterwards, who say old Queen Elizabeth was a man; and that Bacon wrote the immortal plays of Shakespeare; and that Washington did tell lies, and did not cut down a cherry tree.

Let us let the Indian girl, Sacajawea, rest in peace in her grave at old Fort Washakie, where Reverend John Roberts who knew her and performed the services at her burial certified to this fact; where Miss Grace Raymond Hebard, a most reliable and painstaking researcher, who was the University of Wyoming historian, says she is buried; and where relatives and grand children and numerous old Indians testified to her burial in Fort Washakie, her old home.

Professor T. A. Larson wrote in *History of Wyoming* that most scholars agree that Sacajawea's grave is in South Dakota. Irving W. Anderson's article, "Probing the Riddle of the Bird Woman," in the autumn 1973 issue of *Montana: The Magazine of Western History,* provides the best presentation of the evidence. In that article Anderson quoted Russell Reid, then superintendent of the North Dakota State Historical Society:

> In order to support this theory much evidence has been collected in the forms of interviews, statements and affidavits. Most certainly no one has a right to question the motives nor the honesty of individuals who gave such testimony, but it should be pointed out that evidence of this kind is not always reliable. Far too often

1. Dedication of the Sacajawea Monument in 1941. At the microphone was the Reverend John Roberts, Episcopal missionary to the Shoshone Indians and founder of the Shoshone School for Indian Girls in 1883. Roberts officiated at the burial services of Sacajawea.

2. Dedication of the Sacajawea Monument in 1941. On the left was Quantan Quay, an Indian over 100 years old, who spoke of knowing Sacajawea very well and attending her funeral. The Historical Landmark Commission tried to validate the burial site of Sacajawea with legendary witnesses.

3. Two great grand-daughters of Sacajawea, Irene Large and Gloria Isis, unveiling the Sacajawea Monument, September 26, 1941. On the left is L. L. Newton, Master of Ceremonies and Editor of the *Lander Journal*.

1.

2.

3.

individuals are apt to confuse fact with fiction and stories they have heard with some of their own experiences.

Anderson also paraphrased a general maxim of the legal profession: "one scratch of the pen at the time of an event is worth tenfold the testimony of many witnesses relying upon memory subsequent to the event." And so it happened that on December 20, 1812, at Fort Manuel in South Dakota, one Mr. Luttig made the following entry in his journal: "This evening the wife of Charbonneau, a Snake squaw, died of a putrid fever. She was the best woman in the fort, aged abount twenty-five years. She left a fine infant child."

The Historical Landmark Commission prepared biennial reports of its activities. Throughout the late 1920s and 1930s the reports were complete, informative, and grandiose. They reflected the marker dedications of that same era. The splendid and showy events—complete with banquets, picnics, bands, and pageants—reflected not only the participants' patriotism but a strong desire to memorialize the past. In the 1940s and 1950s, the reports became shorter and less informative, more business-like and less friendly. The commission was beset by historical challenges and conflicts. No longer were the commissioners the absolute authorities of Wyoming history.

On June 25, 1955, the Landmark Commission held a special meeting welcoming three new members: Mrs. Keith Blackner, Mr. Cyrus Blair, and Mr. Jules Farlow, Sr. These three replaced T. Joe Cahill, Ernest Dahlquist, and Col. E. A. Froyd. Warren Richardson and Joseph Weppner remained on the commission. During that meeting, Richardson suggested that "a brochure be printed covering every monument erected by the Commission, its location, a brief history of the event commemorated and the inscription on each."

During the commission's meeting the next year, Mrs. Blackner initiated a proposal placing "signs one-half mile on both approaches to all monuments and markers on highways and roads, wording to be 'Historical Marker One-Half Mile'." The commission passed a motion to erect a monument west of Dubois marking the location where the Old Trail crossed over Union Pass. They also chose to erect a monument to the memory of Chief Washakie on the highway at Fort Washakie. In 1957, two markers were built in Cheyenne—the Camp Carlin Monument (Laramie County #3) and the Cheyenne-Fort Laramie-Deadwood Trail Monument (Laramie County #6).

Perhaps the first of several spats with State Engineer L. C. Bishop surfaced in 1956 when Bishop wrote a newspaper editorial criticizing the placement of the Oregon Trails Fork monument (False Parting of the Ways Monument—Sublette County #16). In 1957 Bishop won some political backing from George C. Bermingham, co-chairman of the Joint Ways and Means Committee. Apparently, Bermingham suggested in a letter that the engineer's services could benefit the Landmark Commission. The Thirty-Fourth Wyoming State Legislature agreed that assistance was needed for making historical surveys. Warren Richardson explained that

> after 30 years on the Commission. . .we have marked most all of the important spots on the Oregon Trail,

Bozeman Trail and Overland Stage Station Route and felt that Mr. Bishop's services were not required; however, if and when it was needed, we would call on him.

In June 1958, the final commission meeting was led by Richardson and Weppner, but two new members were appointed by Governor Milward Simpson. Warren B. Lott from Buffalo and D. H. Buscher replaced Blair and Blackner. Farlow asked the commission to reconsider the suggestion to employ Bishop to help with historical surveys. There must have been a good debate because the attorney general's office was asked for an opinion. The new voices—Farlow, Buscher, and Lott—carried the vote against Richardson and Weppner. The two older commissioners—members since 1927—were defeated by new ideas and younger historians. But the setback was a minor one compared to the loss they suffered at the hands of the Wyoming State Legislature in 1959.

In February, the legislature reassigned the responsibilities of the Landmark Commission to the State Library, Archives and Historical Board (Ch.77, Session Laws of Wyoming, 1959). Although few details concerning either the reorganization or the legislative intent of the reassignment have survived, the 1958-1960 Archives and Historical Department reports suggested some of the problems:

> The work of the preservation of historic sites under the control of the State is being revitalized. Much effort has been put into a program to obtain the cooperation and aid of local and state agencies and organizations in developing, maintaining, preserving and restoring these historical landmarks. Special mention should be made of the cooperation of the State Historical Society and County Chapters of the Society, State Highway Department, State Penitentiary, County Commissioners of all counties, Mayors and Chambers of Commerce.

Obviously, the Landmark Commission had lost the cooperation of both federal and state agencies. Perhaps it failed to grow with the changes in historical research and preservation; perhaps it could not cope with change in general. In any case, a reorganization took place, a new plan for historical marking was made, and the Historical Landmark Commission of Wyoming was no more.

The Era of the Wyoming State Archives and Historical Department, the Wyoming State Historical Society, the State Parks Commission, the Wyoming Recreation Commission, and the State Historic Preservation Office

A new era began when the Landmark Commission was disbanded. All of the commission's records and property were transferred to the Wyoming State Archives and Historical Department. Under the guidance of Director Lola M. Homsher and Katherine Halverson, the new department began the long and tedious task of rebuilding the markers program. In 1959, working closely with the State Historical Society and its local chapters, the Archives and Historical Department organized a program to erect historic signs across Wyoming. Together, they sponsored an historical marker style and design contest, won by the Campbell County chapter, which proposed a 4' X 6' wooden sign with a legend carved into it. Many of Wyoming's beautiful markers of today were made in accordance with those plans.

By 1960 several of the new signs had already been erected. Cold Springs Informative Sign (Goshen County #2), Fort Fetterman Information Sign (Converse County #6), and Historic Guernsey Sign (Platte County #6) were some of the first. The Union Pacific Railroad assisted with the construction of a sign at Ames Monument, and the Cheyenne Chamber of Commerce put up markers for each main highway entrance into their city.

Between 1960 and 1962 many more signs were built. Twenty-one of Wyoming's twenty-three counties erected markers, including Leigh Creek Informative Sign (Washakie County #2), Bozeman Trail Informative Sign (Campbell County #2.1), Encampment, Wyoming, (Grand Encampment) Informative Sign (Carbon County #6), and Bear River City Sign (Uinta County #1).

The wooden signs were romantic and beautiful, but they also required a great deal of yearly maintenance. The first signs were carved at the state penitentiary in Rawlins and maintained by the Highway Department. In 1962, the Archives and Historical Department proposed that cast aluminum signs replace the wooden ones. The department went on to suggest that aluminum signs were more attractive—but that was probably a matter of debate.

Also in 1962 the department issued a brochure prepared by Halverson entitled "Wyoming Historical Sites and Markers and Museums," listing 208 historical markers, 115 historic sites and 25 museums. Although the Landmark Commission had suggested a similar brochure in 1955, this publication was the first to gather such information.

The State Parks Commission, created in 1937, became active with the Archives and Historical Department between 1962 and 1964. Paul Henderson, one of the most knowledgeable historians of western trails, was the historian for the Parks Commission in 1962. The markers program now had a new partner, one who assumed some of the responsibilities previously held by the Historical Society and county chapters. The Parks Commission erected and maintained markers while the Archives and Historical Department approved the titles, and researched, compiled, and authenticated the inscriptions used. Although the Historical Society still actively supported the markers program, and also reviewed the legends for monuments and markers, their formal relationship with the Archives and Historical Department changed. Under the leadership of the department, fifty-six markers were erected from 1959 to 1966. Eagle's Nest Stage Station (Park County #7), Killing of Champion and Rae Informative Sign (Johnson County #4), and Fremont's Week in Sublette County (Sublette

County #6), for example, were erected between 1962 and 1964.

The National Historic Preservation Act of 1966 established the National Register of Historic Places. Under this legislation, each state was to designate an historic preservation officer to administer the policies of the register. Responding to the federal mandate, the Wyoming Legislature created the Wyoming Recreation Commission in July 1967. That signaled the beginning of another significant era of historical marker activity for Wyoming. The responsibilities of the state historic preservation officer resided in the Historic Section of the Wyoming Recreation Commission. Absorbed into the new commission and preservation office was the old State Parks Commission and all of its responsibilities for historical landmarks, sites, and markers. The State Archives and Historical Department now worked with the Wyoming Recreation Commission to manage the monuments and markers program.

New names, which would become synonymous with Wyoming historical marker activity, grew from the creation of the commission. Paul Westedt, the first state historic preservation officer, became the director of the Recreation Commission in 1969. Under his guidance, the commission published *Wyoming: A Guide to Historic Sites* in 1976. The book provided information on more than two hundred historic sites and was dedicated to a man well-known to Wyoming historians: Ned Frost—"citizen, historian, and the architect of Wyoming's historic preservation program."

In 1967 Frost, an outfitter from Cody, headed the Historical Section of the Wyoming Recreation Commission. He and Pete Lange of Wheatland surveyed the state's monuments and markers and provided the first numbering system for historical markers in Wyoming. Their survey laid the groundwork upon which the marker system now grows. Although cumbersome and not easily altered, the 1967 survey has guided monument and marker research since then.

Lange became the supervisor of marker maintenance, and developed a vast knowledge of and respect for historical markers before resigning in 1984. Frost provided the flamboyant, colorful, and often-criticized language found on many of the markers erected from 1967 to 1978.

Before Frost's involvement with site interpretation, the Archives and Historical Department had researched and produced legends. But Frost's zeal for markers gave him the lead in sign design. Mark Junge, an academic researcher and understudy of Frost's, provided him with the necessary historical information to make correct site interpretations. Frost wrote the legends, then asked Katherine Halverson at the Archives and Historical Department for approval.

Words and phrases attributed to Frost were: "an epic of fortitudinous exploration"; "What manner of men and beasts impelled conveyances weighing on those grinding wheels?"; "John Colter, veteran of the Lewis and Clark Expedition, notably self-sufficient mountain man and indefatigable explorer, was the first white man known to have reconnoitered this locale"; "The wayfarer's penchant for inscribing names and dates on prominent landmarks excites

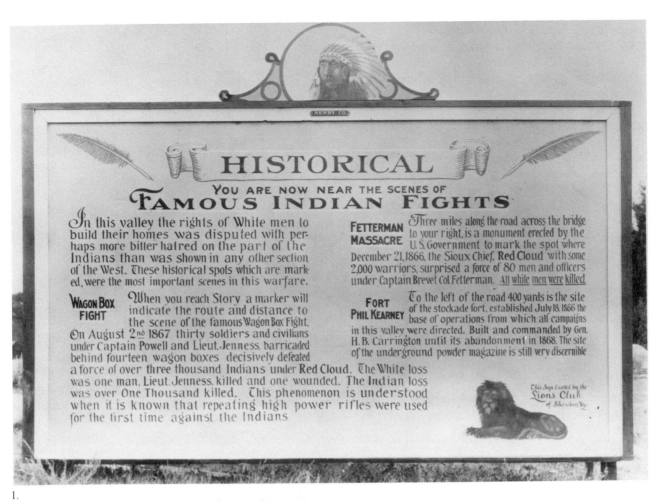

HISTORICAL
YOU ARE NOW NEAR THE SCENES OF
FAMOUS INDIAN FIGHTS

In this valley the rights of White men to build their homes was disputed with perhaps more bitter hatred on the part of the Indians than was shown in any other section of the West. These historical spots which are marked, were the most important scenes in this warfare.

WAGON BOX FIGHT   When you reach Story a marker will indicate the route and distance to the scene of the famous Wagon Box Fight. On August 2nd 1867 thirty soldiers and civilians under Captain Powell and Lieut. Jenness, barricaded behind fourteen wagon boxes decisively defeated a force of over three thousand Indians under Red Cloud. The White loss was one man, Lieut. Jenness, killed and one wounded. The Indian loss was over One Thousand killed. This phenomenon is understood when it is known that repeating high power rifles were used for the first time against the Indians

FETTERMAN MASSACRE   Three miles along the road across the bridge to your right, is a monument erected by the U.S. Government to mark the spot where December 21, 1866, the Sioux Chief, Red Cloud with some 2,000 warriors, surprised a force of 80 men and officers under Captain Brevet Col. Fetterman. All white men were killed.

FORT PHIL KEARNEY   To the left of the road 400 yards is the site of the stockade fort, established July 18, 1866 the base of operations from which all campaigns in this valley were directed. Built and commanded by Gen. H.B. Carrington until its abandonment in 1868. The site of the underground powder magazine is still very discernible

This Sign Erected by the
Lions Club
of Sheridan Wyo.

1.

2.

3.

1. Historical billboard erected by the Lions Club of Sheridan, Wyoming.

2. Ned Frost supplied the flamboyant and colorful language found on many markers erected 1969-1978. When criticized for using words like "fortitudinous" and "indefatigable," Frost would respond, "Let the little bastards learn!"

3. Ned Frost on the left and Paul Henderson in the center. Frost headed the Historical Section of the Wyoming Recreation Commission in 1967. Henderson, one of the most knowledgeable historians of western trails, was historian for the State Parks Commission in 1962. Both men were responsible for efforts to mark historic sites in Wyoming.

the interest of his descendants. Regrettably, marks of historic value are often effaced by later opportunists."

It has been said that Frost was advised to write the signs so that a fourth grader could read them. However, he was himself inclined to write for a higher level of education. When criticized, Frost would respond, "Let the little bastards learn!" Ned Frost made historical markers entertaining and educational. He was fondly remembered by all who worked with him.

When Frost died in 1978, Mark Junge replaced him as head of the Historical Section. Junge said that losing Ned Frost was like losing the spirit and heart of the markers program. Still, Junge led the program through some controversial and troubling times.

In the early 1980s, the Wyoming Recreation Commission and the Archives and Historical Department began to compete for management and control of some historic sites. The markers and monuments program was one of those areas where the two agencies were expected to cooperate, as there was no separate department assigned to that responsibility. Before that time, the Recreation Commission and the Archives and Historical Department had worked reasonably well together. But disagreements and troubles arose. Disputes flourished with respect to maintaining, managing, and interpreting historic sites. An "inside-outside" arrangement evolved, and Governor Ed Herschler commented on the inter-agency squabbles: if a broken window at a state historic site fell inward, then the responsibility to repair it would lie with one agency; if the broken window fell outward, then the responsibility would lie with the other.

In reality, the conflict affected monuments and markers very little; it simply became more difficult to get legends reviewed and approved. The Archives and Historical Department and the Recreation Commission had grown apart and now acted independently of each other. However, changes were underway for both the State Historic Preservation Office and the markers program. Since its inception in 1967, the Preservation Office had resided within the jurisdiction of the Wyoming Recreation Commission. In 1985, reorganization took monuments and markers and the Preservation Office on a journey to another state agency.

Under Executive Order No. 1985-4, Governor Herschler transferred the State Historic Preservation Office—staff, funding, and responsibilities—from the jurisdiction of the Wyoming Recreation Commission to the Archives and Historical Department. Included in the executive order was specific funding for a monuments and markers position. The repository for the position was the Preservation Office's survey and registration program managed by historian Sheila Bricher-Wade. Prior to 1985, work on monuments and markers represented only a small part of the responsibilites of any permanent staff member at either agency. Through reorganization, a state-funded and fully dedicated position for monuments and markers evolved. It wasn't to be long-lived, however. In an effort to downsize government, the legislature cut the position the following year.

Prior to the state-funded monuments and markers position,

grant funding had sustained some full-time staff. In 1982 and 1983, Steve Whissen investigated legal descriptions and locations for many markers.

In 1984, Bruce Noble further identified legal descriptions for each marker. He produced a database of monuments and coordinated the restoration work done by the Wyoming Recreation Commission. Noble's work led him to become an expert on markers and monuments in Wyoming. During the national convention of the Oregon-California Trails Association at Scottsbluff, Nebraska, in August 1985, he presented a paper describing the history of Wyoming's efforts to mark the Oregon Trail. The paper was later published in the summer 1986 issue of the association's official magazine, *Overland Journal.* When the legislature failed to fund the monuments and markers position, Noble left Wyoming for a position in Washington, D.C..

Since 1986, the legislature has, for all practical purposes, left the monuments and markers program unattended and unfunded. Although markers have been placed at various sites, no momentous developments or accomplishments have occurred.

Sheila Bricher-Wade has nursed the program along. She was responsible for erection of markers during Wyoming's centennial year in 1990. Funding was made available through the Centennial Commission, and new markers were placed at several locations, including Camp Devin in Crook County, Jim Bridger Historic Trail in Washakie County, Almy in Uinta County, Wamsutter in Sweetwater County, The Riverton Project and The Sweetwater Valley in Fremont County, and Miners' Monument in Lincoln County.

Perhaps the real heroes of the monuments and markers program have been the men and women who maintained the markers. Known to Preservation Office personnel as "the state parks guys," these employees of the Recreation Commission have shown great care and concern. They have refurbished the deteriorating wooden signs, repaired granite markers that were fractured or knocked over, and assisted with general maintenance around the marker sites. In spite of inter-agency fighting and lack of funding, they have been a stabilizing force for the program.

Historical Marking by Other Organizations

Utah Pioneer Trails and Landmarks Association

The Oregon Trail Memorial Association, as previously discussed, was organized by Ezra Meeker and others prior to Meeker's death in 1928. That organization saw the need to form preservation groups in each state along the old pioneer trails. The Historical Landmarks Commission, formed in 1927, and the Oregon Trail Memorial Association worked well together in Wyoming. Six other western states had, at that time, organized similar commissions. In April 1930, Dr. Howard R. Driggs, president of the Oregon Trail Memorial Association, went to Utah to urge the formation of a preservation group in Utah. With enthusiasm, the Utah Pioneer

Trails and Landmarks Association was formed under the guidance of George Albert Smith, president, and John D. Giles, executive secretary. Giles—referred to as "Utah's Famed Mr. Monuments"—was the right man to contact. He had become interested in pioneers as a boy growing up in Provo and had spent many years studying the history of the Mormon Church and early Utah pioneers.

. The new Landmarks Association worked with the Mutual Improvement Association to raise money for monuments. As in Wyoming, Oregon Trail Memorial Coins were sold to finance the new wave of marker enthusiasm that was spreading over Utah.

The Utah Pioneer Trails and Landmarks Association also built many markers in Wyoming, including several beautiful monuments commemorating the Mormon pioneers that lived in or passed through the state. Each bronze tablet bears at the top a relief of a buffalo skull—the insignia of the association. Local Mormon churches and the State of Wyoming assisted in erecting these monuments.

The first marker erected in Wyoming by the Utah Landmarks Association was the one dedicated at Independence Rock on June 21, 1931. A caravan of about seventy-five cars traveled from Salt Lake City to witness the dedication. As previously mentioned, the bronze plaque memorialized the 80,000 Mormons who passed on their way to the Great Salt Lake Valley, and Heber J. Grant, president of the Mormon Church, dedicated the monument. The Landmarks Association was represented by Smith and Giles, the Wyoming Historical Landmark Commission by Bryant Brooks, and the Natrona County Historical Society by Thomas Cooper. Howard Driggs, president of the Oregon Trail Memorial Association, also was in attendance.

The Mormon Ferry Monument (Natrona County #7)—erected on the Fort Caspar parade grounds and dedicated in 1932—was the thirteenth marker to be placed by the Utah Association. A dedicatory tour similar to those of the Wyoming Historical Landmark Commission brought about fifty Salt Lake City residents to southwest Wyoming in June 1933. George Albert Smith and Heber J. Grant accompanied the trek along the old Mormon California Trail. The association's twenty-fifth marker was dedicated on June 25, at the Mormon Wall Monument (Uinta County 6.10). It commemorated the struggles of the early Mormons at and near Fort Bridger. Dedicated during the previous week were the Willie's Handcart Company Monument (Fremont County #38) and the Martin's Cove Monument (Natrona County #13)—the twenty-seventh and twenty-eighth markers placed by the association. These two monuments marked the sites of tragedies for Mormon pioneers. The Mormon Colonists Monument (Big Horn County #5) was erected September 29, 1935, west of Lovell—the fifty-eighth association marker.

The Utah Pioneer Trails and Landmark Association no longer exists. Before its demise however, the association left a legacy of beautiful historical markers across Wyoming and many other states.

The Daughters of Utah Pioneers

On April 11, 1901, the Daughters of Utah Pioneers began with fifty charter members. Membership was limited to female descendants of the pioneers who arrived in Utah prior to the driving of the Golden Spike at Promontory Point on May 10, 1869. Their purpose was clearly stated:

> The object of this association shall be to perpetuate the names and achievements of the men, women and children who were the pioneers in founding this commonwealth; by preserving old landmarks, marking historical places, collecting relics and histories, establishing a library of historical matter, and securing unprinted manuscripts, photographs, maps and all such data as shall aid in perfecting a record of the Utah pioneers;...thus teaching their descendants and the citizens of our country lessons of faith, courage, fortitude, and patriotism.

During the first years of the organization, historical data collection was the main emphasis. Personal biographies were written and filed. As the files grew, the organization published monthly pamphlets of sixty to seventy-five pages dealing with one subject. In 1930 the pamphlets were incorporated into book form. Twelve volumes of "Heart Throbs of the West" were printed in the following decade. By 1951 a second series became necessary—the six-volume "Treasures of Pioneer History." In 1958 another series entitled "Our Pioneer Heritage" was started.

The sale of these books helped finance the work of the organization. In October 1933, the national convention voted to create a fund for historical marker purposes. In the spring of the next year, the Daughters erected their first marker. By 1987 the organization had furnished 433 plaques. Most of their marking efforts were in Utah, but several markers were erected in Wyoming.

On August 25, 1939, The Daughters of Utah Pioneers erected the First Schoolhouse Plaque (Uinta County #6.18) on the grounds of Fort Bridger. The marker was the organization's fifty-second and commemorated the school that Judge William A. Carter established for the education of children, including his four daughters and two sons, at the fort. The First Brick Church Marker (Uinta County #11) was erected on November 1, 1941. The Mormon Monument (Teton County #5) in Jackson was the 123rd marker erected by the Daughters. Dedicated in 1948, that monument memorialized the five Mormon families who pioneered Jackson Hole in 1889. The Star Valley Marker (Lincoln County #21) was erected in 1956 to memorialize the pioneers of Star Valley. The First Post Office Monument (Lincoln County #1.1) in Thayne, Wyoming, was erected by the Daughters in 1963—the 277th marker dedicated by the organization. In December 1968, Daughters of Utah Pioneers marker No. 357 was erected in Laramie to commemorate the last of the organized emigration companies of Latter-day Saints. The Daughters erected the Osmund Marker (Lincoln County #14) in 1970—their 371st. This marker commemorated the site of the first school in the area between Afton and Smoot.

1.

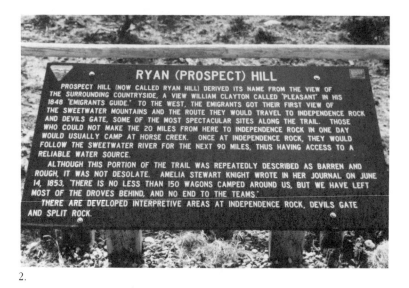

2.

3.

5.

4.

1. Beginning in 1959 Wyoming's historical markers took on a new appearance. Wooden signs, four feet by six feet, were suspended from a large beam and posts.

2. The Ryan Hill BLM sign was erected by the Bureau of Land Management along the Oregon Trail southwest of Casper.

3. Cast aluminum signs were proposed in 1962 to replace the wooden signs requiring yearly maintenance. This sign was erected during Wyoming's Centennial, 1990.

4. Markers erected by the Daughters of Utah Pioneers followed a similar design. This marker depicting the oxen yoke and beehive was erected in Lincoln County.

5. The Utah Pioneer Trails and Landmarks Association was formed in 1930 and erected several markers in Wyoming. Association markers all had bison skulls at the top, as did this marker near Lovell.

United States Department of the Interior—Bureau of Land Management and National Park Service

In November 1978, the Congress of the United States designated the Oregon and Mormon Pioneer Trails as National Historic Trails. The concept involved the cooperation of two agencies of the Interior Department: the National Park Service and the Bureau of Land Management (BLM). The Park Service directed the general planning to protect, interpret, and manage the trails. The BLM carried out the recommendations of the comprehensive plans for the trails system, including interpretation and protection of the historic sites.

Certified historic sites and segments of the Oregon and Mormon Pioneer National Historic Trails were designated in the initial planning. The sites in Wyoming were Emigrant Gap, Bessemer Bend, Devil's Gate, Split Rock, Ice Slough Spring, Rocky Ridge, South Pass, Martin's Cove, and Parting-of-the-Ways. Certified segments of the trails included seventy-two miles at South Pass in Fremont County and sixteen miles near Bear River Divide in Lincoln County. Shorter segments were designated at Independence Rock and Split Rock in Natrona County, and Dry Sandy in Sublette County. Interpretive signs and markers have been placed at many of these sites. They have been listed in the second part of this book under their respective counties.

In 1988 the BLM in Wyoming distributed the "Oregon/Mormon Pioneer National Historic Trails Gift Catalog." The catalog invited interested organizations and persons to contribute money to the BLM's efforts to protect and interpret the trails across Wyoming. Forty-five historic sites were listed with cost estimates for the signing, parking, foot trails, and pamphlets to be placed at each. The sites in the catalog corresponded to those designated in the planning concept for the National Historic Trails. Interpretive signs had already been located at sites such as Emigrant Gap, Ryan (Prospect) Hill, the Oregon Trail just west of Fort Laramie, Pacific Springs, and Plume Rocks. Treated wooden posts—with trail names routed into the surface—marked the trails. For instance, one post had Oregon Trail on one face and Sublette Cutoff on the back; another had Oregon Trail, Mormon Trail, and Pony Express on three different sides. However, much of the signing of sites in the catalog was unfinished, if begun at all, when the catalog first came out. Many more wooden posts were to be placed along the 345 miles of national trails in Wyoming. Under this plan, funding determined the speed and extent of marking efforts.

Oregon-California Trails Association (OCTA)

After the demise of Meeker's Oregon Trail Memorial Association in 1939, and its grandchild—the American Pioneer Trails Association—in 1954, no national group took over the task of preservation until the formation of the Oregon-California Trails Association in 1982. Both during and after the era of the Oregon Trail Memorial Association, interest in the Trail had remained high. Many historians examined emigrant diaries, piecing together stories of hardship and courage. Gravesites and the trails themselves were also subject to study. However, no concerted effort to mark, interpret, and preserve the Oregon Trail had emerged.

Gregory M. Franzwa—author, publisher, and trail buff—invited concerned persons to discuss the formation of an organization to do just that. Attending that meeting were Dr. John A. Latschar, Robert D. Tucker, James F. Bowers, Robert Rennells, Bertha Rennells, Troy Gray, Billie Gray, Merrill J. Mattes, Roger Blair, Dr. Merle W. Wells, and James P. Johnson. Franzwa was elected president of the new organization, and Merrill Mattes elected executive vice president. Troy Gray suggested that the organization be called the Oregon-California Trails Association (OCTA). Its "Statement of Purpose" was broadly defined to include "the identification, preservation, and interpretation of trail remains and associated historic sites and landmarks along the great central migration corridor to the Pacific Coast." The new association published a quarterly magazine—the *Overland Journal*—"as a forum for scholarly articles adding to the sum of knowledge about trails along the central route."

Gregory Franzwa served as president for three years, until 1985, and on the board of directors for two more years. Because of "fundamental differences in philosophy," he submitted his resignation from the organization in June 1987.

The members of OCTA were a distinguished and knowledgeable group. Merrill Mattes, who was also Superintendent of Scotts Bluff National Monument, proved to have vast information about the Oregon Trail system. He authored several books, including *The Great Platte River Road, Platte River Road Narratives,* and *Fort Laramie Park History 1834-1977.* Dr. E. G. Chuinard was "past president of the Lewis and Clark Trail Heritage Foundation and the author of *Only One Man Died,* a study of the medical aspects of the Lewis and Clark expedition." Stanley Kimball was "professor of history at Southern Illinois University, Edwardsville, historian for the Mormon Pioneer Trails Foundation, and the editor of *The Latter Day Saints' Emigrants' Guide* by William Clayton." Dr. John A. Latschar was an "historian with the National Park Service in Denver and co-author of the 'Comprehensive Management and Use Plan for the Oregon Trail'." Dr. Merle Wells was a distinguished historian from Idaho and "served many years as that state's State Historic Preservation Officer." Other individuals, like Troy and Billie Gray, Bob and Bertha Rennells and Charles Martin, Sr., also contributed expertise they had learned in their studies of the Trail.

The initial work of the organization dealt with preservation. In 1983 OCTA prevented further damage by a bulldozer to the Trail near the Nancy Hill grave in Lincoln County. Karen Buck led OCTA in protecting three and one-half miles of Oregon Trail ruts which would have been lost if a proposed U.S. Bureau of Reclamation dam on Big Sandy River had been built. The association also participated with the Wyoming Highway Department in planning State Route 28 between Farson and State Route 372. OCTA's work to preserve the Oregon Trail continued beyond the successes of the first year, leading trail preservation efforts in all of the states from Missouri to Oregon.

Its first attempt at markers occurred in 1983, with a drive to

1.

2.

3.

1. The Wyoming Tie and Timber Company erected and dedicated the Tie Hack Monument in 1946.

2. The Laramie County Historical Society dedicated the Cheyenne Corner Stone in 1960. The Wyoming State Historical Society and its local chapters have always supported efforts to place historical markers and monuments.

3. Dedication of the Overland Trail Marker at the Colorado-Wyoming border on July 4, 1917.

4. Dedication of the Inyan Kara Church, August 1, 1950.

4.

honor the late Paul Henderson. In August 1985, Merrill Mattes led the dedication of the Paul Henderson Memorial at the Oregon Trail Cemetery in Bridgeport, Nebraska. Since 1987, OCTA has also been very active in marking the Trail in Wyoming. It has erected many markers on both private and public lands. Lee Underbrink of Casper promoted the program, receiving help from Karen Buck Rennells of LaBarge and Randy Brown of Douglas. OCTA designed permaloy plaques with a contemporary appearance to detail the lives of emigrants or soldiers who died on the Trail. Markers were placed at the gravesites of Mary J. Hurley, Bennet Tribbett, and Joel Hembree, for example. Other markers, such as Reshaw's Bridge and McKinstry Ridge, interpreted historical sites. Overall, the Oregon-California Trail Association has been concerned more with the people of the great migration and sites along the Trail than with historic battles or fights.

A Few Interested Residents

In the introduction, I discussed the reasons why people built markers. They had a need to preserve the past, a need to pass a memory or heritage on to children or grandchildren. In this book many people important to the history of marking in Wyoming were named; many, unfortunately, were also left out. Inscriptions like "The Citizens of Lingle and Friends," "Town of Cokeville," "Citizens of Kemmerer," "Citizens of Torrington," and "A Few Interested Residents" have appeared on markers. And so, it seems only appropriate that a few interested residents be credited here at the end.

No one named the people who helped erect the monument at Fort Laramie in 1915 on which "A Few Interested Residents" was engraved. It was not important to name them in 1915 and has remained so today. What is important, however, was that some were interested in historic preservation. Because of their concern, Wyoming has received an irreplaceable legacy.

A note on marker numbers:

In June 1967, Ned Frost and Pete Lange, Wyoming Recreation Commission historian and maintenance foreman, respectively, began a systematic inventory of all the historical markers, monuments, and signs. Never before had such a cataloging been done, and the marker numbering system was born.

The numbering system used in this book maintains that original inventory scheme even though questions about its usefulness arose. For instance, when markers were added to the system, they were placed between two existing markers. In that case, a decimal between the two original markers was used, such as 18, 18.5, and 19. In some cases, markers were vandalized and never replaced; sometimes markers were removed because of poor taste in content of the legend. Such circumstances left holes in the numbering system.

ALBANY COUNTY

AMES MONUMENT-1.1

North Face:
TITLE: None
LEGEND: "In Memory of Oakes & Oliver Ames"
East Face: (Bust of Oakes Ames):
TITLE: None
LEGEND: Born January 10, 1804. Died May 8, 1873.
West Face: (Bust of Oliver Ames):
TITLE: None
LEGEND: Born November 1807. Died March 7, 1877.

LOCATION: About 1.5 miles south of I-80 near the summit between Cheyenne and Laramie.

Much of the history below is from the National Register of Historic Places Inventory-Nomination Form prepared by Mark Junge in November 1971.

Oakes and Oliver Ames were ambitious men from Massachusetts with interests in politics and business. In 1855 they jointly built the Easton Branch Railroad in Massachusetts. When financial trouble halted construction and progress of the transcontinental railroad, Oakes Ames was urged to help complete the project. Credit Mobiler of America, the construction company building the transcontinental railroad, was led by Oakes and Oliver Ames, then prominent stockholders.

Oakes Ames, himself a Massachusetts representative to Congress, sold shares of the company's stock to other members of Congress in order to finance the construction. The Credit Mobiler, then under Congressional control, was in a position to influence politicians for the company's benefit. Three years after completion of the railroad, allegations arose accusing the Credit Mobiler and Oakes Ames (Oakes Ames was then the firm's senior partner) of defrauding the government. The House of Representatives, although it did not expel him, condemned his conduct. He died ten weeks after the Congressional condemnation.

On March 10, 1875, the stockholders of the Union Pacific Railroad adopted a resolution to erect a permanent monument in recognition of Oakes Ames' services in the construction of the railroad. The resolution and monument not only reflected the close relationship between Oakes and the Union Pacific Railroad, it vindicated the work of Oliver Ames, and especially that of Oakes Ames.

This magnificent sixty foot-high granite pyramid was completed in 1882 at a cost of $64,773. Union Pacific trains stopped at the monument and the nearby lively community of Sherman before descending the steep grade into the Laramie Plains. In 1901, the railroad was re-routed three and one-half miles south of the monument. The town of Sherman quickly faded, and the monument became a lonely and quiet reminder of the recent past. Sixteen years after the route change, the Union Pacific voted to move the monument to a location near the new tracks. The move was never made, and the monument still stands undisturbed on the high and windy summit between Cheyenne and Laramie. On September 14, 1983, Upland Industries Corporation, the land development subsidiary of Union Pacific Corporation, donated the land, the monument, and funds to the State of Wyoming in order to maintain and perpetuate this historic monument.

AMES INFORMATIVE SIGN-1.2

TITLE: The Ames Monument
LEGEND: Completed in 1882 at a cost of $65,000, this monolithic, 60 foot high granite pyramid was built by the Union Pacific Railroad Company. It stands on the highest elevation (8,247 feet) of the original transcontinental route. Until 1901, when the railroad was relocated several miles to the south, it passed close by the north side of the monument where once stood the rail town of Sherman.

The monument serves a memorial to the Ames brothers of Massachusetts, Oakes (1804-1873) and Oliver (1807-1877), whose wealth, influence, talent, and work were key factors in the construction of the first coast to coast railroad in North America. The contribution made

by Oakes was especially significant even though in 1873 he was implicated in a scandal relative to financing the construction of the railroad.

Ames Monument was designed by the distinguished American architect Henry Hobson Richardson (1838-1886). Located further west than any of his works, this memorial typifies the Richardsonian style by its energetic elemental characteristics. His love for native construction materials is demonstrated by the monument's great, rough hewn granite blocks, quarried from "Reeds rock" one-half mile west. A Richardson biographer has called the monument "perhaps the finest memorial in America...one of Richardson's least known and most perfect works. The bas-relief medallions of the Ames brothers were done by the prominent American sculptor, Augustus Saint-Gaudens.
LOCATION: Adjacent to Ames Monument (Albany County #1.1).

This sign was erected by the Wyoming Recreation Commission in 1973. The Sherman Cemetery and Marker is about one-half mile north of Ames Monument.

BIG LARAMIE STAGE STATION INFORMATIVE SIGN-2

TITLE: One Mile South
LEGEND: Site of Big Laramie Stage Station and river crossing of Overland Trail, 1862-68 which became in 1869 part of the first established cattle ranch on Union Pacific Railroad. This ranch known as Hutton or Heart Ranch was owned by a Charles Hutton, Tom Alsop and Edward Creighton after completing a Union Pacific grading contract.
LOCATION: On Hwy 230 about 4.7 miles southwest of the 130/230 Junction west of Laramie.

COMO BLUFFS-3

TITLE: Como Bluffs
LEGEND: The National Register of Historic Places—Wyoming Place #53
LOCATION: North side of Hwy 30/287 at the Albany/Carbon County line.

This area was rich in fossils from the Cretaceous and Jurassic periods of the Mesozoic era 70,000,000-180,000,000 years ago. Pioneer paleontologist Dr. Othniel C. Marsh did extensive work in the area in the 1870s and 1880s. According to John H. Ostrom and John S. McIntosh in their book *Marsh's Dinosaurs*, "Como Bluff was the site of the first major discovery of dinosaur remains anywhere in the world. From this place were collected many of the fine skeletons now displayed in the Peabody Museum at Yale, the National Museum of the Smithsonian Institution in Washington, D.C., and the American Museum of Natural History in New York."

Adjacent to this marker is Dinosaur Graveyard Informative Sign (Carbon County #4).

FIRST WOMAN JURY-4

TITLE: None
LEGEND: This tablet marks the site where the first woman jury served during March 1870
Placed in 1922 by the Jacques LaRamie Chapter Daughters of the American Revolution
LOCATION: Northeast corner of the park adjacent to the north end of the Union Pacific depot in Laramie.

The jurors were Miss Eliza Stewart, Mrs. Amelia Hatcher, Mrs. G. F. Hilton, Mrs. Mary Mackel, Mrs. Agnes Baker, and Mrs. Sarah A. Pease. See Laramie City Historical Plaques-Plaque #4 (Albany County #6.1).

FORT SANDERS MARKER-5

TITLE: None
LEGEND: This monument marks the site of Fort Sanders established September 5, 1866

ALBANY COUNTY

1.1 Ames Monument
1.2 Ames Informative Sign
2 Big Laramie Stage Station
  Informative Sign
3 Como Bluffs
4 First Woman Jury
5 Fort Sanders Marker
6 Ivinson Mansion
6.1 Laramie City Historical Plaques
7 Laramie Informative Sign #1
8 Laramie Informative Sign #2
9 Abraham Lincoln Monument
9.1 The Dwight D. Eisenhower
  Highway Marker
9.2 Telephone Canyon
10 Overland Trail Marker
11 Overland Trail Marker
12 Overland Trail Marker
13 Overland Trail Marker
14 Rock River Monument
15 Old Sherman Cemetery Marker
15.1 Sherman Mountains
  Informative Sign
16 Original Summit Marker
17.1 Tree Rock
17.2 Tree Rock Informative Sign
18 Mormon Monument

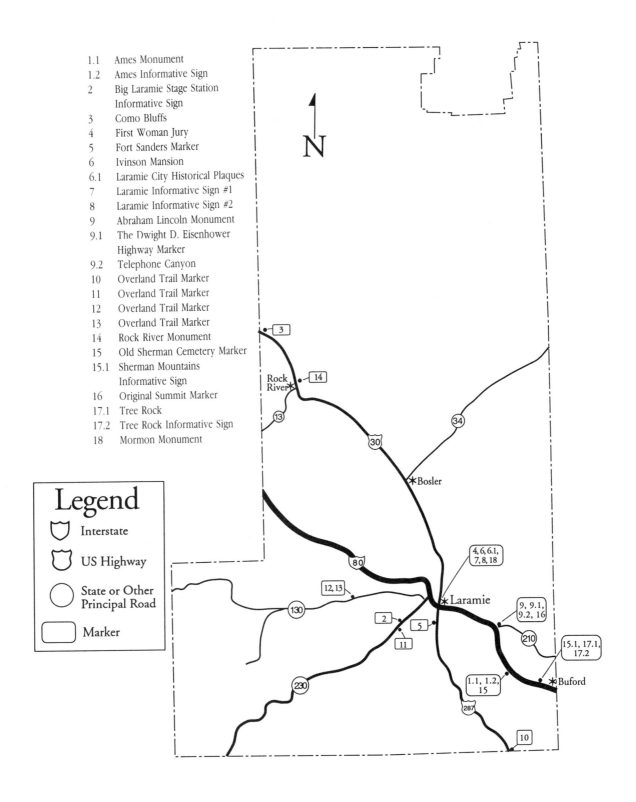

Legend
- Interstate
- US Highway
- State or Other Principal Road
- Marker

Abandoned May 18, 1882. Named in honor of Brigadier General William P. Sanders.

Erected by the State of Wyoming and Jacques Laramie Chapter Daughters of the American Revolution June 1914.

From July 10, to September 5, 1866 known as Fort John Buford.

LOCATION: On Kiowa Street northeast of the cement plant on old U.S. Hwy 287; marker within the fenced enclosure surrounding the Fort Sanders guard house.

This post was established as Fort John Buford on July 4, 1866, for the purpose of protecting the transcontinental railroad and Overland Stage route. At that time, Captain John T. Mainer, who commanded Company F of the Fifth U.S. volunteer infantry and Company A of the Sixth U.S. volunteer infantry, transferred the companies to this post from Fort Halleck about sixty miles to the north and west. The name was changed to Fort Sanders on September 5, 1866, in honor of Brigadier General W. P. Sanders. It initially protected stage lines and emigrant trails using the Lodgepole Creek route to the Oregon Trail. Later, it afforded protection for the Union Pacific workers and ranchers moving in to settle the new land. The post was abandoned on May 18, 1882.

IVINSON MANSION-6

TITLE: Ivinson Mansion and Grounds
LEGEND: The National Register of Historic Places—Wyoming Place #50
LOCATION: 603 Ivinson Avenue in Laramie, Wyoming.

The information below was taken from the National Register of Historic Places Inventory-Nomination Form prepared by Mark Junge in 1971.

The Ivinson Mansion was the home of Jane and Edward Ivinson, who were prominent citizens of Laramie. Construction began on May 3, 1892. Upon completion at the end of that year, at a cost of approximately $40,000, it was probably the finest home in all of Laramie. Today, it serves as the home of the Laramie Plains Museum.

Jane Ivinson was instrumental in establishing Laramie's first school in 1868. She also helped organize the first lodge for women in Laramie, the Rebekahs. She and her husband were active supporters of the Episcopal parish. Their physical gifts to the church were: property; a generous cash gift toward the $75,000 stone Cathedral, which the Episcopal parish erected in 1896; the towers, steeple, clock, and chimes which were added to the Cathedral in 1916; a stained-glass window; and two paintings which had once been in the Ivinson's own home.

Edward Ivinson arrived in Laramie in the spring of 1868 and built a store which would house a general merchandise business. He later became a successful businessman and banker. Ivinson's philanthropic work exemplified his love for Laramie. He provided money to the county to erect the Jane Ivinson Memorial Hospital in memory of his wife. In 1921, he deeded his mansion, carriage house, and the 1.7-acre property to the Episcopal Diocese of Wyoming for the purpose of establishing "Jane Ivinson Memorial Hall, the Cathedral School for Girls." Ivinson served as a member of the first Board of Trustees of the University of Wyoming from 1886 to 1890 and may have helped to locate the university at Laramie.

LARAMIE CITY HISTORICAL PLAQUES-6.1

Plaque #1 (South side of pillar)
TITLE: Laramie Woman's Club
LEGEND: Laramie Woman's Club, organized in 1898, honors Laramie's "First Ladies" who pioneered civic and political responsibility by woman in this country and the world.

Louisa Gardner Swain made world history as the first woman to vote in a general election. She cast her ballot early in the morning of September 6th, 1870 in Laramie, Wyoming.

Plaque #2 (East side of pillar)
TITLE: Mary Godat Bellamy
LEGEND: Mary Godat Bellamy, the first woman elected to the Wyoming State Legislature, represented Albany County in 1911. She worked effectively for laws benefiting woman and children and became a nationally known speaker for woman suffrage.

Plaque #3: (North side of pillar)
TITLE: Martha Symons-Boies
LEGEND: The first woman bailiff in the world, Mrs. Martha Symons-Boies, was appointed to arrange accommodations for the first woman jurors when the Grand Jury met in a building located at First and Garfield Streets in Laramie, March, 1870.

Plaque #4: (West side of pillar)
TITLE: None
LEGEND: World wide attention focused on Laramie in March, 1870 when the first women in history to serve on a jury dealt stern justice in cases of murder, horse-stealing, and illegal branding. They were Miss Eliza Stewart, Mrs. Amelia Hatcher, Mrs. G. F. Hilton, Mrs. Mary Mackel, Mrs. Agnes Baker, and Mrs. Sarah A. Pease.

LOCATION: Concrete pillar on the Ivinson Mansion grounds southeast of the mansion, 603 Ivinson Avenue in Laramie, Wyoming.

LARAMIE INFORMATIVE SIGN # 1-7

TITLE: Laramie
LEGEND: Founded in 1868 upon the arrival of the Union Pacific Railroad, Laramie was named after the fur trader Jacques LaRamie. The first female juror served here in 1870 after Wyoming Territory, in 1869, for the first time in history, gave women full rights of suffrage. Humorist Bill Nye founded his Boomerang newspaper in 1881, and the University of Wyoming opened its doors in 1887. At the south edge of the city lie the ruins of Fort Sanders, 1866-1882. West of the city can be seen the first intermountain ranch (1869) and the ruts left by Ben Holladay's stagecoaches on the old Overland Trail.
LOCATION: 1502 S. 3rd Street in Laramie, Wyoming.

LARAMIE INFORMATIVE SIGN # 2-8

TITLE: Laramie
LEGEND: Founded in 1868 upon the arrival of the Union Pacific Railroad, Laramie was named after the fur trader Jacques LaRamie. The first female jurors served here in 1870 after Wyoming Territory, in 1869, for the first time in history, gave women full rights of suffrage. Humorist, Bill Nye founded his Boomerang newspaper in 1881, and the University of Wyoming opened its doors in 1887. At the south edge of the city lie the ruins of Fort Sanders, 1866-1882. West of the city can be seen the first intermountain ranch (1869) and the ruts left by Ben Holladay's stagecoaches on the Overland Trail.
Erected 1964 by Wyoming State Archives and Historical Department and Wyoming State Historical Society
LOCATION: On the lawn directly south of the Union Pacific depot in Laramie, Wyoming.

ABRAHAM LINCOLN MONUMENT-9

TITLE: "We must think anew and act anew"
        —Abraham Lincoln, 1809-1865
LEGEND: This monument commemorates the sesquicentennial of Lincoln's birth by the State of Wyoming in 1959. Wyoming State Parks Commission—Jack E. Lewis, President; Harold S. Odde, Director; James A. Chapman; Charles M. Smith; Milward L. Simpson, Governor 1955-1959; J. J. Hickey, Governor, 1959; Charles W. Jeffrey, M.D., Rawlins, Wyoming—donor; Robert I. Russin, sculptor.
LOCATION: Summit Rest Area on the north side of I-80 between Cheyenne and Laramie, Wyoming.

This site marked the highest elevation along the Lincoln Highway (old U.S. Hwy 30). When traffic began to flow on Interstate 80, the bust became isolated on old U.S. Hwy 30. In 1968 it was moved to Summit Rest Area several hundred yards north of its original location.

THE DWIGHT D. EISENHOWER
HIGHWAY MARKER-9.1

TITLE: Father of the Interstate Highway System.
LEGEND: In August, 1973, the U.S. Congress designated a cross-country stretch of Interstate as the "Dwight D. Eisenhower Highway" in tribute to President Eisenhower's early recognition of the need for a national network of highways to enhance the mobility of a growing nation. His dream originated in 1919 on an Army convoy from Washington, D.C. to San Francisco, California, a journey that took sixty-two days.

On June 29, 1956, President Eisenhower signed the historic legislation that created the national system of Interstate and Defense Highways and the Federal Highway Trust Fund, the pay-as-you-go mechanism through which U.S. motorists have funded the construction and upkeep of the U.S. Highway system. Today, that system stands as a monument to Eisenhower's vision as a young Army officer—a legacy of safety and mobility that has brought all Americans closer together.

This sign commemorating the Eisenhower Highway was made possible by the following organizations: American Traffic Safety Services Association and the Road Information Program.
LOCATION: Summit Rest Area on the north side of I-80 between Cheyenne and Laramie.

TELEPHONE CANYON-9.2

TITLE: Telephone Canyon
LEGEND: The first in the west through which a telephone line was run. The first conversation over this line was held in 1882 between Bill Nye at Laramie and Hon. F. E. Warren at Cheyenne.

Tablet erected by Jacques Laramie Chapter D.A.R. and S.A.R. of Wyoming 1930.
LOCATION: Fenced enclosure at Summit Rest Area on the north side of I-80 between Cheyenne and Laramie. Adjacent to Original Summit Marker (Albany County #16).

Today, I-80 courses through Telephone Canyon to the summit between Laramie and Cheyenne. On January 7, 1882, the *Laramie Sentinel* announced the formation of the Wyoming Telephone and Telegraph Company. The *Sentinel* reported on the progress of the line and on May 20, 1882, devoted a half-column to instructions on using the telephone.

OVERLAND TRAIL MARKER-10

TITLE: None
LEGEND: This stone marks the place where the Overland Stage Line, on its way to the west, June 1862-1868 crossed the Colorado-Wyoming boundary line.

Erected by the State of Wyoming and the Chapters of the Daughters of the American Revolution, the Cache La Poudre, Fort Collins, Colo., the Centennial, Greeley, Colo., the Jacques LaRamie, Laramie, Wyo. 1917
LOCATION: East side of Hwy 287 at the Colorado/Wyoming state line; about 26 miles from Laramie, Wyoming.

In 1825, William Ashley of the Rocky Mountain Fur Company and a group of his trappers followed the South Platte River and crossed to what is now Virginia Dale, Colorado. They went north to Tie Siding, Wyoming, and continued to the Laramie River and present town of Laramie. They crossed the Medicine Bow River at Elk Mountain and the Divide at Bridger's Pass. They were the first white men to follow this route, which would later become known as the Overland Trail.

John Charles Fremont used the route in 1843 on his second expedition to the far West. In 1849 a party of Cherokee, headed by Captain Evans of Arkansas, went to California by the route, which afterwards was known as the Cherokee Trail.

When Ben Holladay purchased the contract and transportation facilities for the overland mail in 1862, he changed the route from the Oregon Trail south to the Cherokee Trail to avoid Indian troubles. Renamed the Overland Trail, it became the principal mail, stage, and emigrant route after 1862. The trail was

heavily used between 1862 to 1868, though it was used to some extent as late as 1900.

The unveiling and dedication of this monument took place July 4, 1917. Mrs. James Mathison, regent of the Jacques LaRamie Chapter, unveiled the stone marker. Several people from Colorado and Wyoming presented historical topics, such as "The Overland Trail Through Laramie County," "The Stage Station of Virginia Dale," "First Things in Colorado," and "Wyoming Fifty Years Ago."

OVERLAND TRAIL MARKER-11

TITLE: None
LEGEND: The first stone erected in Albany Co. to mark the Old Overland Trail 1862-1868

Erected by Jacques LaRamie Chapter Daughters of the American Revolution, Laramie, Wyoming 1911
LOCATION: South side of Hwy 230, 6.2 miles southwest of the junction of Hwy 230 and 130. 1.5 miles southwest of the Big Laramie Stage Station Informative Sign.

OVERLAND TRAIL MARKER-12

TITLE: The Overland Trail
LEGEND: 1862 to 1868
LOCATION: At a wide turnout on the north side of Hwy 130, 10 miles west of the Junction of Hwy 130 and 230.

This marker was erected by the Kiwanis.

OVERLAND TRAIL MARKER-13

TITLE: Overland Trail
LEGEND: None
LOCATION: About 100 yards north of Overland Trail Marker (Albany County #12) in the field north of Hwy 130.

This marker was erected by the Kiwanis.

ROCK RIVER MONUMENT-14

TITLE: None
LEGEND: In memory to those who passed this way to win and hold the West on the Fort Halleck-Fort Laramie road. Frontier town of Rock Creek, 10 miles northeast

Erected by the Historical Landmark Commission of Wyoming 1953
LOCATION: 1.5 miles north of Rock River on the east side of Hwy 30/287.

The town and stage station on Rock Creek was a focal point for freight wagons traveling to points such as Medicine Bow, Fort Fetterman, or Montana. It served as a stop on the Union Pacific route from 1868. The Rock Creek station was abandoned in 1900.

OLD SHERMAN CEMETERY MARKER-15

TITLE: Old Sherman Cemetery
LEGEND: 1867 to about 1880. Most bodies have been removed.

Erected by the Historical Landmark Commission of Wyoming 1958
LOCATION: One-half mile north of the Ames Monument.

In 1867, the town of Sherman became the winter camp of the Union Pacific Railroad. Until 1901 it was the highest point on the Union Pacific Railroad. In that year the tracks were moved farther south and the town of Sherman was deserted.

1.

2.

3.

1. Ames Monument was the first historical marker in Wyoming. It was erected by the Union Pacific Railroad in 1882.

2. Sherman Mountains Informative Sign was placed by the Wyoming State Archives and Historical Department 1960-1962.

3. Fort Sanders Monument was erected July 18, 1914, by the Jacques LaRamie Chapter of the Daughters of the American Revolution and the Wyoming Oregon Trail Commission.

4. Lincoln Monument was dedicated in 1959, 150 years after Abraham Lincoln's birth.

4.

SHERMAN MOUNTAINS INFORMATIVE SIGN-15.1

TITLE: Sherman Mountains

LEGEND: The Sherman Mountains are erosional remnants rising above the general level of the surface of the Laramie range. The flat topped characteristic of the range resulted from beveling during an ancient erosion cycle. Bedrock here is granite, a crystalline rock made up of pink feldspar, glassy quartz, black mica and hornblende, which originated deep in the earth's crust over a billion years ago.

The peculiar rock forms of the Sherman Mountains are controlled by three sets of joints, or plains of weakness, cutting the granite and dividing into large blocks. Weathering has rounded off corners and has enlarged joint plains, resulting in irregular block-rock masses, many of which are capped by balanced rocks.

Wyoming Recreation Commission

LOCATION: At the Tree Rock Rest Area on I-80 between Cheyenne and Laramie.

ORIGINAL SUMMIT MARKER-16

TITLE: NONE

LEGEND: C.R. 27

        Laramie 9 1/2 ►

        ◄ Sherman 9 1/2

LOCATION: Adjacent to the Telephone Canyon Marker (Albany County #9.2) at the Summit Rest Area between Cheyenne and Laramie.

This is an original mileage marker for the road between Cheyenne and Laramie. It dates possibly to the 1870s.

TREE ROCK-17.1

TITLE: NONE

LEGEND: This tree was growing out of a crevice in the rock when the Union Pacific Railroad built its original mainline fifty feet south of this rock in 1868. The fence and cable were provided by the Union Pacific Railroad Co. at the request of the Historical Landmark Commission of Wyoming.

LOCATION: At Tree Rock Rest Area in I-80 between Cheyenne and Laramie.

TREE ROCK INFORMATIVE SIGN-17.2

TITLE: Tree In Solid Rock

LEGEND: The original line of the Union Pacific Railroad passed within a few feet of this point and supposedly was deflected slightly to avoid destruction of this phenomenon. The fireman of each passing train never failed to drench the tree with a bucket of water.

Dept. of Com. & Ind.

LOCATION: At Tree Rock Rest Area on I-80 between Cheyenne and Laramie.

MORMON MONUMENT-18

TITLE: To Utah in 1868

LEGEND: Daughters of Utah Pioneers

        No. 357

        Erected 1968

In July 1868 the shifting terminal of Union Pacific Railroad reached Laramie and nearby Benton, Wyoming. Approximately 5,000 old world converts to the Church of Jesus Christ of Latter-day Saints were met at these points by about 500 teamsters sent in June by Pres. Brigham Young to take wagons and supplies for the Saints journey to Utah. Returning in Aug. and Sept. they were the last of the organized emigration companies. In 1869 the railroad spanned the continent.

Laramie Camp

LOCATION: On the L.D.S. Church grounds on 15th Street in Laramie, Wyoming.

BIG HORN COUNTY

FIRE FIGHTERS MONUMENT-1.2

TITLE: None
LEGEND:

DEDICATED TO THE MEN
TRAPPED IN SHOSHONE FOREST
FIRE AUGUST 21, 1937
DIED IN LINE OF DUTY

FOREMEN
JAMES A. SABEN   PAUL E. TYRRELL

ENROLLEES

CLYDE ALLEN	MACK T. MAYABB
ROY BEVENS	GEORGE H. RODGERS
AMBROICO GARZA	EARNEST K. SELKE
JOHN B. GERDES	RUBIN D. SHERRY
WILL C. GRIFFITH	WILLIAM H. WHITLOCK

BURNED IN LINE OF DUTY
ENROLLEES

TIMATCO ALMAGER	RAYMOND PRAZAH
WILLIAM C. BARNES	OLIVER RANDLE
WOODROW DUTY	LEE ROY REED
HUBERT FERRIS	DAVID RODRIQUEZ
LEWIS GARCIA	JULIAN RODRIQUEZ
JUAN GOMEZ	ANDON SANCHEZ
AMOS HEFNER	ALCARIO SERROS
JOHNNIE LEVINE	HENRY SPOMER
WELDON MACKEY	JAMES T. SULLIVAN
WILLIAM O. MUELLER	DAVID B. THOMPSON
ALTON J. MURRAY	JAMES TOUCHSONE
JAMES OTTMER	VICENTE VALLE
HERMAN F. PATZKE	JOHNNIE WISNESKI
JOSE PEREZ	CHARLIE WHEELUS
JOHN D. PHILLIPS	HAVEL ZASKODA
HENRY POEHLS	JOE ZAVALA

ERECTED SEPTEMBER, 1937
BY
COMPANY 1811 C.C.C. CAMP F-35-W
TENSLEEP, WYOMING

LOCATION: About 8.5 miles west of Powder River Pass on west side of U.S. Hwy 16 at Meadowlark Lake overlook.

In addition to these killed or injured fire fighters, three other men were killed in the Blackwater Fire: Alfred Clayton, forest ranger from Lander and Dubois, Wyoming; Billy Lee, Bureau of Public Roads foreman from Sherwood, Oregon; and Rex Hale from Afton, Wyoming. Most of the men were from Texas. James Saben, foreman of the Tensleep Civilian Conservation Corps, was from Hyattville, Wyoming.

See Fire Fighters Memorial #1, Fire Fighters Memorial #2, Post Point Blackwater Fire Memorial (Park County #8, 8.1, and 8.2), and Wyoming Fallen Firefighter Memorial (Fremont County #41).

LOWER BIG HORN BASIN INFORMATIVE SIGN-2

TITLE: None
LEGEND: John Colter visited this area in 1807. Many trappers and hunters followed later. The first wheeled vehicle was brought into this region in 1860. Permanent ranches were established near the mouth of the Shoshone River before 1888. Other ranchers soon settled along the Shoshone and Big Horn Rivers, and on Crooked, Gyp and Sage Creeks.

Later homeseekers settled in the lower Shoshone Valley, notably a large Mormon colony in 1900 which constructed irrigation systems and thriving towns. This log house, erected before 1894, and once occupied by one of Big Horn County's first officers, William F. Hunt, is typical of the homes built by the early settlers of this region.
LOCATION: South side of U.S. Hwy 14A, about 0.7 miles east of the junction of U.S. Hwy 310/789 and U.S. Hwy 14A.

MEDICINE LODGE CREEK-3

TITLE: Medicine Lodge Creek Site
LEGEND: The National Register of Historical Places—Wyoming Place #70
LOCATION: About 6 miles northeast of Hyattville, Wyoming. Site is located about 1.7 miles off of Cold Spring Road.

The information below was taken from the National Register of Historic Places Inventory-Nomination Form completed in 1973 by Mark Junge, historian with Wyoming Recreation Commission, and from the Interpretive Guide from the Medicine Lodge State Archaeological Site.

The Medicine Lodge Creek prehistoric site has been recognized for over half a century as an outstanding manifestation of Indian petroglyphs and pictographs, picture stories etched or painted upon the face of a sandstone bluff. In the summer of 1969 Dr. George Frison, Wyoming State Archaeologist and Head of the Department of Anthropology at the University of Wyoming, began archaeological digs in the sand deposits at the base of this bluff. His work has become a key to archaeological interpretation in the area. The discovery of over sixty different cultural levels spanning some 10,000 years of human occupation at Medicine Lodge Creek has enabled archaeologists to examine both the particular types of life styles and how these styles have changed over time.

Wyoming State Parks & Historic Sites, as a division of the Wyoming Department of Commerce, manages the site. There are camping and picnicking areas, restrooms, and a restored ranch house and barn.

MEDICINE LODGE CREEK INFORMATIVE PLAQUES-3.1

Plaque #1
TITLE: Nature's Storehouse
LEGEND: For at least 10,000 years, this area where the Medicine Lodge Creek flows out of the Big Horn Mountains has provided a home for man. From the earliest hunter-gatherers to today's ranchers, Medicine Lodge is an ideal site for human habitation. Everything man needed is located at or near this site. Fruits, berries, greens and roots from the lush plant growth surrounding the creek bottom provided food, medicine, firewood and material for weapons and building. The abundance of animal life from wood rats to bison were an important part of the native diet. Within a few miles of the site there are excellent sources of high quality quartzite and chert—a rock resembling flint. These materials were used to make projectile points, arrowheads and other weapons and tools. The eastern exposure of the sandstone cliffs creates warm, sunny winter mornings and the slight overhang causes cool, shady summer afternoons at the base of the cliff. Add the constant availability of running water and you have an ideal camping spot that has been used throughout the ages.

Plaque #2
TITLE: Petroglyphs and Pictographs
LEGEND: Rock art at Medicine Lodge and throughout the Big Horn Basin falls into two categories—PETROGLYPHS which were pecked into the sandstone surfaces and PICTOGRAPHS that were painted onto the surfaces. Human-like figures and animals were common motifs. The meaning of rock art is difficult to decipher, but most archaeologists agree that the drawings are symbolic and represent the complex mythological and religious concepts of the artists. The figure illustrated here is located above you on the cliffs and has probably been chalked at some point in time and appears bluish in color. This type of figure

BIG HORN COUNTY

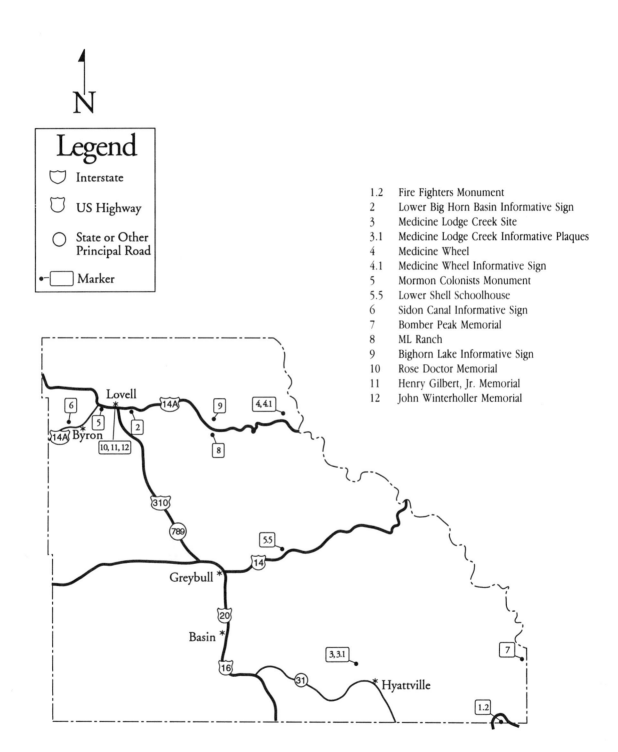

Legend

Interstate

US Highway

State or Other
Principal Road

Marker

1.2   Fire Fighters Monument
2   Lower Big Horn Basin Informative Sign
3   Medicine Lodge Creek Site
3.1   Medicine Lodge Creek Informative Plaques
4   Medicine Wheel
4.1   Medicine Wheel Informative Sign
5   Mormon Colonists Monument
5.5   Lower Shell Schoolhouse
6   Sidon Canal Informative Sign
7   Bomber Peak Memorial
8   ML Ranch
9   Bighorn Lake Informative Sign
10   Rose Doctor Memorial
11   Henry Gilbert, Jr. Memorial
12   John Winterholler Memorial

petroglyphs appear throughout Wyoming and may symbolize the importance of hunting to the prehistoric economy. Rock art is extremely difficult to date, but art at this particular site is probably no more than 1000 years old.

Petroglyphs and pictographs are a priceless legacy from the Indian people who inhabited this area in years gone by. The elements are gradually dimming these fragile drawings and vandalism such as the carving of initials, painting over the figures and even chalking to make the art visible are leading to their destruction. Please let your foot-prints be the only sign of your visit!

Plaque #3
TITLE: Excavating and Recovery
LEGEND: Beginning in 1973, Medicine Lodge Creek was the scene of one of the most significant archaeological excavations in North America. For 2 years, anthropologist from the University of Wyoming carefully excavated the layers of silt and clay to depths of well over 20 feet below where you are standing. Thousands of artifacts, bones, and seeds were recovered, and cooking and heating hearths, food storage pits, and evidence of these structures were unearthed. These discoveries revealed over 60 cultural levels, documenting the entire history of human occupation in the Big Horn Basin. The information gleaned by the anthropologist along with the geological, chemical, botanical, and related studies are being used to reconstruct the life ways of man and how he adapted to changing environmental conditions from the end of the Ice Age to modern times. Some physical evidence of the remains, such as the rectangular depressions at the base of the cliff which have been backfilled for preservation purposes.

Plaque #4
TITLE: Clues from the Past
LEGEND: Thousands of years ago, while the Indians camped here, the banks of Medicine Lodge Creek were only a few feet away from the base of the cliff. Throughout the years, the creek changed its course and meandered across the width of the valley. Massive rockfalls from the cliffs, such as the one before you, diverted the creek back out into the middle of the valley, thus preserving the silt and clays which held the remains of the campsite of the ancient hunter-gatherers. Only through this accident of geological action has any evidence of human habitation at Medicine Lodge Creek been preserved. From the stratigraphy exposed during the excavations, geologists and archaeologists can interpret the history of the valley. Each layer exposed produced clues that give us information on past environmental conditions and the cultural activities that took place. You can envision the original slope of the valley before it was leveled for corrals and before archaeological excavation began by looking at the undisturbed land adjacent to the rockfall and the line of red earth on the cliff approximately 10 feet above the existing ground level.

LOCATION: Same as Medicine Lodge Creek National Register Plaque (Big Horn County #3).

See Medicine Lodge Creek National Register Plaque (Big Horn County #3) for more discussion of this archaeological site.

MEDICINE WHEEL-4
TITLE: Medicine Wheel
LEGEND: The National Register of Historic Places—Wyoming Place #22
LOCATION: About 22 miles west of Burgess Junction on U.S. Hwy 14A between the junction and Lovell, Wyoming.

The information below was taken from the National Register of Historic Places Nomination-Inventory Form prepared by George S. Cattanach, Jr., an archaeologist with the National Park Service, in 1970.

The Medicine Wheel is the largest and most elaborate of known Indian

structures of its type found east of the Rocky Mountains from southern Canada to Oklahoma. Although very little is known about its builders and their purpose, it is known that prospectors and hunters visited the site in 1880s.

The Medicine Wheel, along with about eighty surrounding acres, is preserved to protect its archaeological values. It is dramatically situated on a 9,642-foot ridge, forming a western peak of Medicine Mountain and providing a commanding view of the Bighorn Basin, Wind River, and even the Teton mountain ranges.

MEDICINE WHEEL INFORMATIVE SIGN-4.1
TITLE: Medicine Wheel
LEGEND: The builders and purpose of the Medicine Wheel are unknown. It is currently thought that it was religious in nature, or it may have had astronomical implications, or both. It is constructed of stones laid side by side, forming an almost perfect circle 74 feet in diameter with 28 spokes. An associated radio-carbon date is about 1760. Crow Indian legend says that when they came, the wheel was there. They migrated to the Big Horn Basin around 1776.

Modern Indians use the Medicine Wheel for religious ceremonies. At times, flags, or offerings are left about the wheel, signifying that a ceremony has taken place. The Forest Service does not interfere with these ceremonies, so please do not destroy, or remove the objects. As part of their ceremonial activities the Indians may build an open fire and you may see evidence of this. However, open fires by the general public are prohibited.

The Medicine Wheel is designated a National Historic Landmark, which means it has national significance. It is not only the responsibility of the Government to protect this national landmark but also every American.
LOCATION: About 22 miles west of Burgess Junction on U.S. Hwy 14A between the junction and Lovell, Wyoming.

MORMON COLONISTS MONUMENT-5
TITLE: Official Marker
Utah Pioneer Trails and Landmarks Association
No. 58
Erected: Sept. 29, 1935
LEGEND: In honor of the Mormon Colonists of the Big Horn Basin who, under the leadership of Abraham O. Woodruff, first camped near this site in May 1900. These pioneers, under many difficulties, established towns, notably Byron, Cowley and Lovell, organized the Big Horn Stake of Zion, constructed the Sidon Canal, built railroads and pioneered education through founding the Big Horn Academy.

The Aaronic Priesthood Quorums of the Big Horn Stake and Utah Pioneer Trails and Landmarks Association.
LOCATION: South side of U.S. Hwy 14A/310/789 about 0.4 miles west of the Shoshone River just west of Lovell, Wyoming.

LOWER SHELL SCHOOLHOUSE-5.5
TITLE: None
LEGEND: The Lower Shell Schoolhouse was one of the first non-log community buildings built in the Big Horn Basin. Using a classic one room schoolhouse design, it was constructed on this site in 1903 on land which had been donated to the Odessa School District. The school district was named for the nearby Odessa Post Office which had operated from 1891 to 1895. Local homesteaders quarried sandstone from the surrounding hills and assisted in the construction of the 24' by 46' building. During the 1905-1906 school year forty students were enrolled here demonstrating the early settlers' high regard for education.

Although the building was mainly used as a school, it also functioned

1.

2.

3.

1. The Fire Fighters Monument, located near Meadowlark Lake in the Big Horn Mountains, was erected in 1937 to memorialize those who were killed while fighting a forest fire west of Cody.

2. The Utah Pioneer Trails and Landmarks Association erected the Mormon Colonists Monument on September 29, 1935.

3. The Sidon Canal Informative Sign represented the newer cast-aluminum signs.

as a church for traveling preachers and as a community dance hall. A wide variety of organizations, from cemetery boards to the farm bureau, held meetings here as well. Use as a school ended in the early 1950's, but the building continued to be used as a meeting hall until the early 1970's.

In 1980 the foundation received new footings and the roof was reshingled as an effort was made to stabilize the building after nearly a decade of neglect. The addition to the rear of the building was completed in 1988, using the same architectural design as the original construction. The historical appearance was thus retained, while at the same time the building could serve as an art gallery, bookstore and information center.

The simple form of the schoolhouse epitomizes the austere life of the region's early pioneers. Shell Valley's lush irrigated farm fields contrast with the arid topography of the basin demonstrating the current results of their earlier endeavors. As one of a few remaining one room schoolhouses in Wyoming the "old stone school", as it was often called, has received recognition by enrollment in the National Register of Historic Places.

LOCATION: About 6 miles east of Greybull, Wyoming, on U.S. Hwy 14.

The building houses the Stone School Gallery & Bookstore which has books, maps, and artwork of the region.

SIDON CANAL INFORMATIVE SIGN-6

TITLE: Sidon Canal

LEGEND: Following Mormon settlement of the Salt Lake Valley beginning in 1847, church leaders envisioned colonization of the entire inter-mountain region. In following decades, Mormons emigrated from Utah into Idaho, Arizona and Wyoming.

Seeking to improve their economic status and following Mormon

pioneering tradition, several hundred people in 1900 emigrated from Utah and Idaho to Wyoming's Big Horn Basin, where they built a canal and a community.

Under the Carey Act of 1894 states were encouraged to sell arable public land cheaply following reclamation. But private reclamation projects required capital, and some were aborted as investors lost faith. Unlike other privately-financed projects, the Sidon Canal was built without a large amount of capital.

Emigrants were organized into the Big Horn Colonization Company, an irrigation cooperative which offered company shares in return for labor. Upon arriving in the Basin workers plunged into canal construction, excavating with horse-drawn plows and slip scrapers. Near this point work was blocked by a sandstone boulder known as "Prayer Rock". According to legend, prayer and divine intervention caused the rock to split, allowing construction to continue and strengthening the emigrant faith in the canal project.

The 37-mile long canal was completed in less than two years. It still transports water from a headgate on the Shoshone River near the Big Horn-Park County line to a land segregation of approximately 20,000 acres. It's successful completion serves as an outstanding example of the cooperative effort and spirit of determination exhibited by Mormon pioneers in the American West.

LOCATION: About 3.2 miles west of Byron, Wyoming, on U.S. Hwy 14A.

Mormons settled other areas of Wyoming. They came to the Big Horn Basin in the 1880s. According to T. A. Larson in *History of Wyoming*, a few hundred Mormon families settled on the north side of the Greybull River beginning in 1893. They completed an irrigation project and harvested crops in 1895 without Carey Act land. They established the small Wyoming towns of Burlington and Otto.

BOMBER PEAK MEMORIAL-7

TITLE: Memorial

LEGEND: The following officers and enlisted men of the U.S. Army Air Force gave their lives while on active duty in flight on or about June 28, 1943. Their bomber crashed on the crest of the mountain above this place.

Lieutenants	Sergeants
William R. Ronaghan	Charles E. Newburn, Jr.
Leonard H. Phillips	Ferguson T. Bell, Jr.
Anthony J. Tilotti	Lewis M. Shepard
Charles J. Suppes	James A. Hinds
	Jake F. Penick
	Lee V. Miller

Dedicated by American War Dads & Auxiliary, Sheridan Chapter No. 4, Sheridan, Wyoming August, 1945.

LOCATION: Cloud Peak Primitive Area near the Florence Pass Trail.

ML RANCH-8

TITLE: Mason-Lovell Ranch

LEGEND: 1883-1902

LOCATION: About 15 miles east of Lovell, Wyoming, on U.S. Hwy 14A.

The Bighorn Canyon Visitor Center, located at the junction of U.S. Hwys 310 and 14A, has a nice brochure about the ML Ranch, from which comes the following information.

Henry Clay Lovell, born in Michigan, learned the cattle business in north Texas, the Indian Territory, and Kansas. Lovell formed and financed a partnership with Anthony L. Mason of Kansas City, Missouri, who provided the skills and knowledge necessary for the risky business of cattle ranching. In 1880, Lovell trailed in two Kansas cattle herds and established a ranch along the Bighorn River, a few miles above the mouth of Nowood Creek. He established a second ranch on Shell Creek the following year and, in 1883, a third at the Five Springs site along the Bighorn River. This last site became the headquarters for the ML cattle kingdom.

The ML (Mason-Lovell) Ranch was the largest and most prominent of the ranches in the eastern Big Horn Basin of the Wyoming Territory.

The "Big Outfit" temporarily ceased operation with Mason's death in 1892. Lovell kept the deeded land and a few horses, restocked the range with several thousand cattle from Washington, and resumed operation until his death in 1903. The nearby community of Lovell, Wyoming, is named after this pioneer cattleman.

BIGHORN LAKE INFORMATIVE SIGN-9

TITLE: Bighorn Lake

LEGEND: Before you is Bighorn Lake. Yellowtail Dam at Fort Smith, Montana backs up the Bighorn River 71 miles to this point. Completed in 1968, the dam provides hydroelectric power to the region, water for irrigation and opportunities for recreation.

Fluctuation in river flow and differing demands in electric power will cause extreme change in the lake elevation. At this location a 30 foot change in water level could move the lake shore 5 miles.

At normal pool, the surface of the entire lake covers 12,685 acres. At this time the area before you is under water to the left of the causeway. This represents a 30 foot rise over the normal annual low water level, a difference amounting to 90 billion gallons of water capable of producing 111 million kilowatt hours of electricity at the dam.

For several months each year the water level is too low to cover this area of the reservoir. While the reservoir is drawn down, the ground exposed by the receding water provides breeding habitat for amphibians and aquatic insects, which provide food for fish in Bighorn Lake.

Bureau of Reclamation, U.S. Department of the Interior.

LOCATION: About 13-14 miles east of Lovell, Wyoming, on U.S. Hwy 14A.

ROSE DOCTOR MEMORIAL-10

TITLE: Dr. W. W. Horsley
The "Rose Doctor"

LEGEND: The beauty of these gardens is an enduring tribute to Dr. W.W. Horsley, the "Rose Doctor", whose enthusiasm, dedication, and service to our community made Lovell the...Rose Town of Wyoming.
Dedicated by The Lovell Womens Club 1970

LOCATION: At Main and Pennsylvania Streets on the east side of Lovell, Wyoming.

William Watts Horsley was born in Price, Utah, in 1896. At an early age he was interested in and loved roses. He won his first six plants by selling subscriptions to *Country Gentleman*, and his interest grew from that day. While living in Lovell, Dr. Horsley served as Director of Parks on the Lovell Town Council for thirty-one years. During that time he and a close friend, Phil Smith, conceived the idea of rose parks at either end of the town.

Dr. Horsley was an expert in the field of American roses, and was known as one of the foremost rose authorities in the United States in the 1940s. He served as director of the American Rose Society for twelve years and in 1945 helped to christen the famous "Peace Rose."

Dr. Horsley studied medicine at Utah University in Salt Lake City, Utah, and Harvard Medical School in Boston, Massachusetts. He visited Lovell in 1924 to help his physician father-in-law, Dr. Ed Croft. He remained for the next forty-five years, caring for and devoting himself to the community of Lovell. Every baby he delivered received a rose, as did his older children patients for being good.

HENRY GILBERT, JR. MEMORIAL-11

TITLE: Henry Gilbert, Jr. Memorial
September 23, 1919-December 23, 1941

LEGEND: The Flying Tigers were American boys from 41 of our states, fighter pilots trained in our own Army and Navy, who became members of the new A.V.G. (American Volunteer Group) employed by the government of Generalissimo Chiang Kai-shek to protect the lifeline of China, the Burma Road. The Flying Tigers began under the leadership of Claire Lee Chennault with 100 Curtiss-Wright P-40B Tomahawks and the volunteer pilots to fly them.

They went on from there. They went on in smoke and flame and blood and death to compose their epic—one of the most spectacular in the annals of air warfare. They saved Rangoon and the Burma Road for 65 precious days. They became the demigods of fighting China.

Wingman Henry Gilbert, Jr. of Lovell, Wyoming was the youngest of the Flying Tigers at the age of 22.

On December 23, 1941, two waves of Japanese bombers accompanied by fighters were approaching Mingaladon. Fourteen P-40's and 16 Brewsters of the R.A.F. took off to meet the attack.

Gilbert dived on one of the bomber formations, shooting out bursts and striking two of them but without hitting vital spots in the attack. His P-40 was hit by a cannon shell and streamed out of the battle to crash into the jungle below.

There had been no parachute, and Henry Gilbert was the first Flying Tiger to die in combat.

Dedicated June 29, 1985

Dedicatory remarks by A.V.G. Squadron Leader David L. "Tex" Hill, A.V.G. Flight Leader Noel R. Bacon and the World War II Anniversary Committee.

LOCATION: At Main and Pennsylvania Streets on the east side of Lovell, Wyoming.

Henry Gilbert, Jr. was born September 23, 1919, at Temple, Oklahoma. His family moved to Lovell in 1929 after his father homesteaded in Frannie.

Henry graduated from Lovell High School in 1937. After one-year stays at New Mexico A & M and Washington State University, he entered Navy Flight School in 1940. After graduating in 1941, he was stationed aboard the USS Saratoga out of Pearl Harbor.

In 1985, as part of Lovell's annual summer celebration called "Mustang Days," the World War II Anniversary Committee dedicated both the Henry Gilbert, Jr. Memorial and the John Winterholler Memorial.

JOHN WINTERHOLLER MEMORIAL-12

TITLE: John Winterholler Gymnasium

LEGEND: John Winterholler was born February 3, 1916 in Billings, Montana of Russian immigrants. He came to Lovell, Wyoming in 1932. John graduated from Lovell High School in 1935. While attending LHS he excelled in sports and was named All-State in basketball and football.

John started his meteoric rise to athletic fame at the University of Wyoming in the fall of 1935. "The Cowboy campus has produced no athlete who has attained the Lovell youth's heights," wrote Larry Birleffi of him in 1939. Birleffi noted "He is the athlete's idea of an athlete and a coach's answer... He earned a first berth in every all-conference selection among Big Seven's offerings for All-American honors...His achievements were in baseball, football and basketball."

During World War II he was captured at Corregidor and was a Japanese prisoner of war for 34 months, subsequently becoming paralyzed. John was a recipient of the Silver Star and promoted to a full colonel, all by the age of 30.

John captained a wheelchair basketball team after the war and was once again a leading figure in sporting news, termed "Spider", "Demon on Wheels" and "The Accurate Shooting Colonel Winterholler."

His Alma Mater, UW, called him home to Laramie for "Johnnie Winterholler Day" October 31, 1964. John's brief but poignant words of award acceptance were followed by thunderous applause, as John seemed to all to represent that flag of liberation, "The Stars and Stripes", "Old Glory."

Dedicated June 28, 1985 by the World War II Anniversary Committee

LOCATION: Johnny Winterholler Gymnasium in Lovell, Wyoming.

John Winterholler was present for the dedication of this plaque. While much could be said about the athletic accomplishments of this one-time Lovell resident, it was his patriotism and service to the United States during World War II that ingrained him in the hearts of Lovell residents.

CAMPBELL COUNTY

ASTORIAN OVERLAND EXPEDITION INFORMATIVE SIGN-1

TITLE: 1811 ASTORIAN OVERLAND EXPEDITION

LEGEND: The Astorians, first organized white expedition to enter this region, passed near this point on August 25, 1811. The party, under the leadership of Wilson Price Hunt, was composed of 60 men, 1 Indian squaw and 2 children and was bound for the mouth of the Columbia River to help establish the Pacific Fur Company, headed by John Jacob Astor.

Leaving the Missouri River near the mouth of the Grand River in South Dakota, they traveled overland having one horse for each two men. After many hardships they reached their destination on February l5, 18l2. Edward Rose acted as guide through this area.

LOCATION: About 50 yards west of the post office at Spotted Horse, Wyoming, on U.S. Hwy 14/16.

John Jacob Astor, a New York fur baron, organized the American Fur Company in 1808. A branch of this company was to be started on the Pacific Coast. This so-called Pacific Fur Company was to link the Columbia River valley with the Missouri River, St. Louis, the Great Lakes, and New York. Wilson Price Hunt was assigned the task of organizing and leading an overland party to the Columbia River.

The group set out in the spring of 1811 and planned to use the same route as the Lewis and Clark Expedition (following the Missouri River through South Dakota, North Dakota, and Montana). However, Hunt decided to change the route in order to avoid any confrontation with Blackfeet Indians. The party followed Indian trails across northern Wyoming, crossed or skirted the Big Horn Mountains, and reached the Wind River Mountains. They crossed the Continental Divide somewhere near Union Pass in Fremont County and descended to the head waters of the Green River. After crossing the Gros Ventre range, they followed the Hoback River to its junction with the Snake. The party then built canoes and followed the Snake River out of Wyoming.

BOZEMAN TRAIL INFORMATIVE SIGN-2.1

TITLE: 1863 Bozeman Trail

LEGEND: John Bozeman and John Jacobs laid out this route from Fort Laramie to the Virginia City, Montana gold fields. In 1865 the Powder River Military Expedition under Gen. P. E. Connor, established Ft. Connor on the Powder River. In 1866 Forts Reno, Phil Kearny, and C. F. Smith were built for its protection against the Indians who fought bitterly to hold their last hunting grounds. It became known as the Bloody Bozeman. Portugee Phillips rode over this trail to Ft. Laramie to report the Fetterman Massacre. In 1866 Nelson Story trailed the first herd of Texas longhorns to cross Wyoming along this road. Indian hostiles forced abandonment of the trail in 1868.

LOCATION: South side of State Route 387 about 7.75 miles west of Pine Tree Junction.

The Bozeman Trail passed through several Indian hunting grounds. The Crow Indians lived and hunted in the area before the Sioux, Cheyenne, and Arapaho claimed it as their hunting grounds. The Sioux conceded in an 1866 treaty at Fort Laramie that they would not interfere with travel on the Bozeman Trail. In 1868 "the Crows signed away their rights to the lands south of Montana, retaining only the right to hunt on those lands so long as game remained in sufficient numbers to justify the chase." The Fort Laramie Treaty of 1868 gave the Sioux all of what is now South Dakota west of the Missouri River. It also gave them hunting rights in the land north of the North Platte River and east of the Big Horn Mountains. However, clashes between the white man and the Cheyenne, Arapahoe, and Sioux Indians over the great hunting grounds continued, hence the nickname "The Bloody Bozeman." Travel along the trail ended in August 1868 when the forts were abandoned.

1. The Bozeman Trail Informative Sign, erected in 1960-1962, lies adjacent to a granite marker placed by the Wyoming Oregon Trail Commission in 1914.

BOZEMAN TRAIL MARKER-2.2

TITLE: Bozeman Trail

LEGEND: Marked by the State of Wyoming 1914

LOCATION: South side of State Route 387 about 7.75 miles west of Pine Tree Junction.

See Bozeman Trail Informative Sign (Campbell County #2.1).

WYODAK INFORMATIVE SIGN-3.0

TITLE: Wyodak Resources Development Corp.
Wyodak Coal Mine
A Wholly Owned Subsidiary of
Black Hills Power and Light Company

LEGEND: This open pit coal mine is the source of fuel for generating electricity in northeastern Wyoming, southeastern Montana and the Black Hills region of South Dakota.

The coal was first mined in 1923 by removing the overburden with horse drawn scrapers and then hauling coal to the surface with horse drawn wagons.

The Marion shovel and the P & H crane seen here were used 40 years ago and were some of the first mechanized pieces of equipment purchased for the mine. Wyodak Resources Development Corp. was incorporated in 1958 at which time it purchased mining equipment and leased coal reserves from Homestake Mining Company.

Located in the upper portion of what is known geologically as the Fort Union Formation are three important and remarkable coal seams. The three seams are composed of the upper Wyodak with a thickness of 40 feet, the middle Wyodak with a thickness of 12 feet, and the lower Wyodak with a thickness of 40 feet.

The coal lies in a practically continuous bed varying in thickness from 70 feet to about 110 feet. It is classified as subbituminous coal with an average heat content of 8,000 BTU's per pound. The present coal reserves will provide home heating for the Gillette area and electrical generation until the year 2027.

Upon removal of the coal the area will be reclaimed providing rangeland for cattle grazing and additional habitat for deer and antelope.

LOCATION: About 8 miles east of Gillette on State Route 51 (old U.S. Hwy 14/16).

CAMPBELL COUNTY

Legend

- Interstate
- US Highway
- State or Other Principal Road
- Marker

1   Astorian Overland Expedition Informative Sign
2.1   Bozeman Trail Informative Sign
2.2   Bozeman Trail Marker
3   Wyodak Informative Sign

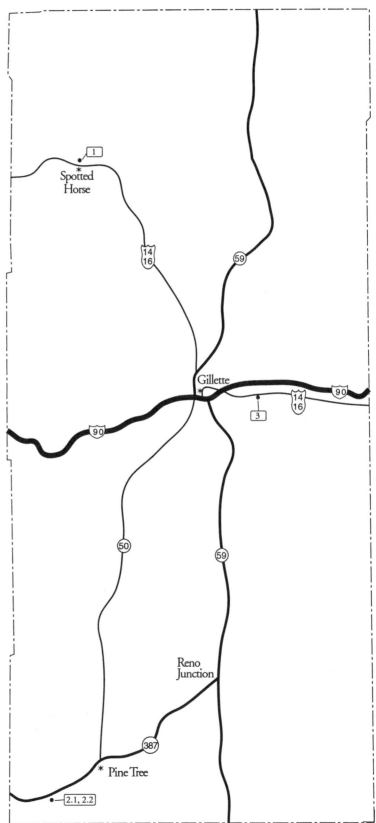

CARBON COUNTY

CATTLE TRAIL INFORMATIVE SIGN-1

TITLE: None
LEGEND: None
LOCATION: East of the railroad depot in Medicine Bow, Wyoming. It is next to Owen Wister Monument (Carbon County #18).

Many cattle brands have been burned into this wooden sign, a monument to the various ranches in the area.

CHEROKEE TRAIL MARKER-2

TITLE: The Site of Old Cherokee Trail
LEGEND: This monument is erected by Mrs. R. D. Myer
Hanna, Wyoming June 1914
LOCATION: Travel 1 mile west of the Wagonhound Rest Area on dirt service road. Marker is on west side of service road.

The first men to follow this route were a group of trappers with William Ashley of the Rocky Mountain Fur Company in 1825. John Charles Fremont used the route in 1843 on his second expedition to the West. In 1849, a party of Cherokee Indians, headed by Captain Evans of Arkansas, followed in en-route to California. The trail was known thereafter as the Cherokee Trail. In 1862, however, when Ben Holladay began to use the trail for the overland mail and transportation route, it became known as the Overland Trail and thereafter served as the principal mail, stage, and emigrant route. Related markers can be found in Albany, Carbon, Sweetwater, and Uinta Counties.

COAL MINERS MONUMENT-2.1

TITLE: None
LEGEND: Dedicated to all coal miners in the Carbon-Hanna area in memory of those who lost their lives in mining accidents.
Erected by Hanna Basin Historical Society May 27, 1984
LOCATION: Near the Hanna Recreation Center in Hanna, Wyoming.

The information below was taken from *History of Wyoming* by T. A. Larson.
The Union Pacific Coal Company began operations at the Hanna coal mines in 1893. Major tragedies occurred in 1903 and 1908. On June 30, 1903, 171 men were killed during an explosion deep within Union Pacific Coal Company's Mine Number One. All but one of the bodies were removed from the mine by Christmas, and the mine reopened in 1904. Almost 150 women were widowed, and 600 children lost their fathers in the accident.
On March 28, 1908, another tragedy struck the mine, as two explosions killed 58 men, leaving 33 widows and 103 fatherless children.
The Wyoming press and the *Denver Times* were angry at the inadequacy of safety measures and compensation paid to the surviving families. Said the *Times*, "Martyrs not to our civilization, but to our ignorance, thoughtlessness and greed!" The Wyoming press reported compensation figures of $800 to each widow and $50 additional for each child under fifteen.
The names of the miners killed in the Hanna coal mines are listed on the marker.

DALEY FLAGPOLE AND MARKER-3

TITLE: None
LEGEND: The pioneer William Daley (1844-1922) built both the original 1866 Fort Phil Kearney flagstaff for the Bozeman Trail fort and this replica which is placed here in memory of the Daley family in 1965.
LOCATION: Southwest corner of the Carbon County Courthouse square in Rawlins, Wyoming; northeast corner of 5th and Pine Streets.

DINOSAUR GRAVEYARD INFORMATIVE SIGN-4

TITLE: Dinosaur Graveyard
LEGEND: The bluff lying 1.3 miles to the north is Como Ridge, just beyond the crest of which lies "The Dinosaur Graveyard", one of the greatest fossil beds of dinosaur skeletons in the world. One of the largest skeletons ever unearthed, measuring 70 feet in length, was taken from this fossil bed. Hundreds of dinosaur skeletons and the bones of early mammals were unearthed and shipped from this area between 1880 and 1890. These dinosaurs lived from about one hundred million to two hundred million years ago.
LOCATION: North side of U.S. Hwy 30/287 at the Carbon/Albany County line.

This marker is adjacent to Como Bluffs (Albany County #3).

THOMAS A. EDISON MONUMENT-5

TITLE: Thomas A. Edison
LEGEND: Camped near this spot in 1878, while on a fishing trip. It was here that his attention was directed to the fiber from his bamboo fishing pole which he tested as a suitable filament for his incandescent electric lamp.
Born February 11, 1847—Died October 18, 1931 Age 84.
Placed by the Historical Landmark Commission of Wyoming 1949
LOCATION: South side of State Route 70 between Encampment and Savory. Overlooks Battle Lake.

ENCAMPMENT, WYOMING, INFORMATIVE SIGN-6

TITLE: Encampment, Wyoming
(Grand Encampment)
Elevation 7,323 feet.
LEGEND: Gateway to the sites of ghost towns of the Copper Country. Once a favorite hunting ground of Prehistoric man, later "Camp le Grand" became a noted rendezvous of Indians and trappers. In 1897 the town site was laid out by Willis George Emerson and associates; in 1897 Ed Haggarty made his big strike on the Continental Divide. In 1902, during the mining boom, the longest aerial tramway in the world was built to convey ore 16 miles from the great Ferris-Haggarty mine to the smelter at Encampment. In 1908 the industry collapsed. Encampment is now a beef, timber, hunting, fishing and resort center.
LOCATION: North end of Main Street in Encampment, Wyoming.

The information below was taken from *Wyoming: A Guide to Historic Sites* published in 1976 and from the brochure provided by the Grand Encampment Museum.
The Grand Encampment region was once a gathering place for Indians and mountain men during the Rocky Mountain fur trade. At the close of the 1800s it became a booming copper region centered around the Ferris-Haggarty Mine. The towns of Rudefeha, Dillon, Copperton, Rambler, Battle, and Elwood grew up quickly near the mines. East of the mining region the towns of Riverside and Encampment served as the miners' commercial hub.
The boom was followed by the bust. Natural hardships (such as storms, snow, and mud), smelter fires in 1906 and 1907, and copper price fluctuations doomed the mining business to failure. When the United Smelters, Railway, and Copper Company, which had produced two million dollars in copper ore, was indicted for overcapitalization and fraudulent stock sales in 1908, the final blow had been made, and the mines closed.
The Grand Encampment Museum in the town of Encampment, Wyoming, houses a wealth of history of the copper boom. Historic buildings, equipment, and memorabilia, including a wooden tower from the 10,000 foot high aerial tramway, can be seen at the museum complex.

CARBON COUNTY

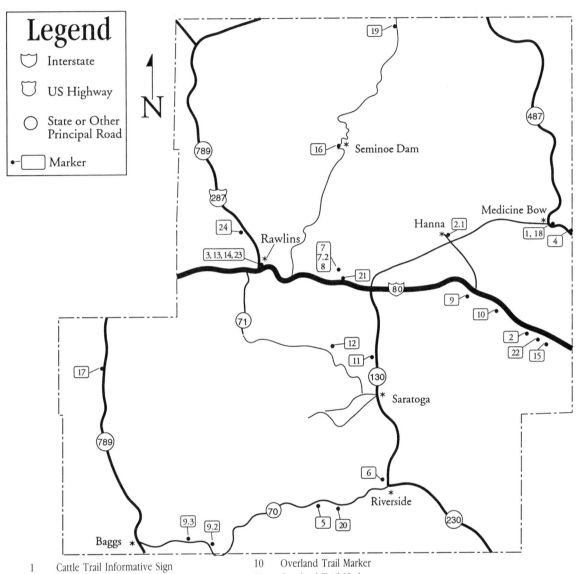

Legend
- Interstate
- US Highway
- State or Other Principal Road
- Marker

N

1	Cattle Trail Informative Sign	10	Overland Trail Marker
2	Cherokee Trail Marker	11	Overland Trail Marker
2.1	Coal Miners Monument	12	Platte River Crossing—Overland Trail Monument
3	Daley Flagpole and Marker	13	Rawlins Springs Marker
4	Dinosaur Graveyard Informative Sign	14	Rawlins Springs Marker
5	Thomas A. Edison Monument	15	Rock Creek Crossing—Overland Trail Marker
6	Encampment, Wyoming, Informative Sign	16	Seminoe Dam Plaque
7	Fort Fred Steele Informative Sign	17	Overland Stage Station Marker
7.2	Fort Fred Steele Interpretive Display	18	Owen Wister Monument
8	Fort Fred Steele Marker	19	S. Morris Waln Monument
9	Fort Halleck Marker	20	Battle Monument
9.2	Jim Baker's Trading Post	21	Blue Star Memorial Highway Marker
9.3	Jim Baker Grave	22	Wagonhound Tipi Rings
		23	Wyoming State Penitentiary Sign
		24	Rawlins Uplift Informative Sign

FORT FRED STEELE INFORMATIVE SIGN-7

TITLE: Fort Fred Steele Historical Overview

LEGEND: The south central portion of Wyoming has long been a travel corridor for prehistoric and historic people. Native American tribes from the Great Basin region to the west crossed this area to hunt buffalo on the eastern plains.

From 1810 until the decline of the Rocky Mountain fur trade in the late 1830's, fur traders and trappers traversed this region on their way west in quest of beaver pelts, then retraced their route east laden with furs. These men left little evidence of their passing, but they explored the routes used by thousands of future settlers destined for locations west of Wyoming.

Although suggestions to build a transcontinental railroad had been made in the 1840's, no decision was reached until after the outbreak of the Civil War when Congress selected a central route through southern Wyoming. The Union Pacific Railroad, chartered by Congress, built track westward from Nebraska through Wyoming to Utah.

The military constructed a series of forts along the Union Pacific route to protect construction crews against attack by hostile Indians. Fort Fred Steele, named in honor of Civil War hero Major General Frederick Steele, was established in June, 1868 where the railroad crossed the North Platte River. Until 1886, when it was decommissioned, the garrison at Fort Fred Steele performed a variety of policing activities involving both Indians and civilians.

The railroad also promoted mercantile development, and livestock, lumber and mining industries. After the departure of the military, these industries continued and the town of Fort Steele survived. Completion of the transcontinental Lincoln Highway through Wyoming in 1922 contributed to a brief economic revival. However, rerouting of the highway in 1939 and the demise of the tie industry in 1940 ended the town's function as a commercial center.

LOCATION: Fort Steele Rest Stop north of I-80. About 12 miles east of Rawlins, Wyoming.

FORT FRED STEELE INTERPRETIVE DISPLAY-7.2

Plaque #1

TITLE: Bridge Tender's House

LEGEND: The bridge tender's house was constructed by the Union Pacific Railroad to serve as an employee surveillance point. The bridge tender could respond quickly to locomotive-caused fires and could remove flood debris which might damage the bridge and cause interruptions to railroad traffic. The photograph shows the present bridge under construction in 1910.

Restored by the Wyoming Recreation Commission in 1983, the one and one-half story, clapboard-sided structure was probably built before 1887. The replacement of steam by diesel locomotives in the mid-1900's eliminated the necessity for a bridge tender and the house was abandoned.

Plaque #2

TITLE: Fort Fred Steele After 1886

LEGEND: Officially abandoned in 1886, the fort came under the jurisdiction of the Department of the Interior in 1887. In 1892 and 1893 most of the buildings were sold at public auction. In 1897 the land, opened to homesteading, was patented by the Union Pacific Railroad.

Primary industries in the town of Fort Steele after the turn of the century were sheep ranching and tie processing. The Lincoln Highway, the nation's first transcontinental highway, passed through the town and boosted the economy between 1920 and 1939. When the highway was moved in 1939 most commercial activity ended. The number of residents declined rapidly and the town became practically deserted.

In 1973 the Wyoming Stage Legislature created the Fort Fred Steele State Historic Site. Although the number of structures has declined dramatically over the years what remains standing is mute testimony to the flourishing and subsequent passing of several frontiers.

Plaque #3

TITLE: Brownsville and Benton

LEGEND: During construction of the Union Pacific Railroad land speculators and a large contingent of undesirables kept pace with or moved ahead of the construction crews and their military escorts. Townsite speculators tried to anticipate depot locations, purchasing land, selling lots and constructing tent towns.

Before the railroad reached the North Platte crossing at Fort Fred Steele, speculators set up the town of Brownsville on the river's east bank. Commanding Officer, Major Richard I. Dodge, issued an order July 2, 1868 proclaiming all lands within a three mile radius of Fort Fred Steele to be part of the military reservation and prohibiting civilian residence. Benton thus grew up on the west edge of the reservation. In a matter of days Brownsville's population resided in Benton. The tent town of Benton lasted only a few months when its population moved west to Rawlins Springs.

Plaque #4

TITLE: Officers' Quarters

LEGEND: The collapsed sandstone building west of the sign is all that remains of the once imposing eight room, one and one-half story Commanding Officer's quarters. Residences for staff officers were four, wood-framed double quarters with a captain in one-half and two lieutenants in the other half. Compared to enlisted men's barracks, the officers' quarters were luxurious. Amenities included lath and plaster walls, kitchens with cellars and large enclosed yards.

Officers' salaries greatly exceeded those of enlisted men. They could hire servants and support a family, activities prohibited to the enlisted man. Social activities at Fort Fred Steele included dinner parties, card games, theatrical presentations, dances and outdoor activities such as fishing, hunting, ice skating and sledding. Even with these diversions, daily military life was monotonous. Opportunities for promotion were limited and usually occurred upon the retirement or death of a superior.

Plaque #5

TITLE: Fort Steele Schoolhouse

LEGEND: After the fort was decommissioned and the military buildings were sold at auction, the residents of the Fort Steele community converted some of the old structures into homes and businesses or built anew on top of bare foundations. The schoolhouse was built in 1919 over the foundation remains of the fort hospital. The one-story, gable-roofed structure with clapboard siding served as a library, church, and community meeting house as well as an education center for the town.

Work and leisure time at Fort Steele did not change drastically with the closing of the fort. The trains continued to stop daily supplying the community with fresh produce and other necessary goods while carrying local timber and wool to points beyond. The North Platte River still provided the town folk with a pleasant location for their leisure activities.

Plaque #6

TITLE: Enlisted Men's Barracks

LEGEND: Two stone foundations and chimneys remain of the five enlisted men's barracks once at Fort Fred Steele. The walls were constructed of logs and boards and battens while a shingled roof

1.

2.

3.

1. The Wyoming Oregon Trail Commission placed this marker at Fort Fred Steele on July 30, 1916. Many other interpretive plaques have been placed at the historic site since then.

2. The Historical Landmark Commission of Wyoming placed many granite markers similar to this Overland Trail marker.

3. The Rawlins marker erected in 1957 by the Carbon County Chapter of the Wyoming State Historical Society told how Rawlins received its name.

4. The Rock Creek Crossing-Overland Trail marker was made possible by a $50 donation from Mrs. Inez L. Kortes of Elk Mountain, Wyoming.

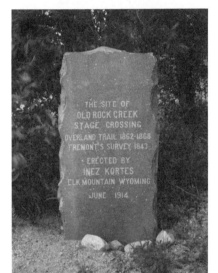

4.

protected pine floor boards. Tar paper covered interior walls. Kitchens doubled as mess and washrooms, and iron bedsteads took up most of the floor space.

Enlisted life in the frontier army could only be characterized as boring, with inadequate salaries and a monotonous diet. Most soldiers spent their days drilling and digging ditches. Social activities for enlisted men were limited and alcohol consumption prompted periodic orders from the commanding officer restricting saloon activities.

In 1892 the barracks buildings, sold at auction with other fort structures, were purchased by private citizens. Only the two central barracks remained when the first transcontinental auto road, the Lincoln Highway, passed through the town of Fort Steele in the 1920's. The road bridged the Platte River directly north of the town and passed close by the old army barracks, one of which was given a new function as a gasoline station.

The last two barracks were destroyed by fires set by vandals on New Year's Eve, 1976.

Plaque #7
TITLE: Sheepherders' Community
LEGEND: Sheep were introduced to Wyoming in the 1850's near Fort Bridger, about 180 miles west of Fort Steele. By 1880 the number had grown to over 350,000 head ranging primarily along the route of the Union Pacific Railroad. The Cosgriff Brothers owned one of the largest sheep ranching operations in Wyoming at that time, and they established herds in the Fort Steele area in 1881. After the fort was decommissioned they acquired many of its buildings and in 1903 constructed one of the largest sheep shearing plants in Wyoming. In 1905 over 800,000 pounds of wool was shipped to Boston, the single largest shipment of wool ever sent out of Wyoming.

L. E. Vivion, owner of the Leo Sheep Company, purchased most of the Cosgriff land holdings including the land at Fort Fred Steele in 1915. The house, lean-to, and shed in this area are the remains of a sheepherders' community.

Plaque #8
TITLE: Powder Magazine
LEGEND: The powder magazine housed the fort's munitions and therefore was located away from the main military complex. Ironically, it is one of the few fort structures remaining. It replaced the original magazine, a dugout constructed when the post was established in 1868.

The structure was built in 1881 from locally quarried stone and from materials fabricated at the Department of the Platte Headquarters in Omaha and shipped by rail to Fort Fred Steele. With sturdy walls on random-coursed ashlar sandstone, the powder magazine remains essentially the same as it was in 1881, although the tin roof has been replaced with shingles and internal shelving has been removed.

Few artillery pieces and only small quantities of ammunition were kept at the post. Fort Fred Steele generally had only a single mountain howitzer, and sometimes a Gatling gun on hand. Other explosive and combustible materials such as powder, fuses and signaling fireworks probably also were stored in this building.

Plaque #9
TITLE: Major General Frederick Steele
1818-1868
LEGEND: General Steele commanded a division of the Union Army at Vicksburg. Later he commanded all Union forces on the line of the Arkansas, exercising President Lincoln's policy of conciliation and reconstruction. At the end of the war he served in Texas, on the Mexican border. He then was sent to Oregon and Washington as commander of the Department of the Columbia.

Shortly following his death, Fort Fred Steele was named in his honor.

Plaque #10
TITLE: Post Trader Residence
LEGEND: This site is the remains of the Post Trader's residence. The photograph taken of the building later in the army's occupation of the fort attests to the prosperity enjoyed by the Post Trader.

The Post Trader was appointed by the Secretary of War, and the position was highly prized because of its profit possibilities. In 1868 J. W. Hugus established dry goods, liquor, freighting and ferry operations, all welcomed by travelers and local residents including the fort's soldiers. Alcohol use apparently caused the Post Commander concern as he frequently ordered Hugus to limit sales to soldiers.

Hugus, one of the area's leading merchandisers, continued as Post Trader until 1884 when he sold his business to Fenimore Chatterton, a long-time employee. Chatterton later held the office of Wyoming Secretary of State and served as Acting Governor from 1903 to 1905.

Plaque #11
TITLE: Carbon Timber Company
LEGEND: Construction of the Union Pacific Railroad stimulated the growth of the timber industry in southern Wyoming. Two companies began supplying ties to the railroad in 1868, but the firm of Coe and Carter was the leading supplier to the Fort Fred Steele collection yards until 1896.

Cut and shaped in the Medicine Bow Mountains to the south, ties were floated downriver during spring run-off and were gathered behind a boom here. Coe and Carter also supplied timbers for coal mines at Carbon, Hanna, and Dana to the east, and lumber for buildings at Fort Fred Steele and the surrounding area. The Carbon Timber Company, successor to Coe and Carter, floated over 1.5 million timbers down the North Platte in 1909.

Directly across the North Platte River east of Fort Steele are the remains of the Carbon Timber Company tie processing facility, a privately-owned site.

Plaque #12
TITLE: Cemetery
LEGEND: The post cemetery served as a graveyard for soldiers, their dependents, and civilians during army occupation of Fort Fred Steele (1868-1886). Although some soldiers died during the Indian Wars of the 1860's and 1870's, most of the military deaths at the fort were the result of accidents and disease. Civilians and travelers who expired in the vicinity of Fort Steele also were interred in the cemetery.

Although the Fort Steele hospital provided medical services to military personnel and their dependents, the lack of refined medical techniques often resulted in death from infection and diseases like pneumonia and tuberculosis. The infant mortality rate was particularly high and 25% of the graves in the cemetery were occupied by children.

The 100' X 140' cemetery was enclosed by a picket fence and contained eighty irregularly spaced graves. Each grave was numbered, the number appearing on a painted wooden peg at the foot of the plot. Gravesite markings included wood headboards for the military but they proved impractical as inscriptions soon became obliterated by weathering. Although few persons of historical fame were buried in the Fort Fred Steele cemetery, an exception was Jefferson J. Standifer, who participated in many western gold rushes including the brief 1867 boom at South Pass City, Wyoming.

Not all those who perished at Fort Steele were buried in the post cemetery. Rather than surrender their loved ones to an eternity on this wind-swept riverbank, some chose to ship the deceased by rail to other final resting places. Military families occasionally requested official assistance with the shipments. Officers reported civilian requests for coffins and embalming materials, complaining that to supply them was not a military responsibility.

When the post was decommissioned in 1886, the Secretary of the Interior declared the cemetery exempt from sale or transfer to public because of the military burials. In 1892 the graves of the soldiers, their dependents and some civilians were moved to Fort McPherson National Cemetery near Maxwell, Nebraska. Civilians continued to use the cemetery after the departure of the military and the last documented burial took place in the 1920's. The land occupied by the cemetery is still owned by the United States government.

Plaque #13

TITLE: Acknowledgement
LEGEND: The State of Wyoming and the Wyoming Recreation Commission thank Charles Vivion, Herman Werner, and Alvina Ducolon for their generous donation of land at Fort Steele State Historic Site. These donations have made possible the preservation of historic Fort Fred Steele for the education and enjoyment of the public.

Plaque #14

TITLE: None
LEGEND: The markers placed here honor Charles G. and Grace M. Vivion, husband and wife, who for more than a generation kept the traditional charge of the flockmaster. In seasons of gentle rains and warming sun, or through time of searing drought and driving blizzards, they cared for their flocks. In successfully developing their ranching operation they enriched a heritage which included the frontier military establishment, Fort FredSteele. They have shared it with the citizens of Wyoming by giving this portion of their land, including the fort site, to encourage awareness of the historic past of the grazing industry.

Placed by the State of Wyoming, 1977

LOCATION: About 12 miles east of Rawlins, Wyoming, and 1.25 miles north of Ft. Steele Rest Area just off of I-80.

FORT FRED STEELE MARKER-8

TITLE: Fort Fred Steele
LEGEND: U.S. Military Post June 30, 1868 to August 7, 1886
Marked by the State of Wyoming 1914
LOCATION: At the Fort Steele State Historic Site. About 0.1 miles northwest of the Union Pacific underpass and the Bridge Tender's House.

This monument was made of the same polished granite as the Fort Halleck Marker. The Fort Fred Steele Marker was placed at the site on July 30, 1916.

FORT HALLECK MARKER-9

TITLE: Fort Halleck
LEGEND: U. S. Military Post   July 20, 1862   July 4, 1866
This monument is erected by the State of Wyoming and the Jacques LaRamie Chapter D.A.R. 1914
LOCATION: In a hay meadow on the ranch headquarters of the Palm Livestock Company. About 4 miles from Elk Mountain interchange off of I-80. Private land; permission needed.

The information below was taken from the National Register of Historic Places Nomination-Inventory Form prepared by Bill Barnhart, Assistant Historian with the Wyoming Recreation Commission.

Fort Halleck was the single strategic military establishment on the Overland Trail. Established on July 20, 1862, the fort defended against hostile Indian warfare and helped keep the transportation line open between the East and West. It was named in honor of Major General Henry W. Halleck of Civil War fame.

The high point of Indian disturbances along the Overland Trail was in 1865. But with the end of the Civil War, migration to the gold fields of Montana by way of the Bozeman Trail diverted Indian pressure off of Fort Halleck, and the fort was officially abandoned on July 4, 1866. Materials and supplies from Fort Halleck were taken to Fort Buford (later called Fort Sanders), a new fort located near present-day Laramie, Wyoming.

This marker was made of the identical stone and style as three other Overland Trail markers: Fort Fred Steele (Carbon County #8), Old Cherokee Trail (Carbon County #2), and Old Rock Creek Stage Crossing (Carbon County #15).

JIM BAKER'S TRADING POST-9.2

Upper Plaque
TITLE: Jim Baker's Trading Post
LEGEND: This cabin was erected by Jim Baker, famous mountain man, plainsman, hunter, trapper, guide, scout, and Indian fighter on the Little Snake River in Carbon County, Wyoming, in 1873. Acquired by the State of Wyoming in 1917 and transported to Cheyenne, Wyoming, to be preserved as a lasting memorial to this brave pioneer citizen.

The Historical Landmark Commission of Wyoming 1939
Lower Plaque
TITLE: None
LEGEND: Returned to the Little Snake River Museum from the State Historical Society of Wyoming July 1974
Re-erected near the original site Sept. 1976. Re-dedication of Jim Baker's Memorial Day July 4, 1977.

LOCATION: At the Little Snake River Museum in Savery, Wyoming.

Jim Baker was Wyoming's last great mountain man and fur trapper. This cabin was his last permanent home in the Rocky Mountains. After Baker's death in 1898, interest in preservation of his cabin as an historic building stimulated an effort to have the building moved to a Denver city park.

Controversy developed as Wyoming public sentiment demanded that the cabin remain in Wyoming. In 1917 Wyoming Senator Allison introduced a "Jim Baker Cabin" measure in the Fourteenth State Legislature. The cabin was purchased by the State of Wyoming, removed from the valley, and reconstructed in Frontier Park in Cheyenne. Here, the cabin deteriorated and was preserved several times. Eventually, interested citizens of the Little Snake River Valley brought the cabin back to Savery, Wyoming, not far from the cabin's original site.

The Jim Baker Cabin was enrolled on the National Register from July 24, 1972, until 1978. When the cabin was moved from Cheyenne back to Savery, it was taken off the Register. However, it was re-enrolled on November 1, 1982.

JIM BAKER GRAVE-9.3

South Face
TITLE: Jim Baker
LEGEND: Here lies Jim Baker
Born in Illinois Dec. 19, 1819 Died May 15, 1898
West Face
TITLE: None
LEGEND: One of the oldest Pioneers of the Rocky Mountains.
Contemporary of "Kit" Carson, Jim Bridger, Freemont, and the rest who helped to civilize this district. A government scout, guide, and Indian fighter. His memory should be respected forever by those who live in all this region, the fighting land of the Indian tribes.

LOCATION: Baker Cemetery west of Savery, Wyoming.

The information below was taken from the National Register of Historic Places Nomination-Inventory Form completed by Mark Junge and Sheila Bricher-Wade in February 1981.

Jim Baker lived and worked in the Rocky Mountains of Wyoming and Colorado. He came to the Rocky Mountains at the age of twenty on an expedition with the American Fur Company, led by Jim Bridger.

On August 21, 1841, Jim Baker, other trappers, and several Snake Indians battled with a war party of Cheyenne, Sioux, and Arapahoe Indians. From

Baker's own account of the fight found in the *Denver Tribune-Republican* of July 10, 1886:

> Old Frappe (Fraeb) was killed, and he was the ugliest looking dead man I ever saw, and I have seen a good many. His face was all covered with blood, and he had rotten front teeth and a horrible grin. When he was killed he never fell, but sat braced up against the stump, a sight to behold. Well, when the fight was over there were about a hundred dead Injuns. There were three of our party killed.

Several geographic features, such as Battle Lake and Battle Mountain, take their names from this fight.

OVERLAND TRAIL MARKER-10

TITLE: Overland Trail
LEGEND: Marked by the State of Wyoming 1914
LOCATION: East of the town of Elk Mountain, 0.5 mile east of the Medicine Bow River bridge.

See Overland Trail Markers (Albany County #10, 11, & 12) for information about the Overland Trail. This marker and the Cherokee Trail Marker (Carbon County #2), and Rock Creek Crossing-Overland Trail Marker (Carbon County #15) were erected in Carbon County in 1914 to memorialize the Overland Trail.

OVERLAND TRAIL MARKER-11

TITLE: None
LEGEND: This marker on the Overland Trail. Platte River Crossing nine miles west. 1861 to 1868.
   Erected by The Historical Landmark Commission of Wyoming
LOCATION: West side of State Route 130, 11 miles north of Saratoga, Wyoming.

See Platte River Crossing-Overland Trail Monument (Carbon County #12) for more information.

PLATTE RIVER CROSSING—OVERLAND TRAIL MONUMENT-12

TITLE: Overland Trail Platte River Crossing
LEGEND: Erected in memory of those brave pioneers who passed this way to win and hold the West.
   This site a gift to Wyoming from Ella Mary Davis and Family in memory of her husband a pioneer banker merchant and stockman of Carbon County.
LOCATION: 9 miles west of Overland Trail Marker (Carbon County #11).

The information below came from the National Register of Historic Places Inventory-Nomination Form prepared by Bill Barnhart, Assistant Historian with the Wyoming Recreation Commission.

The Overland Trail passed over the North Platte River at this site. Emigrants who traveled over the Overland Trail found this site a particularly good place to ford the river, facilitated by a large island in the middle of the river. The site, remotely located in a natural desert of sagebrush and grasses, was used before the coming of the white man as the traditional warring grounds of the Cheyenne, Arapahoe, and Ute Indians.

The most significant of early-day explorations was the Stansbury Expedition, which camped at the Crossing in 1850. The writings of Captain Stansbury told of the area and the hardships getting there:

> The cottonwoods around our camp are the first trees, worthy of the name, that have greeted our eyes for more than a year. They seem to us like old friends, and, as they waved in the fresh breeze over our heads, reminded us of those beloved woodlands from which we had been so long separated. Oh! With what longing desire we had looked forward to such a sight; while our souls, sick of rolling prairies, barren plains, bald and rocky ridges, muddy flats, and sandy wastes, sought in vain for the forest shade and those hills of living verdure which gave the charm to every landscape. Day after day, week after week, had we journeyed over that desolate basin, without

a tree to be seen in the whole horizon. But now the rustling sound of embowered leaves assured us that we had once more reached a spot fitted by nature for the habitation of man. The place we now occupy had long been a favourite camp ground for the numerous warlike parties which annually meet in the region to hunt buffalo and one another. Remains of old Indian stockades are met with scattered about among the thickets; and the guide informed us, that four years since there were at one and the same time, upon this bottom, fifteen or twenty of these forts, constructed by different tribes. Most of them have since been destroyed by fire.

Although the Crossing was in one of the most dangerous sections of the Trail, apparently there was not a great deal of conflict with the Indians. Emigrants did die at or near the site, however, and a pioneer cemetery containing eight known graves and headstones lies just south of the monument. The dates on the headstones for the men and women buried there ranged from 1863 to 1865.

Ed Bennett and Frank Earnest established a ferry at this site to aid emigrant crossings when high water made travel treacherous. Some then referred to the Crossing as Bennett's Ferry.

Platte River Crossing declined in importance when the Union Pacific Railroad completed its tracklaying through the area in 1868. Today the area is devoted to ranching interests. Although the land and marker are owned by the State of Wyoming, access to the site is through private land and permission is necessary before entering.

An Oregon Trail Memorial Association plaque is embedded in the top of this granite monument. It is another testimony to the strong ties between the association and early Wyoming leaders of historical marking.

RAWLINS SPRINGS MARKER-13

TITLE: Rawlins
LEGEND: In the summer of 1867, a survey party led by General Grenville M. Dodge seeking a route for the Union Pacific Railroad, stopped one half mile southwest of here.
   General John A. Rawlins, a member of the party, spoke of the spring there as the most gracious and acceptable of anything he had had on the march and said that if anything was ever named after him he wanted it to be a spring of water.
   General Dodge replied: "We will name this Rawlins Springs."
   This tablet designed by the Carbon County Chapter of The Wyoming State Historical Society 1867-1957.
LOCATION: In front of the Rawlins City Hall in Rawlins, Wyoming.

RAWLINS SPRINGS MARKER-14

TITLE: Rawlins Springs
LEGEND: In the summer of 1867, a survey party led by General Grenville M. Dodge seeking a route for the Union Pacific Railroad stopped here.
   General John A. Rawlins, a member of the party, spoke of the spring as "the most gracious and acceptable of anything he had had on the march" and said that if anything was ever named after him he wanted it to be a spring of water.
   General Dodge replied: "We will name this Rawlins Springs."
   Tablet designed and placed 1957 by the Carbon County Chapter of the Wyoming State Historical Society. Neal E. Miller, President; Alex Gordon, 1st Vice Pres.; L. D. Rettstatt, 2nd Vice Pres.; Lovina Pierson, Secy.; Kleber H. Haddsell, Treas.; and A. H. MacDougall, Repr.
   In grateful recognition of the material aid and technical assistance of the Union Pacific Railroad Company, the Sinclair Refining Company and the University of Wyoming.
LOCATION: Rawlins Springs Park just west of the intersection of Bennett and West Davis Streets in Rawlins, Wyoming.

ROCK CREEK CROSSING—OVERLAND TRAIL MARKER-15

TITLE: None
LEGEND: The site of old Rock Creek Stage Crossing
    Overland Trail 1862-1868
    Fremont's survey 1843
    Erected by Inez Kortes Elk Mountain, Wyoming June 1914
LOCATION: 0.2 miles south of I-80 at the Arlington exit.

The Rock Creek Crossing and Stage Station was one of many way stations along the Overland Trail in the 1860s. Rock Creek became both a commercial and entertainment center for emigrants traveling along the trail. It continued to thrive as a supply and social center for the growing agricultural and timber interests in the surrounding area, even when travel along the trail declined with completion of the Transcontinental Railroad. In 1882, the Rockdale post office was constructed at the site. In the latter part of the 19th century Rock Creek Station owners turned to stock raising for economic purposes. During the early 20th century Rock Creek was renamed Arlington, but its dual commercial and agricultural role continued.

This marker, Fort Halleck Marker, and Cherokee Trail Marker (Carbon County #9 & 2) were erected in 1914 by the Daughters of the American Revolution. Grace Raymond Hebard wrote of the marker: "The Kortes marker is located in front of the old Arlington summer resort, now called 'Wildwood Resort,' about three and a half miles from the new oil fields. This site is where the General Fremont Survey (1843), the Overland Trail and the Cherokee Trail cross Rock Creek."

SEMINOE DAM PLAQUE-16

TITLE: Seminoe Dam and Powerplant   1939
    Kendrick Project
LEGEND: Built by and for the people of the United States for conservation, control, and use of water resources.
    Height above streambed 210 feet
    Length of crest 530 feet
    Reservoir capacity 1,012,000 acre feet
    Powerplant rating 32,400 K.W.
    Bureau of Reclamation United States Department of the Interior
LOCATION: Wall of the powerplant building at base of Seminoe Dam.

OVERLAND STAGE STATION MARKER-17

TITLE: The Overland Stage Station Route
LEGEND: Operated 1862 to 1868
    Washakee Station four miles east. Barrel Springs Station fourteen miles west.
    Erected by the Historical Landmark Commission of Wyoming 1951
LOCATION: 10.5 miles south of I-80 on State Route 789.

OWEN WISTER MONUMENT-18

TITLE: Owen Wister
LEGEND: "When you say that, smile"
    Owen Wister whose writings acquainted the nation with pioneer Wyoming ranch life, made Medicine Bow the beginning of his most popular novel, "The Virginian".
    Dedicated by the Historical Landmark Commission of Wyoming July 2, 1939
LOCATION: East of the train depot in Medicine Bow, Wyoming; next to the Cattle Trail Informative Sign (Carbon County #1).

The statement, "When you call me that, smile!" was one of the most famous lines in Western literature, and came from a Medicine Bow saloon scene in Wister's novel.

S. MORRIS WALN MONUMENT-19

TITLE: None
LEGEND: To the glory of God and sacred to the memory of S. Morris Waln, of Philadelphia, Penn'a. Born September 12th, 1861. Murdered by his guide July 23rd, 1888.
LOCATION: About 15 miles south of State Route 220 on the Alcova-Seminoe Road. Marker is located off of the Pedro Mountain Estates road.

Alfred J. Mokler's *History of Natrona County* (1888-1932) indicated that Morris Waln, of Haverford, Pennsylvania, and C. H. Strong, of New York City, New York, came West in the early spring of 1888 on a hunting, prospecting, and pleasure trip. They hired Thomas O'Brien as a guide and cook. In August, O'Brien murdered both Waln and Strong, took the outfit, and fled the country. He later paid the price for his murders.

The cross is made of Pennsylvania granite. It stands eight feet above the ground, is fourteen inches thick, and has arms four and one-half feet in length. It was put in place December 23, 1889, by Mr. Boney Earnest and others.

BATTLE MONUMENT-20

TITLE: Battle Country
LEGEND: The year is 1841. This country was teaming with beaver and other fur-bearing animals, and it was jealously guarded by Indians. Because the lure of beaver was so great, a group of American Fur Company trappers invaded these mountains determined to trap the streams.

On August 20, Henry Fraeb, with thirty-two trappers under his command, had a desperate battle with an overwhelming force of Cheyenne and Sioux Indians. On that day, ten men were sent out from camp to drive buffalo. Those remaining in camp would head off the bison after the ten started them running in their direction. By accident, the ten men ran onto a large body of Indians, and were attacked with great fury. One trapper was wounded badly in the fight and he turned his horse in the direction of camp, which he reached safely. Fraeb ordered twenty of his men to mount, and he led them to the rescue of the nine who were desperately fighting the unequal conflict. The arrival of the reinforcements decided the battle and the Indians retreated.

The Indians' resentment of their defeat was immediate. Retreating northeast, they fired the forest, thus serving notice that they would make the country a wasteland rather than let the white men take it. The immediate area was denuded.

From this trapper-Indian conflict, Battle Creek, Battle Lake, the town of Battle and Battle Mountain received their name.

The battle occurred where the creek in front of you joins the Little Snake River, about eight miles south.

    Medicine Bow National Forest
LOCATION: Battle Lake Overlook on State Route 70 between Encampment and Savery, Wyoming.

BLUE STAR MEMORIAL HIGHWAY MARKER-21

TITLE: Blue Star Memorial Highway
LEGEND: A tribute to the Armed Forces that have defended the United States of America.
    Sponsored by Wyoming Federation of Garden Clubs in cooperation with The Wyoming Highway Commission
LOCATION: Fort Fred Steele Rest Area about 12 miles east of Rawlins, Wyoming.

WAGONHOUND TIPI RINGS-22

TITLE: Wagonhound Tipi Rings
LEGEND: The stone circles or "Tipi Rings" at this site mark the location of a prehistoric Native American campsite. The stones were probably used to anchor the skins of conical tents, known by the Sioux word "Tipi". The stones were placed around the base of the tipi to hold down the skins as well as to provide additional support to the

tipi in high winds. After the introduction of the metal ax, wooden pegs gradually replaced the stones for holding down the skins.

The tipi was used for shelter and sleeping. Most daily activities occurred outside the structure. A hearth in the center of the tipi was used for heat and cooking in poor weather.

In prehorse times, tipis averaged approximately 12 feet in diameter, and poles used in their construction were up to 15 feet long. Eight to 12 buffalo hides were needed for the construction of a tipi. The hides of buffalo killed during the summer were preferred because they were thinner and lighter in weight. A smudge fire was built inside a new tipi, and the smoke was allowed to permeated the leather. This process waterproofed the leather and aided in its preservation.

It has been estimated that there are over 1 million tipi rings in the western United States. As such, they are one of the most common archaeological features to be found in this part of the country. The features at this rest area have been preserved by the Wyoming Highway Department and the Office of the Wyoming State Archaeologist for your benefit. Please feel free to inspect the tipi rings up close, but do not disturb the rocks.

LOCATION: Wagonhound Rest Area west of Arlington, Wyoming.

WYOMING STATE PENITENTIARY SIGN-23

TITLE: Wyoming State Penitentiary

LEGEND: Before Wyoming was granted statehood, prisoners were incarcerated at the territorial prison located in Laramie. This was by Act of Congress of January 24, 1873 and the territorial prison was completed December 23, 1873. It housed 67 prisoners in a formidable stone barn with gabled roof and heavily barred windows. The National Territorial Building Act of 1888 provided that a penitentiary building for the use of the territory shall be erected in the City of Rawlins at a cost not exceeding $100,000.00 Construction of this territorial prison was begun July 23, 1888 and was named The Wyoming State Penitentiary by the Act of Admission July 10, 1890. It is situated on 65.31 acres of land within the City of Rawlins, Carbon County. Great slabs of stone and rock, observed on the outside structure, were wagoned from the Larson Stone Quarry south of Rawlins. The first prisoner recorded into this institution was on July 16, 1891. Starting in December of 1901 prisoners were transferred from Laramie to Rawlins and this transfer was completed in 1904. Of all prisoners incarcerated in this institution, probably the most publicized was Bill Carlisle the great train robber. The total capacity of inmates that could be incarcerated was 373.

LOCATION: 5th and Walnut Streets in Rawlins, Wyoming.

RAWLINS UPLIFT INFORMATIVE SIGN-24

TITLE: Rawlins Uplift

LEGEND: The Rawlins Uplift, an upward fold in the earth's crust, rises a thousand feet above the surrounding plains. It displays a wide array of geological features and a succession of rock strata that range in age from 2.6 to 10 million years. The high granitic rocks visible from the southwest are the oldest. They are covered on the north and east by the reddish Flathead Sandstone of the Cambrian Period (520,000,000 years) and the overlying gray Madison Limestone of the Mississippian Period (360,000,000). To the right of the colorful Flathead Sandstone one can see a fault (break in the earth's crust) along which rock strata have moved vertically. Quarries on the eastern slopes provided stone for many buildings including the old State Penitentiary in Rawlins. The stone, along with hematite, a red iron mineral, was extracted from the Flathead Sandstone. The hematite was used as a pigment in "barn red" paint. Local legend states that Rawlins paint was once used on the Brooklyn Bridge.

LOCATION: Along U.S. Hwy 287 just north of Rawlins, Wyoming. At the time of this writing, the marker was not yet erected.

CONVERSE COUNTY

AYRES NATURAL BRIDGE INFORMATIVE SIGN-1

TITLE: Ayres Natural Bridge Park

LEGEND: Ages ago Wyoming was covered by seas. Through a period of millions of years the land gradually rose, leaving the present landscape of plains, mountains and rolling hills. As the land emerged, erosion began and through eons of time, formed Ayres Natural Bridge as it exists today.

The bridge is 20 feet high and has a 90 foot span at the base. A trout stream flows beneath. The setting is in the center of a high red sandstone walled amphitheater, which provides a fine shady picnic ground.

All facilities are free and maintained by Converse County. Visitors welcome.

The bridge is 4-3/4 miles south from this point on an all weather road.

LOCATION: Location: South of I-25 on the west side of Natural Bridge Road, between Glenrock and Douglas, Wyoming.

It has been said that frontiersmen in the 1700s and 1800s discovered gold in LaPrele Creek. They inhabited the area after marrying local Indian women. Before scientific explorers came to survey West, the natural bridge had significance in Indian history and legend.

Early emigrants traveling the Oregon Trail recorded their visitations to the area. In 1843, Matthew Field wrote in his diary and sketched the bridge as he visited the area with William Drummond Stewart. Field reproduced the picture in a book, *Prairie and Mountain Sketches*. Ferdinand V. Hayden, an explorer, geologist, and director of the U.S. Geological Survey, first saw the bridge in August 1869.

In 1881, after hearing stories about the natural stone bridge, Alva Ayres traveled to the area and purchased the land which included the bridge on LaPrele Creek. In 1953 Alva Ayres's son, Clement Ayres, donated the bridge and land around it to Converse County.

BIG MUDDY OIL FIELD INFORMATIVE SIGN-2

TITLE: Big Muddy Oil Field

LEGEND: Big Muddy oil field is a typical Wyoming oil producing structure. The field, discovered in 1916, has produced over 30 million barrels of high quality oil. Strata here were arched upward at the time the Rocky Mountains originated about 60 million years ago, to form an anticline, or dome. Because oil is lighter than water, it rose to the crest of the dome where it was trapped in pore spaces between sand grains. The Wall Creek sand lies at a depth of near 3,000 feet and the Dakota sand at about 4,000 feet.

The first oil well in Wyoming was drilled in 1884. There are now about 100 oil fields in the state.

LOCATION: About 3.7 miles east of the Converse/Natrona County line, at a paved turnout on the north side of I-25.

BOZEMAN TRAIL MARKER-3.1

TITLE: Bozeman Trail

LEGEND: Marked by the State of Wyoming 1914

LOCATION: About 18 miles south of State Route 387 on east side of Converse County Road #93 (Ross Road).

The information below was taken from *The Bozeman Trail—Highway of History* by Robert A. Murray and *Marking The Oregon Trail, The Bozeman Road, and Historic Places in Wyoming 1908-1920* by Grace Raymond Hebard.

When gold was found in the early 1860s in southwestern Montana, gold seekers coming from the East had no direct road to follow. Some traveled the route along the Missouri River, as Lewis and Clark had done in 1804 to 1806. Some took the Oregon Trail along the North Platte River to South

Pass and Fort Bridger. Others followed the Overland Route (known also as the Cherokee Trail) from Denver, across the Laramie Plains and Bridger Pass to Fort Bridger. But each route was too long and circuitous for the eager and impatient emigrants seeking fortunes in gold.

One of those gold seekers was John M. Bozeman, a Georgian who described himself as a speculator. In 1863 he and John Jacobs teamed up to develop a trail along the eastern foothills of the Big Horn Mountains from the Oregon-California Trail. However, a threatening band of Sioux Indians stopped the white men at the Clear Fork of the Powder River, and the expedition never proceeded. Even though Bozeman failed to traverse the trail in 1863, he and many other emigrants succeeded in 1864.

Travel on the Bozeman Trail peaked in 1864. Between the present-day Wyoming cities of Douglas and Casper, the Bozeman Trail branched off the Oregon Trail. However, after 1867 the departure point was opposite the site of Fort Fetterman. The trail passed into Montana and on to Fort C. F. Smith on the Big Horn River. It then traveled to the present-day city of Livingston, Montana, through Bozeman Pass, and then southwest into the Beaverhead Valley mining district in Montana:

> The land from the North Platte and Fort Fetterman to Fort C. F. Smith was the cherished and coveted home and hunting ground of the Sioux, who, under Chief Red Cloud and his warriors, determined that no white man should invade their territory. The Indian wars along the Bozeman Trail were the most savage, continuous and unrelenting of any fought on the Western plains, a contest for supremacy between the redman and his enemy, the invading white man. *(Marking The Oregon Trail, The Bozeman Road, and Historic Places in Wyoming 1908-1920 by Grace Raymond Hebard)*

Historical names such as Fetterman, Carrington, and Phillips; Chiefs Red Cloud, Dull Knife, and Black Bear; Forts Reno, Phil Kearny, McKinney, and C. F. Smith; the Fetterman Fight, Wagon Box Fight, the Hayfield Fight, and the Connor Battlefield all developed their notoriety along the Bozeman Trail.

See Bozeman Trail Informative Sign (Campbell County 2.1) for more information about the Bozeman Trail.

LITTLE BOXELDER CREEK MARKER-3.2

TITLE: None

LEGEND: Three men named Sharp, Franklin and Taylor, and one unknown man were killed by Indians, July 12, 1864 where the Oregon Trail crosses Little Boxelder Creek 2 1/2 miles S.W. of here. They are buried four miles S.W. by the grave of Mary Kelly, who also was killed July 13, 1864.

Erected by the Historical Landmark Commission of Wyoming 1954

LOCATION: North side of I-25 about 1.1 miles west of exit to Natural Bridge Road. About 8.5 miles east of Glenrock, Wyoming.

The following information was taken from an article written by Randy Brown in the Winter 1987 issue of *Overland Journal*, the official magazine of the Oregon-California Trails Association.

The Kelly-Larimer wagon train was headed for the Montana gold fields in the summer of 1864. The wagon train met Indians just after crossing Cottonwood Creek. The Indians, most of them Oglala Sioux, followed the wagons down into the valley of Little Box Elder Creek. At dusk, the Indians motioned the train to stop and prepare supper for the Indians. Apparently, the Indians attacked while the emigrants were preparing the camp. Three men fell dead immediately and two others, although wounded, were able to find cover in the bushes in a nearby ravine. The three men who died were Noah Daniel Taylor, who was driving a wagon for William and Sarah Larimer; the Reverend Mr. Sharp, who was described as "a Methodist clergyman" and "aged and nearly blind"; and a black man known only as Franklin. The Indians then seized Fanny Kelly and her niece, Mary Hurley, from the Kelly wagon and Sarah Larimer and her son, Frank Larimer, from the Larimer wagon.

As the women and children were taken captive, another wagon and a lone rider came into view from the east. The Indians immediately went after this group, killing the unidentified lone rider. The four men killed that day were buried in a mass grave near the conflict.

It is not known why Mary Hurley joined the wagon train going to Montana. In her early writings, Fanny Kelly described her as her niece. Later, however, Fanny Kelly described Mary as an adopted daughter, hence

CONVERSE COUNTY

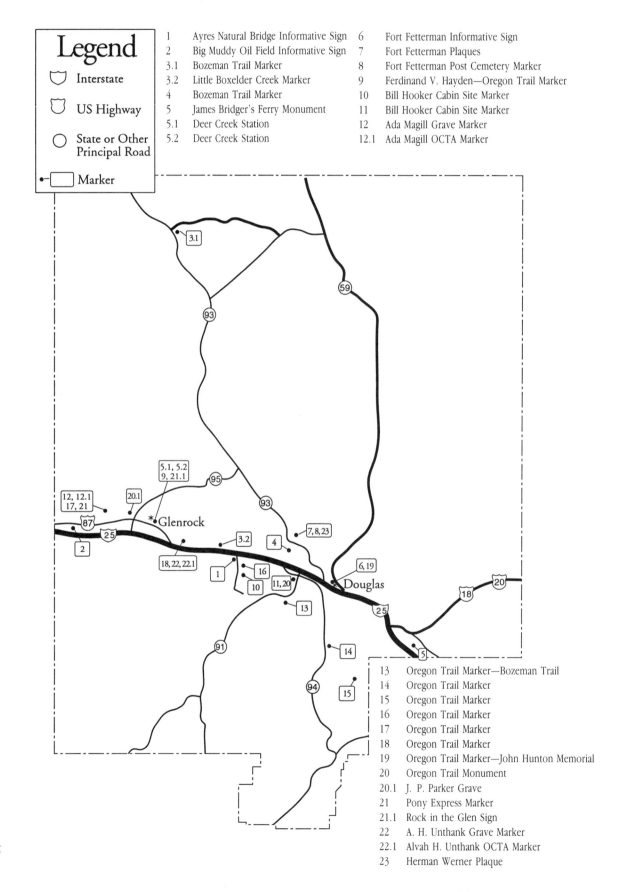

Legend

- ⬡ Interstate
- ⬡ US Highway
- ◯ State or Other Principal Road
- •▭ Marker

1   Ayres Natural Bridge Informative Sign
2   Big Muddy Oil Field Informative Sign
3.1 Bozeman Trail Marker
3.2 Little Boxelder Creek Marker
4   Bozeman Trail Marker
5   James Bridger's Ferry Monument
5.1 Deer Creek Station
5.2 Deer Creek Station

6   Fort Fetterman Informative Sign
7   Fort Fetterman Plaques
8   Fort Fetterman Post Cemetery Marker
9   Ferdinand V. Hayden—Oregon Trail Marker
10   Bill Hooker Cabin Site Marker
11   Bill Hooker Cabin Site Marker
12   Ada Magill Grave Marker
12.1 Ada Magill OCTA Marker

13   Oregon Trail Marker—Bozeman Trail
14   Oregon Trail Marker
15   Oregon Trail Marker
16   Oregon Trail Marker
17   Oregon Trail Marker
18   Oregon Trail Marker
19   Oregon Trail Marker—John Hunton Memorial
20   Oregon Trail Monument
20.1 J. P. Parker Grave
21   Pony Express Marker
21.1 Rock in the Glen Sign
22   A. H. Unthank Grave Marker
22.1 Alvah H. Unthank OCTA Marker
23   Herman Werner Plaque

1.

2.

3.

4.

5.

1. In the early 1960s, the Wyoming State Archives and Historical Deparment designed signs similar to Ayres Natural Bridge Park sign.

2. This large marker listed soldiers who died while at Fort Fetterman and civilians who died in the area even after the fort was abandoned.

3. Several granite markers identical to the one above were placed along the Bozeman Trail by the Wyoming Oregon Trail Commission.

4. The Historical Landmark Commission of Wyoming established this James Bridger Ferry monument in 1937.

5. William H. Jackson, a life member of the Oregon Trail Memorial Association, presented this Association marker and plaque to commemorate his friend and pioneer of the Oregon Trail, Ferdinand V. Hayden.

1.

2.

1. Many markers were made possible by donations from members of the Oregon Trail Memorial Association. Mr. F. W. LaFrentz donated this marker and plaque in honor of Bill Hooker.

2. At first, the Oregon Trail and the Pony Express were the only signs of white man's presence. Oil wells and pumps changed the scenery after white man "civilized" the area.

Mary Kelly. Fanny said that Mary "was the star and joy of our whole party." Mary escaped from the Indians and was able to reach Box Elder Creek the next day. She was spotted by returning Indians at the same time that three soldiers saw her. Fearing that she had been tactically placed there by the Indians, the soldiers did not rush to her assistance. It wasn't long until the Indians killed her.

This historic site on the Oregon Trail was all but forgotten until W. W. Morrison of Cheyenne, Wyoming, began investigating the Little Box Elder Creek conflict in 1945. He located and marked the mass grave of the four men and the grave of Mary Kelly. When a dam was built across the Little Box Elder Creek in 1954, the remains of Sharp, Taylor, Franklin, and the unknown rider were moved to a site near Mary Kelly's grave, and sandstone slabs now mark the grave sites.

The granite marker listed above was originally located on old U.S. Hwy 20/26. When Interstate 25 was built, the marker was removed and placed in storage, all but forgotten. In 1986 Randy Brown, acting on behalf of the Oregon-California Trail Association, and Bruce Noble, then of the Wyoming State Historic Preservation Office, re-erected this monument at its present location.

See Mary J. Hurley OCTA Marker (Converse County #3.3) for more information.

MARY J. HURLEY OCTA MARKER-3.3

TITLE: Mary J. Hurley
LEGEND: On July 12, 1864, a small Montana-bound wagon train was attacked by Sioux Indians a half-mile east of Little Box Elder crossing. The four men buried here were killed immediately: Noah Taylor of Coffey County, Kansas; Mr. Sharp, a Methodist minister probably from Wilson Co., Kansas; one unknown; and Franklin, sixteen-year-old Negro servant of Josiah and Fanny Kelly.

The Kellys, from Allen, Co., Kansas, were accompanied by their niece, seven-year-old Mary J. Hurley. Fanny and Mary, with Sarah Larimer, and son, were taken captive. Mary escaped that night and found her way back to the trail near here but was overtaken and killed just as she was about to be rescued by passing soldiers. Her body was discovered and buried here a few days later.

These graves were identified and restored in 1946 by W. W. Morrison of Cheyenne. When the dam across Little Box Elder was built in 1954, the remains of the four men were removed from their original burial place in the valley and reinterred beside the grave of Mary Hurley.

Research and signing by the:
Oregon-California Trails Association
1988
This is a part of your American heritage. Honor it, protect it, preserve it for your children.
LOCATION: Private land along the Oregon Trail in Converse County.

BOZEMAN TRAIL MARKER-4

TITLE: Bozeman Trail
LEGEND: Marked by the State of Wyoming 1914
LOCATION: About 0.3 miles from the Orpha Road (State Route 93) on Converse County Road 29 just before the bridge over LaPrele Creek.

See Bozeman Trail Markers (Converse County #3.1 and Campbell County #2.1).

JAMES BRIDGER'S FERRY MONUMENT-5

TITLE: James Bridger's Ferry
LEGEND: Established in 1864, was located 1500 feet up the river from this monument.

Erected by the Historical Landmark Commission of Wyoming 1937
LOCATION: About 1 mile south of U.S. Hwy 20/18 at Orin Junction on State Route 319.

From 1866 into late summer 1867, Bridger's Ferry was the most important starting point for the Bozeman Trail traffic. Here in 1865, the government furnished the materials and equipment with which Jim Bridger and his associates built a cable ferry across the dangerous North Platte River. At times of particular trouble, the army stationed a company of men at this point and at least one skirmish with Sioux horse raiders took place here. (*The Bozeman Trail—Highway of History* by Robert A. Murray)

DEER CREEK STATION-5.1

TITLE: Deer Creek Station
LEGEND: Deer Creek Station, which once stood on the site of present-day Glenrock near the confluence of Deer Creek and the North Platte River, became a familiar landmark along the Oregon-California-Mormon Trail between 1857 and 1866.

The station began with Joseph Bissonette's Trading Post, also known as Dakota City. The mountain man's store, post office, blacksmith shop, corrals, and hotel-saloon, served the needs of a variety of visitors. They included photographer William Henry Jackson during his days as a freighter, stage passengers such as British author, Sir Richard Burton, a party of Lutheran missionaries who remained in the area from 1859-1864, troops en route to Salt Lake City during the Utah war and in the winter of 1859-1860, an expedition of the Army Corps of Topographical Engineers under Captain William F. Raynolds. From 1857 to 1861, the post also was a trading center for the nearby Upper Platte Indian Agency, located about 3 1/2 miles upstream along Deer Creek.

Beginning in April of 1860, Pony Express Riders exchanged mounts here at Deer Creek Station. The Pony Express experiment, however, ended abruptly in October 1861. The completion of the first transcontinental telegraph meant that clicking telegraph keys quickly replaced pounding hooves.

Indian-white hostilities escalated after the Civil War began, prompting troops from Fort Laramie to erect a military installation across the road from the trading post in 1862. From Deer Creek, troops sought to protect the telegraph line and travelers along the trail. Intensifying conflicts between the soldiers and Indians ultimately forced Bissonette to abandon his establishment in the fall of 1864. Indians finally burned Deer Creek Station on August 18, 1866. This incident marked the closing of an important chapter of Wyoming's early history.

LOCATION: At Fourth and Cedar Streets in Glenrock, Wyoming.

DEER CREEK STATION-5.2

TITLE: Deer Creek Station
LEGEND: 1860
LOCATION: East side of Third Street and one block north of Birch Street in Glenrock, Wyoming.

See Deer Creek Station (Converse County #5.1) for more information.

FORT FETTERMAN INFORMATIVE SIGN-6

TITLE: Fort Fetterman
LEGEND: Seven miles north of this point Fort Fetterman, named for Bvt. Col. W. J. Fetterman was established in July 1867. After the Fort Laramie Treaty of 1868 it was the last army outpost along the Indian border. An important military and trading post, it served as a supply point for the army. From here, General Crook launched his Powder River Expedition against the Sioux and Cheyennes in 1876, which ended in his defeat on the Rosebud. One of his guides was Frank Grouard and one of his teamsters, Calamity Jane. Abandoned in 1882, Fetterman became a rowdy outfitting point for nearby ranches and was deserted after Douglas was founded in 1886.
LOCATION: North side of Yellowstone Road at turnout just east of Riverbend Drive. Just east of the Orpha Road to Fort Fetterman and south of the Holiday Inn in Douglas, Wyoming.

Fort Fetterman was located on the North Platte River at the crossroads of the Bozeman Trail and the Oregon Trail. After the abandonment of Forts Reno, Phil Kearny, and C. F. Smith in 1868, Fort Fetterman became the primary protective establishment in the heart of hostile Indian country. Its strategic location made it a supply base, a headquarters, and a marshalling point for several major military expeditions during the final "Indian Wars" on the Northern Plains.

Fort Fetterman reached a pinnacle of importance in the mid 1870s. In 1876 it was the base for three of General George Crook's Powder River Expeditions. (See Crook's Campaign Informative Sign and Crook's Monument [Sheridan County #8 and 9].) In December 1876 Colonel Ranald MacKenzie's campaign against the Cheyennes originated from Fort Fetterman. (See Dull Knife Monument [Johnson County #8] for more information about MacKenzie's campaign.)

Ironically, helping break the back of the Indian resistance also spelled Fort Fetterman's eventual doom. After the Indians were confined to reservations, the fort was abandoned in 1882. After 1886 most fort buildings were sold or dismantled or moved to other locations. This site later became part of a ranching operation.

FORT FETTERMAN PLAQUES-7

Plaque #1
TITLE: Fort Fetterman
LEGEND: The National Register of Historic Places—Wyoming Place #18

Plaque #2
TITLE: Ft. Fetterman (1867-82)
LEGEND: The post was established as a major supply point for operations against hostile Indians.

This scene, looking northwest, is of Fort Fetterman as it stood in 1878. The arrow points to your position at the southeast corner of the parade ground. The present location of the flagpole and walks conform to the original locations as shown in the picture.

Plaque #3
TITLE: Communications
LEGEND: Depicted above are: on the left, the site of the once-busy guard house; and on the right, the still-standing ordnance building. Headquarters, located nearby, was connected by telegraph to higher commands in the east. The left view-sight points to the route of that line as it approached this post from Fort Laramie. Most of the line was part of the original 1861 transcontinental telegraph link along the Oregon Trail. This line had been abandoned, but was patched up and extended to this point for military use.

The device on the right locates the former route of the heavily-used wagon road out of Rock Creek, which was once a Union Pacific Railroad station 80 miles to the south. It was from Rock Creek that most supplies were freighted to Fort Fetterman. According to records, wagons traveling this road required a military escort, at times more for protection against outlaws than Indians.

Plaque #4
TITLE: Post Hospital
LEGEND: The post hospital once stood near this point. Due to its frontier isolation and location on an exposed plateau, Fetterman received the dubious honor of being called a hardship post. Here the relentless wind carrying biting sand or stinging snow gave the fort a reputation for being desolate, a reputation due to the unfavorable location of the fort rather than the general climate of the region. Because of these conditions and the hard duty, more soldiers were treated for mental disorders, or physical injuries received in brawling, than those hospitalized due to wounds received in combat.

Plaque #5
TITLE: Fetterman Hotel
LEGEND: Located here was a triplex officer's quarters, usually occupied by the younger bachelor officers. Following abandonment by the army in 1882, the post was converted by civilians into the town of Fetterman. That town was given a notorious reputation under the name "Drybone" in stories by Owen Wister, the founder of the western novel and author of *The Virginian*. The building was known as the Fetterman Hotel at that time. Fetterman began to die when, in 1886, the town of Douglas was established by the westward-building predecessor of the Chicago North Western Railway.

Plaque #6
TITLE: Bozeman Trail
LEGEND: From this point, the Bozeman Trail wound a long, twisting northwesterly route to the Montana goldfields. This view points out a portion of that difficult and dangerous road The map shows the locations of forts, rivers and mountains along the trail.

Also leaving the fort at this point was the telegraph line to Fort Reno about 75 miles northwest. Later, with the abandonment of that fort in 1868, the line ended here until it was extended to Fort McKinney, established in 1878, near the present town of Buffalo.

Plaque #7
TITLE: Stables and Shops
LEGEND: Fort Fetterman had extensive stables, with corrals enclosed by a six-foot adobe fence. Teamsters' quarters were also located within the walls. The device on the left shows the location of those structures.

The device on the right locates the repair shops including those of blacksmith, wheel-right, saddler and carpenter. Due to the isolation of the fort, there was provision for all types of repair work.

Plaque #8
TITLE: Hog Ranch
LEGEND: Above is an artist's conception of the interior of the Fort Fetterman version of a "Hog Ranch," a common frontier term used to describe certain off-post facilities which catered to the lonely soldier's desire for wine, women and song. A cluster of cabins, the "ranch" was typical of similar establishments located outside the bounds of many western military reservations. This one was among the most notorious in the history of the west. The device on the right shows its former location.

The viewing device on the left pinpoints the probable former site of a ferry crossing the North Platte River. Because the Hog Ranch was off-limits, soldiers who desired to visit it usually swam the river. Later a bridge was built not far from the present highway crossing.

Plaque #9
TITLE: Water Supply
LEGEND: From this location, where the water reservoir once stood, one can see several interesting points. The sighting device points out the location of the pump used during later years to supply the fort with water. Prior to installation of the pump the water detail was usually a punishment duty, water having been dipped from the river and hauled in a wooden tank wagon to the fort. There were never any wells on the grounds of the post.

Plaque #10
TITLE: Crook's Campaign
LEGEND: It was from this post that General Crook, in the spring of 1876, led the southern unit of the three-pronged Big Horn and Yellowstone Expedition against the Sioux, Cheyenne and Arapaho Indians. Severe losses were sustained by Crook on June 17th, in the stand-off Battle of the Rosebud. Shortly thereafter, on June 25th, the same Indians annihilated Lt. Col. George A. Custer and the 220 men of the 7th Cavalry which he personally led in the Battle of the Little Big Horn. Fort Fetterman figured prominently in the final wars with these tribes and, following termination of hostilities, the post was abandoned in 1882. The sighting device points to Crook's camp at the beginning of his campaign.

Plaque #11
TITLE: Soldiers' Rations
LEGEND: Behind the row of barracks which paralleled this walkway, were kitchens and mess halls. Cooking duties were supposedly rotated; actually the most competent man usually held the job. Campaign food customarily consisted of the unleavened biscuit called hardtack; wild game when available, otherwise salt-pork; bacon, often moldy and/or wormy; and a watery soup ladled from a stock of canned vegetables mixed and boiled with hardtack. In garrison, baked bread, occasionally beef, and fruits such as raisins and dried apples and peaches offered variety. Raw onions were used as a means of preventing and curing scurvey, supplemented at established posts by fresh vegetables from the garden.

Plaque #12
TITLE: Barracks
LEGEND: Shown below are three identical enlisted men's barracks which stood in a row parallel to the walk. Bunks were double-decked, with springs made of rope stretched on a wooden frame. Mattresses consisted of large bags filled with prairie hay. Clothing and other gear was hung on pegs or stored on wall shelves near each bunk.

Plaque #13
TITLE: Post Trader's Store
LEGEND: This sighting device is focused on the space once occupied by the Post Trader's Store. To the garrison of a frontier army post the Trader's Store was a commercial and social enterprise which today is duplicated by the separate functions of Post Exchange, Officers' Club, NCOs' Club and Enlisted Men's Club. In addition, the store was an unofficial headquarters for civilian scouts, news reporters, trappers, Indians and other travelers desiring to trade for goods or seeking business or social contact with members of the military command. Depicted below is the south side of the parade ground.

LOCATION: On the grounds of Fort Fetterman, about 8 miles north of the intersection of Yellowstone Road and Orpha Road in Douglas, Wyoming.

This area has well-marked paths around the Fort grounds and markers. It is a very good site to visit.

FORT FETTERMAN POST CEMETERY MARKER-8
West face
TITLE: Fort Fetterman Post Cemetery
LEGEND: Beginning in 1867, this area served as the post cemetery. The soldiers, whose names are listed here, were reinterred in the Fort McPherson National Cemetery near Maxwell, Nebraska, May 3, 1883.

Sgt. James A. Malarky	Pvt. Thomas Dolan	Pvt. Benjamin Leach
Sgt. Patrick Sullivan	Russell Emery	John A. McCallister
Cpl. Francis Conrad	Gustave Frosberg	George McKenna
Pvt. William P. Barton	Joseph Hoffman	James M. Newman
Louis P. Bauer	William Howe	Henry Reynolds
William J. Berry	Alexander Johnson	John Ryan
Robert Blackwood	Joseph Jordon	Walter C. Smith
Thomas Bourke	Michael Kearney	James W. Sullivan
Jefferson W. Brabham	James Keating	Horatio Titeau
James Davis	T. W. Kellor	James Webb

East face
TITLE: Pioneers
LEGEND: Many civilians were buried here during the time of military occupancy. After Fort Fetterman's abandonment in 1882 the cemetery continued to be used by local settlers up until the early 1900's.

William I. Bacon	Ella Harrington	Picaqune
"Barney"	May Henry	Mary Potter
Johnny Boyd	Edward Hildebrand	Baby Reynolds

Jim Bridges	James Andrew Howard	William Rust
William H. Brown	Christian Jensen	John (Jack) Saunders
J. H. Capps	Francis Lamming	Archie Andrew Schaus
George Clinton	Jennie Lane	Sophia Schaus
James Daley	John S. Lane	Baby Schlicter
"King David"	Jeremiah Mahoney	Lily Ellen Slichter
Thomas Diamond	Michael McDonald	Springer
Richard P. Elgin	McDougall	Andrew Sullivan
John Feney	Timothy McGerry	Joseph Sullivan
William E. Fox	Moses Odiode	George Throstle
Raphel Galligos	Patrick O'Farrell	Eva Walker
Emerson Greene	John Ottens	Thomas Walker
Griffins	William H. Parks	Ella Hunter Weaver
George W. Hadley	James H. Payne	Benjamin Wilson
Byron Hambleton	Frank Peacock	James Wright
Jesse Hamzon	C. O. Pease	Charles Wyley
August Werner	Andrew Peck	

LOCATION: Just southeast of Fort Fetterman about 0.5 miles east of the Orpha Road, Douglas, Wyoming.

FERDINAND V. HAYDEN-OREGON TRAIL MARKER-9

Granite marker
TITLE: None
LEGEND: To all pioneers who passed this way and in memory of pioneer geologist Ferdinand V. Hayden
    Chief U. S. Geological Survey of the Territories 1867-78
    Born at Westfield, Mass. 1829.

Bronze plaque
TITLE: None
LEGEND: Erected by William Henry Jackson, a member of the Dr. F. V. Hayden Expedition 1870-1878. 1931

LOCATION: Behind the Higgins Hotel in Kimball Park in Glenrock, Wyoming. East side of South Fifth Street, 0.5 block north of Birch Street.

The information below was taken from Wyoming-A Guide to Historic Sites published through the efforts of the Wyoming Recreation Commission in 1976.
Ferdinand Vandeveer Hayden began his exploration of the West in 1853. Although he was a graduate medical doctor, Hayden devoted his life to the geographic and geologic survey of the territories. Among those who participated in Hayden's surveys was William Henry Jackson, who achieved notoriety as a pioneer artist and photographer of travel along the Oregon Trail and was an energetic member of the Oregon Trail Memorial Association. As a friend of Hayden and as research director of the Association, Jackson worked with the support of the people of Westfield, Massachusetts to recognize Hayden's pioneering work.

BILL HOOKER CABIN SITE MARKER-10

TITLE: None
LEGEND: Site of Bill Hooker Cabin 1874-75.
LOCATION: On private land about 5 miles south of I-25 on the Natural Bridge Road. Permission to access site is required. Inquire locally.

The information below came from an article in *The Casper Tribune-Herald* on July 8, 1930.
In July 1930, R. S. Ellison, the first Chairman of the Historical Landmark Commission of Wyoming, and others marked the site of Bill Hooker's cabin on LaBonte Creek and dedicated a red sandstone marker. Other persons attending the marking were L. C. Bishop of Douglas, secretary of the Wyoming Pioneer Association; Bill Hooker; William Jackson, member of the U.S. Geological Survey in Wyoming; and Guthrie Y. Barber, one of the original directors of the Oregon Trail Memorial Association.

BILL HOOKER CABIN SITE MARKER-11

TITLE: None
LEGEND: Commemorative of Bill Hooker, bullwhacker, who built and lived in a cabin on LaBonte Creek ten miles from this point on the Bozeman Trail in 1874.
    Erected by F. W. Lafrentz, pioneer of Wyoming 1931
LOCATION: South side of State Route 96 within highway right-of-way about 0.9 miles west of State Route 91.

At the top of this marker is an Oregon Trail Memorial Association plaque. F. W. Lafrentz, who financed this marker and others, was a New York native and a lifetime member of the Oregon Trail Memorial Association.

ADA MAGILL GRAVE MARKER-12

TITLE: None
LEGEND: Ada, the daughter of C. W. & N. G. Magill. Died July 3, '64.
LOCATION: Next to the railroad tracks about 0.3 miles southwest of the old brick railroad building at Parkerton, Wyoming. Adjacent to Oregon Trail Marker (Converse County #17) and Pony Express Marker (Converse County #21).

This three year old girl apparently contracted dysentery near Fort Laramie and died at this location. Death of emigrants along the Oregon Trail was not unexpected, and the trail was marked by the hardships and tragedies of that era.
Grace Raymond Hebard wrote the following in her summary of marking efforts by the Oregon Trail Commission, the State of Wyoming, and the Daughters of the American Revolution of Wyoming:

> Near the center of the Big Muddy field, a few feet South of the Oregon Trail, is a lonely grave, covered with stones and marked by a rough headstone on which is rudely chiseled the name, and date of death, July 3, 1864, of a little girl, Ada Magill, a member of the party of Ezra Meeker, who passed this way en route to Oregon more than 56 years ago. The party camped for the night on the bank of the North Platte. The child was taken ill, died and was buried by the edge of the trail. Stones were heaped on the grave and a rude fence erected about it to keep off wolves and coyotes. The fence long ago disappeared, but the stones remain. Nearby is a red stone marker, an official Oregon Trail post. Hundreds of automobiles pass over this highway every day en route to Yellowstone Park. For more than half a century canvas covered wagons, headed westward, crossed the rich oil sands of the Big Muddy, the owners little realizing that there were riches under their feet as well as at the far end of the trail. Over this lonely grave the noon day sun beats down, and not one in a thousand of those who pass by know of its existence. The snows cover it with a mantle of white in winter. In spring the winds whisper and the birds sing above it. And in the watches of the night the stars keep vigil over this tiny God's acre in a treeless land.

Hebard's statement that Magills were in a party with Ezra Meeker was incorrect. Meeker crossed in 1852.
See Ada Magill OCTA Marker (Converse County #12.1) for more information.

ADA MAGILL OCTA MARKER-12.1

TITLE: Ada Magill
LEGEND: Caleb and Nancy Magill with their six children were part of a wagon train traveling from Brown County, Kansas, to Dallas, Oregon, in 1864. After leaving Fort Laramie their three-year-old daughter Ada was taken sick with dysentery. At Deer Creek Station she worsened. An hour before dawn on July 3, 1864, Ada died. In "Sunday best tiny calico dress" she was buried on a small rise of ground just south of here.

In 1912 a new highway under construction was to have passed directly over Ada's grave. Her remains were moved thirty feet north to this spot. Wyoming's state engineer, Loren Clark Bishop, fashioned the headstone which now marks the final resting place of this pioneer child.

The Oregon Trail is about fifty feet south of this spot.
Research, Signing, and Funding by   1987
Oregon-California Trails Association

This is a part of your American heritage. Honor it, protect it, preserve it for your children.
LOCATION: Next to the railroad tracks about 0.3 miles southwest of the old brick railroad building at Parkerton, Wyoming. Adjacent to Ada Magill Grave Marker (Converse County #12), Oregon Trail Marker (Converse County #17), and Pony Express Marker (Converse County #21).

OREGON TRAIL MARKER—BOZEMAN TRAIL-13

TITLE: None
LEGEND: This monument marks the junction of the Oregon Trail and the road to old Ft. Fetterman nine miles north of this spot, Established July 19, 1867; Abandoned May 25, 1882.

Erected by the State of Wyoming and Citizens of Converse County to commemorate the early history of Wyoming 1913
LOCATION: Within the fence line (private property) on the south side of State Route 91, 3.8 miles south of State Route 96.

The information below was taken from Grace Hebard's report, *Marking the Oregon Trail, The Bozeman Road, and Historic Places in Wyoming 1908-1920.*

On Saturday, September 20, 1913, the Daughters of the American Revolution, the citizens of Douglas, and members of the State Federation of Women's Clubs participated in the unveiling of this monument. Participated in the ceremonies were Helen McWhinnie; C. H. McWhinnie, Mayor of Douglas; Mr. B. J. Irwin; Mr. Al Ayers, who helped build and dismantle Fort Fetterman; and C. A. Duniway, President of Wyoming State University.

OREGON TRAIL MARKER-14

TITLE: Oregon Trail
LEGEND: Marked by the State of Wyoming 1913
LOCATION: East side of State Route 94 (Esterbrook Road) about 10 miles south of Riverbend Drive.

In September, 1913, the Commissioners of Converse County placed five red sandstone posts (Converse County #14-18) to mark the Oregon Trail, which emigrants followed enroute to California, Utah, and Oregon in the 1830s to 1860s.

OREGON TRAIL MARKER-15

TITLE: Oregon Trail
LEGEND: Marked by the State of Wyoming 1913
LOCATION: About 10.6 miles south of Riverbend Drive on State Route 94 (Esterbrook Road), turn east. Follow dirt road 1.9 miles until reaching old LaBonte Stage Station and stream crossing. Marker is 6 miles further. Land is privately owned; permission to enter is required.

See Oregon Trail Marker (Converse County #14) for more information.
According to Randy Brown, Oregon Trail expert and member of the Oregon-California Trails Association, this location was a key point on the Oregon Trail, as three major branches of the trail merged here. The river route followed the North Platte River north of present-day Glendo, Wyoming. Near the site of Orin Junction, the trail followed a ridge to this point. The second, or middle, route left the North Platte River near present-day Glendo and followed Horseshoe Creek for several miles. It then cut across hills, gullies, and creeks to reach this merge point. The third and last major branch left the main trail near Warm Springs just west of Guernsey, Wyoming. It crossed hills farther to the south and then followed the ridge from the south to reach the merging point.

OREGON TRAIL MARKER-16

TITLE: Oregon Trail
LEGEND: Marked by the State of Wyoming 1913
LOCATION: Between Glenrock and Douglas, on the east side of the Natural Bridge Road 2.6 miles south of I-25.

See Oregon Trail Marker (Converse County #14) for more information.
This marker was originally on Spring Canyon Road about one and a half miles to the east of its present location. The marker was erected in September 1913 at the La Prele School House, the first school house erected in Converse County. It was later moved to the present site where the Natural Bridge Road crossed the trail.

OREGON TRAIL MARKER-17

TITLE: Oregon Trail
LEGEND: Marked by the State of Wyoming 1913
LOCATION: Next to the railroad tracks about 0.3 miles southwest of the old brick railroad building at Parkerton, Wyoming; adjacent to Ada Magill Grave Marker (Converse County #12) and Pony Express Marker (Converse County #21).

See Oregon Trail Marker (Converse County #14) for more information.

OREGON TRAIL MARKER-18

TITLE: Oregon Trail
LEGEND: Marked by the State of Wyoming 1913
LOCATION: South of the Dave Johnston Power Plant near Glenrock at a small turnout near the A. H. Unthank Grave Marker (Converse County #22). Being repaired by Glenrock historians, the marker was to be re-erected at the location given above.

See Oregon Trail Marker (Converse County #14) for more information.

OREGON TRAIL MARKER—JOHN HUNTON MEMORIAL-19

TITLE: None
LEGEND: Erected to the memory of John Hunton, first president of the Wyoming Pioneer Association, bullwhacker of the 60's, 1839-1928.
LOCATION: Southeast corner of the Wyoming Pioneer Museum at the fairgrounds in Douglas, Wyoming.

John Hunton established the S.O. Ranch west of Fort Fetterman in 1874. He was the last post sutler (post trader) at Fort Laramie (1888-1890). He purchased a dozen buildings at the auction of Fort Laramie in 1890, including some of Fort Laramie's biggest surviving attractions: Old Bedlam, the Sutler's Store, the Magazine, and two Officers Quarters. He filed for a homestead on a quarter of the section that included these buildings. John Hunton and Joe Wilde, another Fort Laramie grounds homesteader, co-sponsored the Fort Laramie Marker (Goshen County #20). From 1892-1907 Hunton was U.S. Commissioner in charge of homesteads in eastern Wyoming.

Embedded in this marker is a circular Oregon Trail Memorial plaque with a covered wagon being pulled by a team of oxen.

OREGON TRAIL MONUMENT-20

TITLE: The Oregon Trail
LEGEND: The Oregon Trail 1841 four miles south. Fort Fetterman 1867 seven miles north. Highway crosses Fetterman Trail Route here.
Erected by Historical Landmark Commission of Wyoming 1943
LOCATION: South side of State Hwy 96 about 1.0 miles west of State Hwy 91. Adjacent to Bill Hooker Monument (Converse County #11).

J. P. PARKER GRAVE-20.1

Sandstone marker
TITLE: None
LEGEND: J. P. Parker Died July 1, 1860. Age 41. Ys. 10 WA.

Metal sign
TITLE: None
LEGEND: Erected by Howard Jackson of Glenrock Wyo 1924. Restored by B.S.A. Troop 81 Casper Wyo. Aug. 1965.

LOCATION: North side of U.S. Hwy 20/26/87 about 2.2 miles west of Glenrock, Wyoming. Private land; permission is required.

PONY EXPRESS MARKER-21

TITLE: None
LEGEND: Pony Express Trail 1860-1861.
LOCATION: Next to the railroad tracks about 0.3 miles southwest of the old brick railroad building at Parkerton, Wyoming. Adjacent to Oregon Trail Marker (Converse County #17) and Ada Magill Grave (Converse County #12).

In 1859 William B. Russell, Alexander Majors, and William B. Waddell announced their plans for relaying messages and mail from the east coast to the west coast. The Pony Express was inaugurated April 3, 1860, when a rider left San Francisco and headed for St. Joseph, Missouri, while at the same time a rider in St. Joseph mounted a pony bound for San Francisco. The Pony Express was a short-lived venture and was replaced by the transcontinental telegraph in 1861. The last run of the Pony Express was November 20, 1861.

The National Pony Express Association organizes historical and educational programs for the purpose of identifying, marking, and re- establishing the original Pony Express Trail through the eight states it served. The Association sponsors commemorative rides each summer.

See associated markers Goshen County #21, Natrona County #25, 25.1, and 41, and Uinta County #6.2.

ROCK IN THE GLEN SIGN-21.1

TITLE: Rock in the Glen
LEGEND: On July 26, 1842, John C. Fremont's first expedition to the far west, guided by Kit Carson with Joseph Bissonette as interpreter, also L. Maxwell as hunter, camped in this rocky glen.

Names and dates of many of the 300,000 travelers of the Oregon Trail are here.
LOCATION: At park on south side of U.S. Hwy 20/87 at the west end of Glenrock, Wyoming. Just northeast of the "Rock in the Glen."

Many of the early trappers, emigrants, pioneers, and settlers who traveled across what later became known as Wyoming would stop at this formation and carve a name, date, or other remembrance in the soft greyish-yellow sandstone.

Continental Oil Company deeded the property to the town of Glenrock, and the site was dedicated September, 1982.

A. H. UNTHANK GRAVE MARKER-22

Headstone
TITLE: None
LEGEND: A. H. Unthank Wayne.Co.Ind. Died Jul.2.1850

Footstone
TITLE: None
LEGEND: A.H.U.

Metal sign on top rail surrounding gravesite
TITLE: None
LEGEND: Erected by Howard Jackson of Glenrock Wyo 1924

LOCATION: At roadside turnout about 0.5 miles east of U.S. Hwy 20/26/87 intersection south of Dave Johnston Power Plant. About 50 yards south of the old highway. Land is privately owned; permission required.

See Alvah Unthank OCTA Marker (Converse County #22.1) for more information.

ALVAH H. UNTHANK OCTA MARKER-22.1

TITLE: Alvah H. Unthank
LEGEND: Nineteen-year-old Alvah Unthank was one of a group of young men who left Newport, Wayne County, Indiana, for the gold fields of California in 1850. On June 23 the wagon train passed Register Cliff, south of Guernsey. There Alvah inscribed his name: A. H. Unthank 1850.

In the early evening hours of June 28 the party made camp here by the North Platte River on account of the sudden sickness of Alvah. On June 29 a family friend, Pusey Graves, wrote: "Lay by today to doctor and nurse Alvah. June 30 Alvah getting worse it's quite hopeless complaining none. July 1 Alvah is rapidly sinking. July 2 In the morning hours Alvah died." Cholera had taken its toll.

Graves wrote: "Alvah lay clam bore his suffering patiently and uttered not a murmer or groan. Bid his father to be of good cheer. His child has paid the great debt of nature. Procured a large neat headstone. Solomon Woody carved the inscription." At noon Tuesday, July 2, 1850, the solemn task of burial took place.

Research, Signing and Funding by the:
Oregon-California Trails Association
1988

This is a part of your American heritage. Honor it, protect it, preserve it for your children.
LOCATION: At a roadside turnout about 0.5 miles east of U.S. Hwy 20/26/87 intersection south of Dave Johnston Power Plant. Permission required. About 50 yards south of the turnout on private land. Adjacent to Oregon Trail Marker (Converse County #18).

HERMAN WERNER PLAQUE-23

TITLE: Herman Werner 1892-1973.
LEGEND: Born here, at Fort Fetterman, son of an emigrant soldier serving on the Western Frontier, Herman Werner commenced his career as an open range cowboy and went on to develop one of the most notable ranching operations recorded in Wyoming's history.

Prominently known throughout the state as a rancher, a businessman, a sportsman and a philanthropist, Herman Werner remained at heart a cowboy. Surely, in his own estimation, his greatest success was that ranch workers everywhere recognized him to be "one of the boys".
LOCATION: Memorial shelter at the Fort Fetterman Site.

Although Herman Werner was a wealthy and successful rancher, he was the key figure charged in 1971 by U.S. Attorney Richard Thomas in the deaths of 700 eagles.

McKINSTRY RIDGE-24

TITLE: McKinstry Ridge
LEGEND: On June 26, 1850, portions of two emigrant companies, the Upper Mississippi Ox Company and the Wisconsin Blues, passed this way enroute to the gold fields of California. They are believed to be the first wagon trains to follow a route beyond Fort Laramie that remained north of the N. Platte River. This trail segment, ending at the ferries of the Platte at present-day Glenrock and Casper, is known as Child's Cutoff, named for Andrew Childs of Waukeshaw, Wisconsin, whose emigrant guidebook was published in 1852.

School teacher Byron N. McKinstry of McHenry County, Illinois, was, like Andrew Childs, a member of the Upper Mississippi Ox Company. His diary entry for June 26 describes this stretch of trail:

"After following the river for 5 or 6 m. we crossed some very rough ground. Following a kind of divide first rising in a Northerly direction to the summit, then turning S.W. and descending to the Platte—the crookedest road possible. These hills are bare and have a wild savage appearance, but little vegetation on them. Camped on the Platte. Poor grass. 20 m."

McKinstry's diary, published in 1975 and edited by his grandson, Bruce L. McKinstry, has become a classic trail account. This stretch of Childs Cutoff, described so vividly by Byron, is named McKinstry Ridge in his honor and also for grandson Bruce, who, by tracing his grandfather's journey across the country, has made an invaluable contribution to trail scholarship.

Research, Signing and Funding by the:
Oregon-California Trails Association
Funding by:
Mrs. Viola McKinstry
Riverside, Illinois
1988

This is a part of your American heritage. Honor it, protect it, preserve it for your children.

LOCATION: Private land on the Childs Cutoff of the Oregon Trail in Converse County.

MARTIN RINGO OCTA MARKER-25

TITLE: Martin Ringo

LEGEND: On May 18, 1864, Martin and Mary Peters Ringo left their home in Gallatin, Missouri, intending to settle in California. With them went their five children, John, Albert, Fanny, Enna, and Mattie.

The wagon train they traveled with—some seventy wagons grouped together for mutual protection—camped here on the night on July 29. Early the next morning, as Ringo climbed up his wagon, his shotgun went off in his own hands, killing him instantly. He was forty-five years old.

A friend, William Davenport, wrote: "He was buried near the place he was shot, in as decent a manner as was possible with the facilities on the plains."

The family eventually reached San Jose, California, the home of Coleman and Augusta Younger, brother-in-law and sister of Mary Ringo. Mary Enna Ringo, daughter of Martin and Mary Ringo, became an outstanding teacher in the San Jose school system for over fifty years.

Buried next to Ringo is J. P. Parker. Parker's tombstone tells all that is known of his life and death.

Research and Signing by:
Oregon-California Trails Association
Funding by:
San Jose Adult Education Argonauts in Memory of Ferne V. Gale
1987

This is a part of your American heritage. Honor it, protect it, preserve it for your children.

LOCATION: Private land along the Oregon Trail in Converse County.

JOEL HEMBREE OCTA MARKER-26

TITLE: Joel Hembree

LEGEND: Joel Jordan Hembree, his wife Sara (Sally) and their eight sons from McMinnville, Tennessee, were part of the estimated 1,000 men, women and children who left Fitzhugh's Mill near Independence, Missouri, in May 1843, for Oregon.

On July 18, between Bed Tick Creek and here at LaPrele Creek, six-year-old Joel Hembree, the second youngest son, fell from the wagon tongue on which he was riding and was fatally injured.

Diarist William T. Newby wrote, July 18: "A very bad road. Joel J. Hembrees son Joel fel off the waggeon tung & both wheels run over him. Distance 17 miles." July 19: "Lay buy. Joel Hembree departed this life about 2 o'clock." July 20: "We buried the youth & ingraved his name on the headstone." Dr. Marcus Whitman described the fatality as "a wagon having passed over the abdomen." This is the oldest identified grave along the Oregon Trail.

Joel's body, originally buried 1/4 miles east, was moved here March 24, 1962, and placed beside Pvt. Ralston Baker, who was killed in an Indian skirmish on May 1, 1867.

North 400 feet is the site of the 1860's LaPrele Stage and Pony Express station.

Research and Signing by:
Oregon-California Trails Association
Fencing and Sign Funding by the Paul C. Henderson Memorial Fund
1987

This is a part of your American heritage. Honor it, protect it, preserve it for your children.

LOCATION: Private land along the Oregon Trail in Converse County.

CROOK COUNTY

CROOK COUNTY INFORMATIVE SIGN-1

TITLE: Crook County

LEGEND: Serving as a western gateway to the Black Hills, Crook County, Wyoming is a place of beauty and diversity. The varied terrain includes the state's lowest elevation, 3,125 feet, situated north of the town of Aladdin, while rugged Warren Peak rises to a height of 6,800 feet. Among the county's many communities is nearby Sundance from which famous desperado Harry Longabaugh took the name "Sundance Kid" after being imprisoned there for horse stealing.

Long a favorite hunting ground of Plains Indian tribes, a few white men had entered what is now Crook County before 1874. In that year an elaborate military expedition led by Lieutenant Colonel George A. Custer passed near this point prior to discovering gold in the Black Hills. Hoards of gold hungry prospectors quickly descended on the area, although the Fort Laramie Treaty of 1868 had reserved the Black Hills for the Sioux Nation. Bloody conflict ensued, but General George Crook, for whom the county is named, played an instrumental role in defeating the Indians and confining them to reservations. Crook County was thus opened to white settlement.

In 1876, gold seekers founded Beulah, Crook County's oldest town. Despite the initial lure of gold, ranching provided the county's enduring wealth. After the Civil War, great cattle drives brought Texas Longhorns to the Northwestern plains. Herds were driven through Moorcroft and western Crook County on the Texas Trail, leaving in their dusty wake the beginnings of a cattle kingdom in Wyoming. Stock raising, lumbering, oil and tourism all play an important role in the modern day Crook County economy. Tourists enjoy the abundant recreational opportunities offered by scenic Devil's Tower—the nation's first national monument—the Black Hills National Forest and Keyhole State Park.

LOCATION: Sundance Rest Area and Information Center south of I-90 just east of Sundance, Wyoming.

CUSTER EXPEDITION SIGN-1.1

TITLE: The Custer Expedition

LEGEND: Camped here July 22-23, 1874. General George Custer and officers climbed Inyan Kara Mountain.

Two soldiers died while in camp and were buried on the mountain side to the east. Wyoming Highway Department

Wyoming Recreation Commission

LOCATION: East side of State Route 585 about 15.5 miles south of Sundance, Wyoming.

The two soldiers were Privates Joseph Turner and John Cunningham. A fight between Turner and Private William Roller started when Turner cross-hobbled Roller's horse so that the animal could not walk without falling. The quarrel resulted in Turner's death by gunshot. Private Cunningham died of dysentery July 21, 1874. Their graves were marked by employees of the Black Hills National Forest in 1935.

To the west of this marker is Inyan Kara Mountain, which stands alone on the prairie west of the Black Hills. The Indian name Inyan Kara means, "A mountain within a mountain." This mountain was a landmark for early travelers and provided extensive and magnificent views for those with the 1874 Custer Expedition. Custer and his staff climbed the mountain to get a better view before passage into the interior recesses of the Black Hills. From the notes of Professor A. B. Donaldson, a geologist, "Of the extensive and magnificent views from the summit, we can only say nothing; for, unfortunately, on the day of our visit the air was so hazy that nothing could be seen beyond ten miles. A hazy air is unusual in this country." The difficulty which the Custer party had in viewing the horizon from the summit of Inyan Kara Mountain was due to the fact that the Sioux Indians had fired the prairie to the south and west of Inyan Kara.

See Custer Expedition Informative Sign (Crook County #2) for more information about the Custer Expedition.

CUSTER EXPEDITION INFORMATIVE SIGN-2

TITLE: Custer's Expedition

LEGEND: On July 20, 1874, General George A. Custer, leading the first official government exploring expedition in the Black Hills, crossed at this point enroute to the Black Hills to investigate rumors of gold in paying quantities. The trail in the foreground was left by his party which consisted of 110 wagons, 2000 animals and 1000 men, including engineers, scouts, geologists and practical miners. This expedition was in violation of the Treaty of 1868, which guaranteed the region to the Indians. In 1875, after government negotiations with the Indians to purchase the Black Hills broke down, miners and settlers poured into this area.

LOCATION: South side of State Route 24 about 2.8 miles west of Aladdin, Wyoming.

General Custer left Fort Abraham Lincoln on July 2, 1874, on a reconnaissance mission from the fort to Bear Butte in the northern Black Hills and on into the interior of the Hills. Fort Abraham Lincoln was located on the Missouri River near present-day Bismarck, North Dakota. Presumably, the purpose of the reconnaissance was to learn something of the topography and geology of the Hills. However, the prime objective was to ascertain the exact location of the Hills in relationship to Forts Lincoln and Laramie. General Philip H. Sheridan summed up the intentions in his annual report for 1874:

> In order to better control the Indians making these raids toward the south, I had contemplated, for two or three years past, to establish a military post in the country known as the Black Hills, and in my last annual report, recommended the establishment of a large post there, so that by holding an interior point in the heart of the Indian country we could threaten the villages and stock of the Indians, if they made raids on our settlement.

The Treaty of 1868 guaranteed

> to the Indians as a permanent reservation all the territory lying between the Missouri River on the east, and the western boundary of Dakota on the west, and from the north boundary of the State of Nebraska on the south, to the forty-sixth parallel of latitude on the north; Also stipulated that the country north of the Platte River in Nebraska, and east of the summit of the Big Horn Mountains in Wyoming, should be held and considered unceded Indian territory, and that no white person or persons should be permitted to settle upon, or occupy any portion of same, not to pass through without the consent of the Indians;. . .for a term of years, or, as long as the buffalo might range in sufficient numbers to justify the chase, and prohibited soldiers from entering the unceded territory, north of the Platte. (*The Black Hills: or, Last Hunting Ground of the Dakotahs* by Annie D. Tallent)

General Alfred Terry wrote to General Sheridan: "I am unable to see that any just offense is given to the Indians by the expedition to the Black Hills. . .From the earliest times the government has exercised the right of sending exploring parties of a military character into unceded territory, and this expedition is nothing more." General Sherman felt the same and stated, "I also was one of the commissioners to the Treaty of 1868, and agree with General Terry, that it was not intended to exclude the United States from exploring the Reservation for Roads, or for any other national purpose." (*Custer's Gold—The United States Cavalry Expedition of 1874* by Donald Jackson)

The Indians thought otherwise and bitterly devised a name, "That thieves' road," for Custer's trail.

CUSTER EXPEDITION MONUMENT-3

TITLE: None

LEGEND: Commemorating the passage of the Custer Expedition to the Black Hills—1874

Dedicated by the Historical Landmark Commission of Wyoming, July 1940

CROOK COUNTY

1   Crook County Informative Sign
1.1   Custer Expedition Sign
2   Custer Expedition Informative Sign
3   Custer Expedition Monument
4   Devil's Tower Informative Sign #1
5   Devil's Tower Informative Sign #2
6   Inyan Kara Monument
7   Inyan Kara Site
8   Texas Trail Monument
9   Devil's Tower Plaque
10   Camp Devin Informative Sign

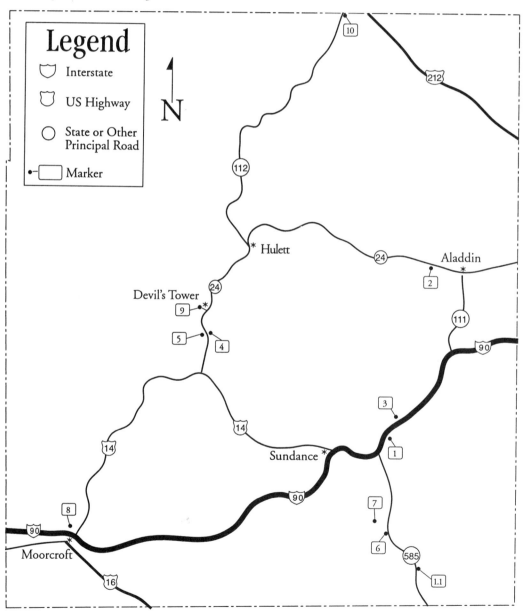

1. The original site of the Inyan Kara Methodist Episcopal Church was located about one mile west of this marker in view of Inyan Kara Mountain to the southwest.

2. This marker near Moorcroft was one of several placed along the Texas Trail in eastern Wyoming.

1.   2.

LOCATION: Original location was north side of U.S. Hwy 14 about 2.3 miles east of the intersection of U.S. Hwy 14 and State Route 585. About 2 miles east of Sundance, Wyoming.

In 1988 this bronze plaque was removed from the pillar of native stone and petrified wood to be relocated to a more visible site. It was not re-erected at the time of this book.

DEVIL'S TOWER INFORMATIVE SIGN #1-4

TITLE: Devil's Tower

LEGEND: Devil's Tower, an important landmark for Plains Indian tribes long before the white man reached Wyoming, was called Mateo Tepee, or Grizzly Bear Lodge, by the Sioux. A number of Indian legends describe the origin of Devil's Tower. One legend tells about seven little girls being chased into a low rock to escape attacking bears. Their prayers for help were heeded. The rock carried them upward to safety as the claws of the leaping bears left furrowed columns in the sides of the ascending tower. Ultimately, the rock grew so high that the girls reached the sky where they were transformed into the constellation known as the Pleiades.

Fur trappers may have visited Devil's Tower, but they left no written evidence of having done so. The first documented visitors were several members of Captain W. F. Raynold's Yellowstone Expedition who arrived in 1859. Sixteen years later, Colonel Richard I. Dodge led a U.S. Geological Survey party to the massive rock formation and coined the name Devil's Tower. Recognizing its unique characteristics, Congress designated the area a U.S. forest reserve in 1892 and in 1906 Devil's Tower became the nation's first national monument.

Rising dramatically to a height of 1,280 feet above the Belle Fourche River, Devil's Tower has become a rock climbing mecca. On July 4, 1893, local rancher William Rogers became the first person to complete the climb after constructing a ladder of wooden pegs, driven into cracks in the rock face. Technical rock climbing techniques were first used to ascend the tower in 1937 when Fritz Wiessner conquered the summit with a small party from the American Alpine Club. Today hundreds of climbers scale the sheer rock walls each summer. All climbers must register with a park ranger before and after attempting a climb.

LOCATION: About 4.3 miles north of Devil's Tower Junction (intersection of U.S. Hwy 14 and State Route 24); about 2.3 miles south of the Devil's Tower National Monument park service gate. East side of road. Across the road from Devil's Tower Informative Sign #2 (Crook County #5).

DEVIL'S TOWER INFORMATIVE SIGN #2-5

TITLE: Devil's Tower

LEGEND: Although Devil's Tower has long been a prominent landmark in northeastern Wyoming, the origin of the mammoth rock obelisk remains somewhat obscure. Geologists agree that Devil's Tower consists of molten rock forced upwards from deep within the earth. Debate continues, however, as to whether Devil's Tower is solidified lava from the neck of an ancient volcano, the wall of which eroded long ago, or whether it is a sheet of molten rock which was injected between rock layers. The characteristic furrowed columns are apparently the result of uniformly-arranged cracks which appeared during the cooling of the volcanic magma. Geologic estimates have placed the age of Devil's Tower at greater than fifty million years, although it is likely that erosion uncovered the rock formation only one or two million years ago.

The unique geological attributes of Devil's Tower stimulated several early preservation efforts. In 1892 Wyoming Senator Francis E. Warren persuaded the General Land Office to create a timber reserve which surrounded the tower. Senator Warren also launched an unsuccessful effort to declare the entire area a national park. In 1906 Congress passed the Antiquities Act, which empowered the President to bestow national monuments status upon federally owned land that contain historic landmarks, historic or prehistoric structures, and other significant historic or scientific objects. President Theodore Roosevelt quickly invoked the Antiquities Act, designating Devil's Tower the nation's first national monument in 1906. The National Park Service was created in 1916 and eventually assumed administrative control of all national monuments.

LOCATION: About 4.3 miles north of Devil's Tower Junction (intersection of U.S. Hwy 14 and State Route 24); about 2.3 miles south of Devil's Tower National Monument park service gate. West side of

67

road. Across the road from Devil's Tower Information Sign (Crook County #4).

INYAN KARA MONUMENT-6
TITLE: Inyan Kara Methodist Episcopal Church
LEGEND: One of the first country churches in Wyoming was built by Rev. O. B. Chassell, pastor of Sundance Circuit, and member of Inyan Kara Community in 1891. Site one mile west.

Erected by the Historical Landmark Commission of Wyoming 1952
LOCATION: West side of State Route 585 about 10.8 miles south of Sundance, Wyoming.

See Inyan Kara Site (Crook County #7).

INYAN KARA SITE-7
East side
TITLE: None
LEGEND: This site thirteen rods square deeded by Fred and Olive M. Clark to William B. H. Van Gundy, Milton A. Lane and Fred Clark and their successors in office

Trustees of Inyan Kara Methodist Episcopal Church to be held in trust for use and benefit of ministry and membership of Methodist Episcopal Church in United States of America, July 10, 1891.

Deed attested by Samuel A. Young

Filed for record August 18, 1891

Inyan Kara Chapter Daughters of the American Revolution and other friends of Inyan Kara Church 1953
West side
TITLE: Original Site
    Inyan Kara Methodist Episcopal Church
LEGEND: First country church in Wyoming. Built in 1891 by Rev. O. B. Chassell, Pastor of Sundance Circuit and members of Inyan Kara Community. The first building for worship erected in this state in a country place away from any settlement.

Dedicated February 7, 1892. Rededicated April 23, 1911 on site on east side of highway one and one half miles southeast.

Removed to Sundance in 1947 and converted into residence.

LOCATION: On private land about 1 mile southwest of Inyan Kara Monument (Crook County #6). Permission required to visit site.

TEXAS TRAIL MONUMENT-8
TITLE: Texas Trail 1866-1897
LEGEND: Along this trail passed herds of cattle from distant Texas to replace the fast vanishing buffalo and build a civilization on the North-Western plains.
LOCATION: Roadside Rest Area just north of I-90 on the west side of Moorcroft, Wyoming.

During the Civil War and afterwards, growth in the larger cities of America brought about a demand for beef. Wyoming offered large areas of grazing land, and the construction of the Union Pacific Railroad provided a means to transport fattened cattle to markets in the East. In the late 1860s large herds of longhorn cattle from Texas were trailed to open ranges in Wyoming, Montana, and the province of Alberta, Canada. The set of trails in Wyoming that brought these cattle to the State were collectively known as the Texas Trail.

The Texas Trail was not an emigrant trail like the Oregon Trail and the Bozeman Trail. It was not well-defined with wagon ruts in sandstone or prairie sagebrush. It was a combination of smaller trails that sometimes came together at river crossings. It entered Wyoming near Pine Bluffs and, after crossing the Belle Fourche River, branched to Montana, the Dakotas, Canada, and northern Wyoming.

The cattle industry soon grew to fill the open ranges. When the Powder River country was opened after 1876, the cattle industry moved in and covered the grasslands north of the Oregon Trail and east of the Big Horn Mountains. Not only did cattle come from Texas, but large herds were also trailed from Oregon eastward over the Oregon Trail.

In 1879 John B. Kendrick, a young cowboy from Texas, trailed a herd into northern Wyoming. Fascinated by the country, he continued to ranch and live in Wyoming, later becoming a Wyoming governor and U.S. Senator.

Five Texas Trail markers have been erected in Wyoming. For more information see Laramie County #24 in Pine Bluffs, Goshen County #17 & #18 in LaGrange and Lingle, and Niobrara County #10 in Lusk.

DEVIL'S TOWER PLAQUE-9
TITLE: Devil's Tower...the first National Monument
LEGEND: President Theodore Roosevelt proclaimed Devil's Tower a national monument on September 24, 1906.

President Roosevelt acted under the authority of the Antiquities Act of 1906 which declared, "that the President of the United States is hereby authorized, in his discretion, to declare by public proclamation historic landmarks, historic and prehistoric structures, and other objects of historic or scientific interest that are situated upon the lands owned or controlled by the Government of the United States to be national monuments..."
LOCATION: On the east wall of the visitor center at Devil's Tower National Monument, north of Devil's Tower Junction (intersection of U.S. Hwy 14 and State Route 24).

See Devil's Tower Information Signs (Crook County #4 & 5).

CAMP DEVIN INFORMATIVE SIGN-10
TITLE: Camp Devin
LEGEND: The Ft. Laramie treaties of 1851 & 1868 set aside the Black Hills for the Sioux, for as long as the grass shall grow and the rivers shall flow. Nevertheless, in 1874 Lt. George Armstrong Custer was sent to investigate rumors of gold in the area giving rise to a flood of goldseekers and camp followers who poured into the hills violating the treaties. Sioux representatives were called to Washington to negotiate, but in November, 1875, before a new agreement could be reached, President Grant used attacks by Sioux on trespassing miners to order the Indians to give up their sacred hills and go to assigned agencies by January of 1876. That spring the military began a campaign to round up all remaining "hostiles" resulting in the Battle of the Little Big Horn, the Dull Knife Battle and the eventual forced surrender of all remaining Indian lands. Native Americans who had once roamed the high plains freely were confined to small reservations, often far from their sacred places.

Two years later the military was still at work protecting settlers and miners. June 1, 1878 Lt. Col. Luther P. Bradley and 520 men left Ft. Laramie following the Cheyenne-Deadwood Stage route to the Black Hills. Their mission was to construct a telegraph line between Deadwood and Ft. Keogh, thus tieing together Montana, Wyoming, and Dakota Territories. At the conclusion of a 30-day march they established a summer bivouac near here. Camp Devin, named for Col. Thomas Devin of the Third U.S. Cavalry, had a life of only two months. Although the existence of the camp was short, its occupants fulfilled their mission. The completed telegraph line resulted in improved communications between forts and white settlements, opening the way for domestication of northeast Wyoming.
LOCATION: East side of State Route 112 at the Wyoming-Montana border.

FREMONT COUNTY

BARR, MASON, MORGAN MEMORIAM-1

TITLE: None
LEGEND: In memoriam, Dr. Barr, Jerome Mason, Harvey Morgan. Killed here by Indians, June 27, 1870.
LOCATION: 5.5 miles southwest of Lander on U.S. Hwy 287 at a turnout on the east side of the road.

Barr, Mason, and Morgan were killed on Willow Creek between the Big and Little Popo Agie Rivers. The three were on their way from the mines to the "valley" for provisions. When attacked, the men turned the wagon-box on its side and used it for a breastworks. The story went that 200 shells were picked up after the fight. It was never known if any of the Indians were killed. When the three were found, Harvey Morgan's skull had the wagon-hammer (others called it the queen bolt of the wagon) driven through it, from side to side. The skull with the spike through it is now part of the Pioneer Museum at Lander, Wyoming.

Captain H. G. Nickerson, a Wyoming pioneer and the first president of the Oregon Trail Commission of Wyoming, engraved and placed this marker in the summer of 1916.

BLOCK HOUSE-2

TITLE: Block House
LEGEND: Built in 1869. A refuge for women and children in times of danger.
Placed by Historical Landmark Commission of Wyoming 1953
LOCATION: About 0.7 mile west of U.S. Hwy 26/287 on Trout Creek Road south of Fort Washakie. South side of the road.

BONNEVILLE CABINS-3

TITLE: Bonneville Cabins
LEGEND: Five hundred yards northwest of this marker stood the Bonneville Cabins, built by Captain B. L. E. Bonneville in 1835 to store his trade goods. Three cabins were constructed and later two more. They were long known as "The Five Cabins," the first mercantile establishment in central Wyoming. In 1866, Major Noyes Baldwin moved a stock of goods into the cabins to trade with Shoshoni Indians, but vacated the following year because of Indian hostilities. In 1868, he located a trading post on Baldwin Creek two miles northwest of Lander, and in 1876 moved to the site of the present M. N. Baldwin Co. Store in Lander.
LOCATION: Southwest edge of Hudson, Wyoming, on State Route 789.

ORIGINAL SITE OF BOYSEN DAM-4

TITLE: Site of original Boysen Dam
LEGEND: Mule teams hauled the material for the original Boysen Dam, built here in early 1900's by Asmus Boysen to provide power for his gold and copper mining interests in this area. A few years later, when the Burlington Railroad built through the Wind River Canyon, rising water behind the dam was declared to be a menace to the operation of the railroad. The railroad sued Boysen, who argued unsuccessfully that the tracks could be raised. He lost the suit and was ordered to remove the superstructure of the dam. Another dam further upstream replaced the original Boysen Dam, the last of which was torn down in 1948, although the abutments of the old dam may still be seen here. Asmus Boysen was a Danish Immigrant, who had risen to a position of wealth and political prominence in Iowa. He lost his fortune in this venture. He died in 1938.

Erected 1965 by the Wyoming State Archives and Historical Department and the Wyoming State Historical Society.
LOCATION: On U.S. Hwy 20 about 0.25 mile south of the southernmost tunnel entering Wind River Canyon.

BURNT RANCH-5

TITLE: None
LEGEND: Burnt Ranch. Oregon-Cal. Trail 1913.
LOCATION: About 10 miles south of Atlantic City via the old Point of Rocks-South Pass Stage Road.

This was a stage and telegraph station along the Oregon Trail and Pony Express Route, the ninth crossing of the Oregon Trail over the Sweetwater River. The Lander Cutoff, a branch of the Oregon Trail, began here and traveled northwest until leaving Wyoming a few miles south of Auborn, Wyoming. Rejoining the main Oregon Trail here at Burnt Ranch, the Seminoe Cutoff of the Oregon Trail began southwest of Ice Spring Slough, staying south of the Sweetwater River to avoid numerous river crossings.

This marker resembles the same work found on the slate slabs at St. Mary's Station and the Spalding and Whitman Monument (Fremont County #26 & 31), which were engraved and placed by Captain H. G. Nickerson, president of the Oregon Trail Commission of Wyoming in 1913.

CAMP BROWN-6

TITLE: None
LEGEND: Site of Fort Augur 1869-70
    Fort Brown 1870-78
LOCATION: A corner stone of the old Montgomery Ward Company Store on Main Street in Lander, Wyoming.

Camp Augur was built in June of 1869 to honor General C. C. Augur who was "at one time Commander of the Mountain Division." In 1870, the fort was renamed Camp Brown in honor of Captain Frederick H. Brown who was killed in the Fetterman battle near Fort Phil Kearny on December 21, 1866. In 1871, Fort Brown was moved fifteen miles northwest near the confluence of the north and south forks of the Little Wind River. On December 30, 1878, the government renamed the post Fort Washakie in honor of the renowned chief of the Shoshones.

CONTINENTAL DIVIDE—OREGON TRAIL MONUMENT-7

TITLE: Old Oregon Trail
LEGEND: 1843-57
LOCATION: From State Route 28, travel about 3.5 miles on the Oregon Buttes Road. Then, follow the Oregon Trail 1 mile south of the Oregon Buttes Road.

Having emigrated to Oregon in 1852, Ezra Meeker was a pioneer of the Oregon Trail, and envisioned its historic preservation. In 1906 he traveled eastward by covered wagon from Oregon to Independence, Missouri, erecting several markers along the way. One such marker was this granite boulder erected in June 1906 on South Pass. See "Ezra Meeker, the Oregon Trail Memorial Association, and the American Pioneer Trails Association" in the first part of this book.

CROWHEART BUTTE INFORMATION SIGN-8

TITLE: Crowheart Butte
LEGEND: In March, 1866, a battle was fought in this vicinity between Shoshone and Bannock Indians on one side and Crow Indians on the other.

The contest was waged for the supremacy of hunting grounds in the Wind River basin. Crowheart Butte was so named because the victorious Washakie, Chief of the Shoshones, displayed a Crow Indian's heart on his lance at the war dance after the battle. The major portion

FREMONT COUNTY

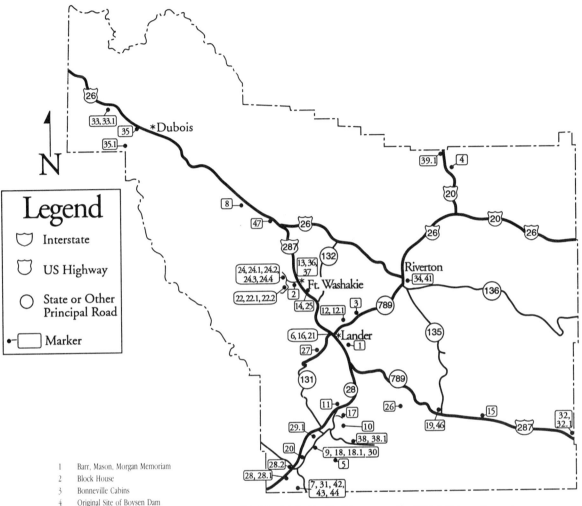

1	Barr, Mason, Morgan Memoriam
2	Block House
3	Bonneville Cabins
4	Original Site of Boysen Dam
5	Burnt Ranch
6	Camp Brown
7	Continental Divide—Oregon Trail Monument
8	Crowheart Butte Information Sign
9	Site of First Masonic Lodge
10	Fort Stambaugh Marker
11	Fort Stambaugh Monument
12	Fort Thompson
12.1	Fort McGraw Site
13	Fort Washakie Marker
14	Fort Washakie Sign
15	Ice Slough Informative Sign
16	Lander Valley Historical Sites Marker
17	Miner's Delight Monument
18	Esther Hobart Morris Monument
18.1	Esther Hobart Morris Plaque
19	Oregon Trail Marker
20	Oregon Trail - Lander Cutoff - South Pass Area Sign
21	Pioneer Monument
22	Shoshone-Episcopal Mission

22.1	Roberts's Indian School for Girls
22.2	Shoshone-Episcopal Mission Sign
24	Sacajawea Grave
24.1	Bazil Grave
24.2	Baptiste Charbonneau Grave
24.3	Richards and Hall Grave
24.4	Fort Washakie Cemetery Chapel
25	Sacajawea Monument
26	St. Mary's Station
27	Sinks Sign
28	National Historic Landmark—South Pass
28.1	South Pass Interpretive Site
28.2	South Pass Marker
29.1	The Sweetwater Mining Region
30	South Pass City Monument
31	Spalding and Whitman Monument
32	Split Rock Marker
32.1	Split Rock Interpretive Site
33	Tie Hack Monument
33.1	Tie Hack Interpretive Display

34	Trapper's Rendezvous Monument
35	Union Pass Monument
35.1	Union Pass Interpretive Plaques
36	Washakie Grave
37	Washakie Monument
38	Willie's Handcart Company
38.1	Willie's Handcart Gravestone
39.1	Wind River Canyon Informative Sign
41	Wyoming Fallen Firefighter Memorial
42	Oregon Buttes
43	South Pass
44	Pacific Springs
46	The Sweetwater Valley Informative Sign
47	The Riverton Project Informative Sign

of the battle was fought near Black Mountain several miles to the north.

Washakie, in his youth and middle age, was a very mighty warrior. He was a wise chief and friendly to the white people. No white man's scalp hung in this chief's tepee.

LOCATION: Along U.S. Hwy 287/26 about 10 miles west of Diversion Dam Junction (Jct. U.S. Hwy 26 and 287). About 4.5 miles southeast of the town of Crowheart, Wyoming.

SITE OF FIRST MASONIC LODGE-9

TITLE: 1869   1925

LEGEND: Site of first Masonic Lodge in Wyoming, No. 28 under jurisdiction of Nebraska, now Wyoming Lodge No. Two, Lander, Wyoming.

LOCATION: In South Pass City at the west end of South Pass Avenue. Found on the east side of a two-story, white, false-front building.

Much of the information below came from *History of Freemasonry in Wyoming* by Alfred James Mokler.

During the early days of South Pass City and the nearby mining region, several members of the Masonic order met and talked about their home lodges. They applied to the Grand Master of the Grand Lodge of Nebraska for a dispensation and were granted it under the Nebraska jurisdiction on November 24, 1869. The lodge became Wyoming Lodge No. 28, at South Pass City, in Sweetwater County, chartered June 23, 1870, by the Most Worshipful Grand Lodge of Nebraska. Not until December 15, 1874, did the first Grand Lodge of Wyoming convene. Shortly thereafter, on February 20, 1875, the lodge at South Pass City was redesignated Wyoming Lodge No. 2. Among the early members were W. M. Hinman, Morris Appel, L. Engler, C. A. Smith, F. Gilman, F. N. Banold, H. C. Sedgwick, E. D. Brown, H. D. Shakespear, W. H. Parpe, Wm. Meyers, John Stone, M. Frank, F. W. Freund, R. K. Morrison, M. T. Park, R. F. Kimbrough, and J. D. Farmer.

Their first lodge meeting, held on December 6, 1869, took place upstairs in the two-story log building known as The Freund Brothers Store. Rent was $50 per month and the lodge room, although large, offered no luxuries.

By the fall of 1878, the mining industry had decreased and people were moving away from the South Pass City area. Many settled nearby in Lander, Wyoming, and it was deemed advisable to move the lodge to Lander. The first meeting in Lander was held January 4, 1879, shortly after which the original South Pass building was razed by fire. The Lander Masonic Lodge completed a replica of the original building in 1969.

A mistake was obviously made in the preparation of this marker. Records indicate that the Cheyenne lodge was actually Wyoming's first Masonic lodge. According to Alfred Mokler, "'The first regularly organized lodge of the Freemasons in what is now the state of Wyoming was known as Cheyenne Lodge, No. 16, chartered October 7, 1868, by the Most Worshipful Grand Lodge, of Colorado." On February 8, 1875, a new charter, with the name of Cheyenne Lodge No. 1, under the jurisdiction of the Grand Lodge of Wyoming, was granted.

FORT STAMBAUGH MARKER-10

TITLE: None

LEGEND: Site of Fort Stambaugh 1870-78

LOCATION: About 2.5 miles northeast of Atlantic City. Inquire locally for further directions.

Endangered by Indian raids, the miners of South Pass City and Atlantic City demanded in 1870 that the government take action to protect them. Named after Lieutenant Charles Stambaugh who was killed by Indians in May of that year, Fort Stambaugh was established in Smith's Gulch two and a half miles from Atlantic City, Wyoming. Abandoned in 1877, the buildings of the fort were put up for public auction in 1881.

FORT STAMBAUGH MONUMENT-11

TITLE: Fort Stambaugh, 1870-1878

LEGEND: Was established to protect from Indians the gold mining camps of South Pass City, Atlantic City, Miner's Delight and others. It was named for 1st Lt. Charles B. Stambaugh, 2nd Cavalry, U.S.A., who

was shot from his horse by Indians when defending a freighting party, May 4, 1870. Site about six miles east.

Erected by the Historical Landmark Commission of Wyoming 1956

LOCATION: Near Highway Department Maintenance shop on State Route 28 at turnout just southwest of the turnoff to Atlantic City, Wyoming.

See Fort Stambaugh Marker (Fremont County #10) above for more information.

FORT THOMPSON-12

TITLE: Site of Fort Thompson or Camp Magraw

LEGEND: In 1856 the United States Congress appropriated money to build the central division of the Fort Kearny-South Pass-Honeylake Wagon Road from Nebraska to California. W. M. F. Magraw was appointed superintendent by the Secretary of the Interior. He was later removed for mismanagement and replaced by W. F. Lander, who staked a new route known as the Lander Cutoff from Gilbert Station, or Burnt Ranch, to City Rocks, Idaho. Winter of 1857-58 overtook the workers at St. Mary's Station on the Oregon Trail. Frank Lowe, guide, led them to this location for winter quarters, officially named Fort Thompson, in honor of the incumbent U. S. Secretary of the Interior. Old timers called it Camp Magraw. The settlement above here, first known as Push Root was named Lander by Lowe, in honor of his friend.

Erected 1965 by the Wyoming State Archives and Historical Department and the Wyoming State Historical Society.

LOCATION: About 2 miles northeast of Lander, Wyoming, on State Route 789 on north side of road. Adjacent to Site of Fort McGraw marker (Fremont County #12.1).

SITE OF FORT MCGRAW-12.1

TITLE: 1857
        Site of Fort McGraw

LEGEND: Rendezvous of Scouts & Trappers. 1812-1835.
        Erected by Lander TR. 17. B.S.A.

LOCATION: About 2 miles northeast of Lander, Wyoming, on State Route 789 on north side of road. Adjacent to Fort Thompson (Camp McGraw) Sign (Fremont County #12).

See Fort Thompson Marker (Fremont County #12) for more details.

FORT WASHAKIE MARKER-13

TITLE: None

LEGEND: Site of Fort Washakie 1878-1909 Capt. T. G. Carson, 10th Cav. Last Comd. Died March 9, 1913.

LOCATION: At Fort Washakie within a fenced yard at the northeast corner of the old parade grounds.

After the Fort Bridger Treaty of 1868 between Chief Washakie of the Shoshones and General Christopher C. Augur of the U.S. government, Camp Augur was established at present day Lander, Wyoming, in 1869 to protect the Shoshones from other Indian raiding parties and whites. Camp Augur was renamed Camp Brown in March 1870, and was moved fifteen miles to the northwest in 1871.

On December 30, 1878, Fort Brown was renamed Fort Washakie, in honor of the Shoshone Chief. The fort had a regular garrison of 115 men until enlarged in 1893 to accommodate more troops. Fort Washakie not only provided protection for the Shoshones, it also served as a stopping off point for expeditions against the Plains Indians and for exploration parties headed for the Big Horn Basin and Yellowstone Park. The post was abandoned in 1909, but the town of Fort Washakie remained.

See Camp Brown Marker and Fort Washakie Sign (Fremont County #6 & 14) for more information.

1.

2.

3.

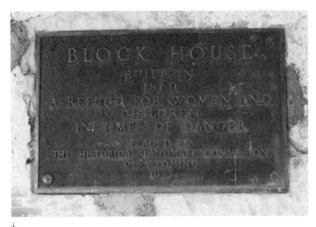

4.

5.

6.

7.

8.

9.

10.

11.

12.

1. Some markers were roughly made and had coarse finishes like this one in Fremont County.

2. Ezra Meeker chiseled this marker in 1906 when he was on one of his trips promoting the preservation of the Oregon Trail.

3. The Daughters of the American Revolution were some of the earliest residents to recognize this site in the Fort Washakie Cemetery as the gravesite of Sacajawea. Although dedications and re-dedications have occurred, facts suggest that she was actually buried in South Dakota.

4. The Historical Landmark Commission of Wyoming occasionally placed bronze plaques on sites rather than larger granite markers. This plaque marks a house that still stands today.

5. Fort Stambaugh was located in barren and lonely country near South Pass City in Fremont County.

6. A contemporary historical marker was placed at the site of the Shoshone Episcopal Mission Boarding School.

7. Miner's Delight Cemetery was located high in the mountains near the old gold mining camp of Miner's Delight.

8. Controversy about the location of Sacajawea's grave followed the dedication of this monument by the Historical Landmark Commission on the Wind River Indian Reservation.

9. Wyoming's 75th Anniversary Commission used native rock and a bronze plaque to commemorate the gold mining city of South Pass.

10. Captain H. G. Nickerson, president of the Wyoming Oregon Trail Commission, chiseled this sign and many others like it between 1913 and 1921. He wrote in a letter, "It took me two days to cut 80 letters in the Whitman-Spalding stone."

11. The decorative Split Rock marker, placed by the Wyoming Historical Landmark Commission in 1956, lies within view of the mountain that guided many emigrants over the Oregon Trail.

12. The Tie Hack Monument was placed overlooking the Wind River along U.S. Hwy 26/287 west of Dubois, Wyoming.

FORT WASHAKIE SIGN-14

TITLE: Fort Washakie

LEGEND: Fort Washakie, headquarters of the Wind River Reservation, was originally established as Camp Augur, on the site of present-day Lander, in 1869, in accordance with the treaty with the Shoshone and Bannock Indians to protect them from Sioux, Arapahoe, Cheyenne and other hostile bands. In 1870 it was re-named Fort Brown, and in 1871 it was moved to the present location, built from adobe and from materials salvaged from the old fort. In 1873, the commanding officer headed a company assigned to explore toward the head of the Big Wind River for a possible wagon route. In compliment to the Shoshone chief, the post was named Fort Washakie in 1878. It was abandoned in 1908.

LOCATION: South of Fort Washakie, Wyoming, on the east side of U.S. Hwy 287 about 0.1 mile south of the turn-off to Ethete. Adjacent to Sacajawea Monument (Fremont County #25).

See Camp Brown Marker and Fort Washakie Marker (Fremont County #6 & 13) for more information.

ICE SLOUGH INFORMATIVE SIGN-15

TITLE: Ice Slough

LEGEND: The Ice Slough is a tributary which drains into the Sweetwater River approximately five miles east of this point. Immediately before you is a slough or low lying wet area from which the tributary takes its name. This marshy expanse is created by a variety of grasses and related tufted marsh plants called sedges which form a patchwork of surface plant life. Water from the tributary flows through unseen beneath the peat-like vegetation. The water freezes solid in the winter and remains frozen during the spring and early summer because of the insulating peat.

Early explorers and the emigrants who traveled to Oregon and California stopped here often, welcoming the ice after having spent many days traversing the hot prairie. One forty-niner, Henry Tappan, wrote in his journal that it was a good place to enjoy a julep. Travelers who arrived late in the summer were disappointed to discover that the ice had finally melted. Today the Ice Slough is nearly dry and very little ice forms in the winter because much of the water has been drained off for irrigation.

LOCATION: North side of U.S. Hwy 287/State Route 789 about 10 miles west of Jeffrey City, Wyoming.

LANDER VALLEY HISTORICAL SITES MARKER-16

TITLE: Lander Valley Historical Sites

LEGEND: Scouts and trappers visited this area in 1811 and rendezvous were held 1829, 1830, and 1838.

Camp Magraw, 1857, site 2.1 miles north.

Fort Thompson, 1857-1858, was located 4.4 miles north of here.

Camp Augur, 1869-1870, became the original Camp Brown, 1870-1871. Location was 1/2 mile west on the south side of Main Street.

Lander was named in 1875 in honor of Gen. Frederick West Lander.

LOCATION: In Lander, Wyoming, at roadside park near the highway maintenance shop at the junction of U.S. Hwy 287/Wyoming Route 789 and Wyoming Route 789.

MINER'S DELIGHT MONUMENT-17

TITLE: None

LEGEND: Anna Anderton 1837-1875

LOCATION: About 6 miles northeast of Atlantic City, Wyoming. Within an enclosed graveyard near the Miner's Delight ghost town.

Gold was first discovered in the South Pass area in about 1842. However, it wasn't until 1867 that lode claims brought the rush of gold miners. In September 1867, Miner's Delight mine was discovered and the city grew based upon gold speculation.

Hamilton City, also known as Miner's Delight, was founded in 1868. It grew and declined with the fortunes of Miner's Delight mine. Newspaperman James Chisolm romanticized the public with stories about the miners at Miner's Delight. He wrote in his diary:

> The miners here are a quiet industrious class of men, mostly old Californians—very intelligent, and affording more practical information on mining matters than one can derive from mere book students and theorists. There are no idlers in the camp—in fact a professional bummer would very quickly perceive that there was no show for him here. In the evenings when the day's labors are over, the men engage in a quiet game among themselves, more for amusement apparently than gain.
>
> What a contrast is there between the quiet life of this mountain camp, and the roaring hells of railroad towns which I have but recently quitted. Cheyenne, Laramie, Benton, Green River—a sketch of these several places would form an interesting study. The very mention of the names calls up a crowd of reminiscences which on the whole are anything but refreshing.

The mines and the town of Miner's Delight were abandoned from 1882 to 1907. The mine was again worked during the Great Depression, from 1932 to 1936, although unsuccessfully.

Miner's Delight is situated in a grove of pine and aspen trees. A steep rock rim rises about a mile east from Beaver Creek. The town, the mine, and the cemetery are all within a quarter of a mile.

ESTHER HOBART MORRIS MONUMENT-18

Granite Marker

TITLE: None

LEGEND: Home & Office Site of Esther Hobart Morris
First Woman Justice of the Peace in the World Feb. 14, 1870
Author with W. H. Bright of the First Equal Suffrage Law Dec. 10, 1869

Bronze Plaque

TITLE: Esther Morris

LEGEND: Erected by the Historical Landmark Commission of Wyoming 1935.

LOCATION: Adjacent to the Esther Morris Cabin on the grounds of South Pass City Historical Site. Also adjacent to Esther Hobart Morris Plaque (Fremont County #18.1).

ESTHER HOBART MORRIS PLAQUE-18.1

Permaloy Plaque

TITLE: Esther Morris

LEGEND: Controversy exists concerning Esther Morris and woman suffrage. In 1869, the legislature passed and Governor Campbell signed a woman suffrage bill authored by William Bright, a South Pass City resident. As a result, Wyoming became the first territory or state to allow women the right to vote.

For eight months in 1870, Esther Morris served as South Pass City's justice of the peace, making her the nation's first woman judge. After her death in 1901, some historians claimed that Mrs. Morris had helped Bright write the suffrage bill. Believing this theory, the Historical Landmarks Commission dedicated the adjacent marker in 1939 on the former location of the Morris family's five room cabin.

However, recent studies indicate that Bright was the only author of the suffrage bill, although he may have received some urging from his wife Julia and some help from Edward Lee, Secretary of the Territory. Morris probably held court in the county building near the center of town.

Today, Esther Morris is recognized as the nation's first woman justice of the peace. The monument and the nearby 1870 period cabin honor Mrs. Morris, who exemplified the spirit of frontier women.
LOCATION: Adjacent to the Esther Morris Cabin on the grounds of South Pass City Historical Site. Also adjacent to Esther Hobart Morris Monument (Fremont County #18).

OREGON TRAIL MARKER-19

TITLE: The Oregon Trail 1841
LEGEND: Continental Divide at South Pass 35 miles west.
 Erected by the Historical Landmark Commission of Wyoming 1943
LOCATION: At Sweetwater Rest Area at junction of U.S. Hwy 287/789 and State Route 135. About 39 miles southeast of Lander, Wyoming.

OREGON TRAIL-LANDER CUTOFF-SOUTH PASS AREA SIGN-20

TITLE: Oregon Trail-Lander Cutoff
 South Pass Area.
LEGEND: This is an old trail used by the Indians and the trappers of the fur period, a short cut to the Snake River country. It was proposed an emigrant road by mountain man John Hockaday in 1854. No emigrant trails crossed the mountains north of here. It was improved as a wagon road for the government by F. W. Lander, in 1859 to avoid dry wastes of the roads to the south and to provide more water, wood and forage. Here it commenced the crossing of the south end of the Wind River Mountains and the Continental Divide and on to the Pacific Northwest. Thirteen thousand people and thousands of domestic animals passed this way in 1859 and for thirty years thereafter it was used heavily, setting the destiny of an empire. These wagon tracks and lonely graves for many miles beyond, a great landmark of history, have been recognized for preservation by:
 U.S. Department of the Interior, Bureau of Land Management, Sublette County Historical Society.
 This trail has been marked at all accessible points with brass caps.
LOCATION: South side of State Route 28 about 30 miles southwest of junction of U.S. Hwy 287/789 and State Route 28. About 39 miles from Lander, Wyoming.

 The Lander Cutoff was a shortcut from South Pass to Fort Hall in Idaho. When the road was surveyed and improved by F. W. Lander in 1857, it became the only part of the Oregon Trail ever subsidized by the government. See also Lander Cutoff and Pioneer Monument (Sublette County #10), Lander Trail Monument (Sublette County #11), Lander Cutoff-Oregon Trail Monument (Lincoln County #9), and Lander Cut-off Sign (Lincoln County #18.2).

PIONEER MONUMENT-21

Southeast Face
TITLE: Fremont Co. Pioneer Association
LEGEND: Names taken from records
 Charter Members and Families

1st Meeting July 5, 1886	3rd Meeting July 2, 1904
H. G. Nickerson-1868	James Kime-1869
L. C. Bliss-1869	R. H. Hall-1873
James I. Patton-1870	Maj. N. Baldwin-1869
Ed Alton-1868	Lizzie Farlow-1869
Alonzo Harvey-1877	Hugo Koch-1867
Archie McFadden	

2nd Meeting July 4, 1887	4th Meeting Sept. 2, 1905
John Fosher-1869	C. P. Cottrell-1869
James Irwin-1869	Ed St. John-1868
William McCabe-1858	Mrs. L. C. Davis-1873

Geo. Jackson-1869	E. F. Cheney-1866
Ben Sexton-1868	Joe Trucky-1868
Wm. B. Gratix-1866	Jas. Couch-1879
August Laucken-1865	F. C. Burnett-1868
Jake Fry-1869	Ernest Hornecker-1869
P. P. Dickinson-1867	Frank Lowe-1870
Louis Poire-1868	
Chas. Fogg-1867	
Wm. Evans-1868	
James A. McVoy-1869	

Special Meeting	Monument Committee
Jan. 27, 1904	August 30, 1953
E. J. Farlow-1878	Jules Farlow-1884
Geo. McKay-1868	Nellie Stratton-1886
Pete Anderson-1869	Anna Scott-1916
Peter Beck	Clair Hall-1880
Sam O'Meara-1874	Essa Fischer-1890
David Jones-1876	Ervin Cheney-1883
Chas. Stough-1879	J. K. Moore Jr.-1876
Abe Fosher-1868	

Brave Pioneer Families Who Came to Wyoming Prior to 1880
(There are 104 names listed in alphabetical order)
Southwest Face
TITLE: Fremont County Pioneer Families
LEGEND: (There are 172 names accompanied by dates of arrival on this side)

LOCATION: Southwest corner of Sixth and Lincoln Streets in Lander, Wyoming. On the entrance sidewalk to the Pioneer Museum.

 Many of the names and dates on this granite pillar are connected with South Pass development in the 1860s. The names were taken from records of the Pioneer Association.

SHOSHONE-EPISCOPAL MISSION-22

TITLE: Shoshone-Episcopal Mission
LEGEND: National Register of Historic Places Wyoming Place No. 60
LOCATION: Two miles west of U.S. Hwy 26/287 on Trout Creek Road south of Fort Washakie, Wyoming.

 See also Shoshone-Episcopal Mission Sign (Fremont County #22.2).

ROBERTS'S INDIAN SCHOOL FOR GIRLS-22.1

TITLE: None
LEGEND: To the glory of God in loving memory of the Rev. John Roberts, D.D., L.L.D. 1853-1949.
 Pioneer teacher, priest, missionary and friend to all.
 Founded the Shoshone School for Indian Girls in 1883 and personally supervised the erection of this building in 1889. Baptized Chief Washakie and remained a faithful pastor to his beloved Indian people until his death in 1949.
 Plaque placed here by resolution of the 54th. Convocation of the Episcopal Church in Wyoming-1963.
LOCATION: Two miles west of U.S. Hwy 26/287 on Trout Creek Road south of Fort Washakie, Wyoming.

 The Shoshone-Episcopal mission was the first Episcopal mission boarding school established in Wyoming. It was made possible through the cooperation of the Reverend John Roberts and Chief Washakie of the Shoshones. See also Shoshone-Episcopal Mission Sign (Fremont County #22.2).

SHOSHONE-EPISCOPAL MISSION SIGN-22.2

TITLE: The Shoshone-Episcopal Mission Boarding School 1890-1945
LEGEND: This school was founded by the Reverend John Roberts.

Born in Wales, in 1853, Roberts was for 66 years a missionary to the Shoshones.

"Our hope is in the children and the young people, the old people can't hear!" So spoke Washakie, Chief of Shoshones, when, in 1889, he gave this land—160 acres of hallowed Shoshone ground, traditional place of solemn assembly and religious ceremony—to his friend the "White Robe", the Reverend Mr. Roberts. Thus the unlettered warrior-statesman, nearing the end of a long life and heavy labors, bequeathed a share of his burdens to an Oxford educated ecclesiastic who, throughout a similarly long lifetime, would similarly labor to lighten the problems of people experiencing transition.

To that end the missionary established his school. Its cornerstone was laid in 1890 and, despite wilderness handicaps, the Georgian building was completed within a year. Here, on soil consecrated by former tribal rituals, Shoshone girls learned a Christian catechism. To their teacher's credit, new knowledge was imparted without disparagement of old beliefs.

Washakie, approaching his centenarian year and having studied the "White Robe's" procedure, submitted to baptism on January 25, 1897. Honored and respected, the Reverend John Roberts D.D., L.L.D. retired from office following 40 years of service. But only death, coming in 1949 in his 96th year, could end his work.

This school, largely self supporting through revenues from its farm lands, was in session 55 years. It closed in 1945.

LOCATION: Two miles west of U.S. Hwy 26/287 on Trout Creek Road south of Fort Washakie. About 50 yards north of the mission building.

SACAJAWEA GRAVE-24

Granite Monument
TITLE: Sacajawea
LEGEND: Died-April 9, 1884
  A guide with the Lewis and Clark Expedition 1805-1806. Identified, 1907 by Rev. J. Roberts who officiated at her burial.

Brass Plaque #1
TITLE: None
LEGEND: Erected by the Wyoming State Organization of the National Society of the Daughters of the American Revolution 1963.

Brass Plaque #2
TITLE: Sacajawea-Bird Woman
LEGEND: Given by Mrs. Josephine Davis Campbell and Mrs. Ruth Scott Hocker in Honor of the Memory of Sacajawea-Bird Woman.
  Rededication by The Wyoming State Society of the National Society of The Daughters of the American Revolution
  August 6, 1984

LOCATION: Southwest corner of the Shoshone Cemetery at Fort Washakie. About 0.6 miles directly north of Shoshone-Episcopal Mission Sign (Fremont County #22.2). Brass Plaque #2 is located on the west side of the Sacajawea Grave.

Sacajawea was an Indian guide of the Lewis and Clark Expedition. Her death and burial site have been points of argument for many years. In the early 1900s, when marking efforts in Wyoming were in their infancy, Grace Raymond Hebard, Professor of Political Economy at the University of Wyoming, researched and claimed that the correct gravesite was in the Shoshone Cemetery at Fort Washakie. The Daughters of the American Revolution, of which Hebard was an active member and leader, dedicated a plaque in 1909. The Wyoming Historical Landmark Commission also dedicated a marker to Sacajawea with help and influence from Hebard.

Controversy ensued as historians challenged the earlier ideas. Many historians now agree that Sacajawea died and was buried at Fort Manuel in South Dakota. See further discussion in "The Wyoming Historical Landmark Commission" in part one of this book.

BAZIL GRAVE-24.1

TITLE: Bazil
LEGEND: Son of Sacajawea Aged 86 years Died 1886. He was reburied here. January 12, 1925.
  1932
LOCATION: North side of Sacajawea Grave (Fremont County #24). Southwest corner of the Shoshone Cemetery at Fort Washakie.

BAPTISTE CHARBONNEAU GRAVE-24.2

TITLE: None
LEGEND: Dedicated in the memory of Baptiste Charbonneau papoose of the Lewis and Clark Expedition—1805-1806 Son of Sacajawea. Born Feb 11 1805. Died on this reservation 1885. Buried west in the Wind River Mountains.
  A.D. 1933.
LOCATION: South side of Sacajawea Grave (Fremont County #24). Southwest corner of the Shoshone Cemetery at Fort Washakie.

RICHARDS AND HALL GRAVE-24.3

TITLE: Sacred to the memory of Mrs. Maggie Richards and Mrs. Hall
LEGEND: Pioneer white settlers killed July 23rd, A.D. 1873 by a raiding band of hostile Sioux Indians in their ranch home on the site of the present City of Lander, Wyoming
  This memorial is here place by Bishop Thomas of Wyoming and other friends, A.D. 1922.
LOCATION: Near the Sacajawea Grave in the Shoshone Cemetery at Fort Washakie.

Mrs. Maggie Richards came from Almion, N.Y., according to James I. Patten, an early Fremont County pioneer:

> Her husband had in 1850 departed for California....Mrs. Richards was to follow her husband in year....she changed her mind, but in the 70's, Mrs. Richards having raised her family....and being lonely, she was making her way overland when she met one of the officers stationed at old Camp Brown, who informed her that the officers were desirous of obtaining the services of a matron to have charge of their mess....when the Post was abandoned, she had so fallen in love with the Lander valley she concluded to locate a homestead and remain there.
> So she erected a suitable building for a road house....Mrs. Richards was considered the good angel of the district....she found time to devote to the sickness and distress of her neighbors....there had been no Indian raids for some time....At this time there was general feeling of safety in the community.
> There were twenty-five Sioux engaged in the diabolical plot....the Indians became bolder, rushed to the cottage, discharging their arrows through the openings for the windows and doors. The women were speedily slain and the pillage of their home began....The bodies of the women were not touched but left where they had fallen. The house was ransacked.
> A large coffin was made, large enough to contain the two bodies, which were placed therein and the mournful cortege moved to the agency, where a large grave had been prepared into which the remains were sadly laid to rest. Thus ended one of the saddest funerals ever held in the valley.

From "Early Pioneers Always Carried a Gun for Tragedy Stalked on every hand with Red Skins Hunting Scalps" in *Wyoming State Journal*, Lander, Wyoming, July 6, 1932.

FORT WASHAKIE CEMETERY CHAPEL-24.4

TITLE: None
LEGEND: This tablet is erected to the memory of The Right

Rev. George Maxwell Randall, D.D., Bishop of Colorado, Wyoming and New Mexico

Born Nov. 23, 1810   Died Sept. 28, 1873

Who held his last service in this building on its former site at Wind River on August 19, 1873 when he baptized eleven Shoshone Indians including four grandchildren of Sacajawea.

This chapel, originally built by the government as a mission house for the Shoshones and used for many years as a school and house of worship, was moved to this place in March, 1916.

Erected by the Missionary District of Wyoming, Diocese of Colorado and Friends.

LOCATION: At Shoshone Cemetery at Fort Washakie.

SACAJAWEA MONUMENT-25

TITLE: Sacajawea

LEGEND: Guide of the Lewis and Clark Expedition 1805

Dedicated by the Historical Landmark Commission of Wyoming 1941
Grave two miles west

LOCATION: South of Fort Washakie on U.S. Hwy 287, about 0.1 miles south of the turnoff to Ethete, Wyoming. Adjacent to Fort Washakie Sign (Fremont County #14).

See Sacajawea Grave Marker (Fremont County #24) for more information.

ST. MARY'S STATION-26

South side of post

TITLE: None

LEGEND: Oregon Trail 1913 St. Mary Station

East side of post

TITLE: None

LEGEND: H. G. N. 1914

LOCATION: About 11 miles from U.S. Hwy 287 by way of Hudson-Atlantic City Road No. 2302. About 0.5 mile north of the Sweetwater River. Private land; permission required. Inquire locally.

St. Mary's Stage Station was built in 1859 by William B. Russell, Alexander Majors, and William B. Waddell, the developers of the Pony Express, as a stopping point along the Oregon Trail. The station was also used as a small Army outpost during Indian troubles in 1864-65.

The marker was engraved and erected in the summer of 1914 by H. G. Nickerson, president of the Oregon Trail Commission of Wyoming. It was one of several erected by Nickerson and the Commission. Another similar black slate marker was placed at Burnt Ranch (Fremont County #5) further west along the Oregon Trail.

SINKS SIGN-27

TITLE: The Rise of the Sinks

LEGEND: The POPO AGIE RIVER (Pronounced "Po-po-shia" and meaning "Beginning of water") was discovered by French Canadian trappers in 1743.

The river disappears after making an abrupt plunge into a mountainside cavern one-half mile up the canyon from this viewpoint.

Rocks which have been dissolved along cracks and fractures have created channels which carry the POPO AGIE RIVER. These vertical passages are called "sinks".

The pond below is actually the river rising to the surface after dropping 200 feet from the cavern upstream.

This geological phenomenon baffled the Indians and pioneers and today still remains to be fully explained.

This site was donated to the City of Lander in 1969 by Pacific Power & Light Company. The site is now part of Sinks Canyon State Park administered by the Wyoming Recreation Commission.

LOCATION: About 7 miles southwest of Lander, Wyoming, on State Route 131 on the Middle Fork of the Popo Agie River.

NATIONAL HISTORIC LANDMARK—SOUTH PASS-28

TITLE: South Pass

LEGEND: South Pass has been designated a Registered National Historic Landmark.

Under the provisions of the Historic Sites Act of August 21, 1935, this site possesses exceptional value in commemorating and illustrating the history of the United States.

The U.S. Department of the Interior National Parks Service 1965

LOCATION: South side of State Route 28 about 47.8 miles southwest of Lander, Wyoming. About 5.5 miles southwest of the South Pass Rest Area (State Route 28 crosses the Sweetwater River at this point).

Although this marker was officially removed and replaced, it did demonstrate the importance of the area in the history of the United States.

SOUTH PASS INTERPRETIVE SITE-28.1

TITLE: South Pass

LEGEND: John Jacob Astor's "Astorians" are often given credit for the discovery of the "South Pass" route to western territories. Astor sent his "Astorians" by sea and land in 1810 to establish the Pacific Fur Company at the mouth of the Columbia River. He intended to break the British fur monopoly in the Pacific Northwest and bring American territory under American control. The overland party, led by Wilson Price Hunt, crossed northern Wyoming in July of 1811. Robert Stuart, a partner in the company, traveled with others by sea. Stuart later returned overland to New York with dispatches for Astor. It was this journey in October of 1812 which pioneered the route across this natural pass over the continental divide, later to become known as South Pass.

The discovery of South Pass, an important segment of the Oregon-California emigrant trails, hastened one of the greatest mass emigrations in the annals of American history. Restless Americans from all walks of life moved west, crossing this pass, seeking a better life in a new land. Among them were Mormons seeking freedom from religious, social and economic intolerance and aggression. For others, the lure was land available for the taking. The discovery of gold in California in 1848, attracted bands of feverish fortune seekers. An estimated 350,000 people passed this way between 1841 and 1866 on their way to western territories.

CHRONOLOGY

1812 Discovery of South Pass by Robert Stuart and his group of Astorians

1826 First crossing of the pass by a wheeled vehicle

1832 First wagon train crossing, led by Army Captain B. L. E. Bonneville

1836 Narcissa P. Whitman and Eliza R. Spalding, first white women to cross South Pass

1843 Beginning of the great migration

1847 First wave of Mormon emigration

1849-1851 Peak period of emigration to the American West

1860 The Pony Express used this route for its brief nineteen month existence

LOCATION: South side of State Route 28 about 47.8 miles southwest of Lander, Wyoming. About 5.5 miles southwest of the South Pass Rest Area (State Route 28 crosses the Sweetwater River at this point).

See Astorian Overland Expedition Information Sign (Campbell County #1) for more information about the Astorian expedition.

SOUTH PASS MARKER-28.2

TITLE: South Pass

LEGEND: The South Pass, in which you are now located, is perhaps the most significant transportation gateway through the Rocky Mountains. Indians, mountain men, Oregon Trail emigrants, Pony Express riders, and miners all recognized the value of this passageway straddling the Continental Divide. Bounded by the Wind River Range on the north and the Antelope Hills on the south, the pass offered overland travelers a broad, relatively level corridor between the Atlantic and Pacific watersheds.

Mining plays a fundamental role in the history of the South Pass region. Gold may have been discovered as early as 1842, but gold fever did not strike until 1867 when a sample of South Pass ore arrived in Salt Lake City. News of the discovery spread swiftly and hordes of expectant millionaires descended on the new towns of South Pass City, Atlantic City, and Miner's Delight. The boom played out quickly. The easily obtained placer gold was rapidly exhausted and miners began leaving the area in the early 1870s.

Despite the brief duration of the boom, mining activity did not cease. In 1884, an enterprising Frenchman named Emile Granier began organizing the construction of a hydraulic gold mining system which employed many local residents over a ten year period. The Fisher Dredge Company recovered considerable gold ore from the bed of Rock Creek during the 1930s. More recently, the United States Steel iron ore mine operated near Atlantic City from the early 1960s until 1983. Hard rock mines also reopen periodically and some are presently operating. Until the next boom arrives, travelers can experience the flavor of a Rocky Mountain mining town by visiting nearby South Pass City, which has been restored by the State of Wyoming.

LOCATION: At the South Pass Rest Area on State Route 28, about 42.3 miles southwest of Lander, Wyoming. About 0.2 mile from where State Route 28 crosses the Sweetwater River.

THE SWEETWATER MINING REGION-29.1

TITLE: The Sweetwater Mining Region

LEGEND: With the discovery of gold near Willow Creek in 1867, thousands of people rushed into this region, mined the streams and hills, and built some of the territory's first towns—South Pass City, Atlantic City, and Miner's Delight. Even though 3000 people lived in the area and more than 30 mines were operating by 1869, a bust soon occurred, and the towns dwindled in size. Since then, three more booms have sustained the area's mining tradition and sense of community.

The region's history still survives today. Besides several sites in and around Atlantic City, the South Pass City State Historic Site contains 24 historic structures and dozens of exhibits. Located just two miles along the adjacent dirt road, the site is open from May 15 to October 15 and is free of charge.

LOCATION: Southeast side of State Route 28 about 33.2 miles southwest of Lander, Wyoming. Located at turnoff to South Pass City, Wyoming.

The following summarization of the history of South Pass City was taken from an old brochure prepared by the Wyoming Recreation Commission twenty to twenty-five years ago. The South Pass City story has not changed:

SOUTH PASS CITY, WYOMING

GOLD. Many Oregon Trail emigrants were travelling to California to search for gold, which had been discovered at Sutters Mill in 1848. Thousands of people hoped to strike it rich, but only a few succeeded. By the 1860s, discoveries of "Mother Lodes" in Colorado, Nevada, Idaho, and Montana resulted in hundreds of new boom towns. When the Carissa mine began producing gold in 1867, a rush to the South Pass area began, and South Pass City was built in the fall of that year. The boom continued in 1868, and Atlantic City and Miner's Delight were quickly erected. The area's population soared to approximately 2000 residents, and dozens of mines and hundreds of placer claims kept the miners busy.

A BUSY, DYNAMIC COMMUNITY. Businessmen arrived to fulfill the needs of the prospectors, and South Pass City soon developed a main street one-half mile long. A resident could conduct business in general stores, butcher shops, restaurants, sawmills, clothing stores, a sporting goods store, a jewelry store, and a furrier. Visitors could stay at one of seven hotels and seek an evening's entertainment at several saloons and "sporting houses," all supplied with liquid refreshments by two local breweries and a wholesale liquor establishment.

A miner could leave his horse at one of four livery stables and hire any of several blacksmiths to shoe the animal, sharpen his mining tools, or mend his wagon. A gun could be purchased or repaired at the gun shop and be used at the shooting gallery. A miner lucky enough to "strike it rich" could deposit his gold at the local bank or ship it home on a Wells Fargo stage. A stout jail would accommodate troublesome residents, while a school would see to the educational needs of the children. Doctors and lawyers hung out shingles to serve the medical and legal needs of the new frontier community. Ranchers and farmers soon moved nearby.

WOMEN'S SUFFRAGE. This rough and ready frontier community played a role in the women's suffrage movement. In the first territorial legislature, William Bright, a saloonkeeper, mine owner, and representative from South Pass City, wrote and introduced a women's suffrage bill. When this bill passed and the Governor signed it in December, 1869, Wyoming became the first territory or state to allow women the right to vote and hold office.

In February 1870, the county commissioners appointed Ester Morris as the town's justice-of-the-peace, making her the nation's first female judge. Even though her selection was controversial in South Pass City, she was an effective judge and tried twenty-six cases. Esther Morris represents the important and unique role that women played in frontier towns.

MANY BOOMS AND BUSTS. All booms must end. In 1872, a bust hit the Sweetwater Mining District. Most miners became discouraged over the absence of large gold deposits and the lack of sufficient capital. By 1875, less than one hundred people remained in the area. Even Camp Stambaugh, built in 1870, soon closed.

Many prospectors wandered to other boom towns to continue their relentless search for gold. Some folks moved to nearby settlements and played important roles in the founding of such towns as Lander, Pinedale, and Thermopolis.

However, a few persistent miners remained and helped start the area's future gold booms. A large hydraulic operation, a copper mine, a dredge, a strip mine, and the continued speculation in gold created South Pass mining rushes in the 1880's, 1890's, 1930's, and 1960's. The population of Atlantic City and South Pass City bounced between a handful of people and as many as 500 residents. But the busts have always followed the booms. Today, a few prospectors continue to pan for gold, a couple of miners are still digging for ore, and South Pass City has been restored as an historic site. Gold mining has not died. It is still a part of life in South Pass.

In 1967, the Governor of Wyoming appointed a group of Wyoming citizens as Board of Trustees for the Old South Pass Historical Preserve Commission for the purposes of preservation and protection of the valuable site. The group served for two years, expending their own resources to meet the burden of their task, until the following legislative session could appoint an existing state agency for administration purposes, and properly fund the site. Those citizens were as follows: Alice Messick, Douglas; Judge W. J. Nicholas, Lander; Dorthe Cable, Cheyenne; Edness K. Wilkins, Casper; James K. Harrower, Pinedale; Stephen B. Accola, Newcastle; Dr. Donald G. MacLeod, Jackson; Ed Bille, Casper.

The State Historic Site has a very interesting self-guided tour showing locations and describing the history of the old South Pass City buildings. There is also a self-guided nature/historic trail at the east edge of the city.

The following summarization of the history of Atlantic City was written by Philippina Halstead for the Atlantic City Historical Society's brochure entitled "Atlantic City Self-guided Historical Tour":

ATLANTIC CITY, WYOMING

Gold miners poured into this district in the late 1860's and, within a few months, created three typical, frontier, gold camps here—South Pass City, Atlantic City, and Miner's Delight. Today, Atlantic City can easily claim the title as boom/bust capital of Wyoming. Since its official platting in April 1868, the town has experienced a continuing series of mining booms and busts, all but one tied to the fortunes of gold.

When W. H. Jackson took his 1870 photograph of Atlantic City, the town sported a three block main street with business buildings on both sides and heavily populated residential areas on the hillsides and in Beer Garden Gulch.

By 1875, that first boom had already ended. Thousands of gold seekers had moved on to settle other communities in Wyoming and the West. Only about 100 people remained that year. Yet Atlantic City hung on, waiting for a renewed interest in gold.

In the 1880s-'90s, the French capitalist, Emile Granier, raised great hopes with his hydraulic plans. Because of national economic conditions, the Atlantic City population surged as mines were reopened and as Granier's 25-mile ditch from Christina Lake to below Atlantic City was dug. By 1893, Granier was bankrupt and gone. The population fell until 1904 when the Dexter Mill and Mining Company bought Granier's properties and claims and built a large mill, again bringing capital into the town. Within a few years, they, too, were bankrupt. So the cycle continued, always accompanied with hope for another big strike.

During the Great Depression of the 1930s, Atlantic City experienced a small boom as the Fischer-Crawford Dredge churned through Atlantic City on down Rock Creek, successfully extracting a good sum of gold while leaving heaps of rocks still visible today. Many of the nearby mines re-opened. By the start of World War II, this short lived excitement faded. When the government declared gold a non-strategic metal, the mines were forced to close. In their search for metal, scavengers came into the area and dismantled many of the mines in the district. By the 1950s, Atlantic City was listed as a ghost town. During several winters in the 1950s and early 1960s, only three or four people remained in the town.

Later in the 1960s, interest in a different metal—iron ore—brought hundreds of people to the area when U.S. Steel constructed a large, open pit mine three miles northwest of Atlantic City. Although most of the miners commuted from Lander, several settled in Atlantic City. This and the growing interest in vacation homes made the town slowly grow again. In the 1980s the U.S. Steel mine closed, and with economic hard times throughout Wyoming, most of the people in this community left to find jobs.

Each spring, the eternal hope of the gold mining community grows as geologists, promoters, and would-be-investors drift in and out of Atlantic City. The wind of this old gold town always whispers of another boom on its way.

Atlantic City offers an interesting self-guided tour describing the history of the city's buildings and area.

SOUTH PASS CITY MONUMENT-30

TITLE: South Pass City, Wyoming
Founded 1868
A great gold camp.
LEGEND: Part of Wyoming's historical heritage. Acquired for preservation May 18, 1966, with funds raised by Wyoming's 75th Anniversary Commission, Inc., its advisers, county committees and people of Wyoming.

Clifford P. Hansen-Governor, Alice Messick-Chairman, Steven Accola-Secretary, Kerm Kath-Treasurer, Edness Kimball Wilkins, Lewis Bates, James K. Harrower, Earl A. Madsen.
LOCATION: North side of the street at South Pass City State Historic Site. South Pass City, Wyoming.

See The Sweetwater Mining Region Marker (Fremont County #29.1) for more information.

SPALDING AND WHITMAN MONUMENT-31

TITLE: Narcissa Prentiss Whitman.
Eliza. Hart Spalding.
LEGEND: First white women to cross this pass July 4 1836
LOCATION: Travel about 3.5 miles east of State Route 28 on the Oregon Buttes Road, then about 1 mile south of the Oregon Buttes Road following the Oregon Trail.

Captain H. G. Nickerson, president of the Oregon Trail Commission of Wyoming, inscribed and erected the marker in June, 1916. The arduous early days of historic site marking were well characterized in Nickerson's letter addressed on June 24, 1916, to Grace Raymond Hebard, Secretary of the Commission:

I have just returned from the South Pass Continental Divide, taking ten days for the trip. Am badly used up, for I had a hard trip, had cold, stormy weather, hard frosts every night, snow banks everywhere, but I am thankful that we have finished the work desired. We hauled 200 pounds of cement from Lander, and a slate slab from Rock Creek 25 miles. It took me two days to cut 80 letters in the Whitman-Spalding stone. I set both monuments in concrete.

In 1835, Dr. Marcus Whitman and the Rev. Samuel Parker traveled through South Pass with an expedition of the American Fur Company. Parker continued West, but Whitman returned east to try to interest other missionaries to work with the Indians. Whitman and his wife were joined by the Reverend H. H. Spalding and his wife on the return mission to the west with another American Fur Company expedition. On July 4, 1836, the caravan reached South Pass where they "kneeled down, and with the Bible and the American Flag in their hands took possession of the Pacific Coast as the home of American mothers and the Church of Christ."

Of that first journey by white women over the pass into "Oregon country," Spalding wrote:

Hope and joy beamed on the face of my dear wife, though pains racked her frame. She seemed to receive new strength. 'Is it reality or a dream,' she exclaimed, 'that after four months of hard and painful journeyings I am alive, and actually standing on the summit of the Rocky Mountains, where yet the foot of white woman has never trod?'

The Continental Divide—Oregon Trail Monument (Fremont County #7) is adjacent to the Spalding and Whitman Monument.

SPLIT ROCK MARKER-32

TITLE: Split Rock
LEGEND: A famous natural landmark used by Indians, trappers and emigrants on the Oregon Trail. Site of Split Rock Pony Express 1860-61, stage, and telegraph station is on the south side of the Sweetwater. Split Rock can be seen as a cleft in the top of the Rattlesnake Range.

Erected by the Historical Landmark Commission of Wyoming 1956
LOCATION: North side of U.S. Hwy 287/789 about 11 miles east of Jeffrey City, Wyoming. About 10 miles northwest of Muddy Gap.

See Split Rock Interpretive Site (Fremont County #32.1) for more information.

SPLIT ROCK INTERPRETIVE SITE-32.1

Plaque #1
TITLE: Split Rock Station and Site Map
LEGEND: The Pony Express generally followed the Oregon Trail through Wyoming to Fort Bridger, then followed the existing mail route across Utah and Nevada to Placerville and Sacramento, California. Split Rock Relay Station, a crude log structure with a pole corral, was located at the base of the mass of rocks directly in front of you. Come view the site at a trail station a short walk from here.

William C. "Buffalo Bill" Cody exchanged horses at this site on a record ride from Red Buttes Station to Rocky Ridge Station and back.

Due to another rider's untimely death, Cody was forced to add an extra leg to his normal relay and eventually covered a total distance of 322 miles in 21 hours and 40 minutes, using 21 horses in the process. On another occasion, Cody rode one horse at top speed for 24 miles when chased by Indians from Horse Creek Station east of Independence Rock to Plant's Station just east of here.

"Split Rock", the mass of rock on the skyline to the north, was an Oregon Trail landmark. It was visible for a day before it was reached from the east and for two days when it was viewed looking back from the west.

Plaque #2
TITLE: The Oregon Trail
LEGEND: The Oregon Trail, the main route of westward expansion from 1812 to 1869, passed through the valley below. An estimated 350,000 people journeyed past this point in search of new lands and new lives in the West.

Two routes of the Oregon Trail coming from Devil's Gate, twelve miles east, converged below this point on the Sweetwater River where good grass and water were available for the stock. Just west of here, ruts carved in the rocks by iron-tired wagons are still visible.

> (August)17. Smokey But the sun rose over the Eastern Mountains in its usual majesty. Some recent Signs of a war party of Indians ware discovered yestarddy which caused some uneasiness...roled up the Stream on the South side...the most ruged bare granite rocks lay along the North side close to the water...saw some fine herds of Ibex or wild sheep some of which ware taken and found to be verry fine eating...This region seems to be the refuses of the world thrown up in the utmost confusion.
>
> James Clyman, 1844

Plaque #3
TITLE: Split Rock Station
LEGEND: Split Rock Station, used by the Pony Express and the Overland Stage, was located in the meadow below. A small log building later served as the Split Rock Post Office until it was closed in the early 1940's.

Shoshone, Arapahoe, Crow and Sioux Indians occupied this pleasant valley before the Oregon Trail became heavily traveled. Their hunting patterns, culture and life style were changed forever. Friction between the tribes and the newcomers from the East led to tragic warfare and the loss to the Indians of the country they had known as theirs. It was due to such hostility that a division of the Sixth Ohio Cavalry was garrisoned at this site in 1862 to provide escort service for stagecoaches and emigrant wagon trains and to establish protection for the telegraph line.

Plaque #4
TITLE: The Sweetwater Rocks
LEGEND: The "Sweetwater Rocks" date back at least 1,400 million years and are some of the oldest found in the Rocky Mountain area. These Precambrian granites have been re-exposed in recent times by erosion of much younger Miocene and Pliocene sediments. When the sediment pressures were removed, granite slabs peeled off, producing the smooth rock knobs. Erosion along old fractures and shear zones left the large cracks in the rocks.

"Split Rock" served as a well known landmark and navigational aid because of its unique shape. Emigrants were guided by the rock for an entire day's travel when they were approaching from the east. It remained in view as a checkpoint behind them from the west for another two days.

LOCATION: North side of U.S. Hwy 287/789 about 14 miles east of Jeffrey City, Wyoming. About 7 miles northwest of Muddy Gap.

This site is one of several Bureau of Land Management interpretive sites along the Oregon Trail. Please see the discussion about the Oregon and Mormon Pioneer National Historic Trails Management Plan in "Historical Marking by Other Organizations" in the first part of this book.

TIE HACK MONUMENT-33
TITLE: None
LEGEND: Erected to perpetuate the memory of the hearty woods and river men who made and delivered the cross ties for the building and maintenance of the Chicago and North Western Railway in this western country.
Wyoming Tie and Timber Company 1946
LOCATION: On U.S. Hwy 26/287 about 17 miles northwest of Dubois, Wyoming.

See Tie Hack Interpretive Display (Fremont County #33.1) for more information.

TIE HACK INTERPRETIVE DISPLAY-33.1
Lower Level
Plaque #1
TITLE: None
LEGEND: Rough, tough, sinewy men, mostly of Scandinavian origin, whose physical strength was nearly a religion. The millions of cross ties they hacked out of the pine forests kept the railroad running through the West.

The tie hack was a professional, hewing ties to the exact 7 inches on a side demanded by the tie inspector. For years he was paid 10 cents a tie up to $3.00 for his dawn to dusk day. Board and room cost about $1.50 a day.

Mostly bachelors, they lived in scattered cabins or tie camps and ate hearty meals at a common boarding house. Entertainment was simple and spontaneous. A few notes on a "squeeze box" might start an evening of dancing, with hob nailed boots scarring the rough wooden floors. The spring tie drive down the Wind River usually ended with one big party in town with enough boozing and brawling to last them another year back in the woods.

These hard-working, hard-drinking, hard-fighting men created an image that remains today only in tie hack legend. By the end of World War II, modern tools and methods brought an end to an era that produced the proud breed of mighty men—the tie hack.

Plaque #2
TITLE: The Cross-Tie
LEGEND: The tall, slightly tapered lodgepole pine is ideal for a cross-tie. The tie hack chose his tree and felled it with a double bitted ax. Using the same tool, he walked the log from end to end cutting a series of parallel slashes on each side of the log. The slightest miscalculation could mean the loss of a toe or foot. Retracing his steps, he hewed the two side faces smooth with the broad ax. The faces were exactly 7 inches apart and so smooth that not even a splinter could be found with the bare hand.

The tie hack then traded his ax for a peeler and removed the bark from the two rounded sides. The final operation was to cut the peeled and hacked log into the 8 foot sections required by the railroad.

Each tie hack owned and cared for his own equipment; which cost him his first 10 days work.
Here are the tools of his trade!
Double-Bit Ax—with two sharp edges
Broad Ax—an 8 pounder with a broad 12-inch long blade. Looks like an executioners ax!

Peeler—a slightly curved dull blade to slip easily under the bark
Crosscut Saw—designed to cut across the grain of the wood
Peavey—a stout spiked lever used to roll logs
Cant Hook—a toothed lever used to drag or turn logs
Pickaroon—a pike pole with a sharp steel point on one side and a curved hook on the other—used to guide floating logs.

They also carried a sharpening file and a jug of kerosene to clean pitch off their equipment.

Plaque #3
TITLE: None
LEGEND: Cross-ties were in demand by the Chicago and Northwestern Railroad as it spanned Wyoming. The Wyoming Tie and Timber Company was formed in 1916 in Riverton to supply the ties—it took 2500 ties for a mile of track.

The main center of tie production was the lodgepole pine forest that surrounds you. Three to five ties, eight feet in length, were hewn from the clear, limb-free trunks.

Wyoming was undeveloped country with few roads. Water was the most economical method of moving the ties from forest to the railhead at Riverton.

Middle Level
Section #1
TITLE: Flumes
LEGEND: A cut, shaped and peeled tie weighs 120 pounds. Each tie hack was responsible for shouldering his own ties and carrying them to a decking area located by one of the narrow roads through the forest.

The hacks marked one end of the tie with his own symbol—a letter or number, and was paid by the number of ties marked with his symbol.

When winter snows arrived, horse drawn bobsleds moved the ties to a banking area next to a dammed up pond. A bobsled loaded with 120 ties weighed 7 tons and was pulled by two horses.

When the spring thaws came, tie hacks dumped their ties into the ponds on smaller creeks and fed them into flumes for the journey to the Wind River.

Flumes are great V-shaped wooden troughs built to float ties down to the main river—bypassing the rock-choked mountain streams.

Dams were built on the streams to impound enough water to carry the ties down the flumes. When the spring floods came in May or June, tie hacks fed the ties into the flumes for their downward journey.

[Series of pictures of flumes]
A section of the Canyon Creek flume was constructed with a 41 degree grade, and one year they tried to slide the ties down it without water. This dry fluming attempt failed when the friction of the ties shooting down the trough set fire to the flume.

This portion of the Warm Springs Flume was trestled and guyed with steel cables to sheer rock walls. Ties traveling this flume emptied into the Warm Springs Dam. Notice the catwalk used by drivers to prod the ties on their way down the flume.

Part of the famous Warm Springs flume follows the creek underground through a water curved arch. The flume is suspended inside the arch by steel cables anchored in the roof. The last tie to float this flume was in 1942.

The smaller flume on the left brought the ties from the forest flume on the right trasproted ties to the Wind River. [This is exactly as it is on the sign.]

Section #2
TITLE: Booms
LEGEND: Barricades across the stream held the ties together in what is called a log boom. When the danger of spring floods had passed, the trap was sprung and the tie drive was on.

Section #3
TITLE: The Tie Drive
LEGEND: It took an experienced Woods Boss to choose exactly the right time to start the drive. Too early, and the spring floods scattered the ties on the banks. Too late, and there wasn't enough water.

Martin Olson usually picked mid-July to put his half a hundred men on the river with peaveys and pike poles to steer a half million ties 100 miles down stream to Riverton.

A tie-drive looked like a river full of giant shoestring potatoes tumbling and rolling along with ant-like men running over the sea of ties, loosening a tie here or unjamming a pile-up there.

The drivers, half in and half out of the water, punched holes in their hobnailed boots to let the water out as fast as it ran in.

A drive lasted about 30 days, with the largest one having 700,000 ties. In the 31 year history of the Wind River drives, over 10 million ties floated to Riverton. The final drive in 1946 contained only machine sawn ties. The colorful tie hack and his river drives were history.

[Series of pictures of tie drives]
Massive jams occasionally filled the river from bank to bank with tangled piles of ties. A good tie driver could find the "key" tie to "spring" the jam.

Cooks and camp attendants followed the tie drive with loaded wagons of tents and camp gear. This 1918 photo is of a noon meal for the drivers.

Ties arrive at Riverton to be sorted, seasoned, treated with a preservative, and stacked for the Chicago and Northwestern Railroad.

Section #4
TITLE: The Tie Hack Boss
LEGEND: Tie cutting on the Wind River started in 1914. Martin Olson became foreman of all woods operations in 1918. Ricker Van Mercer, of Chicago, formed the Wyoming Tie and Timber Company in 1916 and hired Martin Olson as Woods Boss.

Martin, a Norwegian, was a veteran tie hack of Wyoming's pine forest. He started with a crew of 20 men who turned out 100,000 ties his first year as foreman. The crew grew each year, reinforced by young woodswise immigrants from Norway, Sweden and other European countries, until 100 hacks were in the woods.

Martin Olson was held in respect. He had a way of getting the best from any man. He was boss, also a leader. He worked with, cajoled, humored, mothered or drove any hack that got out of line. Martin's ability as Woods Boss was measured by the number of ties delivered to the railhead at Riverton, Wyoming.

The peak year was 1927 when 700,000 ties were driven down the Wind River to Riverton. The Wyoming T and T Company harvested 10 million railroad cross-ties under Olson's supervision and in cooperation with the Forest Service's timber management plan.

After supervising tie hacks and tie drives for 31 years, Olson retired in 1947, when the Wyoming Tie and Timber Company was sold to the J. N. (Bud) Fisher Tie and Timber Company. The change of ownership brought new ideas and methods to the timber industry, marking the end of the tie-hack era.

Lydia Olson, widow of Martin Olson, furnished the photographs and many of the historical facts presented here at the Tie Hack Memorial.

LOCATION: On U.S. Hwy 26/287 about 17 miles northwest of Dubois, Wyoming.

TRAPPERS' RENDEZVOUS MONUMENT-34
TITLE: None
LEGEND: In memory of the trappers, traders and explorers, who

established the rendezvous at the junction of the Little and Big Wind Rivers.

Dedicated by Historical Landmark Commission of Wyoming July 7, 1940

LOCATION: On large granite boulder at northwest corner of City Park in Riverton, Wyoming.

Mountain men, Indians, and the fur companies would gather annually in a well-known valley where the grass was abundant and the supply of furs was greatest. Two of the annual summer gatherings (1830 and 1838) were held at the junction of the Little and Big Wind Rivers. The marker location was changed from near the Wind River because of construction.

From Richard Fetter's *Mountain Men of Wyoming*, "Except for two sites in northern Utah and Pierre's Hole on the Idaho side of the Tetons, all of the summer rendezvous sites were in Wyoming." A new marker, 1825 Rocky Mountain Rendezvous (Sweetwater County #22), was erected in May 1989 at the site of the first mountain-man rendezvous on Henry's Fork near the Wyoming towns of McKinnon and Burntfork.

UNION PASS MONUMENT-35

TITLE: Union Pass

LEGEND: Westbound Astorians led by Wilson Price Hunt in September, 1811, passed through Dubois region, over Union Pass, and on to the mouth of the Columbia River to explore a line of communication and to locate sites for fur trading posts across the continent for John Jacob Astor. In the party were Mackenzie, Crooks, Miller, McClellan, Reed, 11 hunters, interpreters and guides; 45 Canadian engages, an Indian woman and her 2 children.

Erected by the Historical Landmark Commission of Wyoming 1956

LOCATION: On south side of U.S. Hwy 26/287 about 8 miles west of Dubois, Wyoming.

See Union Pass Interpretive Plaques (Fremont County #35.1) for more information.

UNION PASS INTERPRETIVE PLAQUES-35.1

Plaque #1

TITLE: UNION PASS

LEGEND: At this pass—midst a maze of mountain ranges and water courses which had sometimes baffled and repulsed them—aboriginal hunters, mountain men, fur traders and far-ranging explorers have, each in his time, found the key to a geographic conundrum. For them that conundrum had been a far more perplexing problem than such an ordinary task as negotiating the crossing, however torturous, of an unexplored pass occurring along the uncomplicated divide of an unconnected mountain chain.

Hereabouts the Continental Divide is a tricky, triple phenomenon wherein the unguided seeker of a crossing might find the right approach and still arrive at the wrong ending. In North America there are seven river systems that can be cited as truly continental in scope but only in this vicinity and at one other place do as many as three of them head against a common divide. Indians called this region the Land of Many Rivers and mountain men named the pass Union, thereby both—once again—proving themselves gifted practitioners of nomenclature.

Union Pass is surrounded by an extensive, rolling, mountain-top terrain wherein elevations vary between nine and ten thousand feet and interspersed water courses deceptively twist and turn as if undetermined betwixt an Atlantic or a Pacific destination. This mountain expanse might be visualized as a rounded hub in the center of which, like an axle's spindle, fits the pass. Out from this hub radiate three spokes, each one climbing and broadening into mighty mountain ranges—southeasterly the Wind Rivers, southwesterly the Gros Ventres and northerly, extending far into Montana, the Absarokas.

Plaque #2

TITLE: THE RENDEZVOUS

LEGEND: Twelve thousand foot mountain plateaus dominating this view of Green River and Snake River headwaters seemingly provide a southwesterly buttress for loftier peaks forming the core of the Wind River Range. Beyond them it is 43 miles from Union Pass to where confluence of the Green and its Horse Creek tributary marks the most famed of several "rendezvous" grounds relating to that epoch in American history known as the Rocky Mountain Fur Trade.

"Rendezvous", defined as a trade fair in wilderness surroundings, was held in diverse locations throughout the Central Rocky Mountain region. It required spacious, grassy environs for grazing thousands of horses, raising hundreds of trapper and Indian lodges and for horse races and other spectacles exuberantly staged by mountain men and Indians then relaxed from vigilance against dangers which otherwise permitted no unguarded carrousels. A favorite area for "rendezvous" was along the Green, recognized for producing the primest beaver peltry and for conveniently straddling the South Pass logistic route utilized for transport of trade goods and furs between St. Louis and the mountains. On the Green the finest "rendezvous" grounds—rendered especially famous through Alfred Jacob Miller's paintings of the 1837 scene—were those at Horse Creek.

Depending on arrival of St. Louis supply caravans, "rendezvous" usually extended through early July. At the close of revels—leaving many mountain men deeply in debt—there remained up to two months before prime furs signaled the start of fall hunting. The intervening time was pleasantly occupied in traveling and exploring high mountain terrain; then trails around Union Pass were furrowed by Indian travois only to be leveled again by the beating hoofs of the trapper's pack trains.

Plaque #3

TITLE: CULTURAL HERITAGE

LEGEND: High in mountains where the natural environment changes swiftly, eroding or burying its past, for how long a time can vestiges of man's frailer achievements withstand obliteration? No matter!, for here man has brought or developed cultures which are already heritages—treasured in memory if lost in substance.

Presented is a natural scene, a park surrounded by forest and parted by a virgin stream. But it is crossed by a road and also by a zigzag fence of rotting logs. Reconnaissance might reveal a campsite of prehistoric aborigines or discover a beaver trap once the property of a mountain man. Thus, is a cultural environment incorporated with the natural one.

Indians hunted these environs far into historic time. From exits of Union Pass, tribal trails branch in all directions. The road mentioned above, elsewhere explained, might cover ruts made by travois. Camps of mountain tribes, their chipping grounds, drivelines and animal traps exist throughout the area. Earliest among far western fur traders came this way—possibly Colter in 1807, certainly Astorians under Hunt in 1811. Mountain men camped here, Jim Bridger surely during the 1820's and, much later, guiding Captain Raynolds in 1860. Others, whose camping grounds may some day be ascertained, include: Bonneville, soldier, explorer, fur trader, enigma—recording carefully in 1833; Gannett, of the 1870's Geologic Survey with Yount his hunter-packer; Togwotee, a Shoshone Sheep Eater; Wister, famous author; Bliss, horse thief; Anderson, precursory forester; and, not far distant, Sheridan, a general and Arthur, a President of the United States.

The zigzag fence of rotting logs is a vestige of a continuing culture. Pastoral in nature it relates to the 1920 decade when cattlemen, under U.S. Forest Service permit, fenced rich grasslands to hold beef herds, fattening for the market.

Plaque #4

TITLE: FAUNA OF UNION PASS

LEGEND: Before primitive man discovered this pass between rich hunting grounds native ungulates grazed here during summers, migrating to the river valleys and plains for winters. These high plateaus and mountain meadows then harboured thousands of bison.

Though bison are gone, hundreds of elk (wapiti), mule deer and pronghorn antelope summer on Union Pass and in the near vicinity. Bighorn sheep live the year-round on high peaks and plateaus, venturing occasionally to timbered slopes and mountain meadows. Black bear are much in evidence and Lord Grizzly—"Old Ephraim" to mountain men and, in Indian lore, sometimes "Our Brother"—still occasionally roams the nearby forests and crags. Only the Shiras moose had not yet arrived in the days of mountain men, having only migrated this far south since about 1870.

Around 1900 the canine teeth of bull elk were worth their weight in gold. Northwestern Wyoming, isolated midst an abundance of game, was a favorite base of operations for notorious tusk hunters until early day game wardens, forest rangers and private citizens combined to drive the outlaws out.

Except for loss of bison and gain of moose, native fauna is much the same as it was in the days of fur trade. Beaver and trout still inhabit streams. Occasionally an otter may be seen cavorting along stream banks and mink are common to such environs. Pine Martin their peltry prized next to Siberian Sable and much sought by a later generation of mountain men, porcupines and red squirrels inhabit coniferous forests. Marmots and ground squirrels are found in rocky ledges and grassy meadows along with many lesser four-footed denizens. At Union Pass the prehistoric hunter or the most recent recreationist might have seen:

"A golden eagle in the sky and 'Ole Coyote' on the sly."

and thought:

"All snowshoe hares and the little blue grouse had better peel an eye."

Plaque #5

TITLE: RESOURCES—Ownership-Exploitation-Administration

LEGEND: Aesthetic and economic resources surround Union Pass, extending far to the west, north and southwest. These include grass, browse and forest plus animals living thereby and therein. Ownership of lands and vegetation repose in the nation's people; Wyoming's citizens own the wild animals; livestock, seasonally pastured, are privately owned.

Separate laws enacted in 1869 by Wyoming's first Territorial Assembly pertained to branding livestock and protecting wildlife. An incipient but immediately popularized livestock industry received credit for the first. But sponsors of the second, even following its augmentation in 1870 by a rudimentary wildlife agency, went, in that era of materialism, unnoticed. Few territorial fields of endeavor possessed sufficient background for practitioners to appreciate benefits stemming from conservation. Only the fur trade—flourishing in 1826, impoverished by 1840—had produced a second generation cognizant of dangers inherent in ruthless exploitation. Throughout such environs as Union Pass its diminished members trapped and hunted, sometimes outfitting (guide service, pack trains, supplies) clients attracted to the Territory by both its mountain wildernesses and continuing bonanza in open range livestock operations. From such relationships emerged types of outfitting and mountain valley ranching operations predisposed to conservation practices.

Spearheading a long overdue national conservation movement, Theodore Roosevelt found among such ranchers and outfitters men who played leading roles in organizing the first national forests out of the unwieldy Yellowstone Timberland Reserve and in developing an administrative structure adopted by the subsequent U.S. Forest Service.

Searching for complementary talents the Forest Service and the Wyoming Game and Fish Commission have both recruited personnel experienced in ranching and outfitting as well as the graduates of professional schools. Subject—as are all human efforts—to occasional errors, the administrators of Union Pass surroundings have successfully protected and enhanced its natural environment.

Plaque #6

TITLE: FLORA AT UNION PASS

LEGEND: Union Pass the cultural site must first have been Union Pass the natural site. As a natural site it commenced to produce vegetation and was afterwards inhabited by animals before it ever became attractive to man—for any purpose other than the thrill of exploration.

Development of present flora at Union Pass is an evolvement of recent time. The connection between conspicuous boulders and glaciers lately covering the area is mentioned elsewhere, but lichens still thriving grew on those boulders before all local ice had melted. Other flora, needing more favorable conditions, probably didn't attain a flourishing status until following the altithermal period causing cessation of glaciers—about 7,000 years ago.

The forest's development into a climax, a spruce-fir culmination, has been slowed by wildfires. But forest cover is now expanding through man's protective measures plus continuing evolution of soils as in the filling of ponds and marshes from sedimentation and organic matter.

Fortunately, Union Pass is in a park, not in the forest. From its view the foreground is covered on the drier, higher area by sagebrush, bunchgrasses and forbs favoring semi-arid conditions; low grounds support grassland communities, patches of willows and sedge meadows bordering ponds. Common plants are big sage brush, shrubby cinquefoil, Idaho fescue, slender wheat grass, Indian paintbrush and lupine; along the streams grow willows, sedges, rushes, little red elephant, march marigold and globe mallow.

Southeast-toward the Wind River Range-Engleman Spruce-subalpine fir growth is in wetter areas and whitebark pine along hilltops and ridges. To the west-forward-is a younger growth of Engleman Spruce and lodgepole pine fringing expanding forests while within older lodgepole stands are in various stages of transition to the sprucefir climax. Understory plants are grouse whortle berry, lupine, sedges and grasses.

Plaque #7

TITLE: THE RAMSHORN

LEGEND: Jutting like the topsail of a ship from beyond the apparent horizon, a tip of the Ramshorn is seen. It serves to remind the viewer of the Absarokas, a cragged mountain range broader and longer than the Wind Rivers but slightly less elevated. These mountains take their name from Indians identified as Crows or Ravens in the Journals of Lewis and Clark. Fur traders adopting that appellation passed it along to subsequent generations excepting only Absarokas themselves who, echoing forefathers, Anglicize their name to Bird People.

Tip rather than peak is used advisedly; there are peaks in the Absarokas but they are not a dominant feature of that range. Originating in a typical anticlinal fold, the Absarokas have been capped by lava strata measuring to thousands of feet, a geological evolvement known as a volcanic pile. Accordingly, their summits tend to be flat although simultaneous erosion throughout periods of flowing lava prohibited the forming of an all-encompassing tableland. Continued erosion has resulted in a range marked by deep canyons, precipitous ridges, notched passes and escarpment delimited plateaus. Summits rising above a plateau's general elevation are composed of harder materials and sometimes indicate proximity of a former lava fissure. The Ramshorn is one such plateau but its name derives from its escarpment—3,000 feet of cliffs and talus slopes, curving for miles around its southwestern flank like the horn of a mountain ram.

It is appropriate that this mountain be named Ramshorn. The Absarokas offer habitat to a variety and an abundance of wildlife but escarpments and plateaus, producing grass and browse swept free of snow by winter gales, make ideal mountain sheep ranges. Trails established by sheep-eating Shoshones, now followed by other wilderness enthusiasts, attest to mankind's fascination with the wild sheep of the Absarokas.

Plaque #8
TITLE: ROAD THROUGH A PASS
LEGEND: A road, component of a cultural environment, is the most noticeable feature of this otherwise natural landscape. In present form it is not old, not a pioneer route hacked by frontiersmen. Based and graded to support rapid haulage of ponderous loads of logs, this road was built by specialists operating specialized machines. It is a product of 20th century technological culture.

A road of a sort is an ancient and, originally, a natural feature at Union Pass. Wild animals, some-camels, indigenous horses, mammoths now extinct, found this passageway and, following easiest grades during seasonal migrations, trod out—wide in places as a road—a trail. Perhaps 10,000 years ago progenitors of Nimrod trailed these animals around the edges of a receding glacier and on through Union Pass-leaving along that route its first traces of human culture. Around 1700 A.D. Shoshones, descendants or replacements of the earliest hunters, acquired the horse and, among other impacts made by them on the natural environment, the dragging ends of their travois poles widened and deepened this road.

Chronological stages in the Union Pass cultural environment have been: aboriginal, fur trade, explorations and geological surveys, outfitting (recreational industry) and ranching, and management of natural resources-including forestry. Forestry, defined as "cultivating, maintaining, and developing forests", implying harvesting, came last owing to local patterns of development. Although Wyoming was a bellwether in Theodore Roosevelt's early conservation movement, pressing local concern regarding new national forests centered on livestock grazing and wildlife and watershed protection-forestry waited. Substantial timber harvesting, a tie hack era, only began after 1900; upgrading a Union Pass wagon road to high speed hauling standards was a mid-century project.

Plaque #9
TITLE: WIND RIVER RANGE
LEGEND: Postulating the traverse of the Continental Divide the eye climbs to Union Peak, some four airline miles but nearer six by that tortuous route. At 11,491 feet Union Peak is a nondescript rise that draws attention only because it is the final timberline topping elevation on the northwestern end of the Wind River Range. Appearing slightly behind and more to the right, but actually seven miles further along the traverse of the divide, is Three Waters Mountain. That is as far into the Wind Rivers as can be seen from Union Pass. However, if vision could continue to follow the southeasterly bearing of the divide, the viewer might estimate 20 and 30 miles to where nearer 13,804 foot Gannett Peak and farther 13,745 foot Fremont Peak mark the scope of the heart of that range.

The Wind River Range is the highest mountain mass in Wyoming. Basically it is a broad uplift which originated about 60 million years ago during a period of "mountain building" called the Laramide Orogeny. The core of the range reveals Precambrian crystalline rocks, and Paleozoic and Mesozoic sedimentary rocks are upturned on the flanks. The Wind River Range, although south of continental ice caps, was extensively glaciated during the Pleistocene epoch and such sizable lakes as Newfork, Boulder, Fremont, Bull, Green River and Dinwoody, filling canyons and valleys along its widespread flanks, are dammed behind moraines. Existent glaciers in the highest parts of the Wind Rivers are small by comparison, yet they are often cited as the largest ice fields within the contiguous states of the Union.

Boulders strewing Union Pass environs are surface evidence that this northern margin of the range was subdued by spreading glaciers which have left a blanket of till and moraine material.

Plaque #10
TITLE: THREE WATERS MOUNTAIN
LEGEND: Southeast rises a mountain given a lyrical name, one such as Indians or mountain men discovering a geographical phenomenon might have chosen. Midway of its four-mile long crest is the key point, one of only two in North America, where as many as three of the continent's seven major watersheds interlock.

Here a raindrop splits into thirds, the three tiny driblets destined to wend their separate ways along continuously diverging channels to the oceans of the world. One driblet arrives in the Gulf of Mexico, 3,000 miles distant by way of Jakeys Fork, Wind River, Bighorn, Yellowstone, Missouri, and Mississippi; another joins currents running 1,400 miles to the Pacific through Fish Creek, the Gros Ventre, Snake and Columbia; the final one descends more than 1,300 miles to the Gulf of California; via Roaring Fork, Green River and the Colorado.

Seemingly neither Indians nor fur trappers named this mountain. Locally it has been called Triple Divide Peak, but only a bench mark (11,642 ft.) and lines denoting a junction of divides point to it on the Geological Survey's map of 1906. The Survey's 1968 map (correcting the B.M. to 11,675 ft.) officially names this long crest projecting in a northwesterly descent from the 13,800 foot glacier swathed peaks at the heart of the Wind River Range-Three Waters Mountain. That latter day cartographer, possessing the imagination and finding the inspiration to contrive this name, thus proved himself a worthy disciple of Ferdinand Vandeveer Hayden and his competent assistants who were precursors and, in 1879, helpers in the founding of the United States Geological Survey.

LOCATION: About 8 miles west of Dubois, Wyoming, on U.S. Hwy 26/287. Turn south on Union Pass Road, follow for 15 miles to interpretive site.

This is a very nice area to visit in the summer. Its elevation is 9,210 feet. Check locally about road conditions as the area may not be free of snow until later in June.

WASHAKIE GRAVE-36
East side: Washakie 1804-1900
North Side: A wise ruler
West Side: Chief of the Shoshones
South Side: Always loyal to the government and to his white brothers

LOCATION: Southwest corner of the Old Military Cemetery at Fort Washakie, Wyoming.

Chief Washakie became a sub-chief of the Eastern Shoshones in the 1830s. He advised the tribe not to fight against the white men during their westward emigration. He secured a treaty at Fort Bridger in 1868 which gave the Wind River Reservation to the tribe. Chief Washakie also wanted a military post established on the reservation for protection from traditional enemies and certain whites, and in 1871 Camp Brown was established for that purpose. The post was renamed Fort Washakie in 1878, in honor of the Shoshone leader.

Washakie died February 22, 1900, at an age of about 100 years. Post Commander Clough Overton wrote:

> . . . Washakie was a great man, for he was a brave man and a good man. The spirit of his loyalty and courage will speak to soldiers; the memory of his love for his own people will linger to assist them in their troubles, and he will never be forgotten so long as the mountains and streams of Wyoming, which were his home, bear his name.

WASHAKIE MONUMENT-37

TITLE: Washakie
LEGEND: The great Shoshone Chief, and skilled hunter, strategist, and warrior against his tribal enemies was noted for his friendship towards the white men. He united his people. He was born about 1804 and died February 20, 1900. Shoshone Indian Reservation was created by the Great Treaty of July 3, 1868. Fort Washakie 1879-1909, was a military post.

Erected by the Historical Landmark Commission of Wyoming 1956
LOCATION: On Blackcole Street in Fort Washakie, Wyoming. Inquire locally.

See Washakie Grave (Fremont County #36) for more information.

WILLIE'S HANDCART COMPANY-38

TITLE: Official Marker
    Utah Pioneer Trails and Landmarks Association
    No. 27
    Erected June 23, 1933
    Willie's Handcart Company
LEGEND: Captain James G. Willie's Handcart Company of Mormon emigrants on the way to Utah, greatly exhausted by the deep snows of an early winter and suffering from lack of food and clothing, had assembled here for reorganization by relief parties from Utah, about the end of October, 1856. Thirteen persons were frozen to death during a single night and were buried here in one grave. Two others died the next day and were buried nearby. Of the company of 404 persons, 77 perished before help arrived. The survivors reached Salt Lake City November 9, 1856.

Utah Pioneer Trails Landmarks Association and members of Lyman Stake
LOCATION: On the east bank of Rock Creek about 8 miles southeast of Atlantic City, Wyoming. Inquire locally for directions and road conditions. Adjacent to Willie's Handcart Gravestone (Fremont County #38.1).

WILLIE'S HANDCART GRAVESTONE-38.1

TITLE: None
LEGEND: In memory of those members of the Willie Handcart Co. whose journey started too late and ended too early and were buried here in a circular grave October 24 & 25, 1856.

William James, 46	Bodil Mortinsen, 9
Elizabeth Bailey, 52	Nils Anderson, 41
James Kirkwood, 11	Ole Madsen, 41
Samuel Gadd, 10	James Gibb, 67
Lars Wendin, 60	Chesterton Gilman, 66
Anne Olsen, 46	Thomas Gurldstone, 62
Ella Nilson, 22	William Groves, 22
Jens Nilson, 6	

LOCATION: On the east bank of Rock Creek about 8 miles southeast of Atlantic City, Wyoming. Inquire locally for directions and road conditions. Adjacent to Willie's Handcart Company (Fremont County #38).

WIND RIVER CANYON INFORMATIVE SIGN-39.1

TITLE: Wind River Canyon
LEGEND: First white people thru canyon were those of the Ashley Fur Party in 1825.
    C.B. and Q. R.R. thru canyon in 1911, State Highway in 1925.
    This canyon, site of Boysen Dam.
    Wyoming Highway Department.
LOCATION: On west side of U.S. Hwy 20 about 0.5 miles south of Boysen Dam.

Dorothy Buchanan Milek wrote in *Hot Springs: A Wyoming County History*, "Wind River Canyon is a twelve mile chasm with walls towering 2,000 and 3,000 feet high. Rock in the canyon represents every geological era." The magnificent canyon provided an obstacle to development of the Big Horn Basin, yet it gave the area a rare attraction, rivaled only by the Grand Canyon.

The story of the railroad through the canyon began in 1887 when the Cheyenne and Burlington Railroad was suggested by articles of incorporation. Two railroads competed for the right to place rails through the canyon. Chicago and Northwestern Railroad had rails from Lusk through Douglas, Glenrock, Casper, Powder River, and almost to Shoshoni by June 1906. Burlington had a line from Billings, Montana, to Cody, Wyoming, by 1901; the company assured Big Horn Basin residents that a line would connect Cody with Meeteetse and Thermopolis. Thermopolis was reached in May 1909 and work south to the Wind River Canyon began in July 1909. The Chicago, Burlington and Quincy Railroad Company completed the first line through the canyon in May 1911.

A road survey of the canyon was begun in 1920, and Utah Construction Company began work in 1922. In January 1924, six months before the project was completed, passenger cars traveled the canyon on Sundays. Projected costs were just over $401,000; Utah Construction reported costs of between $750,000 and $1,000,000. The Wind River Canyon Road Marker (Fremont County #40), was moved from the old Boysen Dam to the Wyoming Highway Department headquarters in Cheyenne, Wyoming.

Asmus Boysen, a Danish emigrant, envisioned a dam across the canyon to provide electricity and irrigation water. His plan was met with problem after problem. Although completed in 1910, it failed as an investment. The Bureau of Reclamation authorized a new dam south of Boysen's in 1944. Today it supplies the large reservoir at Boysen State Park.

The river entering the canyon was called the Wind River, its origin high in the Wind River Mountains. The river exiting the canyon was named the Big Horn River. Confusion arose, because explorers approached the canyon from two different directions. "The Wedding of the Waters," that area where the drainages of the Wind River Valley and the Big Horn Basin joined, was the name given the site where the river names changed.

WIND RIVER CANYON ROAD MARKER-40

TITLE: Wind River Canyon Road
LEGEND: Built 1922-1924   Length-21.2 miles
    Initiated and construction started during administration of Governor Robert D. Carey
    M. R. Johnson, L. R. A. Condit, S. W. Conwell, Joe C. Kinney, J. M. Snyder   Members of State Highway Commission
    L. E. Laird   State Highway Supt.
    Z. E. Sevison   State Highway Engineer
    R. L. Silver, C. H. Bowman   District Engineers
    N. T. Olson, G. D. Gorwine   Resident Engineers
    Goyne Drummond   Location Engineer.
LOCATION: Entrance of the Wyoming Highway Department Headquarters in Cheyenne, Wyoming.

See Wind River Canyon Informative Sign (Fremont County #39.1) for more information.

WYOMING FALLEN FIREFIGHTER MEMORIAL-41

Granite Markers
TITLE: None
LEGEND:

Bronze bust of structure firefighter	Bronze bust of wildland firefighter
Wyoming Fire Academy Logo	Fire Department Maltese Cross
John S. Federhen	Michael T. Sullivan
Fred W. Tossie	Elsie Christensen
Henry Larsen	Floyd L. Travis
Alfred G. Clayton	Ike Roberts
Rex A. Hale	Galen M. Northrop

Billy Lea	David L. Stoudt
Paul E. Tyrrell	Wayne A. Garkie
James T. Saban	Robert C. Moore
Clyde Allen	Kenneth D. Double
Roy Bevens	Cecil Lynch
Ambrocio Garza	Gene Ahrendt
John B. Gerdes	Douglas Cuzzort
Will C. Griffith	Steven L. Huitt
Mack T. Mayabb	Darrell D. Staley
George E. Rodgers	Merrin Rodgers
Earnest R. Seelke	Donald Kuykendall
Rubin D. Sherry	Edward L. Hutton
William Whitlock	Alan L. Mickelson

Bronze Plaque:
TITLE: None
LEGEND: Dedicated to those Firefighters who gave the ultimate sacrifice in the service of their community.

LOCATION: West side of the Wyoming Fire Academy located at 2500 Academy Court in Riverton, Wyoming.

The Fallen Firefighter Memorial project was envisioned by Larry L. Lee, Fremont County fire warden, following the loss of five firefighters in the 1988 fire season. The concept was presented to the Wyoming Fire Chiefs' Association and the Wyoming Firemen's Association in January 1989 during Mid-Winter Fire School in Riverton, Wyoming. The Fire Chiefs' Association spearheaded the project, and donations came from fire departments, individuals, union organizations, and equipment vendors.

Ken Metzler, battalion chief of Fremont County Firefighters and training officer of the Wyoming Fire Academy, proposed the design concept. The final plan included bronze reliefs of a wildland firefighter and a structural firefighter atop large marble slabs engraved with the names of fallen firefighters. The monument base was constructed of rocks from all twenty-three Wyoming counties, all Bureau of Land Management Districts and National Forests, the Wind River Indian Reservation, and both National Parks located in Wyoming.

OREGON BUTTES-42

TITLE: Oregon Buttes
LEGEND: To the south stand the Oregon Buttes, a major trail landmark. The name is significant because the Buttes were roughly the beginning of the Oregon Territory and also helped keep emigrants encouraged, even though there were still hundreds of miles of rough going ahead. Today, the Oregon Buttes are an Area of Critical Environmental Concern because of their cultural significance and important wildlife values.

About twelve miles to the southwest of Oregon Buttes is the Tri-territory site. This site is the location where the Oregon Territory, Mexican Territory, and Louisiana Purchase had a common boundary. The large landmark, just to the south of where you are standing, is Pacific Butte. The great height and mass of the butte, combined with a ridge to the north paralleling the emigrant trails, helps to create a visual channel through which travelers migrated on their way through South Pass.
LOCATION: On the Oregon Trail just north of South Pass.

SOUTH PASS-43

TITLE: South Pass
LEGEND: South Pass was discovered in 1812 by a small party of Astorians led by Robert Stuart as they traveled east with dispatches for John Jacob Astor. It was "rediscovered" in 1824 by a party led by Jedediah Smith as they searched for a winter crossing through the Wind River Mountain Range. William Sublette led a small caravan of wagons to South Pass in 1828. While the party did not take the wagons over the pass, they proved that wagon travel was possible.

Captain Benjamin Bonneville took the first wagons over South Pass into the Green River Basin in 1832. But it was Lt. John Charles Fremont who would be credited with widely publicizing the route over South Pass as a result of his expedition in 1842. Scattered references to the easy passage over the Rocky Mountains had appeared in newspapers for a decade, but Fremont ignited enthusiasm for South Pass by explaining that a traveler could go through the pass without any "toilsome ascents."

With the discovery of South Pass, the great western migration began. Thousands of Mormons, future Oregonians and Californians would use the trail in the following years.
LOCATION: On the Oregon Trail at South Pass. See Continental Divide—Oregon Trail Monument (Fremont County #7).

PACIFIC SPRINGS-44

TITLE: Pacific Springs
LEGEND: For many emigrants, the first tangible evidence that they had crossed South Pass was Pacific Springs, "the fountain source of the Pacific streams," according to pioneer Joseph Goldsborough Bruff. The broad expanse of the pass from Pacific Springs was proof that the journey to the Pacific coast was geographically half over. But the event was only a slight consolation, the road ahead was still long and hard.

The springs was a major camping spot along the trail, providing good water and grazing. A number of pioneers also died here, most having succumbed to cholera contracted elsewhere along the trail. Several graves are known in the vicinity of Pacific Springs.

In the 1860's, a stagecoach and Pony Express station was located at the springs probably in the areas of the Halter and Flick Ranch. Some sources indicate that the station was burned by Indians in 1862. The exact location of the station is unknown.

Pacific Springs became an important water source for early livestock operators and they remain so today. The springs lie on private property owned by John Hay. The Hay family has been involved in ranching in southwestern Wyoming for five generations dating to the 1870s.
LOCATION: On the Oregon Trail about 3.5 miles west of South Pass.

BENNETT TRIBBETT OCTA MARKER-45

TITLE: Bennett Tribbett
LEGEND: Private Bennett Tribbett was a nineteen-year-old soldier stationed here at Three Crossings Station. He was a member of Company B of the First Battalion, Sixth Ohio Volunteer Cavalry. On December 14, 1862, Tribbett died of an appendicitis. His burial was described by Pvt. Anthony Barleon in a letter written to Bennett's sister, Arviley, at home in Athens county, Ohio.

"We made a coffin of such lumber that we had which of course were rough boards but we planed them off as smooth as we could. We dressed him up in his best clothes which were new and clean, laid a blanket around him, and we tucked a blanket around the coffin which made it look a little better. . . When the time arrived for his burial he was bore off by the arms of 6 of his former associates accompanied by an escort of six men who performed the usual military escort and ceremony. When we arrived at the grave we put the coffin in and the escort fired three rounds over his grave. So he was buried with all the military honors of a soldier."

In July, 1863, four newly recruited companies were consolidated with the old battalion to form a new regiment, designated the Eleventh Ohio Volunteer Cavalry, which continued to serve on the frontier until the last companies were mustered out on July 14, 1866. By Civil War standards casualties in this regiment were light. Three officers and fifteen men died as a result of actions against Indians; one officer and fifty-eight men, like Bennett Tribbett, died of natural causes.

Research, Signing and Funding by the:

Oregon-California Trails Association

1988

This is a part of your American heritage. Honor it, protect it, preserve it for your children.

LOCATION: Private land along the Oregon Trail in Fremont County.

THE SWEETWATER VALLEY INFORMATIVE SIGN-46

TITLE: The Sweetwater Valley

LEGEND: The Sweetwater Valley is the mid-section of the 2000 mile long Oregon Trail. West of Casper, Wyoming, branches of that trail meld into a single transportation corridor and here, paralleling the serpentine Sweetwater River, the trail approaches the base of South Pass. On the other side is "Oregon Country" where routes diverge toward Utah, California and Oregon.

For a week emigrants plodded this stretch of high altitude, semiarid desert. Everyday, more of the same—alkali, sage and sand—a continuing American Sahara. "How I long for a timbered country" wrote one traveler. "...In a thousand miles I have not seen a hundred acres of wood. All that comes near to arborification is a fringe of cottonwood and willows along the banks of creeks and rivers. These everlasting hills have an everlasting curse of barrenness..."

For others, however, the Sweetwater was a relatively agreeable part of the journey. It was summer, the river was low and clear, and there was grass for stock. Days were bright and mild, and scenery was plentiful. "...Still by the Sweet Water. The valley is becoming more narrow and the stream more rapid. In advance and a little to the north of our trail we can see the Wind River Mountains. Their lofty summits are covered with snow, and in their dazzling whiteness appear truly sublime."

LOCATION: At the Sweetwater Rest Area at junction of U.S. Hwy 287/789 and State Route 135. About 39 miles southeast of Lander, Wyoming.

THE RIVERTON PROJECT INFORMATIVE SIGN-47

TITLE: The Riverton Project

LEGEND: Portions of the High Plains were not settled until the early 20th century because water was needed for irrigation. Responding to pressure for Western settlement, Congress created the Reclamation Service in 1902. Its purpose was to develop water resources making possible cultivation of what was considered desert wasteland. One effort was the Riverton Project. Located in the Wind River Basin it was undertaken by the Bureau of Reclamation in 1920.

The Midvale Irrigation District of the Riverton Project involves 73,000 acres, three dams—Bull Lake Dam to the south and Diversion Dam and Pilot Butte Dam to the east, 100 miles of canals and 300 miles of laterals. Diversion Dam, completed in 1923, diverts water from the Wind River to the Wyoming Canal. It is noteworthy as the first dam in the nation with a road incorporated into its structure and the first to contain a fish ladder.

Historian T. A. Larson describes the Riverton irrigation project as "a perennial object lesson in the formidable difficulties inherent in large-scale reclamation projects in the West." Initially posing financial and engineering problems, it came to involve legal and political issues. During the rise of Native American self determination the Arapaho and Shoshone tribes exercised their right to Wind River water, granted by an 1868 treaty. Court battles were fought over water used to irrigate land opened to homesteading by Congress in 1905. The struggle highlights the importance of water to the West.

LOCATION: Diversion Dam Junction Rest Area (Bull Lake Rest Area) just west of the junction of U.S. Hwys 26 and 287. About 40 miles west of Riverton.

GOSHEN COUNTY

CHEYENNE-BLACK HILLS STAGE ROUTE-1

TITLE: None
LEGEND: The Cheyenne-Black Hills Trail passed near this point between 1876 and 1887. Built to supply the Dakota gold camps, the road was constructed in violation of the Ft. Laramie Treaty of 1868 which reserved the Black Hills for Sioux Indians. Stagecoaches and wagons carrying passengers, freight and gold bullion rumbled through nearby Ft. Laramie, an important stopping point along the line, until the arrival of the Chicago and North Western Railroad rendered the route obsolete.
   Erected by the Wyoming Recreation Commission 1985
LOCATION: North side of U.S. Hwy 26 about 4.5 miles west of Fort Laramie, Wyoming.

   There are several monuments across eastern Wyoming that mark the course of the Cheyenne-Black Hills Trail. Another in Goshen County is found at the Fort Laramie National Historic Site. Four markers in Laramie County (#6, 7, 15, & 18), seven in Niobrara County (#2, 3, 4, 5, 7, 8, & 11), one in Platte County (#2), and three in Weston County (#3.2, 4, & 5) give additional history and insight into the Cheyenne-Black Hills Stage Route.

COLD SPRINGS INFORMATIVE SIGN-2

TITLE: Cold Springs 3/4 mile east from this point
LEGEND: Cold Springs was a popular camping ground on the Overland Emigrant Trail to California, Oregon, Utah and other points in the far west.
   It was a stage station along the Overland Stage Route 1854-1862 and also a pony express relay stop 1860-1861.
   Station tender was M. Reynal.
LOCATION: On east side of U.S. Hwy 85 about 1.6 miles south of the intersection of U.S. Hwys 85 and 26 in Torrington, Wyoming. Adjacent to Oregon Trail Marker (Goshen County #12).

   Before the Civil War, the Overland Stage Route followed the Oregon Trail across the plains of Nebraska and Wyoming. Cold Springs Station was a stopover along that route. When the Civil War broke out in 1861, military strength in the west declined, and stages could not be safely guarded. In 1862, the stage line was acquired by Ben Holladay, and he changed its route to a more southerly path through Colorado and southern Wyoming (see Overland Stage Route Marker, Sweetwater County #10).

FORT LARAMIE BRIDGE MONUMENT-3

Aluminum plaque
TITLE: Old Army Bridge over the Platte River
      Erected in 1875
LEGEND: This bridge was a vital link between Cheyenne, Fort Laramie and the military outposts, Indian agencies and the gold fields of the Black Hills Dakota Region.
   Placed by the Historical Landmark Commission of Wyoming July 1951

Bronze plaque
TITLE: Wyoming Historic Civil Engineering Landmark
LEGEND: Fort Laramie Bridge 1875   Wyoming Section ASCE 1977

LOCATION: North end of the old river bridge on the road to Fort Laramie National Historic Site.

   This bridge was constructed by the King Bridge and Manufacturing Company of Ohio and served as a vital traffic link from Cheyenne to Fort Laramie and on to the Black Hills gold fields. It is the oldest of its kind west of the Missouri River and is listed in the Historic American Engineering Record.

FORT LARAMIE VILLAGE MEMORIAL-4

TITLE: None
LEGEND: To all pioneers who passed this way to win and hold the West. Trail crossed one mile south of this point.
   Erected by the Ft. Laramie Citizens and Friends, 1932
LOCATION: In the town of Fort Laramie, Wyoming, on the southwest corner of the intersection of Main and First Streets.

   This marker was one of the many markers placed under the guidance and support of the Oregon Trail Memorial Association. The Association markers featured a bronze plaque with oxen pulling a covered wagon. See "Ezra Meeker, the Oregon Trail Memorial Association, and the American Pioneer Trails Association" in the first part of this book.

FORT PLATTE MONUMENT-5

TITLE: Fort Platte
LEGEND: A trading post, built by Lancaster P. Lupton in 1841, stood fifty yards to the north.
   Placed by the Historical Landmark Commission of Wyoming July 1951
LOCATION: North side of the Fort Laramie Road about 0.2 miles south of the Fort Laramie Bridge Monument.

   In 1834, William Sublette and Robert Campbell built the first fort on the Laramie River and named it Fort William. This trading post enjoyed a fur trade monopoly on the North Platte River until about 1841, when a rival trading post appeared along the Oregon Trail. Fort Platte was built of adobe on the banks of the river just east of Fort William. Lupton, a veteran of the fur trade in the Colorado region, was only the first of several owners of Fort Platte. In 1845, Fort Platte was abandoned while the trade at Fort John (previously Fort William) remained a brisk one.

GRATTAN BURIAL SITE-6

TITLE: Grattan Massacre
LEGEND: Grattan Massacre 1854   Burials were 40 ft. south.
   Erected by the Historical Landmark Commission of Wyoming, 1953
LOCATION: About 0.5 miles north of the Grattan Monument (Goshen County #7) which is 3.2 miles west of Lingle, Wyoming, on State Route 157. Private land; permission required.

   In retaliation for the killing of a cow belonging to a Mormon emigrant, the commander at Fort Laramie sent Brevet Second Lieutenant John Lawrence Grattan and twenty-nine soldiers to the Brule Sioux camp where the offense had occurred. The Indians would not turn over the brave responsible (a Minneconjou Sioux from another camp), and a fight ensued. Grattan and all of his men were killed by the Indians. Indian-emigrant relations turned for the worse, and "25 years of intermittent warfare began." One year later, a force of 600 cavalry under General W. S. Harney punished the Sioux with an early morning attack of the Indian village at Ash Hollow (about 150 miles east of Fort Laramie), "killing 86 Indians, wounding countless others, and capturing a large number of women and children."
   See Grattan Monument (Goshen County #7) for more information.

GRATTAN MONUMENT-7

TITLE: None
LEGEND: Sioux Indians massacred 29 soldiers with their officer, Brevet 2nd Lt. L. Grattan, on August 19, 1854. Site is 1/2 mile north-west.
   A Indian killed a cow from a Mormon caravan. The detachment of soldiers was sent to receive the offender. In the ensuing fight all soldiers and the Chief of the Brule's Sioux, Martoh-Ioway were killed.
   Erected by the Historical Landmark Commission of Wyoming, 1953
LOCATION: On the north side of State Route 157 about 3.2 miles west of Lingle, Wyoming.

   See Grattan Burial Site (Goshen County #6) for more information.

GOSHEN COUNTY

Legend

⬡ Interstate

⬡ US Highway

◯ State or Other Principal Road

•—▭ Marker

1   Cheyenne-Black Hills Stage Route
2   Cold Springs Informative Sign
3   Fort Laramie Bridge Monument
4   Fort Laramie Village Memorial
5   Fort Platte Monument
6   Grattan Burial Site
7   Grattan Monument
8   Mary Homsley Grave
9   Oregon Trail Marker
10 Oregon Trail Marker
11 Oregon Trail Marker
12 Oregon Trail Marker
13 Oregon Trail Marker
14 Oregon Trail Marker
15 Oregon Trail Marker
15.1 Rural Electrification Sign
16 Stuart Campsite Sign
17 Cattle Trail Monument
18 Texas Trail Monument
19 Thoroughbred Horse Monument
20 Fort Laramie Monument
20.1 Pony Express Marker
21 Oregon Trail Marker
22 Iowa Center School Marker
23 Burge Post Office
24 Oldest Horse Monument
25 Fort Laramie National Historic Site Plaques
27 Old Bedlam BLM Marker

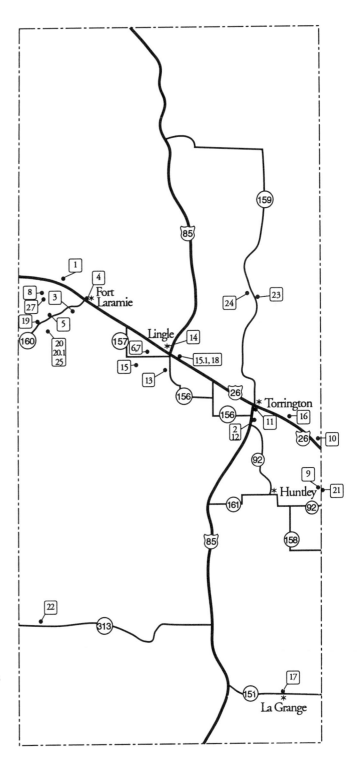

MARY HOMSLEY GRAVE-8

TITLE: None
LEGEND: A pioneer mother of the Oregon Trail
Mary E. Homsley 1823-52.

Headstone
TITLE: Mary E. Homsley
LEGEND: Died June 10/52   Age 28
LOCATION: Near the Laramie Canal road about 1.6 miles north of the Fort Laramie Road. Private land; permission required.

Mary Elizabeth Auden Homsley was born near Lexington, Kentucky, on July 20, 1824. In April 1852, Mary, her husband, Ben, and their two girls started for Oregon Country in covered wagons. While crossing the North Platte River, the wagon, which carried Mary, overturned. Already sick with measles, she weakened that evening and died the next day about five miles west of Fort Laramie.

The *Casper Star Tribune* paid tribute to Mary Homsley (March 31, 1974, page 10C) and recounted the anguish of the last year of her short life.

OREGON TRAIL MARKER-9

TITLE: Oregon Trail
LEGEND: Marked by the Nebraska and Wyoming Sons and Daughters of the American Revolution 1912
27 July 1987 Rededicated.
LOCATION: About 0.5 miles west of Nebraska Hwy L-79C which runs between the Nebraska towns of Henry and Lyman. Directly west of a granite Oregon Trail Marker (Goshen County #21) which is located on L-79C. Private land; permission required.

This marker was dedicated April 4, 1913, one of the first markers dedicated in the State of Wyoming. Despite a snowstorm the night before, the dedication was exemplary of many to follow. Four hundred Wyoming and Nebraska residents attended the ceremony held at the states' boundary.

Mr. H. G. Leavitt of Omaha was Master of Ceremonies. The Torrington Boys' Band under the direction of Mr. Hiram Yoder provided the music. Mrs. Charles Oliver Norton, State Regent of the D.A.R. of Nebraska, and Mrs. H. B. (Emily A.) Patten, State Regent of the D.A.R. of Wyoming, unveiled the monument. Mrs. Patten, who was also Secretary of the Wyoming Oregon Trail Commission, wrote: "So indeed a very wonderful day. The hospitality, the bronzed strong faces, the courtesy, the kindly thought for every detail, the interest in the principal event of the day, the hope that it may mean something more than a mere entertainment all gave us happy hearts as we returned tired for another night at Guersney before reaching our Cheyenne homes."

OREGON TRAIL MARKER-10

TITLE: The Oregon Trail
LEGEND: The Oregon Trail entered Wyoming at this point. 1841. Main trail 3 miles south.
Erected by the Historical Landmark Commission of Wyoming 1943
LOCATION: North side of U.S. Hwy 26 just west of the Wyoming-Nebraska state line. Just west of Henry, Nebraska.

OREGON TRAIL MARKER-11

TITLE: None
LEGEND: To all pioneers who passed this way to win and hold the West.
Erected by the citizens of Torrington, 1931
LOCATION: At the Homesteader's Museum in South Torrington across from the Holly Sugar Plant.

This was one of two electrically illuminated markers. When it was originally placed at the small park near the old Burlington Railroad Depot (where Hardee's Restaurant now stands), an electric light atop the granite marker illuminated it at night. The other electrically lighted marker was the Oregon Trail Marker (Goshen County #14) in Lingle, Wyoming.

OREGON TRAIL MARKER-12

TITLE: Oregon Trail
LEGEND: Marked by the State of Wyoming 1914
LOCATION: East side of U.S. Hwy 85 about 1.6 miles south of the junction of U.S. Hwys 85 and 26 in Torrington, Wyoming. Adjacent to Cold Springs Informative Sign (Goshen County #2).

On June 17, 1915, the Oregon Trail Commission of Wyoming dedicated three markers in Goshen County. The first was the fourteen foot-high concrete monument (Goshen County #20) at Fort Laramie National Historic Site. The other two identical markers were: Goshen County #13, placed just south of the North Platte River south of Lingle, Wyoming; and Goshen County #12, placed south of the North Platte River near Torrington, Wyoming. Governor Joseph M. Carey, who assisted in organizing the Oregon Trail Commission and supported its activities, attended and spoke at these dedications in 1915.

OREGON TRAIL MARKER-13

TITLE: Oregon Trail
LEGEND: Marked by the State of Wyoming 1914
LOCATION: About 2.2 miles south of Lingle, Wyoming, on State Route 156. Southwest of the North Platte River bridge on a hill above the road.

See Oregon Trail Marker (Goshen County #12) for more information.

OREGON TRAIL MARKER-14

TITLE: None
LEGEND: To all pioneers who passed this way to win and hold the West. Trail crossed one mile south.
Erected by the citizens of Lingle and friends 1932
LOCATION: West side of U.S. Hwy 26/85 in Lingle, Wyoming. About 50 yards north of railroad tracks.

The Oregon Trail Memorial Association assisted in the marking of many sites across Wyoming; those sites can be identified by a bronze plaque atop the marker. This marker was one of only two given electrical lighting for night viewing. The other electrically illuminated marker was the Oregon Trail Marker (Goshen County #11) in Torrington, Wyoming.

OREGON TRAIL MARKER-15

TITLE: Oregon Trail
LEGEND: Marked by the State of Wyoming 1914
LOCATION: South side of State Route 157 about 3.3 miles west of Lingle, Wyoming. About 0.1 mile west of Grattan Monument (Goshen County #7).

The Oregon Trail Commission of Wyoming marked Wyoming historical sites in the early 1900s. Several markers identical to this one were placed along the Oregon Trail. The markers were purchased by the State of Wyoming; their placing was done by the citizens of the individual counties.

RURAL ELECTRIFICATION SIGN-15.1

TITLE: Wyoming Rural Electrification
LEGEND: In the early 1930's, fewer than one out of ten rural families in Wyoming had electric power.
The year 1985 marked the 50th anniversary of organized efforts to deliver electric service to the countryside. It began with President Franklin D. Roosevelt's executive order creating the Rural Electrification Administration (REA) on May 11, 1935.
Electrical service was widely available in towns, but rural residents struggled to bring water to their homes in buckets while their children studied by the light of smokey kerosene lanterns.
Cooperatives were formed by people who were determined to have

1.

2.

3.

1. Some of the modern markers, like the Cheyenne-Black Hills Stage Route Marker erected by the Wyoming Recreation Commission in 1985, resembled the old markers placed by the Wyoming Historical Landmark Association 1927-1959.

2. The Mary Homsley Marker commemorated the life and fate of an Oregon Trail emigrant.

3. This marker was placed just about one-half mile east of the Nebraska-Wyoming state line. It was erected by the State of Nebraska to commemorate the Oregon Trail, but "Nebraska Wyoming Monument" was engraved on the granite.

4. The Oregon Trail Memorial Association marker and plaque in Lingle was one of two electrically lit markers. The other electrically lit marker was at the train depot in Torrington.

4.

electricity even though many thought it was not economically practical to build and maintain lines to isolated farms and ranches.

Wyrulec Company in Lingle was the first cooperative formed in Wyoming to bring electricity to the rural people. It started in October of 1937 to supply power to 101 member/consumers in Goshen County and the surrounding area.

In 1985, there were fourteen rural electric systems in Wyoming. Because of the rural electrification program, nearly everyone in rural America can receive electric power.

LOCATION: At the rest area about 1.1 miles east of Lingle, Wyoming, on the north side of U.S. Hwy 26.

STUART CAMPSITE SIGN-16

TITLE: Stuart Campsite
LEGEND: East of Torrington, near the Wyoming/Nebraska state line, is the camp site of Robert Stuart and his party of Astorians. They were the men who laid out and first traveled the route from the West Coast to St. Louis, which later became known as the Oregon Trail. Leaving Astoria, John Jacob Astor's fur trading post at the mouth of the Columbia River, the Astorians got as far as present-day Torrington by December, 1812. According to Stuart's diary, the party constructed a small shack and spent the rest of the winter on the bank of the North Platte River.

Wyoming Recreation Commission
LOCATION: About 4.4 miles east of Torrington, Wyoming, on the north side of U.S. Hwy 26.

See Astorian Overland Expedition Informative Sign (Campbell County #1) and Astorian Incident Sign (Sublette County #1).

Robert Stuart led an Astorian expedition eastward from the Pacific Coast in 1812. His party entered Wyoming through Teton Pass, traveling more southerly than Wilson Price Hunt's earlier expedition in 1811. Stuart's travels led him to cross the Continental Divide in the South Pass area, and he is generally credited with the discovery of this pass. See Astorian Overland Expedition Informative Sign (Campbell County #1) and Astorian Incident Sign (Sublette County #1) for more information about the Astorian expeditions.

The Stuart expedition tried to winter at Bessemer Bend just west of Casper, Wyoming. See First White Man's Cabin Informative Sign (Natrona County #3) and Plaque #4 of the Bessemer Bend BLM Interpretive Site (Natrona County #33). In fear of Indian attack, the party moved on after a two-week stay and wintered at this site east of Torrington, Wyoming.

CATTLE TRAIL MONUMENT-17

Top Plaque
TITLE: None
LEGEND: 1876-1897   In remembrance of the hardy pioneer stockmen and cowboys, who drove their Texas herds across this spot into central and northern Wyoming.

Dedicated by the Historical Landmark Commission of Wyoming July 1941

Lower Plaque
TITLE: Texas Trail
LEGEND: Citizens of La Grange Community and Wyoming Stockgrower's Association.

LOCATION: Opposite the Community Church in LaGrange, Wyoming.

Five markers have been erected in Wyoming (in Laramie, Goshen, Niobrara, and Crook Counties) honoring those pioneers who worked on and about the Texas Trail. See Texas Trail Monument (Crook County #8) for more information.

TEXAS TRAIL MONUMENT-18

Granite
TITLE: Old Texas Trail
LEGEND: Over this trail, from distant Texas, passed the greatest migration of men and cattle in the history of America 1866-1897.

Bronze plaque #1
TITLE: None
LEGEND: In memory of the pioneer cattlemen who passed this way on the Old Texas Trail 1866 to 1897. This plaque was placed by the Historical Landmarks Commission of Wyoming 1948.

Bronze plaque #2
TITLE: None
LEGEND: Sponsored by Lion's Clubs of Lingle and Torrington, Wyoming, Stockgrower's Association, Family of John B. Kendrick, Family of Colonel C. F. Coffee, Warren Livestock Company, Family of John Burns and Citizens of Goshen County.

LOCATION: At the rest area about 1.1 miles east of Lingle, Wyoming, on the north side of U.S. Hwy 26.

Five markers have been erected in Wyoming (in Laramie, Goshen, and Crook Counties) honoring the pioneers who worked on or about the Texas Trail. See Texas Trail Monument (Crook County #8) for more information.

THOROUGHBRED HORSE MONUMENT-19

TITLE: The greatest ride in history
LEGEND: In memory of the thoroughbred horse ridden by John "Portugee" Phillips from Fort Phil Kearny Wyoming to Fort Laramie Wyoming December 24 and 25, 1866. When he sought aid for the garrison at Fort Phil Kearny, which was surrounded by Indians, after the battle with Lieutenant Colonel William F. Fetterman, resulting in the death of Lieutenant Colonel Fetterman and 80 men. The horse died from exhaustion soon after arriving at Fort Laramie, having gone 236 miles in two days, through a blizzard with the temperature below zero.

Placed by the Historical Landmark Commission of Wyoming July 1951

LOCATION: On the Fort Laramie Road about 0.2 miles from the entrance to Fort Laramie National Historic Site.

This marker was challenged by historical critics in the 1950s. The Historical Landmark Commission of Wyoming had grown from infancy in the 1920s to a leading role in historical marking in the 1940s and 1950s. As times changed, critics challenged the Commission's work. Superintendent David L. Hieb of Fort Laramie National Monument sharply criticized the Commission for "erroneous" statements and "exaggerated" language in reference to Phillips's ride. Perhaps as a result of criticism and challenges like this, the responsibilities of the Commission were reassigned in 1959.

FORT LARAMIE MONUMENT-20

TITLE: Fort Laramie
LEGEND: A military post on the Oregon Trail
          June 16, 1849—March 2, 1890.
This monument is erected by the State of Wyoming and a few interested residents 1913
LOCATION: Northeast of the sutler's store at Fort Laramie National Historic Site.

Although the marker legend indicates that it was erected in 1913, the dedication did not take place until June 17, 1915. The State of Wyoming furnished the engraved tablet; Mr. John Hunton and Mr. Joseph Wilde donated the concrete obelisk. Hunton had served as post sutler at Fort Laramie from 1888 to 1890. When the fort was auctioned in 1890, both Hunton and Wilde successfully bid for parcels of the property, evidently envisioning the deterioration of the fort structures and the need for a permanent monument to mark the fort.

PONY EXPRESS MARKER-20.1

Top plaque

TITLE: The Pony Express

LEGEND: 1860-1861   1960-1961

From April, 1860, to October, 1861, Fort Laramie was a major post on the Pony Express route between St. Joseph, Missouri and Sacramento, California.

U.S. Department of the Interior, National Park Service.

National Pony Express Centennial Association

Dwight D. Eisenhower-Chairman   Waddel F. Smith-President

Bottom plaque

TITLE: The Pony Express

LEGEND: Russell Majors Waddell
   Founders Owners Operators

120 celebrated riders rode 650,000 miles with only one rider killed by Indians, one schedule not completed and one mail lost.

National Pony Express Centennial Assn.

Dwight D. Eisenhower-Chairman   Waddell F. Smith-President
Conrad L. Wirth-Director at Large   Lola M. Homsher-Vice Pres.

LOCATION: On the concrete obelisk just northeast of the sutler's store at Fort Laramie National Historic Site.

OREGON TRAIL MARKER-21

TITLE: Oregon Trail

LEGEND: Marked by the State of Nebraska 1913
   Nebraska Wyoming Monument
   N 57° 40'
   W 2086 Ft

LOCATION: Between the Nebraska towns of Henry and Lyman on west side of Hwy L-79C where the Oregon Trail crosses the road.

This monument, about one-half mile east of the Wyoming-Nebraska border, is not actually in Wyoming. However, because it is listed as a Nebraska Wyoming Monument, it is included in this compilation. The marker was noted on a survey of Nebraska historical markers done by Robert Harvey and A. E. Sheldon during the years 1917 to 1923.

IOWA CENTER SCHOOL MARKER-22

TITLE: The Iowa Center School

LEGEND: It began as a one room schoolhouse in 1910. Officially part of district #4 in 1913, consolidation took place in 1920 by moving several school buildings together, just east of here, at the bottom of the hill. The pupils in the 100-square-mile district were bussed to school in farm trucks converted into busses, or by horses and wagon. Enrollment reached its peak in 1925-26 with 98 students. The patrons passed a $12,000 bond issue in 1928 which resulted in the erection of a two story frame structure. This included an auditorium with a regulation basketball court and a stage. The new school burned to the ground in 1929, so the first commencement for the five graduates was held at the Flats Church. The community had a new school built for the 1929 fall term, with an added fire escape.

The elected school board of trustees did an admirable job of providing top-rate education. They kept the school afloat through the depression, health epidemics, and ferocious wind and snow storms. The school was the meeting place for every conceivable type of community activity, some of educational value, church services, and many for pure entertainment.

Iowa Center had 51 graduates from 1929 to its last two in 1944. Due to decreased enrollment, the school could offer only grade school. In 1960 it consolidated with Chugwater, and the students were bussed to town. The land was sold and the school was dismantled. The fifty

year history of the largest rural school in Goshen County had come to an end...

This marker is a joint effort of the descendents of those hardy homesteaders who braved the elements to make this prarie the prosperous farming community it is today. We dedicate it to those who provided this school-centered home which lives in our hearts no matter how far we may roam.

A special thanks to Ed Cotton for donating this property.

LOCATION: North side of State Route 313 about 17 miles west of the junction of U.S. Hwy 85 and State Route 313. About 4 miles east of the Goshen-Platte County line.

BURGE POST OFFICE-23

TITLE: Burge Post Office

LEGEND: Site of Burge Post Office 1913-1928
   Ethel Burge Sheppard—Postmistress

LOCATION: On the east side of State Route 159 about 22 miles north of Torrington, Wyoming.

Several young women came to this area and filed on homesteads in 1913. Ethel Burge (some knew her as Betty Burge) was a young single woman who had moved to Wyoming from Nebraska. She filed on the land across the fence at this marker, built a small building, and began the Burge Post Office in 1913. Prior to this, mail was carried by passers-by on their way to Van Tassell, Wyoming. After the Burge Post Office opened, the mail was handled in a canvas sack and hauled to Van Tassell by wagon. It wasn't until 1917 or 1918 that a regular mail route was established through this ranching area.

Across the road from this sign a Mr. Burdick homesteaded, but was financially unable to keep the land. He relinquished it to Ross Sheppard, a young bachelor who, before long, married Ethel Burge. She moved over to Sheppard's homestead and soon quit operating the Burge Post Office. The post office was moved about one-half mile south, where Hugh Best operated it, along with the Best Store & Cream Station. When Best went out of business, the Sheppards took over the post office and operated it on the homestead were they lived until sometime before 1940 when they moved back to Nebraska.

The two original post office buildings are now clean and whitely painted outbuildings on the original Burdick homestead, which is now owned by Velda Childers.

The marker was placed by Floyd Edwards of Dwight, Nebraska, the nephew of Ethel (Betty) Burge.

OLDEST HORSE MONUMENT-24

TITLE: Babe
   "Little Sweetheart of the Prairie"
   April 1906-June 14, 1958

LEGEND: This monument was erected in memory of "Little Babe"
—The World's Oldest Horse—

Black and white shetland—Height 37 in, weight 330 lbs. She was famous the world over for her unusual age of 52 years and was extremely intelligent. She was active, good eyesight, good hearing until the time of her death. Her fame for her age had spread across the nation. When she became 50 years old, tourists traveling through Wyoming would make special efforts to see the spotted black and white pony.

—Babe was the pet of the community—
Owned by Velda and Wayne Childers

LOCATION: Follow State Route 159 about 25 miles north of Torrington, Wyoming, then travel about 0.5 mile west to the original homestead of Wayne and Velda Childers. Private land; permission requested to visit the monument.

Babe was not always the lovely darling pony portrayed by the legend above. In April of 1936, Babe was a starving pony with bleeding hooves and gashes in the skin on her sides. Wayne and Velda Childers, sympathetic to the animal's needs, asked to buy the mean pony from a Mr. Stickney in Edgemont, SD. Velda nursed the pony along for one year, until Babe became well. The legend above tells the rest of the story.

FORT LARAMIE NATIONAL HISTORIC SITE PLAQUES-25

Plaque #1
TITLE: Sawmill
LEGEND: Through a succession of accidental fires, Fort Laramie's sawmills gained a reputation of being ill-fated. The lime-grout building erected upon this site in 1887 was the last of several such structures that sheltered steam engines used for sawing wood and pumping water.

Plaque #2
TITLE: Site of Cheyenne-Deadwood Stage Station
LEGEND: Cheyenne 93 Miles (arrow pointing to the right)
213 Miles (arrow pointing to the left) Deadwood

Plaque #3
TITLE: The Rustic Hotel
LEGEND: The Rustic Hotel opened in 1876. During that year it probably provided the best accommodations for travelers between Cheyenne and the Black Hills. It also served as a station for the Cheyenne-Black Hills State and Express Line.

By 1883, when this photograph was taken one lady traveler found "horrid little bugs" in the sheets. Three years later, the stage station corrals were polluting the fort's water supply and had to be removed.

ABOVE: Primitive kitchen dugout behind hotel. Building in background is Post Hospital.

Plaque #4
TITLE: The Post Hospital
LEGEND: These walls are all that remain of a twelve-bed hospital built on this in 1873-1874. The 1888 photograph shows the hospital in better days, with spacious verandas, flower gardens and picket-fenced yard. Posing in the garden is Post Surgeon Brechemin and enlisted men of the Medical Department. The site selected for the hospital had been used as a post cemetery prior to 1867. Six burials found within the lines of construction were first moved to a nearby cemetery, and finally to Fort McPherson National Cemetery in Nebraska.

Plaque #5
TITLE: Noncommissioned Officers Quarters
LEGEND: A six-unit apartment, built on this site in 1884, was the best housing available for married enlisted men until the abandonment of the post in 1890. Pictured in 1885, it usually housed ranking NCOs such as Chief Post Musician, Post Quartermaster Sergeant or Regimental Quartermaster Serveant.

Post Ordnance Sergeant Schnyder (RIGHT) and his family lived in the next-to-last apartment during the final two years of his 35-year Fort Laramie residency.

Plaque #6
TITLE: Site of Workshops, Storehouses and Stables
LEGEND: Extending from here to the river was a succession of storehouses and workshops that supplied goods and services to the army. As much as 500,000 pounds of grain were stored here in addition to coal, oil, paint, hay, wood and other quartermaster supplies.

Since soldiers were seldom skilled workers, as many as 100 civilians were hired in Denver, Omaha and Cheyenne to serve as wheelwrights, blacksmiths, carpenters, saddlers and laborers. These men received rations and shelter in addition to $30 to $100 a month.

To the left once stood stables, a constant source of aggravation to the shovel-wielding soldier.

Plaque #7
TITLE: Cavalry Barracks
LEGEND: The building before you is the only surviving enlisted men's barracks at Fort Laramie. The building proper was completed in late 1874 and was designed to provide quarters and other needed support facilities for two companies of soldiers. The veranda, although originally planned, was not added until 1883. As constructed the entire second floor was made up of only two equal, large rooms. These were the company dormitory bays or squad rooms where the enlisted soldiers lived. Each could house about sixty soldiers or one company. On the first floor below each squad room, the building was divided into a kitchen, messroom, cook's room, storage room, wash room, library, armory and orderly room for the N.C.O.'s and non-commissioned officers room.

Plaque #8
TITLE: The Sutler's House
LEGEND: The Victorian-style cottage, built in 1863 and shown in this 1868 photograph, must have been a strange sight on the untamed Northern Plains.

Sometime between 1875 and 1882, the cottage was replaced by a much larger lime-grout structure, used by the Sutler or his agents until the abandonment of the post in 1890.

RIGHT: Families of Post Trader John London and Captain Louis Brechemin. This 1886 photograph reflects the serenity of Fort Laramie's declining years.

Plaque #9
TITLE: Commissary Storehouse
LEGEND: This building was completed in 1884. It was built as a commissary storage facility. As such it would have been primarily divided into two large storerooms: one for meat and one for flour, rice, and beans. Three or four smaller rooms would have been used as offices, an "issue room" and a storage room for canned goods. This building also had a partial cellar with a trap door for use with a hand-operated elevator. Rations and other official Army food items were issued from this building. A commissary officer and sergeant ran the operation.

Plaque #10
TITLE: The Post Bakeries
LEGEND: Four different bakeries operated successively at Fort Laramie. The remains of two bakeries stand before you. The nearer, built in 1876, was used until 1884, when it was converted into a school. A bakery built upon the far site operated from 1884 until 1890. Army bakers produced one eighteen-ounce loaf daily for each man at the fort. With a garrison numbering as many as 700 men, imagine the production that resulted!

Plaque #11
TITLE: Site of Army Bridge
LEGEND: The Laramie River was unpredictable and unchecked by dams. High water during the spring of the year often damaged or washed away existing bridges; therefore, from 1853 to post abandonment in 1890 the river was spanned by several successive bridges on or near this site. The first was constructed by a private firm

which charged tolls to both soldiers and emigrants. In subsequent years they were free to all users. The bridges were well-traveled since a variety of living quarters and a hotel had sprung up on the opposite bank. Bridge sizes varied. They were 14 to 16 feet wide and up to 236 feet long.

Plaque #12
TITLE: Post Laundress

Plaque #13
TITLE: Guardhouse 1850-1868
LEGEND: The remains of the first guardhouse constructed in 1850, at Fort Laramie were discovered by workmen in 1960 during restoration of the "new" guardhouse. This site is a good example of the structural changes that occurred during the forts forty-one year military history. Old buildings were torn down and new ones erected, sometimes directly over old remains. The tiny cells below were only five feet in height and length and were usually reserved for "mill birds" or repeat offenders. Solitary confinement for two weeks on a daily ration of bread and water was not an unusual punishment. This original guardhouse was torn down in 1868.

Plaque #13.1
TITLE: The "New" Guardhouse and Adjacent Barracks
LEGEND: The "new" guardhouse, built in 1876 and shown in this 1887 view, was the last and most comfortable of three such structures at Fort Laramie. It was constructed upon the ruins of the original guardhouse, built in 1849-1850. The "new" guardhouse contained spacious guard quarters and prison rooms, and relatively few prisoners. In 1885, for example, inmates averaged less than three out of every hundred soldiers on the post. Also appearing in the photograph is the two-company, 1866 barracks on the right—an adobe structure with a wooden porch—and the three-company frame barracks on the left, erected in 1868. Foundation ruins are all that remain of these buildings.

Plaque #14
TITLE: General Sink (Latrine)
LEGEND: In the 1880's the Surgeon General determined that the privy vault—"That most objectionable and dangerous nuisance"—was a threat to the soldier's health. His concern had been prompted by the accumulated reports from disgusted post surgeons including several from Fort Laramie. Post surgeon Hartsuff, for instance, had recommended in 1874 that sinks be made bearable at least, so that "The calls of nature shall not go unheeded nor be hurriedly performed." This latrine, constructed in 1886, was hailed as a great improvement. Its contents were flushed through pipes to the river which was regarded as adequate disposal in those days. Only the foundation remains of this lime-grout structure.

Plaque #15
TITLE: Parade Ground
LEGEND: The parade ground was the center around which a variety of utilitarian buildings were constructed between 1849 and 1885.

Though intended as a center of activities for the post with its parades and drills, Fort Laramie's parade ground was not in constant use. Soldiers were kept busy with a broad array of duties related to the upkeep of the post and security of the region.

The parade ground saw two types of formations. Guard mount, or changing of the guard, occurred daily at 9:00 a.m. A full dress parade was held once a week on Sunday.

Plaque #16
TITLE: Administration Building
LEGEND: The large structure built on the site in 1885—pictured shortly after completion—was put to many uses. The section on the far right was used as a schoolroom for officers' children. The central portion housed the Headquarters offices. The left part contained a large auditorium often used for theater productions.

Below: Guard Mount in front of Administration Building around 1889.

Plaque #16.1
TITLE: Captain's Quarters
LEGEND: Originally intended as housing for the commanding officer, this building was divided into a duplex, when the C.O. chose to remain in another new dwelling. As such, the quarters was completed in 1870 at which time high-ranking officers and their families took up residency.

Lumber for the quarters was hauled from Laramie Peak and Denver. Adobe brick was made on site on sunny days. Often during twenty years of military use, the structure required whitewashing and substantial repairs.

After military tenure, the quarters was occupied by a local family and later returned to federal hands. Partial reconstruction and repairs began in 1956.

Plaque #17
TITLE: Fort John (Fort Laramie), 1841
LEGEND: You are standing on the approximate location of Fort John built in 1841 by the American Fur Company at a cost of $10,000. Constructed of sun-dried "adobe" bricks, it was 128 feet by 168 feet. The post had walls which were 12 to 15 feet high and contained storehouses, shops, stables and quarters for the employees of the American Fur Company.

In June of 1849, the United States Army purchased Fort John for $4,000. Fort John served the army as temporary barracks, storehouses, and (even) as a hospital throughout the decade of the 1850's. By the late 1850's the walls were crumbling. In 1862 the army razed it to the ground to make room for new officers quarters.

Plaque #17.1
TITLE: Fort Laramie and The Westward Movement
LEGEND: In addition to being an important fur trading post and later, a strategic military installation, Fort Laramie was the most significant outpost of civilization on the Oregon Trail.

The first (true) covered wagon party embarked from what is now Kansas City, Missouri in 1841. Between 1841 and 1867 an estimated 350,000 emigrants crossed the continent on their way to Oregon, California and the Salt Lake Valley.

Fort Laramie was a place to replenish supplies, repair wagons, mail letters (home) and acquire fresh animals for the trail ahead. Here many abandoned their cumbersome wagons and continued the journey with pack mules or on foot. Others lightened their loads, keeping only bare essentials.

As you look across the river you will notice a large, flat, open area. This was a choice campsite for weary travelers.

Imagine, (as far as you can see) covered wagons, cattle and horses grazing and the activities of the evening camp—men unyoking oxen and discussing the trail ahead, women and children building fires and making preparation for the evening meal.

Construction of the first trans-continental railroad in 1867 diminished animal powered overland travel along the trail and led to its eventual abandonment.

Plaque #17.2
TITLE: Fort Laramie and The Fur Trade
LEGEND: In the early 1800's the wealth of the wilderness was measured in the furs of wild animals, and the beaver was the most important. During that period a new breed of western explorer appeared upon the scene, the mountain man. Essentially a trapper of beaver, he was a staunch individualist and romantic adventurer who roamed the mountains and explored the rivers.

The river below, once abundant with beaver was named for one such trapper-explorer, a French-Canadian, Jacques La Ramee (Laramie). His arrow-pierced body was found in the spring of 1821 near the mouth of the river that bears his name.

In the 1830's silk replaced beaver in fashionable hat styles. This combined with the increasing scarcity of beaver, signaled the end of the trapping era and the mountain's rendezvous, (where trappers and traders met to exchange furs for goods). A flourishing trade in buffalo hides and robes soon took its place and the need for permanent trading posts to store the bulky hides became apparent. Thousands of buffalo hides were shipped east from Fort Laramie, in the 1840's.

In 1834, during the decline of the beaver trade, Robert Campbell and William Sublette established the first Fort Laramie, christened Fort William. The small fort constructed of cottonwood logs remained in existence for eight years. Fort William was then replaced by Fort John (1841). Like its predecessor it was commonly known as Fort Laramie.

Plaque #18
TITLE: Officers' Quarters
LEGEND: Here stood a frame duplex built in 1858.

Plaque #19
TITLE: Ice Houses
LEGEND: During the winter months ice blocks were cut from the Laramie and Platte Rivers and hauled to ice houses at this and other sites. Thick walled and partially underground, the frame or sod structures could each store as much as 150 tons of ice. Ice distribution began with the onset of warm weather and, if carefully rationed, ice could last until September.

Officers, enlisted men and laundresses, as well as the hospital and butchershops, were among the recipients. The post commander determined who could receive ice and in what order and amount. Immediately after reveille, often on alternating days, those entitled could come to the ice houses to receive their shares.

At left is the headquarters circular of April 20, 1876, announcing the first of ice and determining a generous daily allotment.

Plaque #20
TITLE: C.O.'s Chicken Coop (Built in 1881)
LEGEND: High ranking officers commonly kept chickens for their own use. The consumption of chickens and eggs provided a welcome change from meals of wild game and tough army beef. Individual soldiers and cooks utilizing company funds could purchase chickens and eggs from civilians. However, such items were a luxury which seldom appeared on the enlisted man's table.

Plaque #21
TITLE: Refinement at Fort Laramie
LEGEND: Fort Laramie began as a dusty, drab frontier outpost as pictured above in the 1868 photograph. However, by the 1880's, the Army had embarked upon a major cleanup and improvement campaign. The delightful results are evident in the 1887 view—trees and grass, gaslights, boardwalks, picket fences and vine-covered verandas, modern, comfortable quarters. . .even birdbaths!

Plaque #22
TITLE: Officers Quarters
LEGEND: This 1885 photograph shows the buildings constructed on this site in 1881. Previous adobe structures, built in 1855, were left standing as rear wings. On the far left was the Commanding Officer's residence. Between 1881 and 1890 it was successively occupied by the families of Colonels Merritt, Gibbon, and Merriam and the only one equipped with inside plumbing, with a full bathroom upstairs and water pipes into the kitchen. The other two buildings were customarily occupied by Lieutenants or Captains and their families.

Right: Officers Quarters, 1887, looking southwest from the flagpole.

Plaque #23
TITLE: Old Bedlam
LEGEND: This graceful old structure, built in 1849, is the oldest standing building in Wyoming. It was nicknamed "Old Bedlam" because of boisterous sounds supposedly heard while it was occupied by bachelor officers.

Shown in an 1889 photograph, "Old Bedlam" is generally regarded as a Bachelor Officers Quarters. However, the left half was used as Post Headquarters and Commanders Apartment in the 1860's, and at various times, the building was occupied by married officers.

Plaque #23.5
TITLE: John (Portugee) Phillips
LEGEND: Here on December 25, 1866 John (Portugee) Phillips finished his 236 mile ride to obtain troops for the relief of Fort Phil Kearny after the Fetterman Massacre.

Dedicated by the Historical Landmark Commission of Wyoming 1940

Plaque #25
TITLE: Magazine (Built in 1849)
LEGEND: Restored here to the 1850-1862 period, the magazine is among the oldest surviving structures at Fort Laramie. It was during this early period that George Balch, 1st Lieutenant Ordnance Corps, sent the following report to the Assistant Adjutant General:

"I find all the ordnance property with the exception of the field guns and their cartridges stored in the magazine arranged with much order and preserved with great care. The different kinds of ammunition piled together in such positions as to be easily reached, and the artillery implements and equipments, the small arms and their equipments properly disposed of on shelves and in boxes."

Plaque #27
TITLE: Infantry Barracks
LEGEND: In answer to the perpetual need for housing, construction of an enlisted men's barracks commenced at the opposite end of these foundation ruins. The barracks were extended in this direction as more men were assigned. Kitchens, mess halls, laundress' quarters and latrines were built behind (to your left).

Home to about 150 men, the two-story barracks were sparsely furnished. Bunks, made of wood by the quartermaster, were two tiers high with each tier accommodating two men. The Indian wars term "Bunkie," referring to a soldier's closest comrade, derived from this sleeping arrangement.

The two-story barracks were replaced in 1868 by a one-story barracks.

Plaque #28
TITLE: "Officers Row"
LEGEND: This 1889 winter scene shows buildings along the west side of the Parade Ground which housed Fort Laramie's officer complement— hence "Officers Row".

Right to left, the "Burt" House, the "Surgeon's" quarters, two adobe quarters and "Old Bedlam".

The surgeon's eminent position in the social line at Fort Laramie is reflected in this 1888 view (left).

Plaque #29

TITLE: The Sutler's Store

LEGEND: Parts of this building date from the earliest periods at Fort Laramie. The adobe portion on the left, built in 1849, housed the Post Trader's Store.

In 1852, the right section was added and used at various times as the Sutler's office, the Post Office and a game room. The photograph shows an 1877 view.

The rear portion was built in 1883. The Enlisted Men's Bar and a rustic saloon were on the right; The Officers Club on the left housed the Sutler's Store in 1875. (Courtesy University of Wyoming Archives and Western History Dept.)

Plaque #30

TITLE: Fort Laramie Army Bridge

LEGEND: This bridge was constructed in 1875. It is believed to be the oldest existing military bridge west of the Mississippi River.

Once the then-broad and turbulent North Platte River was spanned, the Cheyenne to Deadwood Route was considered the best road to the Black Hills gold fields. The bridge also influenced the establishment of the famous Cheyenne and Black Hills Stage and Express Line. The bridge remained in use until 1958.

Plaque #31

TITLE: Fort Laramie and The Transcontinental Telegraph

LEGEND: The transcontinental telegraph reached Fort Laramie from the east on August 5, 1861. From then until May, 1869, Fort Laramie was a major station on the telegraph line. Soldiers from Fort Laramie protected the line, made repairs, and operated remote repeater stations from Julesburg, Colorado (150 miles to the east) to South Pass, Wyoming (300 miles to the west).

Dedicated August 5, 1990

By the Denver Section of the Institute of Electrical and Electronics Engineers

Plaque #32

TITLE: Electrical Engineering Milestone Transcontinental Telegraph

LEGEND: Between July 4 and October 24, 1861, a telegraph line was constructed by the Western Union Telegraph Co. between St. Joseph, Missouri, and Sacramento, California, thereby completing the first high speed communication link between the Atlantic and Pacific coasts. This service met the critical demand for fast communication between these two areas. This telegraph line operated until May, 1869, when it was replaced by a multi-wire system constructed with the Union Pacific and Central Pacific Railroad Lines.

August 1990

Institute of Electrical and Electronics Engineers

LOCATION: Fort Laramie National Historic Site.

HENRY HILL OCTA MARKER-26

TITLE: Henry Hill

LEGEND: At least three grave markers, each with conflicting data, have marked this grave of Henry Hill. A wood headboard was found here in the 1870s. In 1972 a headstone was found among the stone debris inscribed HENRY HILL June 8 [?] 1852 59 M.

From the date of his death and the numeral 59, presumed to be his age at death, it is believed that this is indeed the grave of Henry Hill, born in Caroline County, Virginia, in 1793. A veteran of the War of 1812, he sold his 399-acre farm in Monroe County, Missouri, in April 1852, to accompany his daughters, Martha and Clemencia, and son Joseph, with their families to California.

From the North Platte ferry area, on June 15, 1852, in-law James Hill wrote: "...about thirty five miles below Fort Larame we was called on to pay the last tribute of respect to old Father Hill." The cause of death was a cholera-like illness. "next morning we buried little black boy Billy."

Henry's daughter, Clemencia, died on Forty-mile Desert in Nevada. Nancy J. Hill, the sister-in-law of his son, Joseph, died July 5, 1852, on the Sublette Cutoff. Her marked grave is located northwest of Kemmerer, Wyoming.

Research by Mrs. Marilyn Hill Craig and the Oregon-California Trails Association

Funding by Mrs. Marilyn Hill Craig
McMinnville, Oregon
(Great-great-granddaughter of Henry Hill)
1987

This a part of your American heritage. Honor it, protect it, preserve it for your children.

LOCATION: Private land along the Oregon.Trail in Goshen County; permission required.

OLD BEDLAM BLM MARKER-27

TITLE: The Journey West Continues

LEGEND: "We proceeded (westward from Fort Laramie) and encamped outside the boundaries of Uncle Sam." So wrote Dr. J. S. Shepard in 1851 as he began the second leg of his journey west. "To leave Fort Laramie was to cast off all ties with civilization. It was an alien land," he noted.

The emigrants' elation at reaching the "civilization" of the Fort after 650 miles of monotonous, difficult overland travel was soon tempered by the realization that even more troublesome trail conditions lay ahead over the final two-thirds of the journey. "Here comes the ascent to the Rocky Mountains," wrote an apprehensive Cornelius Conway at mid-century.

To lighten their loads many travelers cast off thousands of dollars worth of food and equipment. This was especially true of the "49ers" who, in their haste to reach the gold fields, often invested little effort in planning their trip. Joseph Berrien reached Fort Laramie early, May 30, 1849, yet still referred to it as "Camp Sacrifice" because of the large quantities of abandoned gear and foodstuffs he saw nearby.

Between 1849 and 1854 an annual average of some 31,000 overlanders passed through or near the fort on their journey to Oregon, California, or Utah. Most passed on a trail marked by the ruts before you. Wagon travel near the Platte River, just to the north, was difficult due to seasonal high water and progressively more difficult terrain.

LOCATION: Along the Oregon Trail 1.4 miles west and northwest of Fort Laramie National Historic Site.

HOT SPRINGS COUNTY

HOT SPRINGS STATE PARK INFORMATIVE SIGN-1

TITLE: Hot Springs State Park

LEGEND: In the foreground across the river are Rainbow Terraces, formed of mineral deposits from the world's largest mineral hot spring. Algae forms the multicolor of the terraces. The spring flows 18,600,000 gallons every 24 hours, temperature 135 degrees Fahrenheit. The site was a former Indian shrine where Shoshones and Arapahoes bathed and held ceremonials. Washakie, Chief of the Shoshones, led the tribes in signing a treaty which gave the healing waters to the Great White Father in Washington. An Indian pageant annually depicts the gift of these waters. Now a State Park, with buffalo herd, picnic areas, playgrounds, swimming pools, tourist accommodations. No entrance fee.

LOCATION: On the south side of U.S. Hwy 20/789 about 0.5 miles north of Hot Springs State Park headquarters.

DR. THOMAS G. MAGHEE MARKER-2

TITLE: None

LEGEND: Dr. Thomas G. Maghee of U.S. Army visited this Spring Aug. 15, 1875 and filed report of examination in medical record of Camp Brown of which he was Post Surgeon and also Medical officer to Chief Washakie and his Indians.

LOCATION: About 75 yards south of Washakie Bath House Marker (Hot Springs #5) on the Hot Springs State Park Loop Road.

The following information was taken from the obituary column on Maghee in the *Wyoming State Journal,* October 5, 1927.

Thomas Maghee was a well-known pioneer, army surgeon, physician, and citizen of the West. Born in Evansville, Indiana, on July 18, 1842, his roots in a patriotic family led him to serve two and a half years in Company F, Twenty-fourth Indiana Infantry during the Civil War. After the Civil War he studied medicine, graduating in 1873.

Maghee was assigned to a western post as assistant army surgeon, then became an army surgeon at Camp Brown. He participated in Bates Battle on Bad Water Creek in the southern Big Horn Mountains and Copper Mountains.

In 1878, he resigned his army surgeon post and moved to Green River. Two years later he moved his practice to Rawlins, staying until 1905 when he went back to Lander. In 1905, Maghee organized and was appointed superintendent of the Wyoming State Training School, as provided by the Legislature.

A member of the Fremont County Pioneer Association, Maghee died September 29, 1927.

MERRITT'S PASS MARKER-3

TITLE: None

LEGEND: Merritt's Pass, so named when Gen'l. Merritt, Commanding Fifth U. S. Cavalry, passed through these mountains in September of 1877 upon a scouting expedition. This monument is erected in memory of Col. George M. Sliney, W. N. G., who served under Gen'l. Merritt's command on this expedition. Col. Sliney was so impressed by the beauty and fertility of the Owl Creek Valley, as seen from this point, that he then and there determined to return and make his home in the valley. His plan materialized and on October 3, 1883, the Colonel returned and crossed through this pass accompanied by his wife and three daughters. Erected October 3, 1938. In loving memory of a pioneer/soldier father.

  Mrs. Nellie S. Rankin

  Mrs. Myra May Holdridge

LOCATION: On the Blondy Pass Road near the Hot Springs and Fremont County Line. This marker is on the Wind River Indian Reservation; permission to enter must be obtained from the Joint Council of Shoshone and Arapahoe Indians.

The exact location and legend of this marker was not verified, as permission to enter the Wind River Indian Reservation to visit the marker could not be obtained.

Indians used this Owl Creek Mountains pass to travel between the Wind River and Big Horn Basin; the Red Lodge-Fort Washakie Stage Route also crossed the pass in the late nineteenth century.

SMOKY ROW CEMETERY MONUMENT-4

TITLE: 1890   Smoky Row   1900
                  Cemetery

LEGEND: Ollie Koshear   Jack Berry
             Jesse Burson   Ralph Gellerno
             Augernose Jane   Elton Perry
              J. A. McGrey   Unknown woman
                  Unknown man

Erected by Washakie Chapter Daughters of the American Revolution 1962

LOCATION: About 0.3 miles northeast of Star Plunge swimming pool on the Hot Springs State Park Loop Road.

WASHAKIE BATH HOUSE-5

TITLE: None

LEGEND: Site of bath house used by Chief Washakie
  Erected by Washakie Chapter D.A.R. Sept. 28, 1929

LOCATION: About 0.3 miles north of the Star Plunge swimming pool in Hot Springs State Park.

WOODRUFF CABIN SITE MARKER-6

Upper plaque

TITLE: None

LEGEND: First cabin built in Big Horn Basin
  Erected by John Woodruff on Owl Creek in 1873
  Dedicated by the Historical Landmark Commission of Wyoming, July 6, 1940

Lower plaque

TITLE: The Man

LEGEND: Reminiscence. . .concerning a cabin built in the wilderness and its owner, J. D. Woodruff—a Man.

  The Man

  1867-76—Army Scout, Trapper, Prospector, Cabin Builder

  1876-80's—Livestock Trail Pioneer, Drover and Flock Master

  1880's-1920's—Rancher, Miner, Forester, Industrialist and Statehood Builder

  1867-1925—Friend of Indians and Sheepherders, of Chiefs, Governors, Bishops and cowboys

LOCATION: Travel about 8.6 miles north of Thermopolis, Wyoming, on State Route 120. Turn onto State Route 170 and follow for another 8-9 miles. Follow State Route 174 (Anchor Dam Road) west for another 8-9 miles. Marker is on the old Robertson Ranch on the South Fork of Owl Creek about 0.3 miles north of State Route 170.

Born in 1847 in New York, John Woodruff built the first recorded white man's home in the Big Horn Basin at the age of twenty-three. The event was significant, as the Big Horn Basin was the chief hunting grounds of both the Crow and Shoshone tribes. Woodruff undoubtedly was a friend to Chief Washakie and the Shoshones.

Although Woodruff brought sheep to the Fort Washakie area in 1876, it is not known whether the operation made its way to the South Fork of the Owl Creek. He did bring cattle into the Owl Creek country near the end of the 1870s, using his cabin as the headquarters. In 1880 the ranch was

HOT SPRINGS COUNTY

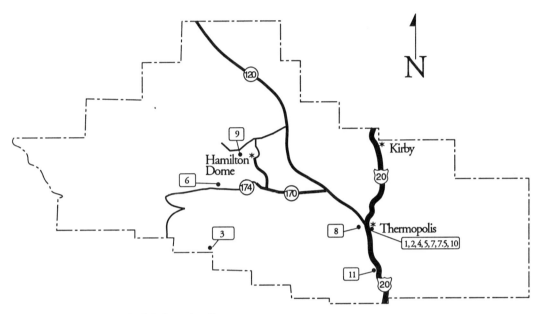

1   Hot Springs State Park Informative Sign
2   Dr. Thomas G. Maghee Marker
3   Merritt's Pass Marker
4   Smoky Row Cemetery Monument
5   Washakie Bath House
6   Woodruff Cabin Site Marker
7   World's Largest Mineral Hot Springs
7.5 Original Hot Mineral Water Marker
8   World's Largest Mineral Hot Springs
9   Legend Rock Petroglyph Site
10   Memorial to Chief Washakie
11   William Barrow Pugh Marker

purchased by Captain R. A. Torrey of Fort Washakie, who branded his cattle with the M—. Woodruff's cabin came to be known as the Embar Ranch, one of the largest ranches in Wyoming.

WORLD'S LARGEST MINERAL HOT SPRINGS-7

TITLE: World's largest mineral hot spring

LEGEND: History: These springs were included in the Shoshone Indian Reservation created by the Treaty of 1868. Later the reservation was also used for the Arapahoes. As information that the springs have "magnitude, health giving properties" became more generally known, Congress was requested to set aside this area for a "National Park or Reservation." In 1896 upon authority from Congress, the Indian Commissioner sent John McLaughlin to negotiate a treaty for the purchase of these springs. He secured an agreement whereby a part of the reservation, approximately 10 miles square was ceded to the United States Government for the sum of $60,000.00. Among the signers of this treaty were the Shoshone Chief Washakie and the Arapahoe Chief Sharp Nose. Chief Washakie said that when game was bountiful in this area, he used to camp near the spring. But by 1890 hunting was so poor in this vicinity that it was seldom visited by the Indian.

Geology: Most of the water in these springs is thought to come underground from the Owl Creek Mountains. Rain falling in the mountains enters porous rock layers, moves slowly downward, and is here forced through crevices in the rocks.

The heat and chemicals in the water are derived from the rock through which it passes and from gases that rise from deeply buried volcanic rocks.

The terraces are made chiefly of lime and gypsum which separate from the cooling water. The colors are due mainly to primitive plants (algae) which grow in the warm water.

Chemistry:

Minerals	Chemical Composition	Parts per million
Silica	$SI\ O_2$	24.0
Aluminum	AL_2O_3	11.6
Iron	FE_2O_3	14.8
Calcium	CAO	624.0
Magnesium	MGO	121.0
Sodium	NA_2O	326.2
Potassium	K_2O	89.6
Sulphur	SO_3	606.8
Chloride	CL	217.6
Carbon Dioxide	CO_2	382.9
Hydrogen sulphide	H_2S	4.5
Total solids		2,396.0

Flow 18,600,000 gallons every 24 hours.
Temperature 135 degrees Fahrenheit.

LOCATION: Just west of Thomas G. Maghee Marker (Hot Springs County #2) on Hot Springs State Park Loop Road.

Congressman Frank Mondell was a leader in the efforts to acquire the mineral springs area from the Indians. There was no interest in Congress or the United States Government for a National Hot Springs (one was already located in Arkansas). On June 7, 1897, Mondell finally convinced Congress to pass the new bill, which stated that of the lands ceded to the United States by the Indians, "one mile square at and about the principal hot spring thereon contained, is hereby ceded, granted, relinquished, and conveyed unto the State of Wyoming." Thus, Big Horn Hot Springs State Reserve became Wyoming's first state park.

ORIGINAL HOT MINERAL WATER MARKER-7.5

TITLE: Thermopolis Hot Mineral Water

LEGEND: 50 mil. Gallons Daily   135 Dgs. Frn.   In springs and wells

it contains 13 of 16 mineral salts which are essential to all life and this water has an alkaline base. Counteracts acids. Removes leidosis the cause of some forty diseases. These soluble mineral solids are similar to those in vegetables and fruit and our system can assimilate them. The two main acid forming salts are left out.

Hydro Therapy (or Hot Bath)

It has been demonstrated in laboratory that Hot Bath kills many germs by producing artificial fever, increases resistance, hastens multiplication white cells of blood. This water contains 8 anticeptics or cleansers. No chance for infection.

Analysis	vans pr. cal.
Silica (SiO2)	727
Oxides Iron (Fe2O3)	105
Oxides Aluminum	222
Carbonate lime	21,584
Sulphate lime	49,402
Carbonate magnesia	15,926
Potassium Sulphates	7437
Sodium Sulphates	5249
Sodium Chlorides	29,920
Carbon dioxide gas (dissolved)	83.6
Oxygen gas (dissolved) pts. pr. mil.	5.7

LOCATION: At Hot Springs County Museum and Cultural Center in Thermopolis, Wyoming.

WORLD'S LARGEST MINERAL HOT SPRINGS-8

TITLE: None

LEGEND: See this natural phenomenon while you are in Thermopolis! Monument Hill, pictured here and visible from this site, overlooks the "Big Spring"—begin your tour of State Park here.

See other springs and beautiful terraces created by the mineral deposits of these healing waters. Learn the history of the Indians' "Gift of the Waters" to the white man. See large buffalo herd. Avail yourself of many park facilities. No entrance fee.

LOCATION: On south side of State Hwy 120 about 0.8 miles from the junction of State Route 120 and U.S. Hwy 20/789.

LEGEND ROCK PETROGLYPH SITE-9

TITLE: Legend Rock Petroglyph Site

LEGEND: The National Register of Historic Places, Wyoming Place #69

LOCATION: About 30 miles northwest of Thermopolis, Wyoming. Inquire locally.

Near Hamilton Dome, three major sandstone outcroppings on the north side of Cottonwood Creek contain a series of petroglyphs (figures carved or etched upon a rock surface) demonstrating the characteristics and beliefs of many prehistoric cultures from 500-1700 A.D. At one area in this site, figures represent early hunting styles of the Late Prehistoric period. Another area is representative of the early Plains Indians. The aesthetic beauty of Legend Rock ranks high among petroglyph sites in the western United States.

MEMORIAL TO CHIEF WASHAKIE-10

TITLE: In memorial to Washakie
Chief of Shoshones

LEGEND: By State Board of Charities & Reform. Gov. John B. Kendrick. Frank L. Houx Sec. of State. Herman B. Gates State Treas. Robert B. Forsythe State Auditor. Edith K. O. Clark Supt. Public Inst. Fred E. Holdrege Superintendent Big Horn Hot Springs State Reserve 1915.

LOCATION: At the Hot Springs County Museum and Cultural Center in Thermopolis, Wyoming.

The mineral hot springs area was known to the Indians for many years.

1.

2.

3.

1. The Thomas Maghee Marker commemorated a Wyoming pioneer physician who worked in the U.S. Army at Camp Brown, practiced privately in Green River and Rawlins, and later became the superintendent of the Wyoming State Training School in Lander.

2. The Smoky Row Cemetery Marker, erected by the Daughters of the American Revolution in 1962, commemorated the early Thermopolis area cemetery.

3. The informative sign in Hot Springs State Park told the history, geology, and chemistry of the hot springs.

Chief Washakie, although a friend of white men and a leader in the treaty giving the area to the whites, had uncertainties in doing so: "If the Great Father thinks that we, his children, had better sell this spring to him, I and my tribe will do what he says and will take whatever he thinks good in payment of them." After the treaty was signed, Washakie said, "I have given you the springs, my heart feels good."

WILLIAM BARROW PUGH MARKER-11

Near side
TITLE: 1889 Reverend 1950
        William Barrow Pugh
LEGEND: Greater love hath no man than this. That a man lay down his life for his friends.
Far side
TITLE: None
LEGEND: Dr. Pugh, Stated Clerk of the General Assembly of the Presbyterian Church in the U.S.A., was killed here on September 14, 1950 as he traveled in the service of his church.

LOCATION: In the Wind River Canyon, about 10 miles south of Thermopolis, Wyoming, on the west side of U.S. Hwy 20/789.

William Barrow Pugh, born January 20, 1889, in Utica, New York, was killed in an automobile accident in Wind River Canyon about fifteen miles south of Thermopolis.

JOHNSON COUNTY

BOZEMAN TRAIL MONUMENT-1

TITLE: Bozeman Trail
LEGEND: Marked by the State of Wyoming
  1865 John Bozeman killed by Indians on Yellowstone 1867
LOCATION: In Buffalo, Wyoming, on the south side of U.S. Hwy 16 in front of Bozeman's Restaurant.

John Bozeman, a speculator from Georgia, came to Montana's Gallatin Valley in 1862 in search of gold. He and John Jacobs explored a trail along the eastern foothills of the Big Horn Mountains south to the Oregon-California Trail along the North Platte River. In 1863 he attempted to lead a wagon train northward from near present-day Evansville, Wyoming, but threatening Sioux Indians turned the party back. He tried again in 1864, the peak year of emigrant traffic along the trail.

While traveling along the Yellowstone River in a trip from the Gallatin Valley to Fort C. F. Smith in March 1867 for supplies, Bozeman was killed by six Indians. He was reburied in 1870 in the town cemetery of Bozeman City, Montana.

Also see Bozeman Trail Marker (Converse County #3.1).

BOZEMAN TRAIL MONUMENT-2

TITLE: Bozeman Trail
LEGEND: Marked by the State of Wyoming 1914
LOCATION: On the west side of the Trabing Road about 0.3 miles north of Crazy Woman Creek. Near the Crazy Woman Battlefield Marker (Johnson County #5).

The State of Wyoming and the Wyoming Oregon Trail Commission were responsible for the ten or eleven monuments erected along the Bozeman Trail from Fort Fetterman to the Wyoming/Montana state line. The Daughters of the American Revolution also played a leading role in placing and dedicating these markers.

See Bozeman Trail Informative Sign (Campbell County #2.1) and Bozeman Trail Marker (Converse County #3.1) for more information on Bozeman Trail history.

BOZEMAN TRAIL MONUMENT-3

TITLE: Bozeman Trail
LEGEND: Marked by the State of Wyoming 1914
LOCATION: West side of old U.S. Hwy 87 about 0.6 miles north of the I-90 overpass. Access via a farm entrance.

See Bozeman Trail Monument (Johnson County #1 and #2).

KILLING OF CHAMPION AND RAE INFORMATIVE SIGN-4

TITLE: Killing of Champion and Rae
LEGEND: About 100 yards west of this point stood the buildings of the Kaycee Ranch, a log cabin and a barn. These buildings were surrounded before daylight on April 9, 1892, by invading cattlemen. Occupying the cabin were Nate Champion and Nick Rae, alleged rustler and two trappers who were captured by the cattlemen, but were unharmed. Rae appeared and was shot down. He was dragged inside the cabin by Champion, who fought off the attackers alone until late afternoon, when the cabin was set afire. He attempted to escape but was shot and killed. Rae died of his wounds during the forenoon.
LOCATION: East side of old U.S. Hwy 87 about 0.1 mile south of the bridge over the Middle Fork of the Powder River.

The events of the Johnson County War have been printed in two very good books. In 1894, Asa Shinn Mercer published *The Banditti of the Plains; or the Cattlemen's Invasion of Wyoming in 1892 (The Crowning Infamy of the Ages)*. In 1967, Helena Huntington Smith published *The War on Powder River—The History of an Insurrection*.

CRAZY WOMAN BATTLE MONUMENT-5

TITLE: None
LEGEND: To the glory of God and in memory of Lieut. N. P. Daniels, U.S.A. Sergt. Terrel, U.S.A. killed on this spot July 20th 1866, by Sioux Indians.
LOCATION: About 0.5 miles east of the intersection of the Smith Brothers Ranch Road and the Trabing Road. Near Bozeman Trail Monument (Johnson County #2).

The following information was taken from the *Buffalo (Wyo.) Bulletin*, August 11, 1966:

In 1866, the Sioux Indians were desperately trying to hold on to their last strong-hold of land in the Powder River. The white man was invading from the south and east while the Crow Indians, the lifetime enemies of the Sioux who were fighting to hold their homeland, were to the west.

In July 1866, a small detachment of soldiers and two civilians left Fort Laramie headed for Fort Phil Kearny. After eight or nine days they reached Fort Reno on the Powder River. Although they picked up several more members there, the detachment was still considered too small to make the dangerous venture into Sioux territory. However, Lieutenant A. H. Wands was determined to proceed, and the party of twenty-six individuals left Fort Reno for Fort Carrington (later known as Fort Phil Kearny) on July 20, 1866.

About sixteen miles from Fort Reno, they found a dead body, a mutilated soldier or courier who had been waylaid earlier by the Indians. At Crazy Woman Creek, another fifteen or twenty miles further, the detachment was attacked by a large band of Sioux Indians. Over half of the soldiers were wounded in the battle that lasted several hours; Lieutenant Napoleon H. Daniels and Sergeant Terrel were killed.

The besieged party was saved by Jim Bridger who led Captain Burroughs and his detachment of two hundred soldiers to Crazy Woman Creek from Fort Carrington. Bridger had noticed signs on buffalo skulls that "there was hell to pay here today at Crazy Woman." If not for Bridger's observation, the entire small detachment would surely have been killed.

FATHER DESMET MONUMENT-6

TITLE: Father DeSmet S.J.
LEGEND: Here 1840. Erected 1940.
  Dedicated by the Historical Landmark Commission of Wyoming July 1940
LOCATION: At a turnout on the east side of old U.S. Hwy 87 about 3 miles north of the Lake DeSmet exit on I-90.

This eighteen foot-high stone marker with a cross overlooks Lake DeSmet north of Buffalo, Wyoming.

Father DeSmet, called "Black Robe" by the Indians, was one of the greatest figures in the history of Indian-white relations in the American Far West. Born in Belgium, he emigrated in 1821 to America where he became a Jesuit. From 1838 to 1870 he played very significant roles with both whites and Indians. Having held the role of peacemaker at the Fort Laramie Council of 1851, DeSmet's services for an 1868 peace mission were requested by General W. S. Harney in a letter to the Commissioner of Indian Affairs:

It is well known that he has almost unbounded influence over them, and his sole object in going among them is to prevent further hostilities and induce them all to meet us at some point in the spring and conclude a permanent peace... You know, I am sure, that he charges nothing for his own individual services—the Priests never do...I wish, my dear General, you would write to him on the subject of his visiting the Indians.

JOHNSON COUNTY

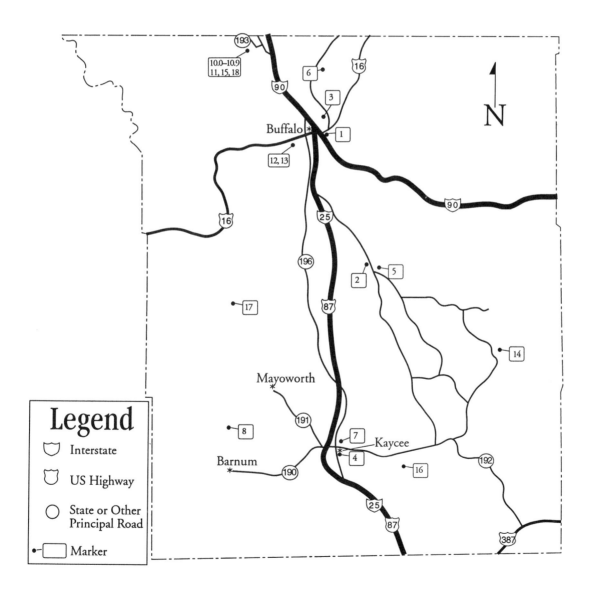

DULL KNIFE BATTLE INFORMATIVE SIGN-7

TITLE: The Dull Knife Battle November 25, 1876.

LEGEND: The final battle of the campaign of 1876 was fought 28 miles west of this point. General McKenzie with 750 cavalry and numerous Indian scouts attacked the encampment of Cheyennes under Chief Dull Knife at dawn.

The camp consisted of about 200 lodges, housing 1400 persons, including about 400 warriors, recently victorious in the defeat of Custer. The Indians fled to the surrounding mountains but fought fiercely all day.

One officer, 6 soldiers were killed, more than 20 wounded. At least 30 Indians were killed, many wounded. The village was destroyed, about 700 horses captured. The Cheyennes, after this disaster, retreated to the nearest agency and surrendered.

LOCATION: About 0.1 miles east of I-90 at the north exit to Kaycee, Wyoming.

From *Wyoming: A Guide to Historic Sites* written by the Wyoming Recreation Commission in 1976:

It was the final phase of Crook's Big Horn Expedition against the Indians, and was part of a plan to strike the Indians in their winter camps. Mackenzie and his forces followed a trail that led toward the Big Horn Mountains and into a sheltered valley that was the location of the Cheyenne camp. At daybreak on November 25, in the beautiful valley of the upper Red Fork, they surprised Dull Knife's tribe, killing between thirty and forty Indians....The Cheyennes were forced to leave their camp as the temperature dropped to thirty-five degrees below zero. Traveling through bad weather with their wounds and lacking adequate supplies, the Cheyennes retreated into the Powder River Basin to look for a friendly Indian camp. Later most of them surrendered at the Red Cloud and Spotted Tail agencies in South Dakota.

DULL KNIFE MONUMENT-8

TITLE: None

LEGEND: Here Nov. 25, 1876 Gen. R. S. Mackenzie with U.S. forces composed of detachments of the 2nd, 3rd, 4th, 5th Cavalry; 4th and 9th Artillery; 9th, 23rd Infantry defeated the Cheyennes under Dull Knife. Lieut. McKinney and six soldiers were killed in battle.

LOCATION: On the Graves Ranch 24.8 miles northwest of Kaycee, Wyoming. Permission necessary to visit marker.

See Dull Knife Battle Informative Sign (Johnson County #7) for more information.

FORT PHIL KEARNY MARKERS 10.0-10.9

LOCATION: Fort Phil Kearny State Historic Site about 1.5 miles west of State Route 193 north of Buffalo, Wyoming.

FORT PHIL KEARNY MARKER-10.0

TITLE: Fort Phil Kearny

LEGEND: Fort Phil Kearny has been designated a Registered National Historic Landmark under the provisions of the Historic Sites Act of August 21, 1935. This site possesses exceptional value in commemorating and illustrating the history of the United States.

U.S. Department of the Interior
National Park Service
1963

FORT PHIL KEARNY MARKER-10.1

TITLE: Fort Phil Kearny
LEGEND: 1866-1868

FORT PHIL KEARNY MARKER-10.2

TITLE: Fort Phil Kearny
       Registered National Historic Landmark

LEGEND: The Land

The land under view, where the Great Plains meet the Rocky Mountains, was once the Red man's land of milk and honey. Then, as now, teeming with wildlife, it was most productive—thus favorite—hunting ground. But it was also a natural route for north-south travel, used from time immemorial by nomadic men and migratory beasts. Lying hundreds of miles beyond the 1860 frontier it was treaty-confirmed Indian Country.

Here came a frontiersman, John Bozeman, pioneering a wagon road which followed buffalo, Indian and trapper trails. His time and energy saving short cut led to the booming mining fields of western Montana. This interloper was followed by others whose habitual frontier callousness easily stifled any scruple over trespass of an Indian passageway. Faint wheel marks soon became a beaten road known as the Bozeman Trail.

High plains and mountain Indians, notably Sioux and Cheyenne, watching this transgression, resented both the physical act and the implied contempt of solemn treaty. They made war. The white transgressors called upon their army for protection. In the end the Indians won a brief respite—partly because of developing railroad far to the south canceled the Bozeman Trail's short cut advantage.

The Fort

On July 13, 1866, Colonel Henry B. Carrington, leading four companies of the 18th Infantry, arrived at this site. Carrington, a competent engineer, immediately put his men to work. Through diligent labor they built, by October of that year, the basic units of what became an outstanding sample of the complete, stockaded, "Indian Wars" military establishment.

From here, as you face across this tablet, extends the ground where Fort Phil Kearny once stood. Replacement posts mark the original corners of the 800' X 600' stockade. Beyond, salient points of contiguous cavalry and quartermaster corrals are marked. At the southwest end an animal watering gap jutted into Little Piney Creek. The Bozeman Trail passed roughly parallel to the northeast side.

Fort Phil Kearny was usually garrisoned by four to six infantry companies, plus one or two companies of cavalry. However, so closely did Sioux and Cheyenne warriors, under the tactician Red Cloud, invest the post that these troops were frequently unable to perform Bozeman Trail convoy duty. Incidents of hostility were the daily rule and several of the most famous engagements of "Indian Wars" relate to this fort.

The military abandoned the fort in August, 1868, and it was burned by a band of Cheyenne.

FORT PHIL KEARNY MARKER-10.3

TITLE: The Bozeman Trail...its approach from the south.

LEGEND: As shown above, so ran, through treaty guaranteed Indian Land, a white man's route of commerce. Like any road it was an environment and ecology disturbing intrusion. Which, in this case, made it a challenge bound to produce a redman's reaction—a resort to arms. Thus the white man's government, supporting it citizens in violation of its own treaty, found justification to found a Fort Phil Kearny.

FORT PHIL KEARNY MARKER-10.4

TITLE: Cemetery site.

LEGEND: Because of a healthy climate plus a short existence, Phil

1.

2.

3.

4.

5.

1. The Crazy Woman Battlefield Marker rested on the barren and lonely prairie along the old route of the Bozeman Trail.

2. The DeSmet Monument in Johnson County overlooked Lake DeSmet. Although distracting, the pipe fence prevented damage to the marker.

3. The Dull Knife Monument commemorated the battle where soldiers attacked a Cheyenne village on a cold November morning.

4. The Fort Reno Monument marked the site of an early fort along the Bozeman Trail. Although the monument was erected through the efforts of the Wyoming Oregon Trail Commission, the site of the fort and the present-day marker was the first acquisition made by the Wyoming Historical Landmark Commission.

5. Erected in 1928, this monument marked the location of one of the first buildings in the state of Wyoming.

Kearny's cemetery might have remained an almost vacant place. But warfare prevented that idea. Here rested eighty-one victims of Fetterman's impetuosity; three heros of the masterful Wagon Box defense; and a few casualties of less celebrated incidents. On June 24, 1896 all bodies not previously exhumed were removed for reinternment in the Custer Battlefield National Cemetery.

FORT PHIL KEARNY MARKER-10.5

TITLE: Pilot Hill Picket Post
LEGEND: Pilot Hill overlooking Piney and Little Piney Creek valleys, the Bozeman Road, the Sullivant Ridge with its wood road was a constantly manned lookout. From this post the sentry signaled to the Fort news of events as they occurred—how the wood detail progressed, what travelers fared the Bozeman Road, where and how a skirmish was developing, who was in desperate need of reinforcements.

FORT PHIL KEARNY MARKER-10.6

TITLE: Site of a sawmill
LEGEND: As explained in No. 1 of this series, wood was the life blood of Fort Phil Kearny. The founding soldiers had carried into this wilderness a sawmill. It was set up without the walls of the stockade as here illustrated. And here, as supplied by logs carried in wagon trains returning from the "Pinery," were sawed the boards from which the Fort's structures were built.

FORT PHIL KEARNY MARKER-10.7

TITLE: Sullivant Ridge
LEGEND: Fort Phil Kearny, built of wood and fueled by wood, required a never ending supply of wood. A supply obtained despite hostile activity by Sioux and Cheyenne. Source was the "Pinery" four miles west against the mountains. The route followed by the crest of Sullivant Ridge—permitting observation of hostiles and preventing opportunity for an ambush.

FORT PHIL KEARNY MARKER-10.8

TITLE: Lodge Trail Ridge
LEGEND: Lodge Trail Ridge divided the drainages of both Piney Creeks with the drainage of Peno (now Prairie Dog) Creek. Up this divide, north beyond Phil Kearny, climbed the Bozeman Trail on its route to Montana. There, December 21, 1866, in violation of explicit orders, Fetterman led his command of eighty-one men. There were no survivors to return.

FORT PHIL KEARNY MARKER-10.9

TITLE: A monument honoring John "Portugee" Phillips.
LEGEND: One of history's great but little celebrated rides was made between midnight December 21 and Christmas night December 25 in the year 1866. From here at Fort Phil Kearny, where annihilation of Fetterman's force had left the garrison in desperate straits, this ride spanned 236 miles to strategic Fort Laramie, the nearest hope for any succor. John "Portugee" Phillips, shrouded in snow and driven by an arctic wind, made that ride. He rode the Commanding Officer's superb thoroughbred and he rode by night and hid by day, or used the bitter yet advantageous storm to hide his movements and blot his tracks. Thus he alluded pursuing Indians who, anticipating a necessary dash for aid, sought to intercept the speeding pair resourceful messenger and courageous steed.

FORT PHIL KEARNY MONUMENT-11

TITLE: None
LEGEND: Site of Fort Phil Kearney
        July 13, 1866—August 1868
Marked by the State of Wyoming

LOCATION: At Fort Phil Kearny State Historic Site near the original entrance to fort. About 100 yards east of the original flag pole site.

In September 1920, the Wyoming-Oregon Trail Commission and the State of Wyoming placed this marker, another at the site of the Wagon Box Fight, and two marking the Bozeman Trail in Johnson County. The spelling of Kearny was obviously an unnoticed error.

FORT MCKINNEY INFORMATIVE SIGN-12

TITLE: Fort McKinney
LEGEND: Fort McKinney—Established at Powder River Crossing of the Bozeman Trail in 1876 as Cantonment Reno was moved to this site in 1878. The fort was built by two companies of the Ninth Infantry, in command of Captain Pollock, for the protection of the Powder River country from the hostile Sioux, Cheyenne, and Arapahoe Indians. The post was named for John McKinney, Lieut. of the Fourth Cavalry, killed in the Dull Knife fight on Red Fork of Powder River November 26, 1876.

It was abandoned in 1894 and the land was deeded to the State of Wyoming for a Soldier's and Sailor's Home.
Wyoming Recreation Commission
LOCATION: On the south side of U.S. Hwy 16 west of Buffalo, Wyoming. About 0.3 miles west of the entrance to the Soldier's and Sailor's Home.

FORT MCKINNEY MONUMENT-13

TITLE: None
LEGEND: Fort McKinney 1877-1894
        Veteran's Home 1903
LOCATION: In front of the flagpole in the small park at the entrance to the Wyoming Soldier's and Sailor's Home west of Buffalo, Wyoming.

FORT RENO MONUMENT-14

TITLE: Fort Reno
LEGEND: U.S. military post established Aug. 28, 1865. Abandoned Aug. 18, 1868.

This monument is erected by the State of Wyoming and the citizens of Johnson County 1914.
LOCATION: About 2 miles north of Sussex, Wyoming, follow dirt road north. Monument is about 8.3 miles from State Route 192 on the west side of the Powder River.

This fort, established by Brigadier General Patrick E. Connor, was originally called Fort Connor. It was renamed Fort Reno in November 1865 in honor of Major Jesse L. Reno who was killed in the Civil War in 1862.

Fort Reno was the first of several Bozeman Trail forts. For three years it provided protection and served as a supply depot. Along with Forts Phil Kearny and C. F. Smith, Fort Reno was abandoned in 1868 under provisions of the Treaty of 1868 between the U.S. Government and the Plains Indians.

In 1913 and 1914, the Wyoming Oregon Trail Commission was involved with erecting this marker and the Bozeman Trail Markers in Johnson County. This marker was originally located near the schoolhouse about two miles north of Sussex, Wyoming, but was moved by the Historical Landmark Commission of Wyoming on September 5, 1927 to the actual site of the fort some ten miles farther north.

The Fort Reno site was the first acquisition of historical property for the State of Wyoming by the Historical Landmark Commission. Mr. and Mrs. Homer L. Payseno of Sussex, Wyoming, deeded 14.21 acres to the Historical Landmark Commission on July 11, 1927.

PHILLIPS MONUMENT-15

South Plaque
TITLE: John (Portugee) Phillips
LEGEND: In honor of John (Portugee) Phillips who Dec. 22-24, 1866, rode 236 miles in sub-zero weather through Indian infested country to Fort Laramie to summon aid for the garrison of Fort Phil Kearny beleaguered by Indians following the Fetterman Massacre.

Erected by the Historical Landmark Commission of Wyoming 1936
East Plaque:
TITLE: None
LEGEND: Fort Phil Kearny 300 yards
West Plaque:
TITLE: None
LEGEND: Fort Phil Kearny 300 yards

LOCATION: About 0.6 miles west of old U.S. Hwy 87 on the route to Fort Phil Kearny State Historic Site.

The Fetterman Fight (also known as the Fetterman Massacre) occurred on December 21, 1866, near Fort Phil Kearny. When Indians attacked a wood train about three miles west of the fort, Colonel Henry B. Carrington ordered a relief party and put Captain William J. Fetterman in command. The relief party of seventy-nine soldiers and two civilians reached the wood train after the attack was broken off. Fetterman chased the Indians to the limits prescribed in his orders. The chase continued over a ridge, where Fetterman was met by an overwhelming force of Sioux Indians led by Chief Red Cloud. The relief party had no survivors.

Colonel Carrington dispatched two riders, Portugee Phillips and William Bailey, to take notice of the Fetterman Massacre to Fort Laramie and to ask for reinforcements. As noted in *The Fetterman Massacre* by Dee Brown, Carrington wrote:

> Do send me reinforcements forthwith. Expedition now with my force is impossible. I risk everything but the post and its stores. I venture as much as any one can, but I have had today a fight unexampled in Indian warfare...Depend upon it that the post will be held so long as a round or a man is left. Promptness is the vital thing...the Indians are desperate; I spare none, and they spare none.

The heroic ride of 236 miles in four days through raging blizzards was an almost incredible feat. Phillips set off the evening of December 21, 1866, and arrived at Fort Laramie Christmas night just before midnight. His horse died soon after, and Phillips suffered for several weeks from exhaustion and frostbite.

The ride of Portugee Phillips was a matter of controversy for the Historical Landmark Commission. In July 1951, the Commission erected a monument near Fort Laramie to the thoroughbred horse Phillips rode (see Goshen County #19). The Commission wrote that Phillips made the ride in two days (they realized that he left December 21 and arrived December 25, but felt he rode for only forty-eight hours of the four-day ordeal). David L. Hieb, the Superintendent of Fort Laramie National Monument in 1952, was troubled by the exaggerations and inaccuracies. A letter written in 1952 from Warren Richardson, Chairman of the Historical Landmark Commission, to Mr. Hieb showed the discord between the two agencies. See "The Wyoming Historical Landmark Commission" in the first section of this book.

PORTUGUESE HOUSES-16

TITLE: None
LEGEND: And he took his journey into a far country. St. Luke XV.

To mark the site of the Portuguese houses the first buildings in the State of Wyoming. Antonio Mateo. 1830. Unsuccessfully besieged for forty days by Indians. Erected in 1928.
LOCATION: About 10.5 miles east of Kaycee, Wyoming. Marker is on private property about 0.5 mile south of State Route 192. Inquire locally.

The following information was taken from the *Buffalo (Wyo.) Bulletin* (August 16, 1951):

This monument marks the spot where the so called Portuguese houses were erected in the fall of 1834. Their architect and builder was a Portuguese fur trader named Antonio Montero, more commonly known as Antonio Mateo. Mateo seemed to know all of the trappers, traders, and Indians in the Powder River country. Not a lot was recorded of Mateo, but James Bridger, James Beckworth, and Captain Benjamin Bonneville apparently had dealings and business with him.

The Portuguese houses were strongly built. The post was of the stockade-type, allowing a very large area to be scanned looking northward from east to west. Jim Bridger stated that one time Mateo's fort withstood a Sioux Indian siege of almost forty days.

Mateo's legend remained at the Portuguese houses; little was recorded about his travels after he left the Powder River country.

STOCK DRIVE MEMORIAL-17

TITLE: Trails from the Past to the Future
LEGEND: None
LOCATION: About 16-17 miles south of U.S. Highway 16 on the hilltop south of Dull Knife Reservoir.

This marker was sponsored in the summer of 1989 by the Johnson County Woolgrowers Association and the U.S. Department of the Interior Bureau of Land Management and was supported by the Wyoming Centennial Commission. It was erected as a memorial to the stock drives of the 1880s.

The following information was taken from *Tales of the Trails: A History and Stories of the Big Horn Mountain Stockdrives* by Sue and Patty Myers:

> The stockdrive cycle included a journey to the mountains in the spring and a return home in the fall. Cool mountain temperatures and abundant grass were felt to be good for the animals and the prairie pastures could lie fallow during the dry summer months, leaving better pasture for winter grazing.

> The Big Horn Mountains have been used for summer grazing since 1883 when D. A. Kingsbury brought sheep into Johnson County. Initially, the movement of sheep and cattle was over open range. Eventually, fences were built leaving roadways along the fencelines for transportation and trail drives. Sheep vastly outnumber cattle on Johnson County trails.

> Stock drives in Johnson County were established early. "In northern Johnson County, two stock drive trails came from the east: one from the Double Crossing near Clearmont/Ucross to Tipperary, and the other from the Red Hills. They joined up near Trabing to head west up Crazy Woman Hill. In southern Johnson County, county roads converge on the Mayoworth Stock Drive near Kaycee."

> Some stock drives took one day and covered only eight miles. Others trailed 120 miles in three weeks. Most stock drives typically began the first part of June. Most days began at 3 a.m. with breakfast snack of coffee and rolls. Usually by 10 a.m. the first rest area would be reached, and a big breakfast was served. Nothing much moved for the next few hours. Trailing would begin again in the late afternoon and carry on until the drive caught up with the camptender and a late supper.

> It has been said that women and children were not generally allowed on the trail. However, most everyone involved in the stock drives has childhood memories of being on the trail. A Basque sheepman was once quoted as saying, "Having one kid on the trail is like having half a herder; having two or more is no herder at all; and with three or more, you might as well stay home."

> Horses and dogs are an important part of a drive. Dogs receive their training from working with other dogs. A dog is invaluable in times of emergency, and a good companion in the lonely life of a herder.

FORT PHIL KEARNY—BOZEMAN TRAIL ASSOCIATION MARKER-18

Upper section
TITLE: Heroic men and women have stood where you now stand
LEGEND: . . .Bravery and courage were their hallmarks.

Bravery and courage are not the possession of men alone for women served here also; both inside the stockade and in the Indian villages. They too shouldered the isolation, grief, loneliness, cold and hardships.

Neither are bravery and courage the possession of white men alone for red men also fought here with bravery and courage.

Bravery and courage have no relationship to whether the cause they serve is "right" or "wrong!"

Wherever, and by whom, bravery and courage are manifested, and in whatever cause they serve, these qualities merit respect and are worthy of honor for themselves alone.

We will do an unforgivable disservice to those, both red and white, who here did their duty if their bravery and courage are not remembered and honored. We will also have failed those who come after us it we do not protect and preserve this ground and provide, as best we can, a means of enabling posterity to KNOW, to APPRECIATE and to FEEL the great events which took place here in the shadow of the Big Horns.

—Charles Weaver Margolf

Lower section

TITLE: In Prayer: Vision of hope

LEGEND: The distant words of memory return to touch upon the battle that was fought here. The memories stir with the thought of that long ago past with the battle cries and the sound of guns of two nations at war.

But the sound of wars have long been silent. The important lessons of learning to accept the fact of existing side by side as two nations has become a way of life.

But today, I choose not to return to the wars of the past. In prayer, I search for the better way in which my people, the Northern Cheyenne, and all Native Americans can accept the life today without losing the spirit of their Indian heritage.

I humble myself before our Creator, the Power of all Creation, and ask a blessing for the good of life to be present today and in the future.

In prayer, I look to the future with hope that the children who have yet to walk upon this land of freedom might also experience the touching of the earth with the same understanding and knowledge we share today.

Finally I gather all the spoken and the many unspoken concerns of the heart. I beg the Sacred Grandfathers to give us their special blessings so that our Creator will give us a new dawn of hope and that the goodness of life will be our constant companion in our pursuit of justice, happiness and freedom for all Americans.

—Bill Tall Bull and Rubie Sooktis

Members of the Sioux, Cheyenne and Arapaho tribes fought the U.S. Army at Fort Phil Kearny.

Fort Phil Kearny/Bozeman Trail Association in cooperation with the Wyoming Archives, Museums, and Historical Department.

LOCATION: Near visitor information center at Fort Phil Kearny State Historical Site north of Buffalo, Wyoming.

This marker was first envisioned by Bill Tall Bull, a history professor at Dull Knife Memorial College. It was dedicated in August 1989 and was the first such memorial honoring the Indian warriors, as well as white men.

LARAMIE COUNTY

BIG BOY LOCOMOTIVE-1

TITLE: None
LEGEND: "Big Boy"—The world's largest steam locomotive
Built in 1941 Big Boy was designed especially for use by the Union Pacific Railroad on its rugged Cheyenne to Ogden, Utah run. The mighty 4004 was one of a series of only 25 locomotives of this type ever built. It was retired from service on December 21, 1956.
Total weight 1,208,750 lbs. Overall length—132' 9 3/8". Fuel capacity—28 Tons. Water capacity—25,000 Gals.
LOCATION: In Holliday Park in Cheyenne, Wyoming.

"Big Boy" was one of a series of only twenty-five of the world's largest steam locomotives. Seven other 4000 Class Locomotives were displayed at other U.S. cities. According to James L. Ehernberger and Francis G. Gschwind, in their book *Sherman Hill*, those locomotives were displayed at: Forney Museum in Denver, Colorado; National Museum of Transport in St. Louis, Missouri; Steamtown U.S.A. in Bellows Falls, Vermont; Los Angeles Fairgrounds in Pamona, California; National Railroad Museum in Green Bay, Wisconsin; Texas State Fairgrounds in Dallas, Texas; and Union Pacific Shopgrounds in Omaha, Nebraska.

DR. RALPH C. GRAMLICH MEMORIAL-1.1

TITLE: In memory of Dr. Ralph C. Gramlich
LEGEND: "Big Boy" the world's largest steam locomotive No. 4004 built in 1941. Designed especially for use by the Union Pacific railroad on its rugged Cheyenne to Ogden, Utah run. Retired from service October 1958. Weight 1,208,750 lbs. Overall length 132 ft. 9-3/4". Fuel capacity 28 tons, water capacity 25,000 gallons, cost of locomotive $265,000.00. 440,545 miles run.

Donors

U.P. Old Timers Club #1	B.P.O. Elks #660
V.F.W. Post #1881 & Auxiliary	Fraternal Order of Eagles #1
Cheyenne Lodge #1 I.O.O.F	
Laramie County Historical Society	Masonic Friends of Dr. Gramlich
Bishop P.A. McGovern Council #801	American Legion Post #6
Retired Railroad Employees Cheyenne Chapter #1	Tri-State Memorial Service

LOCATION: Next to Big Boy Locomotive in Holliday Park in Cheyenne, Wyoming.

ROBERT BURNS MEMORIAL-2

Northeast side
TITLE: Robert Burns
LEGEND: "From scenes like these old Scotia's Grandeaur Springs, that makes her lov'd at home, rever'd abroad. Princes and Lords are but the breath of Kings, 'An honest man's the noblest work of God' ".
Donated by Mary Gilcrest, to the City of Cheyenne, Wyoming, A.D. 1928.
Metal plaque
TITLE: None
LEGEND: William Dubois Architect   W.S. Higman Builder
Trustees for Burns Memorial Marshall S. Reynolds, George E. Brimmer, Daniel W. Gill
Southwest side
TITLE: Robert Burns
LEGEND: Alexis Rudier, Fondeur, Paris
Northwest side
TITLE: None

LEGEND: Henry Snell Camley, R. S. A. sculptor, Edinburgh, Scotland. Born 2nd April 1865. Died 25th October 1928.
LOCATION: Triangular park bounded by Pioneer Avenue, Randall Avenue, and 26th Streets in Cheyenne, Wyoming.

Robert Burns, born in 1759, was a Scottish national poet educated by his father. He wrote "Auld Lang Syne" in 1789. He died of rheumatic fever in 1796.

CAMP CARLIN-3

TITLE: Camp Carlin
LEGEND: Camp Carlin or Cheyenne Depot, 1867-1890, was 2nd largest quartermaster depot in the United States. In Wyoming it supplied Forts Russell, Sanders, Steele, Bridger, Washakie, Fetterman, Laramie, McKinney and Phil Kearny; in Nebraska, Forts Sidney, Omaha Robinson; in Utah, Fort Douglas; in Idaho, Fort Hall; and Meeker Colorado. It supplied annuity goods for Indian tribes. Particularly the Red Cloud and Spotted Tail Agencies.
Site 1/4 mile west. 1/4 mile south.
Erected by the Historical Landmark Commission of Wyoming 1957
LOCATION: North side of Happy Jack Road just west of I-25 in Cheyenne, Wyoming.

Colonel Elias B. Carling chose to site this camp between the new town of Cheyenne and the Army's Fort D. A. Russell. Its official title was the Cheyenne Depot, but became better known as Camp Carling or Camp Carlin.

CAMP WALBACH MONUMENT-4

TITLE: Camp Walbach
LEGEND: U.S. Military Post Sept. 20, 1858 to Apr. 19, 1859.
Marked by the State of Wyoming, the S.A.R. and D.A.R. of Cheyenne, Wyoming 1914
LOCATION: About 4.3 miles northwest of the railroad tracks at Federal, Wyoming. Follow the VL Ranch Road. Private property and permission required.

According to Grace Raymond Hebard in *Marking The Oregon Trail, The Bozeman Road, and Historic Places in Wyoming 1908-1920*, "the placing of a marker on this site was largely due to the suggestion of Hon. Joseph M. Carey and the work of Mrs. J. T. Graham, Mrs. H. B. Patten, Mrs. John F. Carey for the Daughters of the American Revolution and Hon. Maurice Groshon for the Sons of the American Revolution, and a few interested pioneers." The site was dedicated on September 4, 1916.
Camp Walbach (also called Fort Walbach), named for General J. B. Walbach, was placed as "a guard at Cheyenne Pass to protect from Indian depredations." The road was a route for emigrants heading west in search of homes. Roads went from Camp Walbach to Fort Laramie and to Denver; the combination of the two roads being called the Fort Laramie and New Mexico Road.

THE CHEYENNE CLUB-5

TITLE: None
LEGEND: The Cheyenne Club was built on this site in 1882. Most of the members were wealthy cattle barons from the East and Europe. The Club gained world-wide fame. After the blizzard of 1886-1887 the cattle business was ruined, and the Club lost its glamour. The building became the headquarters for the Cheyenne Chamber of Commerce. It was razed in 1936.
LOCATION: Cornerstone in the building at Warren Avenue and 17th Street.

CHEYENNE-FORT LARAMIE-DEADWOOD TRAIL-6

TITLE: None
LEGEND: The Cheyenne-Ft. Laramie-Deadwood Trail started from the

LARAMIE COUNTY

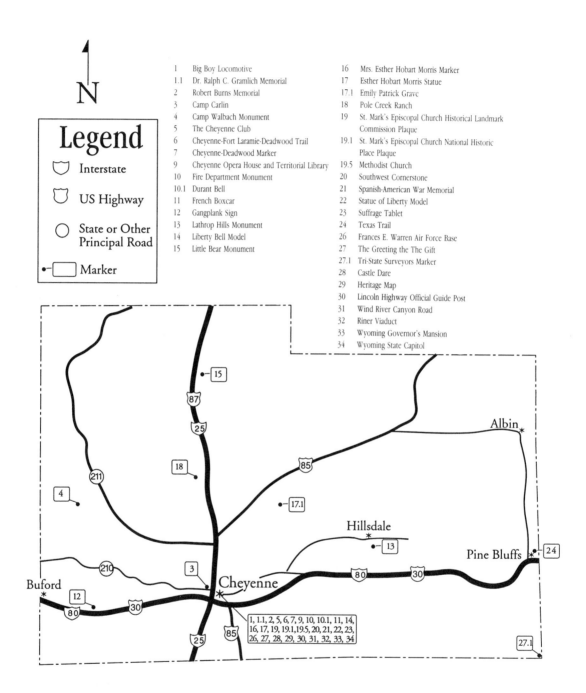

Legend

⬡ Interstate

⬡ US Highway

◯ State or Other Principal Road

•—▢ Marker

1   Big Boy Locomotive
1.1   Dr. Ralph C. Gramlich Memorial
2   Robert Burns Memorial
3   Camp Carlin
4   Camp Walbach Monument
5   The Cheyenne Club
6   Cheyenne-Fort Laramie-Deadwood Trail
7   Cheyenne-Deadwood Marker
9   Cheyenne Opera House and Territorial Library
10   Fire Department Monument
10.1   Durant Bell
11   French Boxcar
12   Gangplank Sign
13   Lathrop Hills Monument
14   Liberty Bell Model
15   Little Bear Monument
16   Mrs. Esther Hobart Morris Marker
17   Esther Hobart Morris Statue
17.1   Emily Patrick Grave
18   Pole Creek Ranch
19   St. Mark's Episcopal Church Historical Landmark Commission Plaque
19.1   St. Mark's Episcopal Church National Historic Place Plaque
19.5   Methodist Church
20   Southwest Cornerstone
21   Spanish-American War Memorial
22   Statue of Liberty Model
23   Suffrage Tablet
24   Texas Trail
26   Frances E. Warren Air Force Base
27   The Greeting the The Gift
27.1   Tri-State Surveyors Marker
28   Castle Dare
29   Heritage Map
30   Lincoln Highway Official Guide Post
31   Wind River Canyon Road
32   Riner Viaduct
33   Wyoming Governor's Mansion
34   Wyoming State Capitol

corner of Capitol Ave. & 16th Street and ran 88 miles north to Ft. Laramie, the most historic fort in the Rocky Mountain west. In 1876 it was extended to Deadwood and the Black Hills gold fields 266 miles from Cheyenne. Indians, trappers, traders, pack trains, cavalry, freighters, cowboys, and stage coaches traveled this way. Road agents and Indians added to the hazards of the road.

Erected by the Historical Landmark Commission of Wyoming 1957
LOCATION: At Capitol Avenue and 22nd Street in Cheyenne, Wyoming.

Three other markers (#7, 15, and 18) in Laramie County commemorate this historic and romantic trail. Two markers in Goshen County (#1 and a Fort Laramie National Historic Site marker), seven markers in Niobrara County (#2, 3, 4, 5, 7, 8, and 11), one in Platte County (#2), and three markers in Weston County (#3.2, 4, and 5) also pertain to the old emigrant, freight, and gold trail.

CHEYENNE-DEADWOOD MARKER-7

TITLE: Fort Laramie Trail
LEGEND: This stone marks that road of romance and adventure traveled by trappers, traders, and troops to Fort Laramie, the most historic spot in the west. 1867-1887.
LOCATION: On the Airport Golf Course at the intersection of Carey Avenue and Kennedy Road in Cheyenne, Wyoming.

CHEYENNE OPERA HOUSE AND TERRITORIAL LIBRARY-9

TITLE: None
LEGEND: The Cheyenne Opera House and Territorial Library was erected on this site in 1882. For twenty years, it was the center of civic, and cultural activity.

In 1902, a fire destroyed the auditorium and stage of the building.

In 1905, the annex was built on the site adjoining the remaining portion of the opera house. The two buildings were razed in 1961.
1963
LOCATION: About 50 feet north of 17th Street on Capitol Avenue in Cheyenne, Wyoming. Located on the side of the old J. C. Penney store.

FIRE DEPARTMENT MONUMENT-10

TITLE: None
LEGEND: Dedicated in perpetuity to those members living and dead of the Alert Hose Company, J. T. Clark Hose Company, I. C. Durant Hose Company, Pioneer Hook and Ladder Company and Phil Sheridan Fire Company constituting the volunteer fire department of Cheyenne.

Instituted in 1868—mustered out in 1909.

Ceremonies held June 22, 1938.
LOCATION: Lost

This plaque was previously located near the City-County Building at 19th Street and Carey Avenue with the Durant Bell. The plaque was lost or taken, but the contents of the plaque are preserved here. The Durant Bell was preserved by Cheyenne resident Ron Harnish and is now the main attraction at the Durant Bell Marker (Laramie County #10.1).

DURANT BELL-10.1

Bell
TITLE: The Jones & Company
Troy Bell Foundry
Troy, N.Y. 1879
LEGEND: None

Plaque at bell site
TITLE: Durant Bell
LEGEND: The Durant Hose Co., and J. T. Clark Co., each purchased huge bells, and boasted the first fire engines in Cheyenne.

Both companies used the fire bells as long as their organizations existed.

The J. T. Clark Bell may be seen at the old Johnson School. Restored 1982

Plaque inside Cheyenne Municipal Building
TITLE: Durant Hose Company
LEGEND: The Durant Hose Company was organized in 1874 and boasted the first fire engine in Cheyenne.

Finally the Durants and J. T. Clarks each purchased huge fire bells which they used as long as their organizations existed. The J. T. Clark fire bell is now located on the Johnson School lawn. The Durant fire bell is located on the lawn of the City Municipal Building.

Mayor Don Erickson May 16, 1983

LOCATION: East courtyard of the City Municipal Building in Cheyenne, Wyoming.

In the 1950s, the American Legion placed the bell, accompanied by a bronze plaque (Laramie County #10), near the City County Building at 19th Street and Carey Avenue. For unexplained reasons the monument was removed; the bell was placed in storage and the plaque was lost. Cheyenne resident Ron Harnish, who worked for the City of Cheyenne, discovered the bell and was instrumental in preserving and displaying it at its present location.

A similar bell, also dating back to 1874, was placed near the old Johnson Junior High School. It had been owned and used by the J. T. Clark Hose Company. It has not been restored or preserved as well as the Durant Bell.

FRENCH BOXCAR-11

TITLE: Merci Boxcar Train
LEGEND: This Boxcar is just one of forty-nine presented to each of the forty-eight states and one to Washington D.C. and Hawaii in 1949.

The Train was an expression of thanks from the citizens of France to the people of the United States for aid rendered during and after World War II. This boxcar was laden with gifts which were distributed throughout the State of Wyoming.

This Boxcar is both a rarity and a remembrance to the Gallant Men and Women who served. The cars were built between 1872 and 1885 and ferried troops, horses, and equipment during both World Wars.

Donated by Republique De France to; The State of Wyoming in care of the Grand Voiture Du Wyoming La Societe Des 40 Hommes Et 8 Chevaux. (40 Hommes—40 Humans, 8 Chevaux—8 Horses)

Voiture Locale
Cheyenne 851   Casper 321   Lander 1437

Contributors to the Restoration of this Artifact
Capital Lumber   Willet's Trucking
Dan-D-Rental   Wyoming Sea Bees (USNR)
Baha Equipment Leasing   F. E. Warren AFB
Voiture Locale 851

LOCATION: In front of the American Legion Hall in Cheyenne at the corner of Lincoln Way and Big Horn Avenue.

GANGPLANK SIGN-12

TITLE: The Gangplank
LEGEND: The granite rocks to the west are more than a billion years old (Pre-Cambrian in age). The sedimentary rocks to the east are some 10 million years old (Late Miocene in age). After the mountains were elevated, some 20,000 feet of rocks were eroded from their crest. Later the younger sedimentary rocks were deposited against the flank of the range.

The time between the formation of the granite to the west and the deposition of the onlapping sediments to the east is measured in terms

1.

2.

3.

4.

1. Little Bear Monument was established by the Wyoming Historical Landmark Commission in 1956. Little Bear Stage Station became a stage station on the Cheyenne-Deadwood Stage Route in 1877.

2. The Greeting and the Gift Marker commemorated Wyoming's participation in the nation's Bicentennial celebration.

3. The Greeting and the Gift Marker, depicting the meeting of an Indian and a mountain man.

4. In 1960 the Laramie County Historical Society erected this sign at Cheyenne's southwest cornerstone which had been set in 1890.

of more than ten hundred million years. You are now standing on the gangplank.

Erected 1962 by Wyoming State Archives and Historical Department and Wyoming State Historical Society

LOCATION: At a turnout on the north side of I-80 about 15.5 miles west of Cheyenne, Wyoming.

General Grenville M. Dodge, chief engineer credited with determining the final route for the Union Pacific Railroad over the Laramie Range, noted the gangplank in 1865. He described a ridge which "led down to the plains without a break" and determined that the natural ridge was most ideal for the Union Pacific.

LATHROP HILLS MONUMENT-13

East face of monument
TITLE: Surveyors Camp
LEGEND: Locating the route of the Union Pacific, the first railroad to the Pacific Ocean.

Lower marker
TITLE: Lathrop Hills, Surveyor for the first transcontinental railroad, killed by Indians.
LEGEND: On June 11, 1867, Lathrop Hills led a party of surveyors up the nearby Lodgepole Creek, staking out the location for the Union Pacific Railroad, the first transcontinental railroad. Hills was riding out in front of the group when he was attacked by Indians and killed. Within minutes his men drove off the Indians and later reported they found 19 arrow wounds in his body. He was 35.

Hills' work lived after him. By November 14, 1867, the track layers had reached Cheyenne and 18 months later a golden spike was driven at Promontory, Utah, completing the first railroad connection between the East and West and opening millions of acres for settlement. The railroad reduced travel time from six months required by wagon train to five days from Omaha to San Francisco.

State of Wyoming Historical Marker
September 1973
Placed by the Hills family

West face of monument
TITLE: None
LEGEND: "General Sherman" granddaddy of all motive power in use on the Union Pacific was this woodburner. Built by Danforth and Cooke of Paterson, New Jersey in 1864-65. It was brought to Omaha by steamboat in June, 1865.

Bottom marker
TITLE: None
LEGEND: Union Pacific Railroad's D D-35 EMD 5,000 H.P. diesel units east bound east of Devil's Slide, Utah.

LOCATION: Just south of the post office in Hillsdale, Wyoming.

LIBERTY BELL MODEL-14

Plaque
TITLE: DEDICATED TO YOU, A FREE CITIZEN IN A FREE LAND
LEGEND: This reproduction of the Liberty Bell was presented to the people of WYOMING by direction of the HONORABLE JOHN W. SNYDER, Secretary of the Treasury, as the inspirational symbol of the United States Savings Bonds Independence Drive from May 15 to July 4, 1950, it was displayed in every part of the state.

The dimensions and tone are identical to those of the original Liberty Bell when it rang out our independence in 1776.

In standing before the symbol, you have the opportunity to dedicate yourself, as did our founding fathers, to the principle of the individual freedom for which our nation stands.

This bell is one of fifty-three cast in France in 1950, and given to the United States Government by:

American Smelting and Refining Company / Miami Copper Company
Anaconda Copper Mining Company / Phelps Dodge Corporation
Kennicott Copper Company / The American Metal Company

Steel Supports by U.S. Steel Corporation's American Bridge Company.
This plaque donated by Revere Copper and Brass Incorporated.

Bell
TITLE: None
LEGEND: Proclaim liberty throughout all the land unto all the inhabitants thereof. By Order of the Assembly of the Province of Pennsylvania for the State House in Philad.A Pass and Stow Prulad A. MDCCLIII

LOCATION: In Cheyenne, Wyoming, at the corner of 24th Street and Carey Avenue on the Capitol Building lawn.

LITTLE BEAR MONUMENT-15

TITLE: None
LEGEND: Cheyenne, Fort Laramie, Deadwood Trail, 1867-1887, started from Camp Carlin and Fort D. A. Russell on the west edge of Cheyenne. This road first ran to Ft. Laramie and in 1876 was extended to Deadwood, Dakota Territory, and the Black Hills gold fields. It also joined the Bozeman Road to Montana. Little Bear stage station, 150 yards east, was opened as a road ranch by Isaac Bard, May 4, 1875. It became a stage station in 1877.

Erected by the Historical Landmark Commission of Wyoming 1956
LOCATION: About 26.7 miles north of Cheyenne, Wyoming, on old U.S. Hwy 87.

Isaac Bard came to Cheyenne in 1867 with a Union Pacific Railroad construction crew. In 1875 he staked a 160-acre homestead on Little Bear Creek. When the Cheyenne and Black Hills Stage and Express Line went into operation in 1876, Bard developed his homestead into a stage station and post office called Little Bear. In 1887 the Cheyenne and Black Hills Stage Line went out of business; Bard's business failed as well.
See Cheyenne-Fort Laramie-Deadwood Trail (Laramie County #6).

MRS. ESTHER HOBART MORRIS MARKER-16

TITLE: Mrs. Esther Hobart Morris
LEGEND: Mother of Woman's Suffrage lived here in 1890. Born August 8, 1814, Spencer, N. Y. Died April 2, 1902 Cheyenne, Wyoming.
Placed by the Historical Landmark Commission of Wyoming 1950
LOCATION: In Cheyenne, Wyoming, at 2114 Warren Avenue.

Esther Hobart Morris was a Wyoming pioneer described as being "heroic in size, masculine in mind," by Grace Raymond Hebard. Hebard and H. G. Nickerson, a Lander citizen and friend of Hebard, developed the story of how Morris, after visiting at a tea party with two candidates for the Legislature, was promised by the winner of the election that a women's suffrage bill would be introduced in the next legislative session.

The story has been refuted, and no evidence today supports the tea party story. T. A. Larson wrote that the verifiable evidence credits William H. Bright, Governor John A. Campbell, and Edward M. Lee for women's suffrage in Wyoming. Lee, the secretary of the territory of Wyoming, had been a leader for women's suffrage while in the Connecticut Legislature. Larson also stated that lessor credit should be given to several other people, including Esther Morris.

ESTHER HOBART MORRIS STATUE-17

South face
TITLE: Esther Hobart Morris
LEGEND: Proponent of the legislative act which in 1869 gave distinction to the Territory of WYOMING as the 1st government in the world to grant WOMEN EQUAL RIGHTS.

North face
TITLE: None
LEGEND: A grateful people honors this stalwart pioneer who also became the 1st woman justice of the peace.

LOCATION: In front of the Capitol Building in Cheyenne, Wyoming.

EMILY PATRICK GRAVE-17.1

Sign over the grave
TITLE: None
LEGEND: Emily Patrick
  Died. Aug. 9. 1867 Age 10

Sign at grave site
TITLE: None
LEGEND: Hither of old strange flotsam drifted
    Born from afar on an age old stream
    Men and women with hopes uplifted
    Stirred and spurred by a splendid dream
    They had their triumphs their gains and losses
    Noons of laughter and nights of care
    Back of the hills are some rough crosses
    A name a date and perchance a prayer
                              Poem from Australia

Bronze monument plaque
TITLE: Emily Patrick
LEGEND: This monument dedicated to the memory of Emily Patrick Died August 9, 1867—Age 10.
  Erected by the VFW Post 1881 & Scout Troop & Post No. 213, Scout Troop No. 102 of Cheyenne, Wyo.—Nov. 11, 1967.

LOCATION: Follow U.S. Hwy 85 northeast from I-25 for about 6 miles. Then follow a dirt road towards Pole Creek Ranch east of U.S. Hwy 85 for about 1.6 miles.

POLE CREEK RANCH-18

TITLE: Pole Creek Ranch
LEGEND: Pole Creek Ranch was the first regular stop of the Cheyenne and Black Hills Stage 18 miles from Cheyenne. A "hotel" was built in 1876.
  Erected by the Historical Landmark Commission of Wyoming 1958
LOCATION: Follow I-25 about 8.5 miles north from turnoff to U.S. Hwy 85. Then travel 1.8 miles west on the Atlas Road (exit 25). Turn south and travel 0.6 miles. The monument is just north of Lodgepole Creek.

Ranches served as stage stops for the Cheyenne and Black Hills Stage. In May 1876, Fred W. Schwartze, who had worked the Pole Creek Ranch since 1871, built a fine two-story hotel offering room and meals to the public.

ST. MARK'S EPISCOPAL CHURCH HISTORICAL LANDMARK COMMISSION PLAQUE-19

TITLE: St. Marks Episcopal Church
LEGEND: The first church edifice built in the State of Wyoming August 23, 1868.
  Placed by the Historical Landmark Commission of Wyoming
LOCATION: South side of St. Mark's Episcopal Church at 1908 Central Avenue in Cheyenne, Wyoming.

ST. MARK'S EPISCOPAL CHURCH NATIONAL HISTORIC PLACE PLAQUE-19.1

TITLE: St. Mark's Episcopal Church
    Pioneer Church of Wyoming
    A National Historic Place

LEGEND: Finding "the wickedness unimaginable and appalling," the Rev. Joseph Cook organized St. Mark's Parish Jan. 27, 1868, in Cheyenne, Dakota Territory, then a railroad winter camp. The first church at 18th and Carey Avenue was dedicated in August 1868 and was the first church building erected and dedicated in Wyoming.
  This present edifice was constructed in 1886 and was patterned after Stoke Poges Church, Buckinghamshire, England.
  The ministry of St. Mark's is historically linked with the settling and development of the frontier west. The church register records the burial service of the cavalrymen killed by Indians, the wedding of an acting governor, and use of the Parish Hall as a social and cultural center.
  The Rev. George Rafter, Rector, was asked to "pray over" Tom Horn during his public hanging in November of 1903.
  In August 1915, the wife and three daughters of the General John J. Pershing were buried with solemn military rites from this church. They lost their lives in a tragic fire at the Presidio, San Francisco. Hundreds of cavalry troops from Fort D. A. Russell participated in the burial procession.
  On Sunday, Oct. 11, 1936, President and Mrs. Franklin D. Roosevelt worshipped here.
  This Historical Marker Erected In 1972 in Loving Memory of Ruth Beggs Parker By Her Family and Friends.
LOCATION: South side of St. Mark's Episcopal Church at 1908 Central Avenue in Cheyenne, Wyoming.

METHODIST CHURCH-19.5

TITLE: First United Methodist Church
LEGEND: Organized—1867   Sanctuary Building constructed—1890
  Entered National Register of Historic Places Wyoming Place No. 84
LOCATION: Corner of 18th Street and Central Avenue in Cheyenne, Wyoming.

The cornerstone of this church was laid in 1890, but the dedication ceremonies did not take place until Easter Sunday in 1894. The cornerstone reads: FIRST METHODIST EPISCOPAL CHURCH 1890-1939. According to *Wyoming: A Guide to Historic Sites* by the Wyoming Recreation Commission:

> In the city hall on Sunday, September 20, 1867 Reverend Baldwin of Burlington, Colorado Territory was the first Methodist clergyman to preach a sermon in Cheyenne. That same day physician D. W. Scott formed a Methodist Society and became the local preacher.

SOUTHWEST CORNERSTONE-20

Plaque
TITLE: Cheyenne Corner Stone
LEGEND: S.W. Corner of site chosen by General Grenville Dodge in 1867 for the division point of the U.P.R.R. and for the location of Cheyenne City. The original 4 sq miles were laid at an angle to give "all houses maximum sunshine throughout the year." This stone was set in 1890.
  Plot and fence donated by Mildred and John Arp
  Laramie County Historical Society 1960
Cornerstone marker
TITLE: Cheyenne City
LEGEND: None

LOCATION: About 200 feet southwest of Goins School near the intersection of Gopp Street and Dey Avenue in Cheyenne, Wyoming.

SPANISH-AMERICAN WAR MEMORIAL-21

South side
TITLE: Taking the Oath
LEGEND: Erected to the memory of the heroes of the Spanish American War by the State of Wyoming and the Ladies Volunteer Aid Society.

West side
TITLE: Battery A, Wyoming Volunteers.
LEGEND: None

North side
TITLE: First Battalion, Wyoming Volunteers.
LEGEND: None

East side
TITLE: Second Regiment, U.S. Vol. Cavalry.
LEGEND: None

LOCATION: Corner of 24th Street and Capitol Avenue in Cheyenne, Wyoming.

There was no draft in the Spanish-American War of 1898. States were assigned quotas of volunteers. Wyoming's quota of 231 for two years was taken from Wyoming's National Guard. One of the most publicized Wyoming soldiers of that war was Colonel Jay L. Torrey who organized the Second United States Volunteer Cavalry, also known as Torrey's Rough Riders. The Spanish American War took sixteen Wyoming casualties, though no Wyoming volunteers died in battle. Five Rough Riders died in an accident.

In 1899, the Wyoming soldiers returned home to great homecoming. The State Legislature appropriated $1500 for this monument, a six foot-high statue of a soldier taking the oath.

STATUE OF LIBERTY MODEL-22

TITLE: None
LEGEND: With the faith and courage of their forefathers who made possible the freedom of these United States.

The Boy Scouts of America

Dedicate this replica of the Statue of Liberty as a pledge of everlasting fidelity and loyalty.

40th anniversary crusade to strengthen the arm of liberty 1950
LOCATION: In front of the Supreme Court Building in Cheyenne, Wyoming.

SUFFRAGE TABLET-23

TITLE: None
LEGEND: This tablet marks the site where the Council of the First Territorial Legislature of Wyoming convened which legislature enacted the first woman suffrage law passed in the United States.

Approved by John Allen Campbell

First governor of Wyoming December 10, 1869

Placed by Cheyenne Chapter Daughters of the American Revolution 1917
LOCATION: South side of 17th Street, about 50 feet east of Carey Avenue in Cheyenne, Wyoming.

Although Wyoming passed the first women's suffrage law in the United States, the U.S. House of Representatives opposed that action when Wyoming was battling for statehood in 1890. On March 26, 1890, speaking before the House in support of his bill to admit Wyoming to statehood, Joseph M. Carey spoke of the unique place of women in Wyoming. Democrats in the House of Representatives complained that women's suffrage should not be permitted. The statehood bill passed the House on that day, by a vote of 139 to 127.

Grace Raymond Hebard wrote in *Marking The Oregon Trail, The Bozeman Road and Historic Places in Wyoming 1908-1920* that the Cheyenne Chapter of the Daughters of the American Revolution, the Sons of the American Revolution of Wyoming, and a few interested citizens of

Cheyenne donated a noble bronze tablet which was placed July 21, 1917. Carey spoke of the history of Wyoming's equal suffrage law at the unveiling ceremonies.

TEXAS TRAIL-24

North side
TITLE: Old Texas Trail
LEGEND: Over this trail from distant Texas, passed the greatest migration of men and cattle in the history of America 1866-1897.

Bronze plaque on the north face of the monument
TITLE: None
LEGEND: In memory of the pioneer cattlemen who passed this way on the old Texas Trail 1866 to 1897.

This plaque placed by the Historical Landmark Commission of Wyoming 1948

Bronze plaque at base of north side
TITLE: None
LEGEND: This monument sponsored by the Lions Club of Pine Bluffs, Wyoming Stockgrowers Association, and the family of Captain D. H. and J. W. Snyder, Texas Trail drivers, who brought the first herds of Texas cattle to Wyoming in 1866.

LOCATION: In Pine Bluffs, Wyoming, in the park at the intersection Market Street, Second Avenue, and Lincoln Street.

Five markers have been erected in Wyoming (Laramie, Goshen, Niobrara, and Crook Counties) honoring the Texas Trail cowboys. See Texas Trail Monument (Crook County #8) for more information.

This memorial was dedicated August 1, 1948. Speakers were Dr. M. L. Morris, mayor of Pine Bluffs, Lester C. Hunt, governor of Wyoming, Dr. Howard Driggs, president American Pioneer Trails Association, and Warren Richardson, chairman Wyoming Historical Landmarks Commission.

FRANCES E. WARREN AIR FORCE BASE-26

LOCATION: Just west of Cheyenne, Wyoming.

From *Wyoming A Guide to Historic Sites* by the Wyoming Recreation Commission in 1976:

More than two hundred neocolonial, red brick structures ranging from a three-story commanding officers' quarters, and great barracks and cavalry stables to a simple powder house are among the features of this midcontinent military base on the eastern fringe of the Rocky Mountains. Originally named Fort D.A. Russell after an Eighth Infantry officer killed during the Civil War, the fort was established along Crow Creek in 1867 by General Christopher C. Augur in order to protect workers building the strategic Union Pacific Railroad across southern Wyoming. It was never a fort in the strictest definition of the term, but rather a military reservation covering approximately 7,500 acres. Temporary log structures were built in September, 1867, but in 1885, when the War Department declared the post to be a permanent military installation, a construction program was begun which has continued to the present.

Many of the buildings are listed in the National Register of Historic Places. Although access to the historic sites on the air base is limited for security reasons, bus tours enable visitors to view the historic buildings and the museum.

THE GREETING AND THE GIFT-27

Informative plaque
TITLE: The Greeting and The Gift
LEGEND: The scene depicts a typical meeting of the Indian and the Mountain Man on the open plains of WYOMING during the time of western discovery and exploration in the early 1800's.

At such meetings offerings of friendship would take place. The Indian is holding out a ceremonial buffalo horn filled with Rocky

Mountain "sweetwater" while the Mountain Man brings several beaver skins stretched on rounds of aspen branches.

Note that the Mountain Man holds his Muzzle Loading "long rifle" well away from his body with his hand over the muzzle to assure that it is harmless.

The Indian stands 12'6' and weighs 3000 pounds. The Mountain Man, whose raised hand reaches to 14', weighs 2500 pounds.

Dedication plaque

TITLE: "The Greeting and The Gift"

LEGEND: A sculptural grouping by Robert I. Russin, Laramie, Wyoming in commemoration of Wyoming's participation in the nation's Bicentennial Celebration. Dedicated January 30, 1977 by the Honorable Ed Herschler, Governor of the State of Wyoming, and the Wyoming Bicentennial Commission.

Peggy Simson Curry Casper, Chairman	Mrs. John U. Loomis Cheyenne	Charles Sharp Torrington
Dr. T.A. Larson Laramie, Vice-Chairman	Mrs. Percy W. Metz Basin	Darwin St. Clair Ft. Washakie
Mary Helen Hendry Casper, Sec.-Treas.	Frank Norris, Jr. Cheyenne	Glenn D. Sweem Sheridan
J. Reuel Armstrong Rawlins	Nora Reimer Sundance	William Taliaferro Rock Springs
Mabel E. Brown Newcastle	Helen L. Reynolds Green River	Randy Wagner Cheyenne
Lee R. Call Afton	Tom Shakespeare Arapahoe	William H. Williams Cheyenne
George F. Guy Cheyenne		Paul H. Westedt Cheyenne

This project was officially endorsed by the American Revolution Bicentennial Administration and was made possible by a federal grant of Bicentennial funds.

LOCATION: Southwest side of Cheyenne, Wyoming, at the Information Center near I-25 and I-80.

TRI-STATE SURVEYORS MARKER-27.1

South side

TITLE: Colorado

LEGEND: 104° 03' 09" W. Long.

Northeast side

TITLE: Nebraska

LEGEND: 41° 00' 06" N. Lat.

Northwest side

TITLE: Wyoming

LEGEND: None

Bronze plaque north side

TITLE: None

LEGEND: Original marker set by Oliver N. Chaffee Aug. 17, 1869. Base added by Art Henrickson August 1981.

Tri-state pillar

South: Colorado

East: 104.72.26

North: 27 W.L.

West: 41 N.L.

LOCATION: Drive about 13 miles south of Pine Bluffs, Wyoming, on the cemetery road, then east across a pasture about 1 mile. Private land; permission required.

Oliver N. Chaffee was contracted by the U.S. Surveyor General to survey and mark Nebraska'a western border. Three of the markers he erected are still in place, near the present communities of Big Springs, Nebraska, and Pine Bluffs and Lusk, Wyoming. Each of these sites has been preserved and

marked. See Surveyor's Marker (Niobrara County #12).

Alonzo and William A. Richards, surveyors from Omaha, Nebraska, reached Pine Bluffs, Wyoming, on June 3, 1873, to begin mapping the southern boundary of the Territory of Wyoming. A record of their work is found in the *Annals of Wyoming*, Volume 7, No. 4, April, 1931. See Tri-State Marker (Sweetwater County #16) and Surveyors Marker (Niobrara County #12).

CASTLE DARE-28

TITLE: Castle Dare 1886

LEGEND: Castle Dare was designed by architect J. P. Julien and built by R. W. Bradley, pioneer stonemason and contractor. The original house was commissioned by cattle baron Alexander Swan as a wedding present for his daughter Louise. Construction was begun in 1886, but the terrible blizzard of that winter caused Swan such financial reverses that the house was sold to David D. Dare who undertook its completion and furnishing. It was for Dare that the house was named.

Later, the house became the property of Bradley, who built the barn carriage house. Both buildings were done in a combination of Norman Revival and Richardson Romanesque architecture. The characteristics include ashlar masonry and towers with crenelated battlements or conical roofs.

The main house served as a boarding house, funeral parlor, and lodge hall until it was razed in 1963 to make way for a parking lot. The carriage house has been used as a private club, shops, and professional offices.

It is a reflection of Cheyenne during the height of the cattle baron days and is representative of the town when it was referred to as the richest small town in America. Renovation of the carriage house began in 1979 and was done almost entirely by volunteer labor.

LOCATION: About 50 yards east of Pioneer Avenue and 20th Streets in Cheyenne, Wyoming.

HERITAGE MAP-29

TITLE: Cheyenne Architectural Heritage Map

LEGEND: August 29, 1986, this Cheyenne Architectural Heritage Map was donated to the City of Cheyenne by the X-JWC Federated Women's Club. The purpose of the map is to preserve the memory of the beautiful historical buildings in the downtown area of Cheyenne. Artists William A. Little Jr., and Randy Hurst. Photographs Courtesy of: Wyoming State Archives, Museums and Historical Department. Constructed by: Western Specialty Mfg. Corp.

LOCATION: Cheyenne, Wyoming, at the corner of W. Lincolnway and Capitol Avenue.

Plaque #1

TITLE: Wyoming State Capitol

LEGEND: The Territorial Legislature authorized $150,000 for the construction of the Capitol's first phase in 1886. The Wyoming Capitol is one of ten gold domed U.S. state capitols.

LOCATION: 24th & Capitol Avenue

Plaque #2

TITLE: Union Pacific Depot

LEGEND: Construction began in 1886, and included a Romanesque clock tower that was a prominent landmark for railroad travelers approaching Cheyenne at the turn of the century.

LOCATION: 121 West 15th Street

Plaque #3

TITLE: Tivoli Building

LEGEND: A fine bar and restaurant was established here in 1883.

Ladies, with or without escorts, were welcomed. The present building was constructed in 1892.
LOCATION: 301 West 16th Street

Plaque #4
TITLE: Atlas Theatre
LEGEND: Constructed in 1887, the Atlas is the oldest standing theatre in Cheyenne. Home to vaudeville performances, in the 1980's the Atlas stage presents live theatre.
LOCATION: 213 West 16th Street

Plaque #5
TITLE: St. Mark's Episcopal Church
LEGEND: Begun in 1886, the 1887 collapse of the cattle industry postponed completion of the church's interior until 1888. Windows include Tiffany stained glass.
LOCATION: 1908 Central Avenue

Plaque #6
TITLE: St. Mary's Cathedral
LEGEND: St. Mary's neo-gothic cathedral, constructed 1906-09, features nine major stained-glass windows. The largest, above the choir loft, was inspired by Raphael's Sistine Madonna.
LOCATION: 2107 Capitol Avenue

Plaque #7
TITLE: First United Methodist Church
LEGEND: The cornerstone of the red sandstone church was laid in 1890, the year Wyoming became a state. Wild Bill Hickock married Agnes Lake Thatcher on this site in 1876.
LOCATION: NE Corner 18th Street & Central Avenue

Plaque #8
TITLE: First Presbyterian Church
LEGEND: The limestone church erected 1923-24, includes Centennial Doors depicting the stained glass Wyoming's great seal, state flag, territorial seal and the Union Pacific emblem.
LOCATION: 220 West 22nd Street

Plaque #9
TITLE: Whipple House
LEGEND: This Italianate brick residence was built in 1883 by Ithamar C. Whipple, Cheyenne merchant, financier and cattleman. Later this was home to Judge John Lacey, distinguished Wyoming counselor.
LOCATION: 300 East 17th Street

Plaque #10
TITLE: Nagle-Warren Mansion
LEGEND: Built in 1887-88 for Erasmus Nagle, faulty sandstone rejected by state Capitol contractors was installed here. Later this mansion was home of U.S. Senator Francis E. Warren.
LOCATION: 222 East 17th Street

Plaque #11
TITLE: Phoenix Block
LEGEND: Completed in 1882 by Francis E. Warren at a cost of $35,000, the Phoenix boasted three stories and a complete plumbing system with water and gas.
LOCATION: SW Corner 16th Street & Capitol Avenue

Plaque #12
TITLE: Hynds Building
LEGEND: Built in 1922 by Harry P. Hynds, a prominent Cheyenne

businessman and philanthropist, this was the site of the historic Interocean Hotel.
LOCATION: 1600 Capitol Avenue

Plaque #13
TITLE: Idleman Building
LEGEND: Constructed in 1884 for wholesale liquor business, customers could walk among barrels and siphon samples through a tube, buying whatever they fancied.
LOCATION: NE Corner 16th Street & Carey Avenue

Plaque #14
TITLE: Commercial Building
LEGEND: Constructed 1883, this building housed federal government offices until 1905. U.S. Deputy Marshall Joe LeFors heard hired gunman Tom Horn's alleged confession here.
LOCATION: 200 block West 16th Street

Plaque #15
TITLE: Warren Mercantile
LEGEND: You are standing on the site of the 1884 Warren Mercantile Company building. 1887 to 1932 Burlington Railroad occupied part of the building for depot use.
LOCATION: SE corner 16th Street & Capitol Avenue

Plaque #16
TITLE: Rocky Mountain Telephone Building
LEGEND: Constructed in 1906 for the new telephone exchange, John Arp purchased this building in 1930 to create a comfortable hotel with running water and private baths.
LOCATION: 1623 Capitol Avenue

Plaque #17
TITLE: Dinneen's Garage
LEGEND: Designed and built in 1927 for W.E. Dinneen, the building includes a water-powered elevator for lifting automobiles to the second floor, still in use in the 1980's.
LOCATION: 400 West 16th Street

Plaque #18
TITLE: Historic Governor's Mansion
LEGEND: Constructed in 1904, the residence was the home of twenty Wyoming first families between 1905 and 1976. Notable visitors were Theodore Roosevelt, Harry Truman and William "Buffalo Bill" Cody.
LOCATION: 300 East 21st Street

Plaque #19
TITLE: Majestic Building
LEGEND: The Majestic Building was constructed in 1907 for the First National Bank. The emergency exit became a social passage, known as Peacock Alley, between the Paramount Theatre and the Plains Hotel.
LOCATION: 1601 Capitol Avenue

Plaque #20
TITLE: Plains Hotel
LEGEND: The Plains Hotel opened in 1911 and was the focus of Cheyenne's social and political events for fifty years. Chief Little Shield's picture became the hotel trademark.
LOCATION: 1600 Central Avenue

Plaque #21
TITLE: Masonic Temple
LEGEND: The cornerstone was placed by the Masons in 1901. Following

a fire in 1903, the interior was rebuilt. The stained-glass windows still show fire damage.
LOCATION: 1820 Capitol Avenue

Plaque #22
TITLE: Ferdinand W. LaFrentz House
LEGEND: The LaFrentz house is representative of the frame cottages built in Cheyenne during the 1880's when Cheyenne was reputed to be the richest little city in the world.
LOCATION: 2015 Warren Avenue

Plaque #23
TITLE: Corson House
LEGEND: Designed in 1883 by George D. Rainsford, this whimsical cottage is almost unchanged in appearance and has been the home of three generations of Corsons.
LOCATION: 209 East 18th Street

Plaque #24
TITLE: Castle Dare
LEGEND: Construction started in 1886. R. W. Bradley moved into the mansion after sales to both Alexander Swan and D. D. Dare failed to close. In 1963 all but the carriage house was razed.
LOCATION: 1920 Carey Avenue

Plaque #25
TITLE: Knights of Pythias
LEGEND: Constructed in 1884, Knights of Pythias Hall was the home of the Ninth Territorial Legislative Assembly in 1886. Portions of the elaborate cornice are still visible.
LOCATION: 312 West 17th Street

Plaque #26
TITLE: Davis Building
LEGEND: Five Cheyenne streets' names titled by General Dodge were changed. The Davis Building, constructed in 1895, remembers Eddy Street by a sign on the west side of the building.
LOCATION: 320 West 17th Street

Plaque #27
TITLE: Boyd Building
LEGEND: Designed by Frederick H. Porter in 1912, the building originally housed the Citizens' National Bank. H. N. Boyd purchased the structure after the bank failed in 1924.
LOCATION: 1720 Carey Avenue

Plaque #28
TITLE: Nettford Apartments
LEGEND: The Greek Revival red brick structure graced with white columns was opened in 1911 as apartments. It was owned by Arthur C. Kingsford and named for his wife, Nettie.
LOCATION: 215 East 18th Street

Plaque #29
TITLE: County Building
LEGEND: Construction began in 1917. This edifice replaced the first Laramie County Court House where, in 1903, the famous hanging of Tom Horn took place.
LOCATION: NW corner 19th Street & Carey Avenue

Plaque #30
TITLE: Grier Furniture
LEGEND: Erected in 1911 by Cheyenne businessman and politician,

Francis E. Warren, this commercial structure was later the funeral home and furniture store of Hobbs, Huckfeldt and Finkbiner.
LOCATION: 1601 Central Avenue

LINCOLN HIGHWAY OFFICIAL GUIDE POST-30
TITLE: The Lincoln Highway
LEGEND:
State Line
The Lincoln Highway
◄ Nebraska
Wyoming ►
◄ New York
San Francisco ►
LOCATION: Entrance to the State Headquarters of the Wyoming Highway Department in Cheyenne, Wyoming.

The transcontinental road, named in honor of Abraham Lincoln, was begun in 1912 and was later designated U.S. Highway 30. The official Lincoln Highway guide post was adopted in 1917 and cast by The Lebanon Machine Co. in Lebanon, NH. See Abraham Lincoln Monument (Albany County #9).

WIND RIVER CANYON ROAD-31
TITLE: Wind River Canyon Road
LOCATION: Built 1922-1924   Length 21.2 miles
Initiated and construction started during administration of Governor Robert D. Carey
M. R. Johnston, S. W. Conwell, J. M. Snyder, L. R. A. Condit, Joe C. Kinney—Members State Highway Commission
L. E. Laird—State Highway Supt.
Z. E. Sevison—State Highway Engineer
R. L. Silver, C. H. Bowman—District Engineers
N. T. Olson, G. D. Corwine—Resident Engineers
Goyne Drummond—Locating Engineer
LOCATION: Entrance to the State Headquarters of the Wyoming Highway Department in Cheyenne, Wyoming.

The canyon is located between Thermopolis and Shoshoni, Wyoming, in Hot Springs and Fremont counties. See Wind River Canyon Road Marker (Fremont County #40).

RINER VIADUCT-32
TITLE: Railing from Riner Viaduct
In service from 1929 to 1982
LEGEND: This piece of wrought iron railing is about all that remains of the historic Riner Viaduct that once bridged Cheyenne's north and south sides separated by the Union Pacific Railroad yards.
Originally an all-wood structure, Riner Viaduct first carried travelers over the railroad yards in 1892. At that time, a significant portion of Cheyenne's commercial district was located immediately south of where the viaduct was built.
Although named after J. S. Riner, Cheyenne's mayor from 1887 to 1891, the structure has also been called the Central Avenue Viaduct. Riner was in his second term when the Kansas City Structural Steel Co. of Kansas City, Mo., replaced the original viaduct with a steel structure in 1929. The replacement was a joint venture by the railroad, Laramie County and federal government.
However, after many years of heavy use and weathering, deterioration set in. Use restrictions became necessary, and replacement became inevitable.
On the morning of July 15, 1982, the last vehicle passed over Riner Viaduct because the first of twin replacement viaducts was ready for traffic. Riner Viaduct was razed during the 1982-83 winter to make way for construction of the second viaduct.

WYOMING GOVERNOR'S MANSION-33

TITLE: Wyoming Governor's Mansion
　　　　Enrolled in the National Register of Historic Places
LEGEND: The 1902 Wyoming Legislature authorized an Executive
Mansion and appropriated $40,000 for the purpose. Under architect
Charles W. Murdock, this Georgian style building was completed late
in 1904 at a total cost, including site, landscaping, construction and
furnishings, of $33,253.29.

Governor and Mrs. Bryant B. Brooks were the Mansion's first
occupants. A society-news item from the *Cheyenne Daily Leader*,
January 4, 1905, said: "Mrs. B. B. Brooks will return from Casper on
Friday evening accompanied by her children. Every effort is being
made by the decorators and furnishers to have the Executive Mansion
in readiness to receive the family Saturday."

The Mansion got its housewarming in official and formal style when,
on January 23, 1905, Governor and Mrs. Brooks entertained at a
reception in honor of State Legislators, State Officials and their wives.
Next day, the *Wyoming Tribune* reported the affair in a page one story
which said, "A Happy Throng of Guests Assemble at the Executive
Mansion to meet the Legislature."

State Executive Mansions were customary structures long before
Wyoming got around to building this one as a home for its governors.
Still, this Mansion had one "first." When Mrs. Nellie Taylor Ross
became Governor of Wyoming in 1925, this was the first Executive
Mansion in the Nation to become the home of a woman governor.
LOCATION: 300 East 21st Street in Cheyenne, Wyoming.

WYOMING STATE CAPITOL-34

TITLE: Wyoming State Capitol
LEGEND: Wyoming State Capitol has been designated a National
Historic Landmark.

This site possesses national significance in commemorating the
history of the United States of Amcrica.

1987
National Park Service
United States Department of the Interior
LOCATION: Just inside the main entry to the Wyoming State Capitol in
Cheyenne, Wyoming.

LINCOLN COUNTY

ASTORIANS MONUMENT-1

TITLE: None
LEGEND: Here in September 1812 the returning Astorians, led by Robert Stuart were attacked by the Indians and their horses stolen. Commemorating the opening of the Snake River Canyon Road. Built by Civilian Conservation Corps.

Dedicated July 4, 1939 by the Historial Landmark Commission of Wyoming
LOCATION: About 1 mile south of Alpine, Wyoming, on Lincoln County Road 101.

The marker was vandalized many years ago, and the bronze plaque has been missing ever since. The pillar of stone and mortar still stands.

Several other Astorian markers are located across the state. See Astorian Overland Expedition Informative Sign (Campbell County #1), Stuart Campsite Sign (Goshen County #16), South Pass Interpretive Site, Union Pass Monument, and Union Pass Interpretive Plaques (Fremont County #28.1, #35, and #35.1), First White Man's Cabin (Natrona County #3), Astorian Incident Sign and On the Ashes of their Campfires (Sublette County #1 and #13).

FIRST POST OFFICE-1.1

TITLE: First Post Office
LEGEND: Daughters of Utah Pioneers
No. 277
Erected 1963

Thayne, formerly called Glencoe, was founded in 1888, at which time mail was brought in to Star Valley by team and wagon and distributed to the people from a log cabin owned by Joseph Thayne. The building was one room 12x15 feet with a dirt roof. Three years later it was moved to the center of town and Henry Thayne and his wife occupied it. This log cabin, located one and one-half rods west of this site, became the first post office May 8, 1891 with Laura Thayne post mistress.

Silver Star Camp
Lincoln County, Wyoming
LOCATION: West side of U.S. Hwy 89 about 0.1 mile north of the intersection of Riggs Avenue and Wright Street in Thayne, Wyoming.

From the settlement of Thayne, Wyoming, in 1888 until 1891, mail was carried by anyone who volunteered to bring it into the valley, and usually was left at the home of Henry Thayne. Mrs. Laura Thayne applied to the federal government to become postmistress at an official post office in Thayne. Its official name was Thayne, Wyoming Post Office.

FOSSIL BUTTE INFORMATIVE SIGN-2

TITLE: Fossil Butte
LEGEND: Fossil Butte is world famous for perfectly preserved fossil fish. The deposits were worked as early as 1877. There are specimens from this locality in museums all over the world.

The rocks in the Butte were laid down about 50 million years ago. Red rocks in the lower part are stream deposits named Knight Formation. Light colored beds in the upper part are of the Green River and are remnant of beds deposited in a lake once covering much of western Wyoming.

The fish-bearing layer and quarries are about half-way up the butte. The Green River Formation has yielded a great many varieties of fossil fish, including herring, perch, catfish and stingrays, as well as fossil insects, birds and bat.
LOCATION: About 10.5 miles west of Kemmerer, Wyoming on U.S. Hwy 30. Sign is about 0.4 miles north of U.S. Hwy 30 on the access road to Fossil Butte National Monument.

GROVER PIONEERS MONUMENT-3

West side
TITLE: None
LEGEND: All honor to the pioneers of Grover 1885-1950.

In honor and memory of the men and women of an earlier day who gave themselves to the building of Grover.
South side
TITLE: Honor Roll
LEGEND: Proudly we pay tribute to the members of our community who answered the call to the colors in World Wars I and II.

LOCATION: On the church grounds, east side of U.S. Hwy 89 in Grover, Wyoming.

NANCY HILL GRAVE-4

TITLE: None
LEGEND: NANCY J. HILL
July 5, 1852
MONROE COUNTY
Miss.
LOCATION: About 17-18 miles northwest of Kemmerer, Wyoming on State Route 233. Road is rough and should be traveled only in good weather. Inquire locally.

Nancy Hill was part of an emigrant wagon train that was apparently besieged and held up by Indians for two to three weeks. After the trouble seemed to be over, the party headed west. After only a few miles, Nancy Hill was stricken with cholera and died shortly afterwards. The Oregon-California Trails Association also placed a marker at this site. See Nancy Jane Hill-OCTA Marker (Lincoln County #19).

ALFRED CORUM GRAVE-4.1

TITLE: Alfred Corum Grave
LEGEND: Within this compound lie the graves of five or six pioneers who lost their lives while traveling to the gold fields of California and the fertile Willamette Valley of Oregon.

Alfred Corum and his brothers John, Herod, and Simeon left Cooper County, Missouri, on April 10, 1849, bound for the gold fields. Their wagon train reached the Hams Fork Plateau on July 3, 1849, and "layed over" as Alfred had been sick for a week or ten days. Some 200 wagons passed them on this day. On July 4 the wagon train pulled out, leaving six men behind to render aid to the dying Alfred. He died at 1:00 p.m. of unknown causes on the 4th of July, 1849.

Margaret Campbell is buried a few yards from Alfred Corum. She died on July 29, 1848 of unknown causes. Historians have been unable to determine the names and circumstances of death of the other emigrants buried here.
LOCATION: About 17-18 miles northwest of Kemmerer, Wyoming on State Route 233. Road is rough and should be traveled only in good weather. Inquire locally. About 0.5 mile down the ridge from Nancy Hill's Grave (Lincoln County #4).

KEMMERER FOUNDERS MONUMENT-5

TITLE: Kemmerer
LEGEND: Founded 1897 by Mahlon S. Kemmerer, 1843-1925 and Patrick J. Quealy, 1857-1930.
LOCATION: Southwest corner of the triangular city park in the center of Kemmerer, Wyoming.

Patrick J. Quealy was an energetic man with interests in the coal and cattle industry. Besides founding Kemmerer, he also spent time in the coal mining town of Carbon (near Medicine Bow, Wyoming), the Union Pacific coal camp known as Almy (north of Evanston, Wyoming), and Rock Springs

LINCOLN COUNTY

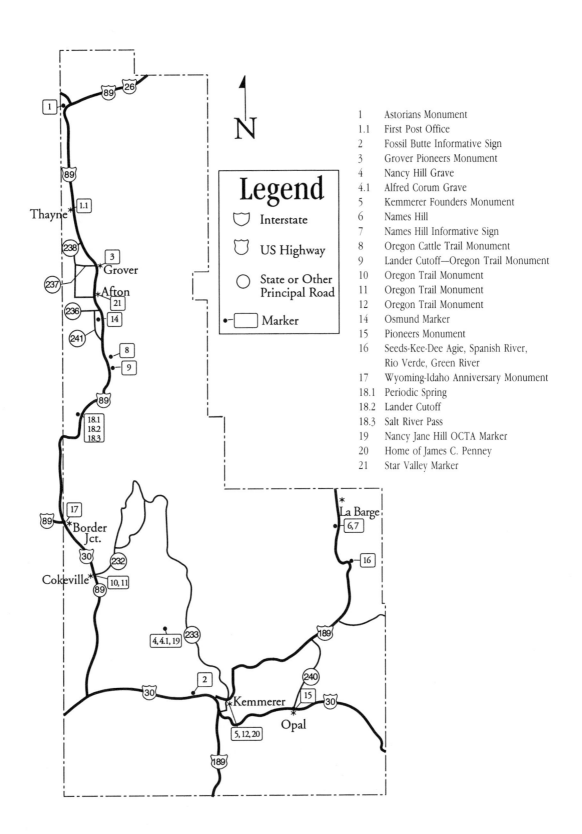

Legend

⬡ Interstate

⛨ US Highway

◯ State or Other Principal Road

•—▭ Marker

1   Astorians Monument
1.1 First Post Office
2   Fossil Butte Informative Sign
3   Grover Pioneers Monument
4   Nancy Hill Grave
4.1 Alfred Corum Grave
5   Kemmerer Founders Monument
6   Names Hill
7   Names Hill Informative Sign
8   Oregon Cattle Trail Monument
9   Lander Cutoff—Oregon Trail Monument
10   Oregon Trail Monument
11   Oregon Trail Monument
12   Oregon Trail Monument
14   Osmund Marker
15   Pioneers Monument
16   Seeds-Kee-Dee Agie, Spanish River,
     Rio Verde, Green River
17   Wyoming-Idaho Anniversary Monument
18.1 Periodic Spring
18.2 Lander Cutoff
18.3 Salt River Pass
19   Nancy Jane Hill OCTA Marker
20   Home of James C. Penney
21   Star Valley Marker

where he helped form the Rock Springs Coal Company in 1887. In 1894, Quealy purchased land and started a cattle business on the Ham's Fork River (flows through present day Kemmerer and Frontier, Wyoming). He also staked out about 2560 acres of what he considered prospective coal land. While he did not have financing for a commercial coal operation, he earned a reputation as one of the region's foremost coal men.

Quealy first met Mahlon S. Kemmerer, the wealthy pioneer Pennsylvania coal man, in 1895. Their friendship was sincere and long-lasting. Kemmerer provided financial backing and added experience that Quealy needed. In 1897 they established four partnerships: The Frontier Supply Company, a general merchandise store; The Ham's Fork Cattle Company; The Frontier Coal Company (known for the first month as The Kemmerer Coal Company); and The Uinta Improvement Company, a land company designed to conduct the partners' real estate concerns. Frontier was the company town established by the partnership; coal production began in October 1897. Just weeks after the partnership was signed, a decision was made to establish the town of Kemmerer. The townsite was formally organized in spring of 1897; house lots began to sell in 1897. Kemmerer was incorporated in January 1899.

An excellent look into the early years of this coal mining area can be found in *Kemmerer, Wyoming: The Founding of an Independent Coal Town 1897-1902* by Dr. Glen Barrett.

NAMES HILL-6

TITLE: Names Hill
LEGEND: The old Green River crossing and rendezvous on the old Oregon Trail.

Gift of First National Bank Kemmerer, Wyo. to the State of Wyoming.
LOCATION: West side of U.S. Hwy 189 about 6 miles south of La Barge, Wyoming.

Names Hill was a well-known Oregon-California Trail landmark, one of three most noticeable locations where emigrants camped and carved their names in soft limestone cliffs a common early day practice. Register Cliff on the North Platte River and Independence Rock on the Sweetwater River were two other familiar sites used for the same purpose.

NAMES HILL INFORMATIVE SIGN-7

TITLE: James Bridger
        Trapper 1844
LEGEND: He little knew that when he cut his name or had it cut in this stone, that it would be engraved in the annals of the history of the west deeper than that of any other man. As one of the world's outstanding explorers, he guided emigrants, railroads and army in the expansion of a nation.

Sublette County Historical Society, Lincoln County Board of Commissioners, Wyoming Highway Dept
LOCATION: West side of U.S. Hwy 189 about 6 miles south of La Barge, Wyoming.

See Names Hill (Lincoln County #6) for more information.

OREGON CATTLE TRAIL MONUMENT-8

TITLE: None
LEGEND: Trail from Oregon, 1875-1890. This way passed great herds of cattle, horses and sheep into Wyoming. Erected in memory of the Trail Driver. Sponsored by Star Valley Chamber of Commerce and The Wyoming Stockgrowers Association.

This plaque placed by the Historical Landmark Commission of Wyoming 1948
LOCATION: On the east side of U.S. Hwy 89 about 3 miles south of Smoot, Wyoming.

Cattle were driven from west to east along the Oregon Trail to stock the ranges of Wyoming and Colorado. The first herds entered Wyoming in 1875 along the Lander Cutoff in the Salt River Valley. The last drive along the trail occurred in 1890.

LANDER CUTOFF—OREGON TRAIL MONUMENT-9

TITLE: Lander Cutoff of the Oregon Trail.
LEGEND: Dedicated to all pioneers who passed this way to win and hold the West.

Erected by the Historical Landmark Commission of Wyoming in 1939
LOCATION: On the east side of U.S. Hwy 89 about 5.6 miles south of Smoot, Wyoming.

The amount of emigrant travel on the Oregon Trail necessitated new travel routes to provide grass, water, and timber, generally scarce along the routes south of South Pass. In 1857, Frederick West Lander surveyed several existing trails but felt that constructing a new trail would serve the intent much better. The Lander Cutoff departed from the main trail at Burnt Ranch just before South Pass, passed along the base of the Wind River Mountains to Salt River, through the Star Valley, and on to Fort Hall in Idaho. The Lander Cutoff was the only part of the Oregon Trail ever federally subsidized.

OREGON TRAIL MONUMENT-10

TITLE: None
LEGEND: To all pioneers who passed this way to win and hold the West.

Erected by Town of Cokeville, Wyo. 1931
LOCATION: In Cokeville City Park at the corner of East Main Street and Park Street in Cokeville, Wyoming.

This marker was erected because of the influence of the Oregon Trail Memorial Association, and more specifically, the Covered Wagon Centennial in 1930. See "Ezra Meeker, the Oregon Trail Memorial Association, and the American Pioneer Trails Association" in the first part of this book.

OREGON TRAIL MONUMENT-11

TITLE: Old Oregon Trail
LEGEND: Used from 1812 to 1912. Monument Erected by Ezra Meeker.

Plaque placed by the Historical Landmark Commission of Wyoming 1950
LOCATION: Southeast corner of the intersection of U.S. Hwy 30 and State Route 232 in Cokeville, Wyoming.

OREGON TRAIL MONUMENT-12

TITLE: None
LEGEND: To all pioneers who passed this way to win and hold the West.

Erected by popular subscription, Citizens of Kemmerer, 1931
LOCATION: Northwest corner of the triangular city park in center of Kemmerer, Wyoming.

This marker, like many others across Wyoming, was erected because of the influence and support of the Oregon Trail Memorial Association. The Covered Wagon Centennial, the nationwide celebration sponsored by the Association in 1930, provided the inspiration for the erection of many Wyoming markers.

OSMUND MARKER-14

TITLE: Osmund
LEGEND: Daughters of Utah Pioneers
        No. 371
        Erected 1970
Dry Creek, later called Mt. Pleasant, was settled in 1886. The first public building erected in this area, 1891, was a log schoolhouse also used as a church. Students furnished their own desks and stools. George Hardman, teacher. Osmund Ward, organized

1.

2.

3.

4.

1. Names Hill Marker erected on the Oregon Trail in July 1940.

2. Inspired by the Covered Wagon Centennial in 1930, the citizens of Cokeville erected this granite marker and bronze Oregon Trail Memorial Association plaque in 1931 to remember pioneers who traveled on the Oregon Trail.

3. Thayne's first post office was in place by 1891. This marker was erected in 1963.

4. Many markers, similar to this one in Lincoln County, were erected in Sublette County along the Oregon Trail. Although the signs were massive and impressive, the expanse of the country through which the Trail pioneers traveled far exceeded the magnitude of the signs.

September 8, 1901, Andrew M. Neilson, Bishop. Named Honored George Osmund, First President of Star Valley Stake, Church of Jesus Christ of Latter Day Saints.
Camp Minnie
LOCATION: About 4 miles south of Afton, Wyoming. About 0.6 miles south of the start of State Route 234.

PIONEERS MONUMENT-15

TITLE: None
LEGEND: To all pioneers who passed this way to win and hold the West.
    Erected by Opal Citizens and Friends
LOCATION: In Opal, Wyoming, just west of the Opal Mercantile Company.

This marker was erected due to the influence and guidance of the Oregon Trail Memorial Association. In 1930 the Association sponsored and directed the Covered Wagon Centennial which celebrated the first covered wagon across the nation. Many markers were erected during that year or just shortly thereafter.

SEEDS-KEE-DEE AGIE, SPANISH RIVER, RIO VERDE, GREEN RIVER-16

TITLE: Seeds-Kee-Dee Agie, Spanish River, Rio Verde, Green River
LEGEND: To the Shoshone Indian, this river was the Seeds-Kee-Dee Agie (Prairie Chicken River). On September 16, 1811 the Astorians near its headwaters termed it the Spanish River. To the Spaniards far to the south, it was the Rio Verde (Green River). Jedediah Smith and his ten mountain men, making the first westward crossing of the South Pass by white men, camped near here Mar. 19, 1824 on the Seeds-Kee-Dee. They trapped the river and its forks which were named for them; Labarge, Ham's, Black's, Smith's, Henry's etc. These waters were considered as the greatest beaver waters ever known. The upper reaches became the center of the fur trade and Rendezvous. In 1841 the fur trade had ceased but the trappers had blazed the trails for emigrants. For forty-nine years over the Oregon and California trails thousands of emigrants going west, crossed these waters near by. The many that drowned and died were buried along the river banks. The mountain men guided, manned the ferries, and traded with the emigrants. Graves, marked and unmarked, names cut in the rocks, and wagon trails worn deep, remain with the legend and lore of a great river of the west, The Green.

Sublette County Historical Society,
Lincoln County Board of Commissioners
U.S. Bureau of Land Management
U.S. Bureau of Reclamation.
LOCATION: East side of U.S. Hwy 189 south of Names Hill and La Barge, Wyoming.

WYOMING-IDAHO ANNIVERSARY MONUMENT-17

Wyoming side
TITLE: Wyoming
LEGEND: Golden Anniversary 1940.
  Admitted to Statehood July 10, 1890.
  Dedicated by the Historical Landmark Commission of Wyoming July 3, 1940
Idaho side
TITLE: Idaho
LEGEND: Fifty years of Statehood 1940.
  Admitted July 3, 1890.
  Dedicated by the 50 Years of Statehood Committee

LOCATION: North side of U.S. Hwy 30 just off U.S. Hwy 89. Near Border, Wyoming, about 12 miles north of Cokeville, Wyoming.

In March 1940, Idaho Governor Bottolfsen suggested a joint Golden Anniversary celebration at the border between the Wyoming and Idaho. Wyoming Governor Nels H. Smith conferred with the Historical Landmark Commission, and plans were made to jointly erect a monument.

PERIODIC SPRING-18.1

TITLE: Periodic Spring
LEGEND: Located 4 miles east of Afton in the Salt River Range, is the largest of three natural springs in the world that naturally turn off and on. Water flow is interrupted from anywhere between 3 to 30 minutes, generally between the months of August-May. It is thought that a cave behind the spring creates a siphon which causes interruption of the water flow. Its ability to turn off and on during low discharge stages has fascinated visitors since prehistoric times. Access to the spring is via the Swift Creek road and requires a 3/4 mile hike by trail.
Bridger National Forest
LOCATION: Salt River Pass on U.S. Hwy 89 about 18 miles south of Afton, Wyoming.

LANDER CUTOFF-18.2

TITLE: Lander Cut-off
LEGEND: The Lander Cut-off left the Oregon Trail at Burnt Ranch on the Sweetwater River near South Pass City, Wy. Frederick Lander surveyed the trail in 1857. Tens of thousands of people passed over the trail during its use. With the Transcontinental Railroad being completed in 1869, emigrant travel over the trail rapidly declined. The last wagons over the trail were observed at Fort Piney Wy. between 1910 and 1912. The Lander Cut-off rejoined the Oregon Trail in Idaho northeast of Pocatello at Ross Fork Creek.
LOCATION: Salt River Pass on U.S. Hwy 89, about 18 miles south of Afton, Wyoming.

SALT RIVER PASS-18.3

TITLE: Salt River Pass
LEGEND: From this point water flows north to the Snake River and thence to the Pacific Ocean or south to the Bear River and into Great Salt Lake.

Sustained yield of high quality water is the primary consideration under the multiple use concept on the Bridger National Forest.

Bridger National Forest
LOCATION: Salt River Pass on U.S. Hwy 89, about 18 miles south of Afton, Wyoming.

NANCY JANE HILL OCTA MARKER-19

TITLE: Nancy Jane Hill
LEGEND: In April, 1852, four brothers, Wesley, Samuel, James and Steven Hill, together with their families, 62 persons in all, left Paris, Monroe County, Missouri, for California.

There were two deaths along the Platte River and here on the Hamsfork Plateau. Nancy Jane Hill, second eldest of the six children of Wesley and Elizabeth Hill, died of cholera, July 5, 1852, age twenty years.

Nancy's Uncle, James Hill, wrote: "She was in good health on Sunday evening taken unwell that knight worst in the morning and a corps at nine o'clock at knight."

On the Forty Mile desert in Nevada Nancy's father, Wesley Hill, died August 24, 1852, and was buried at Ragtown at the Carson River.

The Hill train settled in Soscol Valley, Napa County in California.

Legend has it that Nancy Jane's fiance returned three times over a period of 53 years to tend the grave.

Research by	Funding by
Stephen Jackson	P. Hartwell Gillaspy
Stockton, California	Stockton, California
(Relative of Nancy Jane Hill)	(Great-grand-nephew
and the	of Nancy Jane Hill)
Oregon-California	
Trails Association	
1987	

This is part of your American heritage. Honor it, protect it, preserve it for your children.
LOCATION: About 17-18 miles northwest of Kemmerer, Wyoming. Road is rough and should be traveled only in good weather. Inquire locally.

See Nancy Hill Grave (Lincoln County #4) for more information.

HOME OF JAMES C. PENNEY-20

TITLE: Home of James C. Penney
LEGEND: Founded J. C. Penney Company, Inc. April 14, 1902 in Kemmerer, Wyoming.
  Operated by J. C. Penney Homestead, Inc.
LOCATION: Just northeast of downtown Kemmerer, Wyoming.

James Cash Penney arrived in Kemmerer in 1902 and opened the Golden Rule store. Kemmerer was a coal town and the business faced stiff competition from the company stores at Frontier, Cumberland, and Diamondville. He succeeded in his endeavor and expanded his business throughout the United States. Golden Rule stores later became J. C. Penney stores.

STAR VALLEY MARKER-21

TITLE: Star Valley
LEGEND: Daughters of Utah Pioneers
  No. 237
  Erected 1956
In the spring of 1879 a group of pioneers from Bear Lake settled here. Moses Thatcher explored the area, dedicated it as a home for the Latter-day Saints calling it Star Valley. Freedom and Auburn settled in 1879 and Afton in 1885. The first public building was located on this square. A log house with dirt roof served the settlers as a church, school, and public meeting place from 1886 to 1892 when it was replaced by a large frame building. The bell on this monument calling

Calling the people together could be heard throughtout the valley.
LOCATION: 347 Jefferson Street in Afton, Wyoming.

In 1879, Charles C. Rich and Moses Thatcher were appointed to supervise Latter-day Saint settlement in Star Valley. David Robinson and August Lehmberg settled near the present site of Auburn. In 1880, Charles D. Cazier located a settlement at the present site of Afton on Swift Creek, although Afton was not permanently settled until 1885.

A large frame building built in 1892 housed a bell in a tower. The bell was rung at 9:30 and 9:50 every Sunday morning so that valley residents could set their clocks, an event which continued for forty years until the building was torn down. The bell was removed from storage and placed on the top of the Afton Marker in 1956 by the Daughters of Utah Pioneers.

NATRONA COUNTY

CASPER INFORMATIVE SIGN-1

TITLE: City of Casper

LEGEND: The city of Casper, established near the site of old Fort Caspar, formerly Platte Bridge Station, was named in honor of Lieut. Caspar Collins, who lost his life in an Indian battle there on July 26, 1865. The Fort was one of the small army posts which guarded the Oregon and Emigrant Trail and the transcontinental telegraph line during the mid-1800's. The first railroad came to Casper in 1888, and the town remained "rail's end" until 1905 when the line was extended to Lander. Casper's early economy was based on cattle and sheep raising. Oil had been discovered in the vicinity and in 1895 the first oil refinery was built. The industry has developed since then until Casper is now the principal oil city in Wyoming.

Erected 1965 by Wyoming State Archives and Historical Department and the Wyoming State Historical Society

LOCATION: Casper Tourist Information Center, just south and west of the intersection of North Center Street and I-25.

FIRST WHITE MAN'S CABIN INFORMATIVE SIGN-3

TITLE: First white man's cabin in Wyoming

LEGEND: Approximately 2 miles northwest from here is the location of the cabin built by Robert Stuart's party of Astorians. They were enroute from Astoria to St. Louis to report to John Jacob Astor the fate of his ship, which was destroyed by Indians, and the crew killed. Stuart and six companions left Astoria June 29, 1812, reached Wyoming in November after winter had set in. Footsore and hungry, they found game plentiful here and built a cabin. They had planned to stay until spring, but after Indians discovered their cabin, they left in the night and continued eastward down the river.

LOCATION: Sign no longer exists. Originally was adjacent to Oregon Trail Monument on State Route 220 about 1.7 miles west of the Bessemer Road.

This monument marked the site of the Astorians' camp at Bessemer Bend near Casper, Wyoming. Although in 1978 the supporting chains were cut and the sign was taken, the story of the eastbound Astorians deserves preservation for the sake of Wyoming's early history.

FORT CASPAR CEMETERY—GRAND ARMY OF THE REPUBLIC-4

TITLE: None

LEGEND: In memory of the Grand Army of the Republic. To our fathers who sacrificed lives and fortunes for our freedom and unity.

Presented in 1956 by Betsy Ross Tent No. 19, Daughters of Union Veterans of the Civil War. 1861-1865.

LOCATION: On a small hill just south of the entrance to Fort Caspar.

OLD PIONEER MILITARY CEMETERY MARKER-5

TITLE: Old Pioneer Military Cemetery

LEGEND: Lt. Caspar Collins was killed July 26, 1865 about 3 miles from this spot. His body was removed by relatives to his old home in Hillsboro, Ohio. Bodies of soldiers killed from 1858 to 1867 were reburied at Fort D. A. Russell in 1899. Some still interred here are unknown. The roster shows of 103 men. 92 were under 23 years of age. Lt. Collins was not yet 21. Casper was named after Caspar Collins.

Erected by the Historical Landmark Commission of Wyoming 1957

LOCATION: On a small hill just south of the entrance to Fort Caspar.

PLATTE BRIDGE CEMETERY-5.1

TITLE: Platte Bridge Cemetery

LEGEND: You may be surprised that no one is buried under these stone markers. They represent some of the soldiers who died while stationed at Platte Bridge Station (Fort Caspar). The army removed the bodies originally located here and reinterred them at Fort D. A. Russell in 1899.

In 1936, members of the Civilian Conservation Corps unearthed three skeletons while working at this site. These bodies were reburied under the large monument to your left.

It is almost certain that other people are buried on the fort grounds. During the days of the great emigration along the Oregon Trail, this area served as a pioneer cemetery.

Funded by: Natrona County Historical Society 1988

LOCATION: On small hill just south of the entrance to Fort Caspar.

FORT CASPAR INFORMATIVE SIGN-6

TITLE: Old Fort Caspar

LEGEND: Originally known to trappers and explorers (1830-1847) as Upper Crossing of the North Platte River, it became the Mormon Ferry in 1847. Guinard built a bridge here in 1858, and troops from Platte Bridge Station guarded the telegraph line and protected emigrants on the "Oregon Trail". July 26, 1865, the station was attacked by hordes of Indians. Lt. Caspar Collins led an heroic attempt to rescue Sgt. Custard's wagon train, but sacrificed his life in aiding a fallen soldier. The station was renamed "Ft. Caspar" in his honor. Abandoned in 1867, fort and bridge were burned by Indians. The old fort was restored on its original foundations in 1936.

LOCATION: Entrance to Fort Caspar.

FORT CASPAR-6.1

TITLE: Fort Caspar

LEGEND: Named after Lt. Caspar Collins who was killed while rescuing a wounded comrade July 26, 1865.

Formerly Upper Platte Crossing, Mormon Ferry 1847-59, Platte Bridge Station 1859-1865, Fort Caspar 1865-67.

Oregon Trail 1834-1869, California Gold Trail, 1849, Overland Stage 1851, Pony Express 1860-61 First Trnscont-Telegraph 1861.

LOCATION: On the walkway to the restored buildings at Fort Caspar.

THE BATTLE OF RED BUTTES-6.2

TITLE: The Battle of Red Buttes

LEGEND: A desperate battle to save a supply train ended tragically the same day as the Battle at Platte Bridge. Sgt. Amos Custard and his men were bringing five supply wagons from the Sweetwater Station near Independence Rock. The group came into view of Platte Bridge Station from the direction of Red Buttes about noon on July 26, 1865.

Unaware of the morning's skirmish, Custard barely had time to assume a defensive position when a large group of Indians attacked. The 4 hour battle ended when the Indians overran the soldier's position.

The next day a detachment from Platte Bridge Station found the bodies of Sgt. Custard and 20 of his men. The only survivors were three of the five men on advance patrol from the supply train who made their way here to safety.

Funded by: Natrona County Historical Society 1988

LOCATION: On the walkway to the restored buildings at Fort Caspar.

NATRONA COUNTY

1	Casper Informative Sign	13	Martin's Cove	33	Bates Hole Stock Trail
3	First White Man's Cabin Informative Sign	14	Oregon Trail Marker	34	North Platte River Project Interpretive Site
4	Fort Caspar Cemetery—Grand Army of the Republic	15	Oregon Trail Marker	35	Alcova Reservoir Interpretive Marker
5	Old Pioneer Military Cemetery Marker	16	Oregon Trail Marker	36	Devil's Gate BLM Interpretive Site
5.1	Platte Bridge Cemetery	18	Oregon Trail Memorial	37	Red Buttes Battle
6	Fort Caspar Informative Sign	19	Oregon Trail Monument	38	Emigrant Gap BLM Interpretive Site
6.1	Fort Caspar	19.1	Oregon Trail Monument	39	Ryan Hill BLM Interpretive Site
6.2	The Battle of Red Buttes	20	Oregon Trail—Red Buttes Marker	40	Pony Express Marker
6.3	The Battle at Platte Bridge	21	Oregon Trail Monument	41	The Oregon-California Trail Octa Marker
7	Mormon Ferry Monument	22	Oregon Trail Monument	42	The Armory Marker
7.1	Mormon Ferry	23	Oregon Trail Memorial	43	Reshaw's Bridge Marker
8	Old Platte Bridge—Oregon Trail Monument	23.1	Oregon Trail Memorial	45	Guinard Bridge
9	Hell's Half Acre Informative Sign	23.2	Boy Scouts of America Monument	46	Pathfinder Cemetery
10	Hell's Half Acre Monument	24	Pioneer Monument	47	Pioneer Park Permaloy Plaque
11	Independence Rock Informative Sign	25	Pony Express Monument	48	Town of Mills Permaloy Plaque
12	Independence Rock Plaques	25.1	Pony Express Monument		
		26	Battle of Red Buttes—Oregon Trail Monument		
		27	Red Buttes Battle—Cemetery and Monument		
		29	Salt Creek Sign		
		30	Pathfinder Dam		
		30.1	Pathfinder Dam—Civil Engineering Landmark		
		30.2	Pathfinder Dam—Dedication Plaque		
		31	Bridger Road—Waltman Crossing		
		32	Bessemer Bend BLM Interpretive Site		

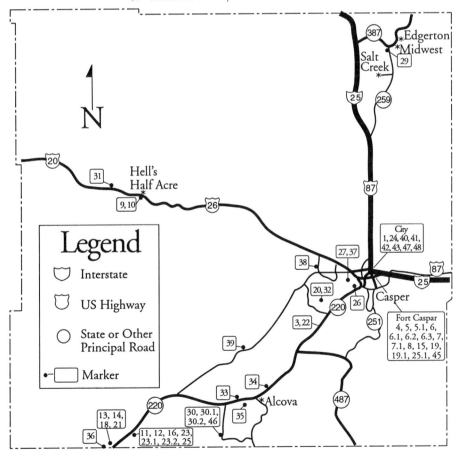

127

THE BATTLE AT PLATTE BRIDGE-6.3

TITLE: The Battle at Platte Bridge

LEGEND: Early on the morning of July 26, 1865 Lt. Caspar Collins led a troop of men to reinforce an army supply train coming into Platte Bridge Station. Only a mile west of the post, the group was ambushed by members of the Sioux, Cheyenne and Arapahoe nations.

The Indians were anxious to avenge the losses they sustained at the Sand Creek Massacre the previous year. They hoped to destroy Platte Bridge Station in this attack.

The Indian force heavily outnumbered the group led by Collins. During the retreat, four men were killed including the twenty-year old lieutenant.

The Army renamed Platte Bridge Station in honor of the young hero. Since a new post in Colorado had recently been named in honor of Caspar Collins' father, Col. W. O. Collins, the name Fort Caspar was chosen.

Funded by: Natrona County Historical Society
1988

LOCATION: On the walkway to the restored buildings at Fort Caspar.

MORMON FERRY MONUMENT-7

TITLE: The "Mormon" Ferry
Official Marker Utah Pioneer Trails and Landmark Association No. 13
Erected 1932

LEGEND: First commercial ferry on the Platte River was established 1/2 mile south of here in June 1847 by "Mormon" pioneers on their way to the valley of the Great Salt Lake. Brigham Young directed nine men to remain to operate the ferry. They were Thomas Grover, Captain John S. Higby, Luke S. Johnson, Appleton M. Harmon, Edmund Ellsworth, Francis M. Pomeroy, William Empey, James Davenport and Benjamin F. Stewart. The first passengers were Missourians bound for Oregon. The ferry was made of two large cottonwood canoes fastened by cross pieces and covered with slabs. It was operated with oars.

Utah Pioneer Trails and Landmarks Association, Natrona County Historical Society and Citizens of Wyoming

LOCATION: Northwest corner of the parade grounds at Fort Caspar.

MORMON FERRY-7.1

TITLE: The Mormon Ferry

LEGEND: Brigham Young, leading the advance Mormon party to the Great Salt Lake, reached this spot on June 12, 1847. He constructed a ferry to transport their wagons across the swift current of the North Platte River. Nine men were left to operate the ferry; a blacksmith was available to help needy travelers. The ferry operated until 1852.

LOCATION: Adjacent to a replica of a ferry, north end of the parade grounds at Fort Caspar.

OLD PLATTE BRIDGE—OREGON TRAIL MONUMENT-8

South side

TITLE: Site of old Platte Bridge

LEGEND: Built by Louis Guinard 1858-59.

Immediately south and west are the sites of Platte Bridge Station. First overland telegraph, stage and Pony Express stations on the old Oregon Trail.

Erected by Natrona County Historical Society, July 26, 1930

North side

TITLE: None

LEGEND: One half mile north and west across North Platte River on the tableland occurred Platte Bridge fight July 26, 1865 in which Lt. Caspar W. Collins, 11th Ohio Vol. Cav., and Privates George W. McDonald, Co. I, George Camp and Sebastian Nehring, Co. K, all of 11th Kan. Vol. Cav. were killed.

Also killed the same day near here were Privates James A. Porter and Adam Culp, both of Co. I, 11th Kan. Vol. Cav.

LOCATION: Northwest corner of the parade grounds at Fort Caspar.

In 1930, the Oregon Trail Memorial Association sponsored and directed the Covered Wagon Centennial to honor the first covered wagons to cross the nation 100 years earlier. Many historical markers were erected and dedicated during that year including this one, identified by the large Oregon Trail Memorial Association medallion at the top. See "Ezra Meeker, the Oregon Trail Memorial Association, and the American Pioneer Trails Association" in the first part of this book.

See Guinard Bridge plaque (Natrona County #45) for more discussion of the bridge.

HELL'S HALF ACRE INFORMATIVE SIGN-9

TITLE: Hell's Half Acre

LEGEND: This unique setting of natural beauty covers approximately 320 acres. Viewed from a point of maximum depth, its walls and pinnacles show soft and varied hues comparable to the Grand Canyon of the Yellowstone.

Investigation has confirmed that in former days the Indians drove great herds of buffalo into this depression for slaughter. Flint arrowheads and buffalo bones have been found here. A detachment of Captain B. L. E. Bonneville's party visited this site in July 1833. This area has been dedicated to Natrona County by the Federal Government.

LOCATION: South side of U.S. Hwy 20/26 at the Hell's Half Acre turnout, about 42 miles west of Casper, Wyoming

HELL'S HALF ACRE MONUMENT-10

TITLE: Hell's Half Acre

LEGEND: Erected by Historical Landmark Commission of Wyoming 1949

LOCATION: South side of U.S. Hwy 20/26 at the Hell's Half Acre turnout, about 42 miles west of Casper, Wyoming.

Although the bronze plaque was taken in about 1980, the crumbling cement pillar that once housed it still stands as a disappearing part of history itself.

INDEPENDENCE ROCK INFORMATIVE SIGN-11

TITLE: Independence Rock

LEGEND: Father DeSmet, early missionary, on July 5, 1841, surnamed this rock "The Great Record of the Desert" on account of the many names and dates carves on its surface.

It was an important landmark and camp site for the emigrants of the Oregon and Utah Trails crossing this territory from 1840 to 1869.

The first Masonic lodge held in Wyoming was opened on this rock on July 4, 1862.

The rock is of igneous origin consisting of red and white feldspar and mica. Marks on the sides show the action of the glacier, which crossed this part of the country in the Pre-Oligocene period.

LOCATION: South side of State Route 220 at the Independence Rock Rest Area.

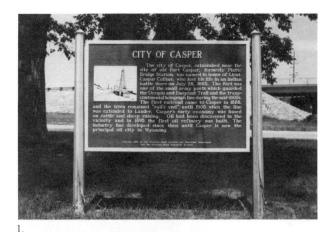

1.

2.

3.

4.

5.

6.

1. Many contemporary signs like the City of Casper Marker were placed in park-like settings.

2. Boy Scouts were very active in marking efforts for the 1930 Covered Wagon Centennial and later in 1931 when this marker was placed.

3. This marker was erected on the east side of Independence Rock during the national celebration of 1930 known as the Covered Wagon Centennial.

4. Many of the markers erected by the Wyoming Historical Landmark Commission were granite markers similar to this one found on the Oregon Trail.

5. Many markers, like the Old Platte Bridge—Oregon Trail Monument, were placed at Fort Caspar Historic Site.

6. The National Pony Express Centennial Association placed beautiful bronze plaques and historical markers like this one at Fort Caspar. Others were placed at Fort Laramie and Fort Bridger.

1.   2.   3.

1. The Historical Landmark Commission of Wyoming was very active from 1927 until 1959 erecting granite markers like this one.

2. Martin's Cove Marker was placed in 1933 by the Utah Pioneer Trails and Landmark Associaton memorializing 145 Mormon pioneers who perished in a snowstorm in November 1856.

3. In the open prairie where some of the markers are located, fences were erected to keep cattle and other livestock from damaging the markers.

INDEPENDENCE ROCK PLAQUES-12

Rest Area Plaques

Plaque #1
TITLE: Early Ranching
LEGEND: By 1869 people gradually began to settle this area. Cattle herds which had multiplied and overstocked Oregon ranges were driven back along the Oregon Trail to graze the empty plains. Other herds came to Wyoming, Montana, and Colorado from the great Texas herds. The journey's end for many herds were well watered valleys such as along the Sweetwater River.

Although the Valley of the Sweetwater was once an active scene of westward migration, today it is a vast grazing land used by owners of working ranches. Independence Rock and the ruts of the Oregon Trail remain as evidence that a nation once passed this way.

Plaque #2
TITLE: Military Involvement
LEGEND: Increased travel along the Oregon Trail and the construction of a telegraph line along this route led the Indians to the realization that their existence was threatened by another civilization. As a result, violence between emigrants and Indians increased. By 1860-61 several small military garrisons were built to protect travelers and keep the communication lines open.

The Three Crossing Station was located about 18 miles North and West of this site. It was a sturdy stockade, manned by one noncommissioned officer and 6 privates. Sweetwater Station, located about 2 miles northeast of Independence Rock was a telegraph relay station, military supply base, as well as a Pony Express and Overland Stage station. Both sites were abandoned in 1866.

Plaque #3
TITLE: The Great Emigration
LEGEND: Independence Rock was one of the most noted Oregon Trail landmarks. Between 1848 and completion of the transcontinental railroad in 1869, the trail was the major route followed by emigrants from Independence, Missouri to California, Utah, and the Willamette Valley of Oregon

Father Pierre DeSmet, a Jesuit missionary, dubbed the rock "The Register of the Desert" for at one time it had an estimated 40,000 names engraved on its surface. Almost all of the names, sometimes applied with a mixture of powder, buffalo grease and glue, are now covered with lichens, mother nature's eraser, which is slowly decomposing the rock.

Plaque #4
TITLE: Fur Trade and Naming the Rock
LEGEND: Eastward-moving Astorian fur traders in 1812 were probably the first white men to discover Independence Rock. Regardless of the date of discovery, the rock was a well-known landmark to the fur trapping mountain men.

Theories about naming the rock vary, but one likely version states that on July 4, 1830, mountain man William Sublette, leader of the first wagon train to cross the overland route, christened Independence Rock in honor of the nation's birthdate.

Plaque #5
TITLE: Prehistory and Geology
LEGEND: The Sweetwater causeway was probably first used by animals. Early North American Indians, following migratory animal herds, also used this overland passage. When their descendants,

including the Shoshone, Arapahoe, and other Plains tribes acquired the horse, the animal hooves and the poles of their travois wore the trail deeper and wider.

The geologic formation of Independence Rock is shown in the 3 diagrams at right.

Early Eocene Time, 50 million years ago.

The Granite Mountains were uplifted. Sedimentary rocks were stripped by streams from this rising fold, causing the granite core to be exposed, a part of which is Independence Rock, shown on the diagram as I.R.

Miocene Time, 15 million years ago.

The broad granite core of the Granite Mountains sagged downward several thousand feet. As a result, most of this once-majestic mountain range became lower than the basins to the north and south and was largely buried by enormous amounts of gray, windblown sand. In some places the sand accumulated to a thickness of 3000 feet.

Independence Rock as you see it today.

Most of the sediments that buried the rounded summits of the Granite Range have been stripped away. Summits such as Independence Rock have been re-exposed and appear today essentially as they were at the time of their burial 15 million years ago.

North end of Independence Rock
Plaque #1
TITLE: None
LEGEND: In Memory of Jason Lee. The Trail Blazer of Methodism in the Northwest. 1834-1844

Plaque #2
TITLE: None
LEGEND: In Memory of Dr. Grace Raymond Hebard 1861-1936. Wyoming historian-author-educator. Erected by Colonial Dames Resident in the State of Wyoming

Plaque #3
TITLE: None
LEGEND: In Memory of Anderson Deckard and party who camped here July 4, 1853. Settled near Albany, Oregon. Erected by his descendants. 1954.

Plaque #4
TITLE: None
LEGEND: In honor of The Mormon Pioneers who passed Independence Rock June 21, 1847 under the leadership of Brigham Young on their way top the valley of the Great Salt Lake and of more than 80,000 "Morman" emigrants who followed by ox teams, hand carts and other means of travel seeking religious liberty and economic independence.

Erected June 21, 1931 by descendants and followers of the pioneers who have made the desert blossom as the rose.

Plaque #5
TITLE: None
LEGEND: In Memory of Father P. J. DeSmet, S.J. 1840 who named this rock The Register of the Desert.

Dedicated July 4, 1930 by Wyoming Knights of Columbus.

Plaque #6
TITLE: Independence Rock
LEGEND: Probably discovered by returning Astorians 1812.

Given its name by emigrants who celebrated Independence Day here July 4, 1825. Capt. Bonneville passed here with first wagons 1832. Whitman and Spalding, missionaries with their wives stopped here in

1836. Father DeSmet saw it and owing to many names upon it called it the "Register of the Desert" 1840. Gen. John C. Fremont camped here with U.S. Army Aug. 2; 1842. Fifty thousand emigrants passed here in 1853. It is the most famous landmark of the Old Oregon Trail.

This tablet presented and placed by Henry D. Schoonmaker 1920

In 1915 Independence Rock was situated on a ranch owned by Henry D. Schoonmaker. He donated the bronze tablet to Wyoming in 1920.

Plaque #7
TITLE: Independence Rock
LEGEND: National Register of Historic Places-Wyoming Place No. 4.

Plaque #8
TITLE: None
LEGEND: In memory of William F. Bragg, Jr. 1922-1988

Independence Rock was considered a milestone as the settlers moved west on their journey across the Great Plains. They rejoiced and celebrated when they reached this spot. The Rock also served as a milestone for athletes. Cyclists from all corners of this Nation crossed the finish line here after a grueling road journey.

This stage has been named in memory of William Bragg, Jr., a Wyoming author and historian. One of Bill's wishes was that someday this National Historic Landmark would receive the recognition it deserved.

Thanks, Bill, for the great memories.
Presented by the Casper Bicycle Classic.

Plaque #9
TITLE: The Preservation of Independence Rock
LEGEND: An important landform like Independence Rock is protected and preserved only through the efforts of many people and organizations. Not all attempts at preservation and commemoration are acceptable by current standards, however, and some actions left permanent scars on the National Historic Landmark.

Past attempts to memorialize an event or person by the placement of a plaque on the Rock damaged the surface. Today, nine bronzed legends, bolted to this igneous summit are mute testimony to us about people of the immediate past and tell us what they believed to be important about their history.

A preservation ethic was fostered by public knowledge of the importance of the site. Public gatherings and celebrations held at the Rock over the years, including Independence Day commemorations, Masonic Lodge celebrations, and a National Boy Scout Jamboree, helped build public awareness.

As part of the United States bicentennial celebration, the State of Wyoming established Independence Rock State Historic Site with administrative responsibilities given to the Wyoming Recreation Commission. In an effort to retain the undisturbed atmosphere surrounding the Rock, development at the site was kept to a minimum. A fence placed around the area of the historical inscriptions reduces contemporary damage.

Hundreds and thousands of people stopped here to rest, to meet, and to picnic and the area continues to serve in the same capacity as Independence Rock State Historic Site, allowing visitors to enjoy the majestic beauty of the landmark while refreshing themselves.

Plaque #10
TITLE: None
LEGEND: To Narcissa Prentiss Whitman and Eliza Hart Spalding. Missionaries. 1st White Women in Wyoming and 1st Women over Oregon Trail 1836.

Placed July 4, 1936, by The Historical Landmark Commission of Wyoming

Plaque #11
TITLE: None
LEGEND: The first Lodge of Masons in what is now the State of Wyoming, was convened on Independence Rock on July 4, 1862 by a body of Master Masons who were traveling west on the Old Oregon Trail.

To commemorate this event Casper Lodge, No. 15, A.F. & A.M. of Casper, Wyoming, held memorial services here on July 4th, 1920.

Plaque #12
TITLE: Ezra Meeker
LEGEND: 1830   Pioneer   1928

LOCATION: On the south side of State Route 220, about 55 miles southwest of Casper, Wyoming.

The five plaques located at the Independence Rock Rest Area no longer are used, but their content is preserved in this book for their historical and geological interests. The remaining twelve markers are located at the north end of Independence Rock State State Historic Site. A walkway from the Rest Area leads to the markers on the north end of Independence Rock. An access road from State Route 220 and a parking area are located at the north end of Independence Rock.

Plaque #12 honored Ezra Meeker, one of the best known early pioneers. Through his efforts from 1906 to 1908, 150 additional markers were placed along the Oregon Trail from St. Louis to the west coast. His influence and guidance helped establish the Oregon Trail Memorial Association in 1926. He saw some of the Association's efforts materialize but passed on before the Covered Wagon Centennial in 1930.

During that national celebration of the Oregon Trail and its pioneers, the Ezra Meeker plaque was dedicated before about 3,500 people on July 4, 1930. Other markers were dedicated at or near Independence Rock that same weekend. Among them were the plaque honoring Father P. J. DeSmet, the Mason's marker, two Oregon Trail Memorial Association plaques at the Tom Sun Ranch just southwest of Independence Rock, two Boy Scout markers on the east side of Independence Rock, and the plaque on the north side of Independence Rock honoring the Mormon pioneers.

MARTIN'S COVE-13

TITLE: Official Marker
        Utah Pioneers Trails and Landmark Association
        No. 28
        Erected June 22, 1933
        Martin's Cove
LEGEND: Survivors of Captain Edward Martin's handcart company of Mormon emigrants from England to Utah were rescued here in perishing condition about Nov. 12, 1856. Delayed in starting and hampered by inferior carts, it was overtaken by an early winter. Among the company of 576, including aged people and children, the fatalities numbered 145. Insufficient food and clothing and severe weather caused many deaths. Toward the end every campground became a grave yard. Some of the survivors found shelter in a stockade and mail station near Devil's Gate where their property was stored for the winter. Earlier companies reached Utah in safety.

Utah Pioneer Trails & Landmarks Association and citizens of Wyoming.
LOCATION: West of Devil's Gate on the north side of the Tom Sun Ranch road about 2.1 miles west of the ranch headquarters. The marker is on private land; permission required to enter.

OREGON TRAIL MARKER-14

TITLE: The Oregon Trail 1841
LEGEND: Devil's Gate one-fourth mile east. Split Rock 20 miles northwest.
        Erected by the Historical Landmark Commission of Wyoming 1943

LOCATION: On the Tom Sun Ranch just west of Devil's Gate. Adjacent to two other markers (Natrona County #18 & 21).

OREGON TRAIL MARKER-15

TITLE: None
LEGEND: Unveiled by Fort Caspar Chapter D.A.R. July 5, 1920.
        Oregon Trail Marked by the State of Wyoming 1914.
        Lieutenant Caspar W. Collins killed by Sioux Indians near this spot July 26, 1865.
LOCATION: On the grounds at Fort Caspar.

This marker was donated by the State of Wyoming, the Caspar Chapter of the D.A.R., and the Commissioners of Natrona County. The marker stands where the Oregon Trail crossed the Yellowstone Highway. According to Grace Hebard in *Marking The Oregon Trail, The Bozeman Trail and Historic Places in Wyoming 1908-1920:*

> The stone stands in the middle of the old trail bed, which is at this point at least fifty feet wide and several feet deep, looking like some ancient irrigation ditch. The excavation of this path was made by human, ox, mule and horse feet, wagon wheels, wheelbarrows, push carts, Indian, wild animal, and the continual winds of a Wyoming climate!

OREGON TRAIL MARKER-16

TITLE: Oregon Trail
LEGEND: Marked by the State of Wyoming 1914
LOCATION: North end of Independence Rock, about 55 miles southwest of Casper, Wyoming, on State Route 220.

This marker was erroneously erected on the east side of the North Platte River in 1914. However, under the direction of the Daughters of the American Revolution and Mrs. B. B. Brooks, State Regent for the D.A.R., the marker was re-dedicated on the north side of Independence Rock on July 4, 1920.

OREGON TRAIL MEMORIAL-18

TITLE: None
LEGEND: In honor of the Pioneer Women buried here in unmarked graves 1836-1870.
        Erected 1930 by Business and Professional Women Club of Casper
LOCATION: On the Tom Sun Ranch just west of Devil's Gate. Adjacent to two other Oregon Trail markers (Natrona County #14 & 21).

The Oregon Trail Memorial Association coordinated the Covered Wagon Centennial in 1930. The July 4, 1930, celebration included the dedication of this marker, with its large circular Oregon Trail Memorial plaque embedded in the granite. Many similar markers were placed at important locations along the Oregon Trail.

OREGON TRAIL MONUMENT-19

TITLE: Oregon Trail
LEGEND: Marked by the State of Wyoming 1914
LOCATION: Southeast corner of the parade grounds at Fort Caspar. Adjacent to Oregon Trail Monument (Natrona County #19.1).

The Oregon Trail Commission, along with the Sons and Daughters of the American Revolution, was instrumental in getting these early Oregon Trail markers made and erected. Although dated 1914, many were erected and dedicated shortly after that year.

OREGON TRAIL MONUMENT-19.1

TITLE: Oregon Trail Memorial
LEGEND: None
LOCATION: Southeast corner of the parade grounds at Fort Caspar. Adjacent to Oregon Trail Monument (Natrona County #19).

OREGON TRAIL—RED BUTTES MARKER-20

TITLE: Red Buttes
LEGEND: Of Oregon Trail fame where westward travelers left the North Platte River.

A tribute to pioneer emigrants from Casper Literary Club, 1930
LOCATION: Rest area about 0.2 miles north of the bridge over the North Platte River at Bessemer Bend. About 2.2 miles from the junction of Bessemer Bend Road and State Route 220. Adjacent to the Bessemer Bend BLM Interpretive Site (Natrona County #32).

This marker was one of three placed under the direction of Dan W. Greenburg and the Natrona County Historical Society during the Covered Wagon Centennial year. The granite marker, vandalized long ago, is missing the Oregon Trail Memorial plaque.

OREGON TRAIL MONUMENT-21

TITLE: None
LEGEND: To all pioneers 1830-1870 buried here on the Tom Sun Ranch.

Ezra Meeker often visited this spot. Erected by Oregon Trail Memorial Association 1930.
LOCATION: On the Tom Sun Ranch just west of Devil's Gate. Adjacent to two other Oregon Trail markers (Natrona County #14 & 18)

Through the leadership of George D. Pratt and the Oregon Trail Memorial Association, this marker was dedicated in the afternoon of July 4, 1930, in tribute to the some three dozen unknown emigrants.

OREGON TRAIL MONUMENT-22

TITLE: The Oregon Trail 1841
LEGEND: Oregon Trail approximately four miles north. On bend of North Platte visible to the north Robert Stuart in 1812 erected the first white man's cabin in Wyoming.

Erected by the Historical Landmark Commission of Wyoming 1943
LOCATION: On the south side of State Route 220 about 1.7 miles west of junction of Bessemer Road and State Route 220.

See First White Man's Cabin Informative Sign (Natrona County #3) for more information.

OREGON TRAIL MEMORIAL-23

Red Sandstone
TITLE: None
LEGEND: B.S.A. Troop 207.
　　　　Buckner Mo.
　　　　July 4, 1930.
Bronze marker
TITLE: None
LEGEND: Parco Troop No. 130 Boy Scouts of America Independence Rock, July 4, 1930.

LOCATION: On the east side of Independence Rock, about 55 miles southwest of Casper, Wyoming, on State Route 220. Adjacent to three other markers (Natrona County #23.1, 23.2, & 25). There is a short walk from the parking area at the north end of Independence Rock.

The bronze marker disappeared years ago. Its legend holds historic significance, as over 800 Boy Scouts dedicated three markers during the Covered Wagon Centennial in 1930. For more discussion of the Covered Wagon Centennial see "Ezra Meeker, the Oregon Trail Memorial Association, and the American Pioneer Trails Association" in the first part of this book.

OREGON TRAIL MEMORIAL-23.1

TITLE: Oregon Trail Memorial
LEGEND: To all unknown pioneers who passed this way to win and hold the West.

Placed here by Troop 21, Boy Scouts of America Woodmere Long Island, New York, Charles A. Hewlett, Scoutmaster.
LOCATION: On the east side of Independence Rock, about 55 miles southwest of Casper, Wyoming, on State Route 220. Adjacent to three other markers (Natrona County #22, 23.2, & 25). There is a short walk from the parking area at the north end of Independence Rock.

In 1930, a group of over 800 Boy Scouts gathered at Independence Rock for the Covered Wagon Centennial, dedicating this and two other markers on July 5th. The marker bears the brass medallion of the Oregon Trail Memorial Association.

BOY SCOUTS OF AMERICA MONUMENT-23.2

TITLE: None
LEGEND: To past-present-future Wyoming State Historical Site dedicated September 12, 1981, courtesy C.W.C. B.S.A. 1930-1976-1981.
LOCATION: On the east side of Independence Rock, about 55 miles southwest of Casper, Wyoming, on State Route 220. Adjacent to three other markers (Natrona County #22, 23.1, & 25). There is a short walk from the parking area at the north end of Independence Rock.

This unique marker was erected during the Covered Wagon Centennial in 1930. Each of the Boy Scout patrols contributed a rock native to his home community. The monument made from these rocks was dedicated July 5, 1930.

PIONEER MONUMENT-24

South face
TITLE: Fort Casper
LEGEND: U.S. Military Post established about 1864 by volunteers. Abandoned Oct. 19, 1867. Situated one mile west of this spot.

Marked by the State of Wyoming 1914
West face
TITLE: Pioneer Monument
LEGEND: Erected on the site of the Old Oregon Trail. In memory of the pioneers who blazed the way. Built by Natrona County Pioneer Association. 1849-1911.

LOCATION: East side of North Center Street just south of East B Street in Casper, Wyoming. Across the street from the Casper City and County Building.

Casper's Pioneer Monument was erected in February 1911 by the women of the Natrona County Pioneer Association. During one of his trips along the Oregon Trail, Ezra Meeker, founder of the Oregon Trail Memorial Association and pioneer of the Oregon Trail, interested the Natrona County Pioneer Association in erecting a monument. The Association women raised $1500 to purchase a large Indiana limestone marker; the freight costs were donated by the Northwestern Railway Company. At the time, the twenty-six foot high marker was one of the largest and most expensive Oregon Trail monuments.

The bronze plaque was unveiled November 20, 1914, by the Natrona County Pioneer Association and the local chapter of the Daughters of the American Revolution. Ex-Governor Bryant B. Brooks gave the address, "The Pioneer Movement to the West," and Erma Patton unveiled the monument. According to Alfred J. Molker's *History of Natrona County,* William H. Lloyd, who cut the stone for Natrona County's court house, the Masonic Temple, and a number of the other public buildings in Casper, cut the inscription for the Association and inserted the bronze tablet in the obelisk for the State of Wyoming.

PONY EXPRESS MONUMENT-25

TITLE: Pony Express
LEGEND: To all pioneers and in memory of James A. Shoemaker of the Oregon Trail Memorial Association.
Erected by Troop 21
Boy Scouts of America
Woodmere, New York 1931
LOCATION: On the east side of Independence Rock, about 55 miles southwest of Casper, Wyoming, on State Route 220. Adjacent to three other markers (Natrona County #23, 23.1, & 23.2). There is a short walk from the parking area on the north side of Independence Rock.

PONY EXPRESS MONUMENT-25.1

Rectangular plaque
TITLE: The Pony Express
LEGEND: Here was bustling Platte Bridge Station (later renamed Fort Caspar) with a relay station for the Pony Express. The bridge was a catalyst drawing together wilderness wayfarers—frontiersmen and immigrants—to learn late news of trail events in civilized regions.
Erected by the State of Wyoming
National Pony Express Centennial Association, Horace A. Sorensen—President, Richard I. Frost—Director.
Circular plaque
TITLE: National Pony Express Centennial Association
1860-61 Trail Marker 1960-61
LEGEND: Russell Majors Wadell
Founders Owners Operators
Pony Express

LOCATION: Northwest corner of the parade grounds at Fort Caspar.

BATTLE OF RED BUTTES—OREGON TRAIL MONUMENT-26

TITLE: Commemorating battle of Red Buttes which occurred across North Platte River July 26, 1865.
LEGEND: Erected by Headquarters 2d Corps Area United States Army, which re-enacted the battle at Governor's Island, N.Y. June 2l, and 22, 1930. H.E. Ely, Major General Commanding.
LOCATION: North side of State Route 220 at paved turnout about 0.6 miles west of Robertson Road in Casper, Wyoming.

A wagon train led by Sgt. Amos J. Custard and twenty-three men started from Sweetwater Station, about 120 miles to the west of Fort Caspar, headed for Platte Bridge Station at Fort Caspar. They were attacked by Indians near Red Buttes on July 26, 1865, with twenty-seven soldiers losing their lives here. The commemorative cemetery is located about two miles north of this marker on private land.

In June 1930, the battle was commemorated in a celebration of the Covered Wagon Centennial at Governor's Island in the harbor of New York. An estimated 40,000 people saw the re-enactment of the Red Buttes Battle.

As part of the Oregon Trail Memorial Association's Covered Wagon Centennial celebration in 1930, an Oregon Trail Memorial plaque was placed atop this marker.

RED BUTTES BATTLE—CEMETERY AND MONUMENT-27

TITLE: Commemorating Battle of Red Buttes July 26, 1865
LEGEND: Erected by Headquarters Second Corps Area United States Army which reenacted the battle at Governor's Island, N.Y. June 21, and 22, 1930. H. E. Ely, Major General Commanding.
LOCATION: Near Casper, Wyoming, on private land accessed from Poison Spider Road. Permission necessary. Inquire locally. Adjacent to Red Buttes Battle (Natrona County #37).

Vandals defaced this marker years ago, and the Oregon Trail Memorial plaque has disappeared. See Battle of Red Buttes—Oregon Trail Monument (Natrona County #26) for more information.

SALT CREEK SIGN-29

TITLE: Salt Creek Oil Field
LEGEND: Stockmen were aware of pools of oil in the creek bottoms during cattle trailing days. These oil seeps led to the discovery of Salt Creek, one of Wyoming's largest oil fields, nine miles long by five miles wide.

In 1883, the first claims were filed in the 22,000 acre Salt Creek Field. The first strike in the field occurred in 1908 at a depth of 1,050 feet. Many wells are still active.

Salt Creek was one of the first unitized oil fields in the United States. Under unitization one company operates properties for all owners and more efficient recovery methods can be used. Improved practices in Salt Creek have recovered many additional millions of barrels of oil.
Wyoming Recreation Commission
LOCATION: Southwest corner of the junction of State Routes 387 and 259 at Midwest, Wyoming.

Pioneers A. T. Seymour and Cy Iba were the first to attempt oil prospecting in the Salt Creek area. The Pennsylvania Oil and Gas Company drilled a well one thousand feet deep in 1889 and began production with a ten-barrel-a-day well. There were difficulties, however, because the oil had to be transported, by wagons pulled by up to twelve horses, to the new refinery in Casper and then eastward. In 1893, the Fremont, Elkhorn and Missouri Valley Railroad (later to be known as the Chicago and Northwestern) carried oil from the refinery to Orin Junction, Wyoming. There the Cheyenne and Northern Railroad (later known as the Burlington Northern) carried the oil south (from *Wyoming: A Guide to Historic Sites*).

PATHFINDER DAM-30

TITLE: Pathfinder Dam
LEGEND: No. Platte River Project 1903-1909
Structure Height 214 feet
Crest Length 432 feet
Reservoir Capacity 1,016,000 acre feet
Bureau of Reclamation
LOCATION: Pathfinder Dam, south of State Route 220, about 50 miles west of Casper, Wyoming.

The Federal Reclamation Act of 1902 and various project authorizing acts passed by Congress permitted the government to build irrigation works and enabled the Reclamation Service (Bureau of Reclamation) to develop the North Platte River for both irrigation water and power production, thus increasing the river's importance.

It took six years and over two million dollars before Pathfinder Dam was completed in 1909. The masonry arch dam was named in honor of General John Charles Fremont, "Pathfinder of the West," a government explorer in 1842 who attempted to run the turbulent North Platte River waters near the Pathfinder Dam location.

PATHFINDER DAM—CIVIL ENGINEERING LANDMARK-30.1

TITLE: Pathfinder Dam
LEGEND: Wyoming Historic Civil Engineering Landmark
Wyoming Section ASCE 1975
LOCATION: Pathfinder Dam, south of State Route 220, about 50 miles west of Casper, Wyoming.

PATHFINDER DAM—DEDICATION PLAQUE-30.2

TITLE: Pathfinder Dam
       1909
       North Platte Project

LEGEND: Built by and for the people of the United States for the conservation, control, and use of water resources.
   Height of Dam 214 feet
   Length of Crest 432 feet
   Reservoir Capacity 1,016,000 acre feet

LOCATION: Pathfinder Dam, south of State Route 220, about 50 miles west of Casper, Wyoming.

BRIDGER ROAD—WALTMAN CROSSING-31

TITLE: Bridger Road—Waltman Crossing

LEGEND: Here the present-day highway crosses what remains of an all but forgotten road. That road led to the remote gold fields of western Montana, booming since 1862.

The Government, in 1859, ordered Captain W. F. Raynolds, Topographic Engineers, U.S. Army, to reconnoiter Rocky Mountain topography and potential routes leading to areas of indicated mineralization. Old Jim Bridger, noted explorer since fur trade days, was Raynolds' guide. In 1864 official energy was still concentrated on the Civil War and that most famous of mountain-men laid out this road himself.

The Oregon Trail was the trunk line of the western roads. Although Montana's mines lay far north of its course, further west—in Idaho a branch-road turned off to those diggings. But that right-angle turn added some two hundred time-consuming, exhausting miles to the shortest feasible roadway. During 1863, John Bozeman had pioneered a road, east of the Big Horn Mountains and up the Yellowstone Valley, cutting across the angle, saving two weeks travel time. Still, by crossing Indian hunting grounds, his road increased the hazard of overland freight and travel.

Bridger's route—west of the Big Horns—reduced danger from Indian attacks while saving ten days time. But the Bridger road was a compromise. It never was as well known as either of its alternatives. Later, it was important in the settlement of northwestern Wyoming.

LOCATION: At the Waltman Roadside Rest Area about 49 miles west of Casper, Wyoming, on the north side of U.S. Hwy 20/26.

BESSEMER BEND BLM INTERPRETIVE SITE-32

Plaque #1
TITLE: The Goose Egg Ranch

LEGEND: The Goose Egg Ranch was established in this area of Wyoming by the Searight Cattle Company of Texas, which stocked it with 14,000 head of cattle trailed in from Oregon. Inspiration for the name of the ranch came when one of the cowboys found some goose eggs on an island in the North Platte River.

The ranch house, built in the fall of 1881, was a large native stone building with a living room, kitchen, five bedrooms and a cellar. Although most materials were freighted by wagon teams from Cheyenne, the stone was cut from nearby rocks.

Famous for its local dances and parties, the house was picked by Owen Wister as the setting for an incident in his western novel, "The Virginian". In this famous story the Virginian switched babies in clothing and cribs while their parents danced at the party. This prank was his reaction to being snubbed by the teacher, Molly Wood, after he rode 100 miles to attend the party.

The ranch house was one quarter mile east of flourishing Bessemer City. It was once used as a hotel, advertised as "the best hotel in central Wyoming with accommodations unsurpassed".

When the Goose Egg Ranch was sold in 1886, it became part of J. M. Carey's spread. Carey and his son, Robert, both were Governor and Senator for Wyoming in the early 1900's. The house was razed in 1951 because it was felt to be a hazard.

Plaque #2
TITLE: Pony Express

LEGEND: Red Buttes Pony Express Station was located a few hundred feet from here on the ridge above the river. The station was constructed for the Overland Stage and shared by the Pony Express. It was along this north bank of the river that the first transcontinental telegraph line was built.

William "Buffalo Bill" Cody, Pony Express rider, made the longest non stop ride from this station. Completing his own run of 116 miles between Red Buttes and Three Crossings, he found his relief rider had met an untimely death, causing Cody to ride an extra 76 miles to Rock Ridge Station. He immediately returned from Rock Ridge to Red Buttes, completing the route in record time.

Plaque #3
TITLE: Pony Express
       April 4, 1860—October 24, 1861

LEGEND: Historic sites have been interpreted along the Pony Express Trail by the Bureau of Land Management in Wyoming, Utah and Nevada. This effort to embrace your understanding of this western heritage is in observance of the American Revolution Bicentennial. "Bessemer Bend" is one of three Bureau of Land Management sites in Wyoming. You are invited westward to the Sweetwater River to visit "Devil's Gate" near Independence Rock via Wyoming 220 and "Split Rock" via Wyoming 287. If you are the adventurous sort, trace the original path of the Pony Express or the Oregon Trail following the route of westward expansion.

SUBTITLE: The Need Was There
LEGEND: Competing with time, harsh climates, long distance, mountains, plains, deserts and the hostility of numerous Indian bands, the Pony Express met the need to carry communication 1600 miles across the West. It was a triumph of organization, determination and courage and was vital to the life of the Nation. The Pony Express kept the far West informed and helped to keep California in the Union at the outbreak of the Civil War, thus playing a part in holding the Nation together. During its eighteen month life, the Pony Express operated at peak efficiency, speeding mail from either end at an average rate of only 10 days. The time was shorter for telegrams as the "talking wire" neared completion from east and west. From April 4, 1860 to October 24, 1861, the California Overland Mail and Pike's Peak Express (Pony Express) was the Nation's vital communication link with the far West.

SUBTITLE: How It Was Done
LEGEND: Stations were set up 10 to 15 miles apart along the route, each manned by two to four men and extra horses. In the desert west, relay stations were often much farther apart. About 300 of the hardiest western horses were bought at prices up to $200 each. Above all, the 80 riders were recruited from the most daring, determined and toughest "wiry young fellows" in the West. Lightly equipped and armed, each rider rode about 35 miles and back, exchanging horses at three relay stations. Over his saddle the rider carried the mochila, a leather cover with four mail pouches. Postage for a single letter was $1 to $5. Each rider rode at top speed to his relay stations. There the precious mochila was placed on a waiting horse and the rider was off again in two minutes. Day and night, good weather and bad, winter and summer, the "Pony" never stopped, averaging 10 to 15 miles an hour across the West.

SUBTITLE: The Pony's Echo

LEGEND: Completion of the Transcontinental Telegraph Line, October 24, 1861, put an end to the Pony Express. The wire now met the need for urgent communication. The Overland Mail Stage Coach service for letters had been intensified so that the high cost of Pony Express mail was no longer justified. In 18 months the story of the Pony Express had attracted world-wide attention that has not faded with time. Its backers, William B. Russell, Alexander Majors, William B. Waddell and Company, lost over $1 million on the venture and never received federal support. Never the less, the Pony Express will remain as an outstanding example of American enterprise, endurance, courage and determination in the westward expansion of the Nation.

Plaque #4

TITLE: Astorians

LEGEND: John Jacob Astor's "Astorians" are often given credit for finding the "South Pass" route to Oregon territory, later crossed by thousands on the Oregon Trail. Astor sent his "Astorians" by sea and land in 1810 to establish the Pacific Fur Company at the mouth of the Columbia River. Astor's dream was to establish a Pacific base for his fur trading business that would become a cornerstone for a great new American state. He intended to break the British fur monopoly in the Pacific Northwest and bring American territory under American control.

Wilson Price Hunt with his party of "Astorians" traveled west, crossing northern Wyoming in July of 1811. Robert Stuart, a partner in the company, traveled with others by sea. Stuart later returned to New York with dispatches for Astor. It was this journey which pioneered the route over South Pass, in October 1812.

The Platte River, being a natural travel route across Wyoming and Nebraska, was first encountered by Stuart above Bessemer Bend. Stuart's party camped near here across the river, from November 1 to November 13, 1812, planning to winter in a crude cabin they built. Fearing Indian attack, the party abandoned the cabin and proceeded down the river.

Stuart's diary describes how he found this place:

> ...we reached a considerable mountain through which the River ran 4 miles, when the Country opening, it made a large bend to the north (Bessemer Bend), to the lower end of which we went in 2 more and encamped in a beautiful bottom of Cottonwoods surrounded with a thick growth of the common Willow—our days journey was 24 miles NE.

Many explorers, mountain men and travelers stopped here, at what they referred to as "Red Buttes". Among them were Andrew Sublette, July 30, 1834, "bound for Laramy's Fork", John Charles Fremont in 1842, and Howard Stansbury, July 27, 1852.

Plaque #5

TITLE: The Oregon Trail

LEGEND: The Oregon Trail was the major corridor of westward migration—the main street of the West from the 1830's to 1869 when the transcontinental railroad was completed. Restless Americans from all walks of life moved west along this corridor seeking a better life in a new land. The Mormons sought freedom from religious, social and economic intolerance and aggression. For others, the lure was land available for the taking. After the discovery of gold in California in 1848, bands of feverish fortune seekers sought the buried wealth of the West. An estimated 350,000 people passed this way between 1841 and 1866 on their way to western territories. For these thousands of men, women and children, the journey was 2,000 miles of plains, deserts and mountains-one step at a time. Their vision of personal freedom and opportunity were vital to national expansion. The long journey to Oregon took emigrants about six months, moving 10 to 20 miles a day with their wagons, carts and packs. Time, distance and hardships seasoned the travelers much as soldiers are seasoned by a long war.

Those who crossed the North Platte River at this point had already traveled nearly 775 miles, most of it near the Platte River. Howard Stansbury passed through here in July of 1852 and noted the difficulties encountered by those who had passed ahead of him. He witnessed eleven broken wagons and much discarded equipment; such as blacksmith's anvils, trunks, ploughs, ovens and grindstones.

Plaque #6

TITLE: Bessemer Bend

LEGEND: Explorers, fur traders, mountain men and emigrants have camped at this site. Although the main route of the Oregon Trail is a few miles north of here, many emigrant travelers crossed the North Platte River at this site for the last time on their trek west. They preferred using this favorable ford rather than waiting in line and paying the tolls and ferry fees required at lower crossings. Ample grass, good water and pleasant surroundings made this a favorite campsite for some travelers, since the route to or from the Sweetwater River was three days of rough, dry country and poisonous alkali water.

Bessemer City, ("Queen of the Plains"), flourished for a short time (1888-1891) a few miles west of the river. Bessemer City was founded by cattle kings anticipating the construction of a railroad. This area was the hub of well-established stock-grazing ranches on major streams and rivers. The residents of Bessemer City staged a campaign for the Natrona County seat and in April of 1890 lost their bid to Casper, another nearby village. Bessemer City died and is now a field of waving alfalfa where once stood hotels, stores, churches, and saloons.

LOCATION: About 0.2 miles north of the bridge over the North Platte River at Bessemer Bend. About 2.2 miles north of the junction of Bessemer Bend Road and State Route 220. Adjacent to Oregon Trail—Red Buttes Marker (Natrona County #20).

BATES HOLE STOCK TRAIL

TITLE: Bates Hole Stock Trail

LEGEND: Stock Driveways were established under a provision of the 1916 Stockraising Homestead Act. Local ranch operators pay for trailing privileges along the Bates Hole Stock Driveway. Trailing occurs annually between May and November, with peak use occurring in June as herds travel to summer pastures in the Deer Creek Range, and in October as they return to home winter ranges. Your courtesy and cooperation towards the users of the stock trail is appreciated.

In cooperation with the Bates Hole Stock Trail Committee, adjoining landowners, and the Bureau of Land Management.

LOCATION: Dirt road (Natrona County 316), north of State Route 220 about 5 miles west of Alcova, Wyoming.

NORTH PLATTE RIVER PROJECT INTERPRETIVE SITE-34

SUBTITLE: Gray Reef Dam and Reservoir

LEGEND: Constructed to regulate rather than store water. Regulation of water flow in the North Platte River is of particular importance for power production, for full benefits for fish life, water quality, municipal and industrial water and irrigation.

Gray Reef Reservoir assures that releases can be made from Alcova Powerplant according to varying needs for power. It provides river flowage with a minimum of daily fluctuation.

The reservoir can store 1,800 acre-feet of water behind the earthfill dam which is 36 feet high and 650 feet long. The outlet gates are electronically controlled from Alcova Powerplant.

SUBTITLE: Alcova Dam and Reservoir

LEGEND: Alcova Dam, 10 miles downstream from Pathfinder Dam, acts as a diversion structure and creates a reservoir from which water is diverted into the Casper Canal for irrigating the Kendrick Project lands. The dam is an earth and rockfill embankment structure 265 feet high with a crest length of 763 feet.

Additional lands downstream are irrigated by water released through the Alcova Powerplant at the base of the dam, or over a controlled spillway. The storage capacity of Alcova Reservoir is 189,000 acre feet.

SUBTITLE: Pathfinder Dam and Reservoir
LEGEND: Constructed for the storage of water on the North Platte River and for irrigation purposes in eastern Wyoming and western Nebraska.

This masonry, arch, gravity-type dam, structurally 214 feet in height with a crest length of 432 feet, is made of granite quarried from nearby hills. Constructed during 1905-1909, Pathfinder Dam is one of the first dams built under the Reclamation Law.

The storage capacity of Pathfinder Reservoir is 1,016,000 acre feet.

SUBTITLE: Fremont Canyon Powerplant
LEGEND: Built to take advantage of a 350-foot 'head' between Pathfinder and Alcova Reservoirs, available water is used to generate electric power. The reinforced concrete powerplant contains two 24,000-kilowatt generators. Construction features also include a conduit 18 feet in diameter and three miles in length; a surge tank 40 feet in diameter and 246 feet (24 stories) high; and a vehicular tunnel 17 feet in diameter and 1,700 feet long for access to the powerplant.

LOCATION: On State Highway 220 about 30 miles west of Casper, Wyoming.

ALCOVA RESERVOIR INTERPRETIVE MARKER-35

TITLE: Alcova Reservoir
LEGEND: Alcova Reservoir, below you, created by Alcova Dam constructed by the Bureau of Reclamation and completed in 1938, is on the North Platte River. The reservoir is 4 miles long, has 2500 acre surface area, and a normal water surface elevation of 5,500 feet. Water from this reservoir is diverted into Casper Canal for irrigating Kendrick Project lands.

Casper Canal with a capacity of 600 cubic feet per second, is 62 miles long and serves 201 miles of laterals and sub-laterals.

The principal crops grown on the 24,000 irrigable acres are corn, alfalfa and feed grains.

Lake Shore Drive, 2 miles back, provides a more complete view of beautiful Alcova Reservoir. There you will find boat launching ramps, fishing, swimming areas, and picnic and camping sites.
U.S. Department of the Interior March 3, 1849
U.S. Department of the Interior Bureau of Reclamation
LOCATION: At scenic turnout on State Route 220, about 4 miles west of Alcova, Wyoming.

DEVIL'S GATE BLM INTERPRETIVE SITE-36

Plaque #1
TITLE: Devil's Gate
LEGEND: Devil's Gate, the 370-foot high, 1500-foot long cleft, carved over the centuries by the Sweetwater River, was a major landmark on the Oregon Trail...A pleasant change for weary travelers coming across the rough, dry country from the North Platte River, a four day trek. Goldrush 49'er, J. G. Bruff, wrote of Devil's Gate: "...some of the boys clambered up the rocks on the north side of the Gate...where they fired pistols and threw down rocks, pleased with the reverberation, which was great. I made a careful sketch of this remarkable gorge."

Plaque #2
TITLE: Oregon Trail
LEGEND: The Oregon Trail was the major corridor of westward migration...the main street of the West from the 1830's to 1869 when the transcontinental railroad was completed. Restless Americans from all walks of life moved west along this corridor seeking a better life in a new land. The Mormons sought freedom from religious, social and economic intolerances and aggression. For others, the lure was land for the taking. After the discovery of gold in California in 1848, bands of feverish fortune seekers sought the buried wealth of the West. An estimated 350,000 people passed this way between 1841 and 1866 on their way to western territories. For these thousands of men, women and children, the journey was 2,000 miles of plains, mountains and deserts...one step at a time. Their visions of personal freedom and opportunity were vital to national expansion.

The long journey to Oregon took emigrants about six months, moving 10 to 20 miles a day with their wagons, carts and packs. Time, distance and hardships seasoned the travelers much as soldiers are seasoned by a long war.

Following Indian trails, fur traders and trappers opened the way. The Stuart party of John Jacob Astor's Pacific Fur Company pioneered this route in 1812 from west to east (Oregon to St. Louis) over South Pass. Until the 1840's, the heaviest use of the route was made by these "mountain men". They scouted the American West and later led missionaries (1836) and the first wagon trains (1841) over the Oregon Trail.

Historic Sites have been interpreted along the Oregon Trail by the Bureau of Land Management in Wyoming, Idaho and Oregon. This effort to enhance your understanding of our western heritage is in observance of the American Revolution Bicentennial.

"Devil's Gate" is one of the Bureau of Land Management sites in Wyoming. You are invited to visit "Bessemer Bend" to the east, near Casper, located on the North Platte River via Wyoming 220 and "Split Rock" to the west, located on U.S. 287. If you are the adventurous sort, trace the original path of the Oregon Trail following the route of westward expansion.

Plaque #3
TITLE: Sweetwater River
LEGEND: From here to Split Rock, a day's trail journey west, the Oregon Trail followed two routes: one close to the Sweetwater River, the other further from it but more direct. Capt. Howard Stansbury comments August 1, 1852:

> ...the road passing occasionally through deep, heavy sand continued up the right bank of the Sweetwater...the valley is here nearly two miles wide, with rolling hills between the two mountain ranges, which...form its limits.
>
> About a dozen burnt wagons and nineteen dead oxen were passed today along the road; but the destruction has been by no means as great as upon the North Fork of the Platte and the crossing over to the Sweetwater.

The Pony Express and Overland Stage coaches followed these routes; the Pony Express changing horses at Plant's Station a few miles from here.

Plaque #4
TITLE: Martin's Cove
LEGEND: Two miles to the northwest, nestled at the foot of the Sweetwater Rocks, is Martin's Cove. Here Captain Edward Martin's exhausted company of Mormon handcart emigrants sought shelter from an early winter storm in November of 1856. Of 576 men, women and

children, 145 had died before rescue parties from Salt Lake City reached them.

> A condition of distress here meet my eyes that I never saw before or since. The (Mormon) train was strung out for two or three miles. There were old men pulling and tugging their carts, sometimes loaded with a sick wife or children, women pulling along sick husbands, little children six to eight years old struggling through the mud and snow. As night came on the mud would freeze on their clothes and feet. We gathered on to some of the most helpless with our riatas tied to the carts, and helped as many as we could into camp...Such assistance as we could give was rendered to all until they finally arrived at Devil's Gate fort, about the first of November. There were some 1200 in all, about one half with handcarts and the other half with teams.
>
> The winter storms had now set in in all their severity. The provisions we took amounted to almost nothing among so many people, many of them now on very short rations, some almost starving. Many were dying daily from exposure and want of food.
>
> —Daniel W. Jones, 1856

Plaque #5
TITLE: Legend of Devil's Gate
LEGEND: Shoshone and Arapahoe legend is one explanation of how Devil's Gate was formed. A powerful evil spirit in the form of a tremendous beast with enormous tusks ravaged the Sweetwater Valley, preventing the Indians from hunting and camping. A prophet informed the tribes that the Great Spirit required them to destroy the beast. They launched an attack from the mountain passes and ravines, and shot countless arrows into the evil mass. The enraged beast, with a mighty upward thrust of its tusks, ripped a gap in the mountain and disappeared through the gap, never to be seen again.
Robert L. Munkres, "Independence Rock and Devil's Gate" in *Annals of Wyoming*, April 1968.

Plaque #6
TITLE: Sun Ranch
LEGEND: Below is the Sun Ranch, one of the first open range ranches in Wyoming. The original building, constructed in 1872, is still on the site and is a Registered National Historic Landmark.

Plaque #7
TITLE: Oregon Trail
LEGEND: The Oregon Trail passed over the ridge to the right of Devil's Gate. Good grass, water and the shelter of the hills made this a popular campsite. Oregon emigrant James Mathers stopped here July 8, 1846, and wrote: "...encamped above the pass of the river, between high rocks. This is the most interesting sight we have met with on our journey."

Plaque #8
TITLE: Devil's Gate Mail Station
LEGEND: The Devil's Gate Mail Station was located here. The Post Office Department contracted monthly mail delivery along this route from Independence, Missouri, to Salt Lake City, Utah. This service, using light wagons in summer and pack mules in winter, remained the sole mail service until late 1858. John M. Hockaday and George Chorpenning established, under contract, this system of relay stations. These pack-mule stations preceded regular stagecoach service to Utah and California. Plant's Station, a few miles west of here, was used later as one of the stagecoach stations on the route to Utah and California.

Plaque #9
TITLE: Tribute to Hardship

LEGEND: Thousands of pioneer settlers enroute to Utah, California and Oregon journeyed over 1,000 miles to this point; illness and death were not uncommon. Here, as well as along the entire trail, many people were buried. Surrounding you on this ridge are over 20 graves. The elevated terrain was safe from trampling feet and iron wheeled wagons.

LOCATION: Interpretive site turnout north side of State Route 220 about 60 miles southwest of Casper, Wyoming. About 12 miles northeast of Muddy Gap.

RED BUTTES BATTLE-37

TITLE: Sgt. Custard Wagon-Train Fight
LEGEND: On July 26, 1865 near this site a U.S. Army Wagon Train under the command of Sgt. Custard, Eleventh Kansas Cavalry was attacked by Sioux, Cheyenne and Arapahoe Indians. In a vicious four hour fight twenty troopers and an unknown number of warriors were killed. All the wagons were burned.
Erected by Paradise Valley Boy Scout Troop 167
LOCATION: Near Casper, Wyoming, on private land accessed from Poison Spider Road. Permission necessary. Inquire locally. Adjacent to Red Buttes Battle-Cemetery and Monument (Natrona County #27).

EMIGRANT GAP BLM INTERPRETIVE SITE-38

TITLE: Emigrant Gap Historical Site
LEGEND: Many emigrant pioneers passed through this gap, or opening, in Emigrant Ridge between the 1840's and the 1880's as they traveled the Oregon-Mormon Trail by oxen-drawn wagons, on horseback, or on foot. The trail generally followed the North Platte River from the Scottsbluff, Nebraska area to crossings near Fort Caspar (just 8 miles east), which was active between 1862 and 1867. The trail departed from the North Platte River near Fort Caspar, meandering overland toward Willow Springs, Ryan (Prospect) Hill, the Sweetwater River drainage, Independence Rock, South Pass, and beyond to Utah, Oregon and California.

From this point the emigrants had a sweeping view to the west, the scene of their next week's journey. Emigrant Gap signified the departure from the North Platte River valley and the beginning of the ascent into the Rocky Mountains. The trail crossed over the Continental divide at South Pass.

From here you can follow Poison Spider Road to Oregon Trail Road, which closely parallels the route of the Oregon-Mormon Trail.
LOCATION: On Poison Spider Road about 10 miles west of Mills, Wyoming. On Emigrant Gap Ridge where Oregon Trail crosses.

RYAN HILL BLM INTERPRETIVE SITE-39

Plaque #1
TITLE: A Look Back
LEGEND: Looking east from this point, the emigrants could see most of the route back to the North Platte River and Casper Mountain. From the point where they left the North Platte River, they could travel to Willow Springs, at the base of Ryan (Prospect) Hill, in two or three days if they were not delayed by sickness or accidents. Willow Springs, with its good water, was the customary campsite after they had passed through Emigrant Gap and Rock Avenue a day or two earlier.

There would be no reliable source of good water again until they reached Horse Creek, 10 miles beyond Willow Springs, on their way to the Sweetwater River near Independence Rock. Upon leaving Willow Springs they faced a 400-foot climb to this point at the top of what they call Prospect Hill, a trying task for draft animals pulling the belongings of emigrants.

From this vantage you can see the remains of the wagon ruts

immediately to the north and east. Please stay on the posted foot trail—remember to enjoy and not destroy.

Plaque #2

TITLE: The Oregon Trail

LEGEND: Ruts of the Oregon Trail are visible at this location. This trail was the great roadway for large covered wagon migrations to Oregon, California, and Utah. An estimated 350,000 people passed this way between 1843 and 1866. 1866 marked the end of the large migration parties; thereafter only small parties traveled the trail. The great migration ended in the 1880's. The trail remains an important transportation corridor today.

The Oregon Trail—trail mileage figures from Emigrants' Guide by William Clayton. 1848

Plaque #3

TITLE: Wildlife and Habitat

LEGEND: The surrounding sagebrush/grassland habitat supports a variety of wildlife species today, just as it did during the active trail use days. Most of the plant and animal species observed and used by the early emigrants still inhabit this area. A notable exception is the buffalo, which is no longer found here.

The grasses fed the emigrants' livestock, and the sagebrush fueled their fires, though not as satisfactorily as they might have wished. William G. Johnson noted in his journal on June 5, 1849, that it had drawbacks—it "sends forth great volumes of blinding smoke, particularly damaging to the eyes of the cook."

The emigrants shot buffalo, sage grouse, and cottontail rabbits as they moved through the area, supplementing their meager diet with the fresh meat. With the exception of the roads, pipelines, and other structures of human origin, this area appears today much as it did in the 1850's and 1860's.

Plaque #4

TITLE: Ryan (Prospect) Hill

LEGEND: Prospect Hill (now called Ryan Hill) derived its name from the view of the surrounding countryside, a view William Clayton called "pleasant" in his 1848 "Emigrants Guide." To the west, the emigrants got their first view of the Sweetwater Mountains and the route they would travel to Independence Rock and Devils Gate, some of the most spectacular sites along the trail. Those who could not make the 20 miles from here to Independence Rock in one day would usually camp at Horse Creek. Once at Independence Rock, they would follow the Sweetwater River for the next 90 miles, thus having access to a reliable water source.

Although this portion of the trail was repeatedly described as barren and rough, it was not desolate. Amelia Stewart Knight wrote in her journal on June 14, 1853, "There is no less than 150 wagons camped around us, but we have left most of the droves behind, and no end to the teams."

There are developed interpretive areas at Independence Rock, Devils Gate and Split Rock.

LOCATION: On the Oregon Trail Road (Horse Creek Road) about 13 miles south of State Route 220 and about 17 miles north of Zero Road.

PONY EXPRESS MARKER-40

TITLE: National Pony Express Centennial Association
   1860-61 Trail Marker 1960-61
LEGEND: Russell Majors Waddell
         Founders Owners Operators
         Pony Express

LOCATION: Outdoor plaza of the First Interstate Bank in Casper, Wyoming. Adjacent to Oregon-California Trail OCTA Marker (Natrona County #41).

THE OREGON-CALIFORNIA TRAIL OCTA MARKER-41

TITLE: The Oregon-California Trail

LEGEND: During the years 1841 to 1867 over 350,000 persons passed through Casper on their way West. The majority of them traveled through what is now the lobby of the First Interstate Bank. The promise of free land, sudden riches, or religious freedom caused these pioneers to endure the great hardships of a very difficult trail. Thousands of persons died in the quest and are buried along the old highway. This was the largest overland migration in history.
   Research and Signing by Oregon-California Trails Association
   Funding by First Interstate Bank of Casper
   1987
   This is a part of your American heritage. Honor it, protect it, preserve it for your children.
LOCATION: Outdoor plaza of the First Interstate Bank of Casper, Wyoming. Adjacent to Pony Express Marker (Natrona County #40).

THE ARMORY MARKER-42

TITLE: The Armory

LEGEND: Casper's unique National Guard Armory was built here in 1930 to house the Headquarters Troop of the 115th Cavalry Regiment. The indoor field provided room for training both horses and men, and even hosted the occasional polo match until the regiment was called to active duty on February 24, 1941.

The first level housed the drill area, horse stalls, blacksmith shop, wagon shop, and equipment room. The second level contained the hay loft, a viewing area, and a ballroom with hardwood floors.

In 1987, the structure was razed to improve traffic flow around Casper College. This monument reflects the fond memories of Armory activities shared by many Casper citizens.
   Presented by: Natrona County Historical Society
   Casper Centennial
   1989
LOCATION: On the campus of Casper College.

RESHAW'S BRIDGE MARKER-43

TITLE: Reshaw's Bridge
      1852-65
LEGEND: Thousands of emigrants following the Oregon-California Trail crossed the North Platte River over a bridge built here by John Richard (Reshaw). The $5 toll during high water saved swimming or ferrying across, and saved countless lives in the process.

Fort Clay, also known as Camp Davis, was established here in 1855 to protect the bridge. Camp Payne was also located here in 1858-59.
   Research and Signing by
   Oregon-California Trails Association
   Funding by
   Wyoming State Historical Society
   1987
   This is a part of your American heritage. Honor it, protect it, preserve it for your children.
LOCATION: At Reshaw Park in Evansville, Wyoming.

QUINTINA SNODDERLY OCTA MARKER-44

TITLE: Quintina Snodderly

LEGEND: A pioneer mother, Quintina Snodderly died near here on

June 25, 1852. A native of Tennessee, Quintina, with her husband, Jacob, and their eight children (five girls and three boys) had lived in Clarinda County, Iowa, for several years before embarking on their trip across the plains. They were members of a wagon train captained by Rev. Joab Powell, which had left St. Joseph, Missouri, in the spring of 1852.

Quintina's grave was discovered and excavated in 1974. An examination of the skeleton revealed the cause of death. Most of the ribs had been crushed, probably by the heavy wheels of a covered wagon. The skeleton was in otherwise perfect condition, with fragments of a green ribbon bow still around the neck. The Powell wagon train probably crossed the North Platte River at this point and the accident may have occurred as the wagons climbed the river bluffs to enter the north bank trail.

Jacob and the children reached Linn County, Oregon, and several descendants still reside in that area.

The grave was restored and fence constructed here in 1987, by the Oregon-California Trails Association. It is a few feet from the original site.

Research and Signing by Katherine and Bill Fritts and the Oregon-California Trails Association

Funding by Natrona County Historical Society

1987

This is a part of your American heritage. Honor it, protect it, preserve it for your children.

LOCATION: Private land on the Oregon Trail in Natrona County.

GUINARD BRIDGE-45

TITLE: Guinard Bridge

LEGEND: The center piece of the Platte Bridge Station and Fort Caspar was the bridge built here by Louis Guinard in 1859-1860 and used until Fort Caspar was abandoned in 1867. The bridge superstructure stood on 28 timber cribbings filled with rock and gravel. Not counting the approaches, the bridge was 810 feet long and 17 feet wide. The total cost of construction was estimated at $40,000 dollars. The toll for wagons to cross was $1.00 to $6.00 dollars, determined by the height of the river. An additional toll was charged for animals and people. This bridge symbolized the changes being shaped by the expansion of America during the middle 19th Century.

LOCATION: Northwest corner of the Fort Caspar parade grounds.

PATHFINDER CEMETERY-46

TITLE: Pathfinder Cemetery

LEGEND: Seven grave sites dating from 1905 to 1912 are located in this tiny cemetery. Barney Flynn and Clint Moor, workers on Pathfinder Dam, died February 9, 1912 in a construction accident. Five men were working on the concrete ladderway on the south side of the canyon when a tram cable directly above them gave way. As the cable fell it knocked the men from their scaffolding to the bottom of the canyon killing them.

The other graves are of residents of the area. The farthest to the right is that of infant Leslie Wolf(e) who died from eating poison meant for coyotes.

Research by Natrona County Historical Society

Funded by Wyoming National Banks

1990

LOCATION: About 1 mile north of Pathfinder Dam alongside the road to the dam. About 50 miles west of Casper, Wyoming.

PIONEER PARK PERMALOY PLAQUE-47

TITLE: None

LEGEND: Originally located 3 blocks south of here, this monument was moved to this location in 1952. In an effort to rectify inaccurate information presented on the monument, the following corrections are provided.

OREGON TRAIL

The 1849 date presented on the Oregon Trail portion of the monument seems to imply that date as the beginning of western migration on the Trail. It is now generally accepted that use of the Oregon Trail by organized trains of pioneers heading west began in 1841 and continued until completion of the transcontinental railroad in 1869.

FORT CASPAR

In 1859/60 Louis Guinard built a trading post and toll bridge across the North Platte River at the site known as the upper crossing, later to be called Platte Bridge Station. In addition to Guinard's trading post and blacksmith shop, the Pony Express and Pacific Telegraph Company used the bridge to cross the river. In 1862 troops of volunteer cavalry from Ohio established a military presence at the site. Renamed Fort Caspar in 1865 (note correct spelling) in honor of Lt. Caspar Collins, the original post and reconstructed fort is actually located 3 miles west of this location.

Research by Natrona County Historical Society

Funded by Wyoming National Bank

1991

LOCATION: East side of North Center Street and south of East B Street in Casper, Wyoming.

Not many historical markers or interpretive plaques were erected to correct erroneous information on earlier markers. Just imagine the discussion at a meeting between members of the Oregon Trail Commission of 1913, the Natrona County Pioneer Association of 1911, and the Natrona County Historical Society of 1991!

TOWN OF MILLS PERMALOY PLAQUE-48

TITLE: The Town of Mills

LEGEND: In 1919 the Mills Construction Company purchased a major portion of this area to mine sand and gravel from the flood plain of the North Platte River. This material was hauled by horse and wagon to the Midwest Refinery (now Amoco) to build roads and tank farm dikes. By 1921 over a thousand people lived in the area along what is now Federal Street.

The people voted to incorporate the Town of Mills in April of 1921. George Boyle was elected Mayor and took office in May. The Town built a new town hall and a highly controversial bond election approved money for construction of a public water system. The Town's first water tank was built on this site in 1924 and stood here until 1975. Mills has grown over the years and today is over a square mile in size and has two thousand residents.

Research by Natrona County Historical Society

Funded by Wyoming National Banks

1990

LOCATION: City Memorial Park in Mills, Wyoming.

NIOBRARA COUNTY

AMERICAN LEGION—BRANSTETTER SIGN-1

TITLE: AMERICAN LEGION
FERDINAND BRANSTETTER POST NO. 1
VAN TASSELL, WYOMING

LEGEND: The American Legion, founded at Paris, France in 1919 holds a long and enviable record of service to the nation and to the veterans of the nation's wars.

Covering those formative years of rapid growth, Legion records are not always exact, but it is determinable that Van Tassell, Wyoming was among the first four posts organized within the nation, their charters all signed on the same day.

Named for Ferdinand Branstetter, resident of Van Tassell community and among the first to cross broad seas and fall on the field of honor, Post No. 1 has led the role of chartered posts throughout the history of the Legion's Wyoming department. It has led that role honorably in service to community, state and nation.

LOCATION: North side of U.S. Hwy 20 at west end of Van Tassell, Wyoming.

Van Tassell, Denver, St. Louis, and Washington, D.C. were the first American Legion posts organized in the United States; their charters were signed the same day in 1919. Ferdinand Branstetter, one of the first men from the area to die in Europe during World War I, homesteaded south of Van Tassell in 1914.

CHEYENNE-DEADWOOD TRAIL INFORMATIVE SIGN-2

TITLE: Cheyenne-Deadwood Trail

LEGEND: Here you stand on the Cheyenne-Deadwood Trail over which freight wagons and stagecoaches traveled between Cheyenne and the Black Hills gold mining area from 1876 to 1887. One of these stages may be seen in the Lusk Museum. The nearby monument is at the grave of George Lathrop, pioneer stage driver. South you can see Rawhide Buttes, west of which was located the home station of the Cheyenne and Black Hills Stage Lines. One and a half miles northeast was Running Water or Silver Cliff's stage station, forerunner of Lusk. Last straggler of the great Buffalo herds in this area was killed nearby in recent years.

LOCATION: West side of Lusk, Wyoming, at the rest area on the south side of U.S. Hwy 18/20. About 1.7 miles west of the junction of U.S. Hwys 20/85 and 18/20. Adjacent to George Lathrop Monument (Niobrara County #4).

There are several other monuments to the Cheyenne-Deadwood Trail from its beginning in Cheyenne to its departure from the state near Newcastle in Weston County. Four markers are found in Laramie County (#6, 7, 15, & 18), while Niobrara County has six (#3, 4, 5, 7, 8, & 11), Platte County has one (#2), and Weston County has three (#3.2, 4, & 5).

FORT HAT CREEK INFORMATIVE SIGN-3

TITLE: Fort Hat Creek

LEGEND: In 1875 soldiers went from Fort Laramie to establish an outpost on Hat Creek in Nebraska.

Confused, they built a fort of logs on Sage Creek in Wyoming. The gold rush to the Black Hills started the Cheyenne-Deadwood Stage Route in 1876.

Bullwhackers freighting salt pork and whiskey to Deadwood, armored coaches hauling gold bricks and passengers to Cheyenne, Indians, and road agents brought adventure to Hat Creek Stage Station. A two story log structure was built near the fort for a telegraph station, postoffice, blacksmith shop, hotel and store.

This building, still standing and used as a ranch home, is two miles east and one mile south.
Wyoming Recreation Commission

LOCATION: East side of U.S. Hwy 18/85 about 13.3 miles north of Lusk, Wyoming.

See Cheyenne-Deadwood Trail Informative Sign (Niobrara County #2) for more information.

GEORGE LATHROP MONUMENT-4

Main Plaque:

TITLE: In memory of "George Lathrop"

LEGEND: Pioneer of the West, Indian fighter, veteran stage driver. Born at Pottsville, Pa., Dec. 24, 1830. Died at Willow, Wyoming Dec. 24, 1915. Buried here. A good man whose life was filled with stirring events.

Marking the Cheyenne and Black Hills Trail

This marker is erected on the old Cheyenne and Black Hills Stage Road, in memory of the operators of the line and the pioneers who traveled it. Operators of the stage line
Luke Voorhees   Russell Thorp, Sr.
Done by popular subscription and unveiled May 30, 1930.

Second plaque

TITLE: None

LEGEND: This memorial financed through sale of "Memoirs of a Pioneer" written by George Lathrop, published gratis by Lusk Herald, first Wyoming newspaper published north of the Union Pacific Ry.
Memorial committee
Tom Black   Russell Thorp, Jr.
E. B. Willson   Geo. Voorhees
R. I. Olinger   J. B. Griffith
Al Rurdquist, Artist
Bronze plate by Newman Mfg. Co., O.

Third plaque

TITLE: None

LEGEND: Accepted August 16th 1940
The Historical Landmark Commission of Wyoming

LOCATION: West side of Lusk, Wyoming, at the rest area on the south side of U. S. Hwy 18/20. About 1.7 miles west of the junction of U.S. Hwys 20/85 and 18/20. Adjacent to Cheyenne-Deadwood Trail Informative Sign (Niobrara County #2).

HAT CREEK MONUMENT-5

TITLE: 1876-1887

LEGEND: In memory of the pioneers who operated the stage line and those who traveled the old Cheyenne-Deadwood Trail.

Erected on the site of old Fort Hat Creek by the Luke Voorhees Chapter Daughters of the American Revolution 1927

LOCATION: Just north of the Fort Hat Creek Informative Sign (see Niobrara County #3) turn east on county road and travel about 2 miles. Then turn southwest on gravel road and travel about 1 mile to sign and old stage station. Marker and log building are easily seen from dirt road, but buildings are on private land.

JIREH SIGN-6

Informative Sign

TITLE: Jireh

LEGEND: The townsite of Jireh and the campus of the Jireh College, 1909-1920, lying to the northeast, marked the location of a pioneer

NIOBRARA COUNTY

N

Legend

⬭ Interstate

⬭ US Highway

◯ State or Other
Principal Road

•—▭ Marker

1   American Legion—Branstetter Sign
2   Cheyenne-Deadwood Trail Informative Sign
3   Fort Hat Creek Informative Sign
4   George Lathrop Monument
5   Hat Creek Monument
6   Jireh Sign
7   Mother Featherlegs Monument
8   Rawhide Buttes Informative Sign
10   Texas Trail Marker
11   Robbers' Roost Sign
12   Surveyors' Marker, Niobrara County
13   Redwood Water Tank

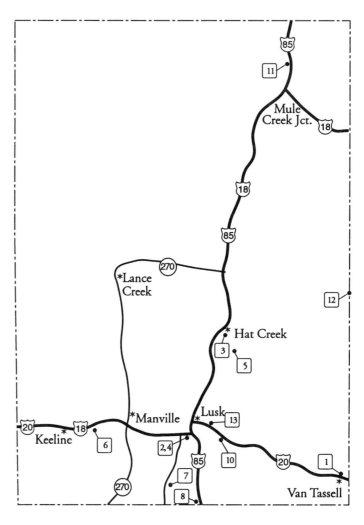

1. A historic building preserved at the original site of the Hat Creek Stage Station on the Cheyenne-Deadwood Trail near Lusk.

2. This Texas Trail marker was dedicated August 15, 1940, east of Lusk.

1.

2.

Denominational Preparatory School and Junior College in Wyoming. Both townsite and campus were established during homesteading days to serve the residents of the Eastern Wyoming Area with the opportunity for an advanced education. Envisioned was not only a Christian College but also a sympathetic Christian Community. Herein was engendered both the pioneering spirit of the early West and a missionary spirit of the dedicated.

Jehovah-Jireh: Genesis XXII 14 "The Lord will provide"

Cornerstone
TITLE: JIREH College
LEGEND: None

LOCATION: About 2 miles east of Keeline, Wyoming, where U.S. Hwy 18/20 intersects with the Jireh Road.

From *Wyoming: A Guide to Historic Sites*, the following portrays some history of Jireh, Wyoming:

Except for a few settlements and small towns, the area of eastern Wyoming lying adjacent the Chicago and North Western Railroad at the turn of the century was ranchland covered with grass and sage. In the midst of that apparent desolation Reverend George Dalzell, pastor of the Lusk Congregational Church, envisioned a Christian college and community. Extolling Wyoming as the 'land of opportunity,' Dalzell and Daniel B. Atkinson encouraged Christians living in central states to come out west where there were free homes on the public domain, fertile soil, good markets, good schools, a healthful climate, and the opportunity to live and work in a Christian Community called Jireh, a name which meant 'The Lord will provide.' (Genesis XXII:14). Response to the call for homesteaders came mainly from ministers and professors in Ohio, Illinois, and Indiana, as the pioneering spirit which had earlier settled much of the West was rekindled by the presence of a new land open to homestead.

The Jireh College that Dalzell and others dreamed about, a two and one-half story frame building constructed in 1909-10, was built mainly upon a foundation of faith. But the economic foundation was not strong, and lack of financial support closed down the denominational college in 1920. Not long afterward the town of Jireh itself was gone, and today a historic marker and a cemetery are among the last reminders of this experiment of Christian living.

MOTHER FEATHERLEGS MONUMENT-7
Granite marker
TITLE: Mother Featherlegs Shepherd
LEGEND: Here lies Mother Featherlegs Shepherd
So called, as in her ruffled pantalettes she looked like a feather-legged chicken in a high wind. Was a roadhouse ma'am here on the Cheyenne-Black Hills Stage Line.
An outlaw confederate, she was murdered by "Dangerous Dick Davis, The Terrapin" in 1879 for a $1500 cache.
Dedicated May 17, 1964.

Brass Plate
TITLE: None
LEGEND: Erected by Jim Griffith and Bob Darrow

LOCATION: On a dirt road about 10 miles south of U.S. Hwy 18/20. Access to dirt road is a turnoff just past the rest area, about 1.7 miles west of the junction of U.S. Hwy 20/85 and 18/20.

RAWHIDE BUTTES INFORMATIVE SIGN-8
TITLE: Rawhide Buttes
LEGEND: Rawhide Buttes, visible west of this point, once served as a favorite camping spot of Indians and fur trappers. Several different tales explain the origin of the name. One account holds that this locale served as a departure point from which trappers sent fur pelts, or "rawhides," east to St. Louis. Another story tells of a reckless young man who killed an Indian woman while journeying to California during the 1849 gold rush. Attempting to avoid trouble, his fellow travelers surrendered the man for punishment and then watched in horror as the Indians skinned him alive at the base of the buttes—thus the name "Rawhide Buttes."

In 1874, a military expedition led by Lieutenant Col. George A. Custer discovered gold in the Black Hills of Dakota Territory. Hoping to capitalize on the ensuing rush of prospectors, the entrepeneurial team of John Gilmer, Monroe Salisbury and Mathewson Patrick organized the Cheyenne and Black Hills Stage and Express line in 1876. The company soon began leasing ranch buildings located at Rawhide Buttes for use as a stage station. When Russell Thorp, Sr. purchased the Rawhide Buttes Station in November 1882, the bustling stage stop had grown to include a grocery and dry good store, stage barn, post office and blacksmith shop.

The arrival of the Chicago and North Western Railroad led the demise of stagecoaching. The last Black Hills-bound stage departed from Cheyenne's Inter-ocean Hotel on February 19, 1887. With the stage no longer rolling, the buildings clustered at the base of Rawhide Buttes reverted from stage station to ranch headquarters. The end of an era had arrived.

LOCATION: West side of U.S. Hwy 85 about 10 miles south of Lusk, Wyoming.

SPANISH DIGGINGS-9

TITLE: Spanish Diggings

LEGEND: The greatest prehistoric workshop on the American Continent lies twelve and one half miles to the South. Covering an area thirty miles long and ten miles wide, it presents a panorama of hundreds of stone shops surrounded by huge piles of chippings left by generations of prehistoric arrow and spearhead makers.

Hundreds of specimens of perfect pottery have been removed from this site to Eastern Museums, many more probably remain for the searcher of today.

LOCATION: Marker no longer standing. Previous location was at turnout on south side of U.S. Hwy 18/20 about 22 miles west of Lusk, Wyoming.

TEXAS TRAIL MARKER-10

Top plaque

TITLE: Texas Trail

LEGEND: Texas to Montana 1876 to 1897. Along this trail passed herds of cattle from distant Texas to replace in Wyoming and Montana the fast vanishing buffalo and build civilization on the northwestern plains.

Dedicated by the Historical Landmarks Commission of Wyoming 1940

Lower plaque

TITLE: None

LEGEND: Sponsored by the Lusk Lions Club. Wyo. Stockgrowers Ass'n., and Stockmen of Eastern Wyo. Plaque by Bill Harwood.

LOCATION: On the south side of U.S. Hwy 20 about 3.4 miles east of the junction of U.S. Hwys 20 and 18/85 in Lusk, Wyoming.

Five other Texas Trail monuments have been erected along the trail. See Crook County #8, Goshen County #17 & 18, and Laramie County #24 for more information.

ROBBERS' ROOST SIGN-11

TITLE: Robbers' Roost Station
   Cheyenne and Black Hills Stage Route

LEGEND: Along the Cheyenne-Deadwood Stage Route, stories still are told of outlaws and buried gold. But the swaying Concord stagecoaches stopped rolling in 1887, eleven years after beginning service to the gold regions of the Black Hills in 1876.

Located at the Cheyenne River crossing, Robbers' Roost was a station of the Cheyenne and Black Hills Stage and Express Company. Built in 1877 on a new shortcut, it derived its name from the many robberies in the area. The crossing was the spot most dreaded by stage drivers; steep river banks slowed the coaches to a crawl and provided concealment from which lurking road agents could watch the approach of their intended victims.

Station agent at Robber's Roost was D. Boone May, also a deputy U.S. marshall and a shotgun messenger for the gold-laden treasure coaches from the "Hills". In September, 1878, south of here, May and

John Zimmerman surprised desperadoes in the act of robbing the southbound coach. The outlaws opened fire and one of them, Frank Towle, was fatally wounded. Outnumbered, May and Zimmerman escorted the coach to safety and the outlaws made their escape. Towle was buried by his companions. May later found the grave, removed Towle's head and took it to Cheyenne in a sack to try to claim a reward.

The era of the gold rush to the Black Hills was a flamboyant one, bringing together a diverse gathering of frontier characters Indians, soldiers; miners, stage drivers; tradesmen, housewives; gamblers, prostitutes and outlaws.

According to legend Robbers' Roost Station was burned by Indians.

LOCATION: West side of U.S. Hwy 85 about 3 miles north of Mule Creek Junction and about 0.5 mile south of the bridge over the Cheyenne River.

SURVEYORS' MARKER, NIOBRARA COUNTY-12

Brass marker

TITLE: The Common Corner to Nebraska and South Dakota on Wyoming Line

LEGEND: The Survey for the boundary between Nebraska and Wyoming Territory began August 17th, 1869, at the intersection of the 41st Parallel of Latitude and the 27th degree of Longitude West of Washington, D.C. Oliver N. Chaffee, Astronomer and Surveyor and his crew surveyed North on the 27th Meridian, 138 miles, 22 chains, and 67 links, and set a white limestone monument here on September 6th, 1869.

In 1874, beginning at the Keya Paha River and ending at the Chaffee monument, Chauncey Wiltse surveyed the 43rd Parallel of Latitude between Nebraska and Dakota Territory.

In 1893, Joseph Jenkins retraced the Wiltse Survey and set a quartzite monument here and at 1/2 mile intervals from the Chaffee monument East to the Missouri River.

In 1908, Edward F. Stahle retraced the Wyoming-Nebraska boundary and set granite posts at mile intervals and brass caps at closing corners.

In recognition of those early Surveyors, the skills they demonstrated and the hardships they endured we dedicate this Plaque on September 6th, 1989.

The geographic position of the Chaffee monument is based on NAD 1983 and determined by the Global Position System method.

Latitude 43° 00' 02" 251
Longitude 104° 03' 11" 315
Elevation 1198.4 Meters (3931.70 feet)

Major Contributors
Professional Surveyors Assn. of Nebraska
Professional Land Surveyors of Colorado
Professional Land Surveyors of Wyoming
South Dakota Society of Professional Land Surveyors
Fall River County South Dakota Historical Society
Nebraska State Historical Society Foundation
Sioux County Nebraska Historical Society
Niobrara County Historical Society of Wyoming
Berntsen, Incorporated, Madison, Wisconsin
Bureau of Land Management
Pine Ridge Job Corps
Citizens of Fall River County, South Dakota
Citizens of Sioux County, Nebraska

Quartzite monument

South face: By. $\dfrac{\text{N.}}{\text{Wyo.}}$

West face: Wyo.

North face: By. $\dfrac{\text{Wyo.}}{\text{S.D.}}$

East face: 1893
         T. Mon.
         224 M. 12.13 C.

White limestone monument
South face: 138 MI. 22 Ch. 67 Lks.
West face: Wyoming
North face: 27.WL.
East face: 43 NL

LOCATION: Access via the Hat Creek Road and Indian Creek Road. The marker is located on private property northeast of Lusk, Wyoming. Permission is necessary to visit the site. Inquire locally.

In the years before Wyoming became a territory, the boundary marking the western end of Dakota Territory varied with the legislation enacted. At times it was set as the 104th longitude (104 degrees west of Greenwich, England). At other times it was set at the 27th meridian (measured from the astronomical observatory in Washington, D.C. and comparable to 104 degrees, three minutes, and two seconds west of Greenwich). When Montana Territory was created in 1864, the boundary was set even further west at the 33rd meridian. In 1866, when the Dakota Legislature established the first county in what was Wyoming country, the boundary was 104 degrees west of Greenwich (104th longitude). When Wyoming Territory was created on July 25, 1868, the 27th meridian (104 degrees, three minutes, and two seconds west of Greenwich) became the boundary between the two territories. The intersection of the 27th meridian and the 43rd latitude became the common boundary for the Territories of Wyoming and Dakota and the State of Nebraska.

Oliver N. Chaffee surveyed the southern and western boundary of Nebraska in 1869. He established the northwest corner of Nebraska on the 43rd Parallel, and erected a fourteen inch-square limestone marker at its intersection with the 27th meridian. The Chaffee monument was placed on September 6, 1869.

Chauncey Wiltse completed the first survey of the Nebraska-South Dakota boundary in September 1874. Jenkins retraced Wiltse's survey in 1893, placing quartzite monuments at half-mile intervals along the entire South Dakota-Nebraska boundary including this marker, placed in 1893.

Approaching the ranch headquarters one can see granite posts along a fence. These mileposts were placed in 1908 by surveyor Edward F. Stahle.

REDWOOD WATER TANK-13

TITLE: REDWOOD WATER TANK

LEGEND: The redwood water tank was built to furnish water for the Fremont, Elkhorn, & Missouri Valley Railroad steam engines. This line, which was part of the Northwestern line, and later became the Chicago Northwestern Railroad, came to Lusk on July 13, 1886.

The original site was several hundred feet to the west of the present location. Water was furnished from a well by a windmill. Later, it came from a hand-dug well by hand and steam power. The tank is one of six left standing in the U.S.

The historical society has been working to preserve the tank since 1971. We had assistance from Chicago Northwestern Railroad, Town of Lusk, and numerous other contributions.

Niobrara County Historical Society

Sign donated by: Fancy Farmers Garden Club

LOCATION: North side of U.S. Hwy 20 just east of Lusk, Wyoming.

PARK COUNTY

ABSAROKA VOLCANIC FIELD INFORMATIVE SIGN-1

TITLE: Absaroka Volcanic Field
LEGEND: The valley of the North Fork of the Shoshone River passes through a series of volcanic rocks over 9,000 feet thick covering 3,000 square miles. The rocks include lava, volcanic ash, and other sorts of volcanic material. Agglomerate is a common type and consists of rounded masses of volcanic rock in a finer matrix.

Numerous dikes which were feeders for lava flows, show in the canyon walls as thin, narrow bands resembling stone walls. The peculiar castle-like forms are the result of weathering and removal of softer material by water.
LOCATION: North side of U.S. Hwy 14/16/20 about 19.5 miles west of Cody, Wyoming. About 1.2 miles west of post office at Wapiti, Wyoming.

AMELIA EARHART MEMORIAL-2

Front side
TITLE: Amelia Earhart in Wyoming
LEGEND: In memory of the world famous aviatrix

First woman to fly across the Atlantic June 17, 1928 and May 20, 1932. Was building a summer home near here when she left to fly around the earth and was lost in the South Pacific July 2, 1937.

Erected by her Wyoming friends.
Back side:
TITLE: Contributors
LEGEND: Cheyenne Zonta Club, Dr. and Mrs. Harold McCracken, Ernest J. Goppert, Dunrud Family, Park County Historical Society, American Legion Post 85, Meeteetse Lions Club, Paul Stock, Charles Webster Family, Henry Sayles Family and Clarence Dollar Family.

LOCATION: Near Meeteetse, Wyoming, on the east side of State Route 120 about 0.25 mile north of the bridge over the Greybull River.

BUFFALO BILL STATUE-3

East face: Buffalo Bill
MDCCCXLVI-MCMXVII
South face: "THE SCOUT"
COLONEL WILLIAM F. CODY
"BUFFALO BILL"
SCULPTED AND PRESENTED BY
GERTRUDE VANDERBILT WHITNEY
JULY 4, 1924

LOCATION: In Cody, Wyoming, at the west end of Sheridan Avenue, just north of the Buffalo Bill Historical Center.

William Frederick Cody was born in 1846 near LeClaire, Iowa. When he was fourteen years old he joined the Pony Express and became one of the most famous riders. In 1867 he contracted with the Kansas Pacific Railroad to provide meat (buffalo) for the 1,200 men working on the railroad. In less than 18 months Cody killed 4,280 buffalo and was thereafter nicknamed "Buffalo Bill." He served as an Army scout and gained a reputation for tracking, hunting, and fighting Indians.

On July 17, 1876, when Buffalo Bill was serving as a scout with the Fifth Cavalry near Fort Robinson, Nebraska, a large force of Cheyenne warriors was met and the Battle of War Bonnet Creek ensued. During the battle, Cody shot and scalped a chief named Yellow Hand.

Cody's fame grew. He helped organize the first "Buffalo Bill's Wild West Show," which toured the United States and Europe for nearly three decades.

He also was interested in the development of Wyoming, investing in the Big Horn Basin and in Sheridan. The county seat of Park County was named in his honor.

When Buffalo Bill Cody died in 1917, the Wyoming State Legislature

appropriated $5,000 to undertake the establishment of a memorial to Cody. This beginning grew into the Buffalo Bill Memorial Association and the Buffalo Bill Historical Center complex.

The Buffalo Bill Statue was another memorial effort. In the early 1920s Mrs. Mary Jester Allen, a niece of Buffalo Bill, proposed that the prominent artist, Gertrude Vanderbilt Whitney, sculpt a statue of Cody. The life-sized statue portrayed "an Indian Wars army scout riding in the lead of a swift-moving cavalry column. The scout suddenly sees a sign and checks his mount to a halt to better observe ground markings. He does this while throwing up his right arm-clutching a Winchester carbine—as a signal for the column to draw rein." The statue was dedicated July 4, 1924.

The impressive statue inspired the two different groups working in the same direction to memorialize William Cody. From that point, the Cody family and the Buffalo Bill Memorial Association coordinated their efforts to develop the large cultural center that exists today in Cody, Wyoming.

GERTRUDE V. WHITNEY MEMORIAL-3.1

TITLE: Gertrude V. Whitney
LEGEND: To Gertrude V. Whitney in appreciation of her art and our gratitude for the wonderful statue of Buffalo Bill, The Scout.

Citizens of Cody, July 4, 1933.
LOCATION: On the south side of the Buffalo Bill Monument (Park County #3).

Gertrude Vanderbilt Whitney was a talented sculptor who had trained under some of the best instructors in the world. Her other works included the Titanic Memorial and Aztec Fountain in Washington, D.C., El Dorado Fountain in San Francisco, and the statue of Columbus at Palos in Spain.

CASTLE ROCK INFORMATIVE SIGN-4

TITLE: Castle Rock
LEGEND: John Colter, famed among the famous breed of "Mountain Men," passed this landmark late in the fall of 1807 while on business for the fur trader Manuel Lisa. Searching for Indians in order to conduct trade, he also hunted salt caves reputedly located near headwaters of this stream, then known as the "stinking water."

On his journey Colter not only discovered this later named Shoshone River but he also became the first recorded white man to visit the upper Wind River, Jackson's Hole and Yellowstone park. His lonely trek, compounding the normal dangers of savage wilderness by mid-winter passage of a broad and lofty mountain range, lives in history and legend an epic of fortitudinous exploration.
LOCATION: On the north side of the South Fork Road (South Fork of the Shoshone River), about 17.3 miles southwest of Cody, Wyoming.

The Park County Chapter of the Wyoming State Historical Society dedicated an earlier sign on September 29, 1957, marking the 150th anniversary of Colter's travels past this point. The original marker was stolen Thanksgiving 1968.

COLTER'S HELL SIGN-5

TITLE: Colter's Hell
LEGEND: John Colter, veteran of the Lewis and Clark Expedition, notably self-sufficient mountain man and indefatigable explorer, was the first white man known to have reconnoitered this locale. In 1807, possibly traveling alone but probably escorted by Crow guides, he crossed the Stinking Water (Shoshone River) via a major Indian trail ford located about a mile downstream from this observation point. Here, extending along both sides of the river, he discovered an active geyser district. Steam mixed with sulfur fumes and shooting flames escaped through vents in the valley floor, subterranean rumblings were ominously audible. Although mineralized hot springs continued to flow along the river's edge, the eruptions Colter watched are now marked only by cones of parched stone.

PARK COUNTY

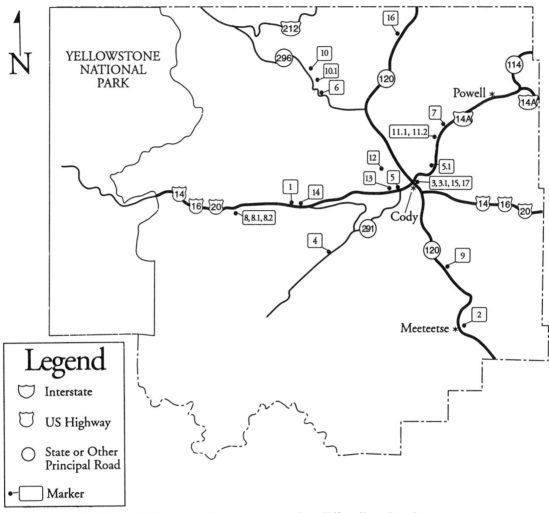

1   Absaroka Volcanic Field Informative Sign
2   Amelia Earhart Memorial
3   Buffalo Bill Statue
3.1 Gertrude V. Whitney Memorial
4   Castle Rock Informative Sign
5   Colter's Hell Sign
5.1 "Corbett's Shebang" at the Stinking Water Crossing
6   Dead Indian Summit Monument
7   Eagle's Nest Stage Station
8   Fire Fighters Memorial #1
8.1 Fire Fighters Memorial #2
8.2 Fire Fighters Memorial #3

9   Halfway House Stage Stop
10   Frank N. Hammitt Memorial
10.1 Donald P. Musso Memorial
11.1 Heart Mountain Relocation Center Monument
11.2 Heart Mountain Relocation Center Informative Plaques
12   Newton Lakes—Trail Creek Ranch Cemetery
13   Shoshone Canyon Informative Sign
14   Wapiti Ranger Station Informative Sign
15   Vietnam Memorial
16   Nez Perce Trail
17   Mountain Man Memorials

This was primarily Shoshone and Crow country but other Indians came to the area. Particularly Bannocks and Nez Perce, journeying eastward over the mountains to hunt the plains buffalo, tarried to test the heralded medicinal values of these "stinking waters" baths. Ranged along bench-lands to the east and north are numerous tepee rings, evidence of former Indian encampments. Heart Mountain, famous landmark and geological oddity, is conspicuous on the northern horizon.

Honoring a respected predecessor, mountain men of the 1820's-1830's fur trade heyday named this place Colter's Hell. Later, early-day officials of Yellowstone Park applied that name to the park's geyser area—thereby causing a degree of historic confusion. The true Colter's Hell is here in view.

LOCATION: West of Cody, Wyoming, on the north side of U.S. Hwy 14/16/20 at a wide turnout overlooking the Shoshone River, about 2.6 miles west of the Buffalo Bill Historical Center.

"CORBETT'S SHEBANG" AT THE STINKING WATER CROSSING-5.1

TITLE: "Corbett's Shebang" at Stinking Water Crossing
LEGEND: On September 10, 1880, Victor Arland and John F. Corbett set up the first mercantile establishment in the Big Horn Basin on the Indian Trace that follows Trail Creek. Looking to the cattlemen for business, they moved to Cottonwood Creek in 1883, then to Meeteetse Creek in 1884 where Arland, their final trading post, was established.

Corbett, doing the freighting from Billings for company enterprises, set up a way station in the river bottom where the freight road crossed the Stinking Water River—later re-named the Shoshone. A bridge, the first of five to span the river at this point, was constructed in 1883 at a cost of $5000 raised by subscription from cattlemen, the Northern Pacific Railroad and Billings merchants.

Accommodations provided were a small store, a saloon and overnight lodging. A post office was established in 1885 with Corbett the postmaster. It was a gathering place and social center long before Cody came into existence twelve years later.

Corbett died in bed at his Meeteetse home December 15, 1910. His partner, Arland, went to his reward in more traditional style—dying with his boots on. In December, 1889, a shot fired through a saloon window in Red Lodge, Montana, killed him while he was playing poker.

The name of Corbett lingers on but the need for "Corbett's Shebang" in the river bottom ended with the arrival of the railroad in November 1901.

LOCATION: Just north of the bridge over the Shoshone River on the west side of U.S. Hwy 14A, about 6 miles north of Cody, Wyoming.

DEAD INDIAN SUMMIT MONUMENT-6

TITLE: Dead Indian Summit
        Altitude 8,000 feet
LEGEND: This pass is the summit of Dead Indian Hill. Through this portal great herds of wild game seasonally migrated from the mountains to the plains. This high pass was the gate way for countless Indian hunting and war parties, and through this portal Chief Joseph, in 1877, led his Nez Perce Indians in a strategic and defensive retreat, persued by U. S. Army soldiers. Over this one and only opening of the valleys to the west traveled a vast army of miners to seek wealth of Cooke City, and down this steep hill the early settlers of Sunlight Basin braved its dangers. The first road improvement was made possible in 1909, by dwellers of Sunlight Valley whose names are here inscribed.

Adophus J. Beam	Oliver Whitney	Mary E. Painter
Wm. V. Campbell	Hervey G. Marvin	Wm. T. Painter
Siras J. Davis	Samual Thompson	Marguerite M. Painter

Wade W. McClung	John R. Painter	John K. Rollinson
Agustus A. LaFond	Evelyn T. Painter	Willard D. Ruscher

This historical marker dedicated 1940.
LOCATION: About 30 miles north of Cody, Wyoming. Travel about 17 miles north of Cody on State Route 120, then turn west onto the Sunlight Basin Road for about another 13 miles.

EAGLE'S NEST STAGE STATION-7

TITLE: Eagle's Nest Stage Station
LEGEND: Established in the 1890's by Tom Lanchberry to accommodate passengers and horses on the Red Lodge to Fort Washakie run, Eagle's Nest Station, one-half mile north, operated until early in the century when railway expansion limited its usefulness. Stout four and six-horse teams, under salty drivers, pulling tough, coach-type wagons, were changed every 15 to 20 miles. Stages traveled 60 to 80 miles a day, tying together cattle ranches and army posts. One dollar a night for supper, bed and breakfast was the usual charge to dust-covered passengers on the long, rough route from Montana's Northern Pacific to the Union Pacific Railroad in southern Wyoming.
LOCATION: On the west side of U.S. Hwy 14A, about 9.5 miles south of Powell, Wyoming.

This marker was erected by the Wyoming State Archives and Historical Department and the Wyoming State Historical Society, Park County Chapter. The logo of each of those organizations was imprinted on the beam supporting the marker.

FIRE FIGHTERS MEMORIAL #1-8

East side
TITLE: Shoshone National Forest Black Water Fire August 20-24, 1937
LEGEND: This marks the beginning of the Fire Fighters' Memorial Trail which follows Black Water Creek five miles to the place of origin of the Fire, and thence to other points of interest. This fire was controlled after burning over 1254 acres of forest. Fifteen fire fighters lost their lives and thirty nine others were injured when the fire was whipped up by a sudden gale on August 21. Signs and monuments mark the important locations along this trail, including the fire camps, the first aid station, Clayton Gulch where eight men were killed, and the rocky knoll where ranger Post gathered his crew to escape the fire.
West side
TITLE: Fire Fighters Memorial
LEGEND: Alfred G. Clayton, Forest Ranger. James T. Saban, Foreman. Paul E. Tyrrell, Foreman. Rex A. Hale, Jr., technician. Billy Lea, Engr. Aid. Clyde Allen, Roy Bevens, Ambrocio Garza, John B. Gerdes, Will C. Griffith, Mack T. Mayabb, George E. Rodgers, Ernest R. Seelke, Rubin D. Sherry, William H. Whitlock.

LOCATION: On the east side of U.S. Hwy 14/16/20, about 34 miles west of Cody, Wyoming.

This striking marker is one of three along Blackwater Creek that pay tribute to the firefighters who died in the Blackwater Fire. The other two markers are located about five miles up the Blackwater Creek Trail. See Fire Fighters Memorial #2 & 3 (Park County #8.1 & 8.2).

Two other Blackwater firefighter memorials are located elsewhere in Wyoming. Fire Fighters Monument (Big Horn County #1.2), erected in September 1937 by Company 1811 of the Civilian Conservation Corps located at Tensleep, Wyoming, was dedicated on the west side of U.S. Hwy 16 overlooking Meadowlark Lake in the Big Horn Mountains. The Fallen Firefighter Memorial (Fremont County #41) was erected in 1990 at the Wyoming Fire Academy in Riverton, Wyoming.

1.

2.

3.

4.

5.

1. The Buffalo Bill Statue was dedicated in Cody on July 4, 1924.

2. The colorful language in the legend on the Castle Rock Informative Sign was written by Ned Frost. Frost was criticized by some who felt that his legends were too complicated for the average person.

3. This marker between Powell and Cody was erected by the Wyoming State Archives and Historical Department, the Wyoming State Historical Society, and the Park County Historical Society.

4. This decorative and rustic wooden marker was placed between Meeteetse and Cody. Many markers of similar design can be found across Wyoming.

5. This bronze plaque, erected in the interest of promoting peace and understanding between people, was placed near the Heart Mountain Relocation Center.

FIRE FIGHTERS MEMORIAL #2-8.1

TITLE: Alfred G. Clayton, Rex A. Hale, George E. Rodgers, Mack T. Mayabb, Will C. Griffith, John B. Gerdes, Roy Bevens, James T. Saban
LEGEND: They gave their last full measure of devotion on the afternoon of August 21, 1937, while fighting the Blackwater Fire. These brave men lost their lives in the gulch to the right of this marker.
LOCATION: The Blackwater Creek Trail about 5 miles from the Fire Fighters Memorial #1 (see Park County #8). Inquire locally (at Blackwater Lodge or Absorka Lodge).

This magnificent marker can only be reached by a five-mile hike along the Blackwater Creek Trail over gentle trail terrain most of the way, although some steep trail hiking tests the experienced hiker. The scenery is as outstanding.

Along each of its eight sides, the marker's large bronze octagon plaque lists the names of the eight men killed in the nearby gulch. The plaque also shows the seals of the U.S. Forest Service and the United States Civilian Conservation Corps. Surrounding the base of this monument is inlaid red stone in a pattern resembling fire. It truly is a magnificent memorial.

Fire Fighters Memorial #3 (Park County #8.2) is located one half mile further along the trail, also a strenuous but very rewarding hike.

FIRE FIGHTERS MEMORIAL #3-8.2

TITLE: Post Point
Blackwater Fire
August 20-24, 1937
LEGEND: Here, on the afternoon of August 21, 1937, thirty seven enrollees of CCC Company 1811 in charge of Ranger Post and Jr. Forester Tyrrell, with seven Bureau of Public Roads employees including Foreman Davis and Fire Cooperator Sullivan in charge, took refuge from the fire. Five men attempted to escape through the fire and four of them—Lea, Allen, Seelke, and Sherry, perished. Ranger Post and all of the forty who remained with him received burns of varying severity and three of these—Jr. Forester Tyrrell and Enrollees Whitlock and Garza died later.
LOCATION: Along the Blackwater Creek Trail about 5.5 miles from Fire Fighters Memorial #1 (see Park County #8). About 0.5 mile beyond Fire Fighters Memorial #2 (Park County #8.1). Inquire locally (at Blackwater Lodge or Absorka Lodge).

This Blackwater firefighter memorial is the highest marker along the trail. It is a strenuous and steep-terrain hiking trail. The scenery is magnificent, with the steep volcanic mountainside dotted with grayed and barren tree tombstones in all directions.

The marker is a large brass plate set down on the volcanic debris high on the trail leading to Clayton Mountain. The seals of the U.S. Forest Service, the U.S. Department of Agriculture Bureau of Public Works, and the United States Civilian Conservation Corps are reminders of the agencies for whom the men worked.

HALFWAY HOUSE STAGE STOP-9

TITLE: Site of Halfway House Stage Stop.
LEGEND: At this spot in 1903 a rock dugout facing south, near a fresh-water spring in the hillside, was established as a stage "noon stop" where horses were changed and meals served. The primitive accommodation was halfway between Corbett Crossing on the Stinking Water River and the bustling frontier town of Meteetsee. In 1904, Halfway Stop had a newfangled telephone, complete with a large "Public Telephone" sign. The station was abandoned in 1908 after automobiles began to use the route, but the spring remained in use for many years, a favorite watering place in this arid country. This marker commemorates early station keepers and travelers who passed this way.
LOCATION: East side of State Route 120, about 19 miles north of Meeteetse, Wyoming.

FRANK N. HAMMITT MEMORIAL-10

TITLE: Frank N. Hammitt
July 25, 1869
July 25, 1903
LEGEND: Served as forest ranger Yellowstone National Park Timberland Reserve, Shoshone National Forest, from 1898 until his death.
LOCATION: On the Sunlight Basin Road, about 41 miles from Cody, Wyoming. About 10 miles north of Dead Indian Summit Monument (Park County #6).

This native stone and metal monument sits under the foot of a small mesa with precipitous cliffs around three sides. Hammitt was riding a horse which spooked over the rimrock and fell two hundred feet to his own and his rider's death.

DONALD P. MUSSO MEMORIAL-10.1

TITLE: In Memory of
Donald P. Musso
December 21, 1942—June 4, 1985
LEGEND: District Ranger on the Clarks Fork District of the Shoshone National Forest, 1977-1984. Don Musso loved this beautiful country. This site is dedicated to the memory of this special man.
LOCATION: About 37 miles northwest of Cody, Wyoming, on the Sunlight Basin Road. Marker is on the south side of the Clark's Fork River bridge.

Dead Indian Summit Monument and Frank N. Hammitt Memorial (Park County #6 & 10) are also located on the Sunlight Basin Road, which offers beautiful scenery. This marker overlooks the narrow and steep canyon where the Clark's Fork River cuts a deep and lonely path.

HEART MOUNTAIN RELOCATION CENTER MONUMENT-11.1

TITLE: Heart Mountain Relocation Center
1942-1945
LEGEND: During the World War II years, Heart Mountain Relocation Center was located on a 740-acre tract of land across the Burlington Railroad right-of-way westward from where you stand facing this monument, and Heart Mountain itself, on the Heart Mountain division of the Shoshone Irrigation Project.

Eleven thousand people of Japanese ancestry from the three west-coast states were loosely confined by the United States Government in the center for about three years. They lived in barracks as singles, or as families, according to their marital status.

The camp was equipped with modern waterworks and sewer system and a modern hospital and dental clinic, staffed with people from the ranks of the evacuees. First rate schooling was provided for the children of the evacuees through the high school grades.

This monument was erected, 1963, by the American Legion Posts of Heart Mountain and Powell, Wyoming, and their Auxiliaries, in the interest of international peace and understanding and as a memorial to the men and women who have died in the service of our country.
LOCATION: On the northwest side of U.S. Hwy 14A, about 12 miles northeast of Cody, Wyoming.

HEART MOUNTAIN RELOCATION CENTER INFORMATIVE PLAQUES-11.2

Plaque #1
TITLE: Heart Mountain Relocation Center Memorial
LEGEND: History
After the bombing of Pearl Harbor on December 7, 1941, many parts

of the West Coast were declared military defense zones. The government ordered the removal of all persons of Japanese ancestry and the War Relocation Authority was established in March 1942 to house them in inland camps. The Heart Mountain Relocation Center was one of ten temporary camps constructed to confine over 110,000 men, women and children forced to leave their homes in California, Oregon, and Washington and part of Arizona. It was the only camp located in Wyoming. Construction on the center began in June 1942 and the first internees arrived in August of that year. At the peak of its population the Heart Mountain Center, which covered over 740 acres, contained nearly 11,000 people housed in 450 barracks. Although surrounded by barbed wire and armed guards, the internees kept the camp functioning as a small city with its own public works, grade school, a high school, hospital and newspaper. At the time it was the third largest city in Wyoming.

The camp was closed in November 1945, the buildings removed and the land, made arable by irrigation ditches completed by the internees, was opened up for homesteading.

A portion of the Heart Mountain Center was listed on the National Register of Historic Places on December 19, 1985. The area listed includes the immediate vicinity of this Honor Roll and the structures located to the east.

Honor Roll

This monument was erected by the internees at the Heart Mountain Relocation Center in August 1944 to honor those from the camp who served in the United States armed forces in World War II. The photographs to the right and below show the Honor Roll as it was in 1944. Although the elements have erased the names of those listed, the structure still remains as it was originally.

In 1978 the Honor Roll was preserved as a memorial not only to those Japanese-Americans who served in the military, but also to recognize the sacrifices of those who were interned here throughout the war.

In 1985 a plaque was erected memorializing those people from Heart Mountain who gave their lives in World War II.

Plaque #2
TITLE: None
LEGEND: September 1985

This memorial plaque is dedicated to the more than 600 internees who left Heart Mountain to serve in the U.S. Armed Forces during World War II, and to the memory of the 22 Heart Mountaineers who gave their lives for our country.

Cpl Yoshiharu Aoyama	Pvt Roy Kawamoto	T/Sgt George Oyama
Sgt Robert Farmer	Cpl Yasuo Kenmotsu	Pfc Toru Seiki
Pfc Ted Fujioka	Pvt Isamu Kunimatsu	Pfc William Taketa
Sgt Tadashi Hachiya	Pfc Hiroshi Kyono	Lt Kei Tanahashi
Pvt Stanley K. Hayami	Sgt George Mayeda	S/Sgt Kei Yamaguchi
S/Sgt Joe Hayashi	Pvt Jim Nagata	Pfc Fred Yamamoto
Sgt John S. Kanazawa	Pfc Akagi Nagaoki	2nd Lt Hitoshi Yonemura
	Cpl James Okubo	

May the injustices of the removal and incarceration of 120,000 persons of Japanese ancestry during World War II, two-thirds of whom were American citizens, never be repeated. Presented by the Heart Mountain High School Class of 1947 on behalf of the 10,700 persons interned here from 1942-1945. With appreciation to the people of Park County who made this memorial park possible.

Plaque #3
TITLE: 1942-1945
    Heart Mountain Relocation Center Memorial Park
LEGEND: This Memorial is dedicated to those people interned here

during World War II, to their sons and daughters who served our country, and to those who gave their lives in that service.
    1977
    Erected through interests of these Heart Mountain organizations: The Extension Club, The Homesteaders' Association, and the Irrigation District, The Powell Bicentennial Commission, The Park County Commissioner, and The Historical Societies of Park County and Wyoming.

Plaque #4
TITLE: 1942-1945
LEGEND: This concrete structure was a Mess Hall Chimney Base in Block 23.
    1987

LOCATION: Follow U.S. Hwy 14A about 12 miles northeast of Cody, Wyoming, and turn onto County Road 19. Follow it for 0.5 mile to the Heart Mountain Relocation Center.

NEWTON LAKES—TRAIL CREEK RANCH CEMETERY-12

Sign
TITLE: Primitive necropolis
LEGEND: The following pioneers were buried here, but not much of a record as to which grave was used and little information regarding the pioneers is available. We are indebted to Charles Hartung, a pioneer cowboy for what we do have. 1882—Tom Heffner, cowboy for Henry Lovell, gassed at springs. 1882—Johnnie Lincoln, murdered at the Trail Creek ranch. Paul Bretache's baby was buried here. The wife and baby of Pete (Black Pete) Enzon, buried in separate graves. An unknown man walked over the cliff at the springs in the dark. 1900—Clarence Veonor Edick, died of internal injuries when crossing to the springs. An unknown invalid from the Red Lodge area died at the springs. 1903—Mrs. Wm. Brown of Bellfrey gassed in hot spring. Louis Wilde from the Greybull Valley died at the springs. His stock was branded with a cotton hook.

Granite stone
TITLE: Trail Creek Ranch Cemetery
LEGEND: Site of seven unknown pioneer graves
    Original homestead of A. C. Newton in 1887
    Dedicated by Brownie Newton 1975.

LOCATION: From its junction with U.S. Hwy 14A, follow State Route 120 for about 3.2 miles. Turn west onto County Road 7 WC and follow it for 1.3 miles to the entrance of Trail Creek Ranch. Turn left before ranch entrance and follow dirt road 1.2 miles to site.

SHOSHONE CANYON INFORMATIVE SIGN-13

TITLE: Shoshone Canyon
LEGEND: Shoshone Canyon is a gorge cut across Rattlesnake Mountain by the wearing action of the Shoshone River over a long period of time. The mountain is an upfold in the earth's crust. Beds of sedimentary rock on the east flank slope eastward beneath the plains. The same units bend up and over the crest of the mountain and stand vertical along the west flank. Granite over two billion years old, is exposed around Buffalo Bill Dam. South of the dam is a vertical fracture, or fault, in the rocks along which the mountain was uplifted over 2,000 feet.
LOCATION: North side of U.S. Hwy 14/16/20, about 3.1 miles west of Cody, Wyoming, just at entrance to Shoshone Canyon.

WAPITI RANGER STATION INFORMATIVE SIGN-14

TITLE: Wapiti Ranger Station

LEGEND: This is the oldest national forest ranger station in the United States. It was built in 1903 as a supervisor and ranger headquarters for the Shoshone Division of the Yellowstone Timberland Reserve. This reserve was established by President Benjamin Harrison on March 30, 1891 and was the first federal forest reservation to be established. In 1902, President Theodore Roosevelt greatly enlarged the original Timberland Reserve and the new reservation was divided into four divisions. One of these divisions has since been considerably enlarged and is now known as the Shoshone National Forest, comprising approximately 2,500,000 acres.

LOCATION: The sign no longer stands, but an information center is located on the north side of U.S. Hwy 14/16/20, about 30 miles west of Cody, Wyoming.

VIETNAM MEMORIAL-15

Granite Memorial #1

TITLE: Wyoming Vietnam Veterans Memorial

LEGEND: This memorial is dedicated to our comrades who gave their lives in Vietnam, Laos, and Cambodia 1965-1972

Erected through the efforts of surviving Vietnam Veterans, families, friends and the people of the State of Wyoming

Built in hope that the memory of the sacrifice of those listed here will never be erased

Dedicated November 11, 1986

Granite Memorial #2

TITLE: None

LEGEND: Carlton J. Holland, Robert W. Grove, David G. Lucas, Alma J. Stumpp, Ernest E. Taylor

Robert F. Guthrie, Craig S. Blackner, Samuel L. Dellos, Barry A. Hansen, Gary E. Bartz, Leonard D. May, Philip O. Robinson

Michael R. Beck, Weldon D. Moss, Gilbert B. Bush, Douglas T. Patrick, Robert L. Shuck, James F. Barnes, Curtis T. Ando, Norman L. Moore, Alva R. Krogman, Pablo Patino

Joseph L. Hart, Jerry D. Byers, Dennis W. Smith, Daniel R. Laird, George R. Harrison, Raymond E. Benson, Daniel J. Orlikowski, Walter Washut Jr., William B. Esslinger, Harold L. Gibson, Timothy J. Saunders, Kenneth L. Brown, William B. Graves

Gilland Corbitt, Bruce A. Jensen, Lawrence D. Torrez, Merrell J. Clayburn, Terrance H. Larson, James C. Wilson, Pedro R. Montanez, Douglas E. Rogers, Orville D. Cooley, Edward F. McNally Jr., Stephen W. Stark, William D. Selders, Dennis D. King, Elmer D. Lauck, Walter E. Handy, Leslie J Landos

Richard S. Brown, Frank M. Darling, James E. Pantier, Charles W. Reberg, Vernon W. Nix III, Richard L. Endicott, Richard M. Martin, Allen L. Faler, Joseph A. Padilla, Gary D. Fox, Kenneth W. King, Robert E. Barnes, Terry L. Fetzer, Edward R. Braun, Charles S. Roy, Richard P. Cazin, Ronald G. Ferris

Donald E. Jarrett, Ronald A. Shadoan, Andrew J. Wantulok, Bennett E. Evans, Dennis W. Wear, Edward L. Lawton, Robert Herrid, Elton G. Anderson, Laurence B. Green, Dale W. Johnson, Donald L. Ford, William J. McAtee, Robert A. Rex, Henry E. Maul, Dennis B. Farris, Victor R. Landes, Robert S. Knalder, Donald B. Schroeder

Daniel W. Margrave II, Richard J. Sweeney, Edward B. Steele, John W. Kobelin II, Ralph T. Sand, James L. Barton, Oliver E. Reynolds, Candelario P. Bustos, Leroy R. Cardenas, Joseph B. Walker, John H. Aldrich, Lonnie A. Dykes, William M. Wilson, Robert F. Maurer, Dennis R. Wartchow, Richard P. Powers

Robert R. Rogers, Lester McCabe, Larry R. Owens, Crag T. Marrington, Albert O. Wayman Jr., Steven Boal, Richard T. Kastner, Walis W. Garst, Robert E. Romero, Roger L. Scott, Edward C. Haggerty, William T. McCormick, Ernest C. Balland

Roy J. Snyder, Thomas W. Skiles, Donald E. Carpenter, Joe W. Green, Ronald R. Stewart, Robert G. Crichton, Donald W. Chipp Jr., Richard E. Tabor, John A. Cukale Jr., Earl E. McCarty

Benjamin E. Stagowski, Gary J. Fuqua, Terry V. Knight, Randall J. Glasspoole, Robert L. Morganflash, Stephen E. Slocum, Emil M. Miltnovich

James E. Steadman, Larry L. Warnock, Dennis C. Cressey, Harry B. Coen, Lawrence G. Evert

LOCATION: In the Viet Nam Memorial Park, about 0.5 mile west of the intersection of U.S. Hwy 14/16/20 and State Route 120 in Cody, Wyoming.

All counties and many cities in Wyoming have erected monuments and memorials to their veterans and to those who gave their lives in wars protecting the freedoms of the United States. Those markers memorialize soldiers from the Spanish-American War, World Wars I and II, the Korean War, and the Vietnam War. Although not included in this book, there was no intent to lessen the sacrifices made during these other conflicts.

In October 1989, the Department of Defense, the Army, and the Department of the Interior approved the addition of the name of Spec. 4 Jose "Leo" Lujan to the Wyoming Vietnam Memorial. He died in May 1968 of injuries received in a plane crash in December 1967.

NEZ PERCE TRAIL-16

TITLE: Nez Perce Trail

LEGEND: In 1877, the Nez Perce Indians of Idaho, led by Chief Joseph, fled the U.S. Army. They crossed the Clark's Fork River near this point, while trying to outrun the soldiers to Canada.

Erected 1987 by Boy Scout Troop 53

LOCATION: At the Edelweiss Campground on the east side of State Route 120 where it crosses the Clark's Fork River, about 28 miles north of Cody, Wyoming.

MOUNTAIN MAN MEMORIALS-17

Granite Marker

TITLE: The American Mountain Man

LEGEND: Dedicated to all Mountain Men known and unknown for their essential part in the opening of the American West.

We gratefully acknowledge the way their unique lifestyle has profoundly influenced our own.

Erected by the Brotherhood of The American Mountain Men June 10, 1978

Plaque #1

TITLE: In Tribute to John Colter

LEGEND: First known white American explorer to enter this locale in the fall of 1807.

Probably crossing the river 1/4 mile east of this point (right), before discovering "Colter's Hell" 1/2 mile to the west (left).

Born and raised in Virginia in 1770's.

A valued member of the Lewis and Clark Expedition to the Pacific Ocean, 1803-1806.

Among the first American "Free Trappers" in the Rocky Mountains, along with Joseph Dickson and Forrest Bancock, 1806-1807.

First to explore Big Horn Basin, Yellowstone Park, and Grand Teton regions, 1807-1808.

Immortalized by his legendary "run for life" escape, from the hostile

Blackfeet Indians, 1808.

Quit the mountains in 1810, married and settled on a farm near St. Louis, Missouri.

Died of disease in 1813, unheralded, but not forgotten. His final resting place has since been lost.

Erected by the John Colter Society 1981

A legacy for all who adventure

Plaque #2

TITLE: George Drouillard
   (c. 1775-1810)

LEGEND: Born to a French Canadian father and Shawnee mother, Drouillard joined the Lewis and Clark Expedition in 1803 as chief interpreter and hunter. Lewis said of him, "I scarcely know how we should exist were it not for the exertions of this excellent hunter." While thus employed, he was possibly the first white man to trap on the upper Missouri River. In 1807, he joined Manuel Lisa's trading expedition. During two solitary winter treks on foot to notify various tribes of Lisa's fort on the Yellowstone, Drouillard journeyed up the Stinking Water (Shoshone River) near this spot. His explorations of this and other major rivers to the east totalled 500 miles, and he produced an important map upon which William Clark and later cartographers relied heavily.

Trapping near the Three Forks with the Missouri Fur Company, he was killed by Blackfeet Indians in May 1810.

Plaque #3

TITLE: Jedediah Strong Smith
   January 6, 1799   May 27, 1831

LEGEND: Born in Jerico, N.Y., the 6th of 14 children, Jed was destined to influence the Westward expansion of the United States as few men have done. Influenced by Lewis and Clark's exploits he joined Ashley's trapping expedition in 1822, soon becoming a partner and then owner in 1827. A natural leader, devout Christian and tireless explorer, Jed's discovery popularized the South Pass crossing of the Rockies. He was the first man to travel overland to California and first to travel the coast from California to the Columbia. He survived near death from thirst and starvation, maulings of a grizzly and attacks by Arikara, Mojave and Kelewatset indians. Killed by Comanches near Fargo Spring, Kansas, his was never found but his legacy lives on as his trails of discovery became the highways for America's westward migration.

Plaque #4

TITLE: Born c 1770   Died 1813
   John Colter

LEGEND: A hunter for Lewis and Clark (1803-1806), Colter remained in the mountains to trap and explore. During his great journey of discovery he found "Colter's Hell" west of Cody, Wyoming. Captured by the Blackfeet in 1808, he was forced to run for his life. Outdistancing the entire tribe for seven miles he survived, naked and weaponless, to become a legend in his own lifetime. John Colter was the first true "Mountain Man."

Plaque #5

TITLE: A Tribute to James "Old Gabe" Bridger
   1804-1881

LEGEND: Mountain man, hunter, trapper, fur trader, emigrant guide, and Army scout. Born in Richmond, Virginia in 1804 and moved to St. Louis, Missouri in 1812. Served as a blacksmith's apprentice from 1818 to 1822. Came west with the 1822 Ashley-Henry Expedition. Discovered the Great Salt Lake in 1824 and visited what is now Yellowstone Park in 1830. In 1833 he became a full partner in the fur trading firm of Sublette, Fraeb, Gervais, Bridger, and Fitzpatrick. Anticipating the influx

of immigrants he established Ft. Bridger to resupply and repair wagon trains. Jim served as a guide and scout for the Army until 1868. After his discharge Old Gabe retired to his farm in Missouri. However, by 1874 his health began to fail and he was blind. Jim's only regret was that he would never see his beloved Rocky Mountains before his death. On July 17, 1881 the Lord laid Old Gabes tired body to rest and set his spirit free to return at last to the mountains he loved.

Plaque #6

TITLE: In Tribute to Jim Bridger

LEGEND: Regarded most famous of the Rocky Mountain trappers and explorers who blazed the American West's early trails of continental destiny and who frequented these environs throughout the mid-1800's.

West 20 miles upriver towers Jim Mountain named for Jim Baker, a well known Bridger protege.

East 30 miles downriver the "Bridger Trail" crosses the "Stinking Water" (Shoshone River). This trail was established across the Big Horn Basin around 1864 by Jim Bridger (then working primarily as an emigrant and Army expedition guide). As a safer alternative route to the "Bozeman Trail" in traveling from the "Oregon-California Trail" to the Montana mines.

Jim Bridger epitomized the "mountain man" and his legacy endures, but only in context with many others. In all this breed never exceeded more than a few hundred. They came seeking adventure and fortune. Over half of them succumbed to the rigors of their profession hostile elements, animals, Indians, and starvation. Their names and remains are forever consigned—unrecorded—to the dust of the mountains and plains where they "went under", often in violent fashion. This marker also stands in their memory.

Erected 1982

Plaque #7

TITLE: Osborne Russell
   1814   1892

LEGEND: Born June 12, 1814 in Bowdoinham, Maine, Russell went to sea briefly at age 16 then for three years was a trapper in Wisconsin and Minnesota. He joined Nathanial Wyeth's 1834 expedition to deliver trade goods to the trappers' rendezvous in the Rocky Mountains. Wyeth met disappointment in his enterprise but moved on to build Fort Hall. Russell helped to build the fort and stayed to maintain it until spring when he joined Jim Bridger's trapping party. He soon declared his independence as a "free trapper" and pursued beaver until 1843.

Russell's travels took him from Montana to Utah Lake as he crossed and recrossed the Rockies many times. All this while he felt an obligation to record his observations in his journal.

In 1843 he moved to the California/Oregon country where he became a miner, a merchant and at one time a judge. He died August 28, 1892 in Placerville, California. He is gratefully remembered by all who read his "Journal of a Trapper" with its daily account of the activities and adventures of a trapper.

Plaque #8

TITLE: Thomas Fitzpatrick
   1799-1854

LEGEND: Mountain man, business man, western guide, Indian agent; born and educated in Ireland, emigrated to America at age 16, he joined Ashley's trappers in 1823 and was appointed to leadership that year. He became a full partner in the Rocky Mountain Fur Co. in 1830. Tom battled with the Arickarees in 1823 and with the Gros Vents at Pierre's Hole in 1832. These same Gros Vents attacked him a few weeks earlier as he rode alone east of the Tetons. His horses and weapons lost in flight, barely alive when rescued many days later, his hair had turned white from the ordeal. Tom had two nicknames, "White Hair" and

"Broken Hand", the latter from an encounter with a rifle ball during a Blackfoot attack. With the decline of the fur trade, Tom served as a guide to west-bound emigrants (1841-42), J. D. Fremont's explorations (1843-44), and Col. Kerney's expedition of 1845-46. Honorably served as Federal Indian Agent from 1846 until his death February 7, 1854.

Plaque #9
TITLE: Hugh Glass
  ? 1832(3)
LEGEND: Tough and independent, Glass had been a ship's captain and impressed pirate, captured and adopted by the Pawnees and finally made his way to St. Louis to join Ashley and his trappers. While ascending the Missouri he was wounded in a battle with the Arikarees (Rees). Several weeks later he was attacked by a grizzly and "tore nearly all to peases." Two men were paid to tend the old man until his death, but after several days they abandoned him knowing his death was certain and a Ree attack was imminent. Hugh recovered consciousness and crawled and hobbled 350 miles to Ft. Kiowa. When sufficiently recovered he headed back to the Rockies seeking those who had abandoned him.

Twice during the next ten months Glass was forced to flee for his life from Ree attack. He left Ashley's men to work the Santa Fe trade for a few years but later returned to the land of his old enemies.

Hugh was finally killed by Rees at a river crossing during the winter of 1832-33.

LOCATION: Historic Trail Town, 2 miles west of the Buffalo Bill Historical Center in Cody, Wyoming.

Old Trail Town is a collection of historic buildings and relics of the Wyoming frontier. Situated on the first site of Old Cody City, the original Red Lodge to Fort Washakie Trail runs through the property.

Part of the collection is a memorial to the mountain men of the fur trade era. There also is a cemetery where five area pioneers and two mountain men were reburied.

The man behind the collections is Bob Edgar, a Wyoming Big Horn Basin native. Besides being an archaeologist, historian and western artist, Edgar has set himself apart as a leader in preserving Wyoming history.

PLATTE COUNTY

BARREL HOOPS SITE-1

South side: Main Oregon Trail 1830-1867
  Marked by E. F. & R. A. P. 1953
West side: Barrel Hoops site
LOCATION: Follow the Esterbrook Road about 6 miles west of Glendo, Wyoming, to the Leo Foy Ranch. The marker is about 3.4 miles west of the ranch on the north side of the Elkhorn River. Permission is required as the land is privately owned.

On August 1, 1876, the wagon train was attacked by a band of Indians ten miles west of the present site of Glendo, Wyoming, on the old Emigrant Road. The following summary of the Barrel Hoops Site story came from an article prepared by Ed Foy, Sr., as related to him by Ves Sherman, who was second wagon boss of the Heck Reel wagon train. The story was given to me by Leo and Ann Foy who live on the ranch where the Barrel Hoops site is located:

A. H. Reel of Cheyenne, popularly known as "Heck," was a widely known freighter and cattleman who operated a freight outfit under contract with the Army. His supply train, headquartered at Camp Carlin, supplied Fort Laramie and Fort Fetterman.

The wagon boss in charge of this specific train was George Throstle, a 35 year old, faithful and hard-working employee. The train was contracted to haul flour, bacon, and other supplies to the fort on Little Goose Creek in northern Wyoming for use by Crook's army. Sixteen men were hired and outfitted with a .45 caliber sixshooter and a .44 Winchester at Mr. Reel's request. The train followed the Cheyenne-Fort Fetterman Trail and Bull's Bend Cottonwood Road because there were no steep grades and few ravines to cross, and it led to a camp on the Elkhorn River (the Foy Ranch), one of the best camping places with plenty of wild grass and water.

On August 1, the laborious task of getting the wagons up the steep hill north of the Elkhorn started. At about 4 p.m. the wagon bosses, Throstle and Sherman, were attacked 300 yards ahead of the wagon train by a band of about 30 Indians. George Throstle was struck 3 times and fell dead from his horse. Sherman made it safely back to the wagons which were then corralled. The freighters needed to unload all of the flour in order to get at the rifles. The fight lasted until evening.

The next morning the damage was surveyed. Wagon boss Throstle had been killed; Irish Pete was shot in the leg; Sherman was injured by a shot which struck the fork of his saddle; 14 horses had been killed and the rear wagon had been destroyed by fire. The wagon train began its journey at 10 a.m. The train was met and escorted to Fort Fetterman by the Army.

At this site for many years were remains of burnt wagon parts, metal parts, and barrel hoops.

"E. F." on the south side of the marker refers to Ed Foy. "R. A. P." probably refers to Bob Peterson. These men were responsible for the erection of this marker.

CHUGWATER DIVISION STAGE STATION-2

TITLE: Chugwater
LEGEND: Chugwater Division Stage Station Cheyenne-Black Hills Trail
  Established March 18, 1876 Abandoned September 1887, Russell Thorpe, owner.
  Erected by Historical Landmark Commission of Wyoming 1937
LOCATION: Just west of the railroad tracks on the main road through Chugwater, Wyoming.

There are several other monuments across eastern Wyoming that mark the course of the Cheyenne-Deadwood Trail. Four markers in Laramie County (#6, 7, 15, & 18), two markers in Goshen County (#1 and a Fort Laramie National Historic Site marker), seven markers in Niobrara County (#2, 3, 4, 5, 7, 8, & 11), and three markers in Weston County (#3.2, 4, & 5) give additional history and insight into the Cheyenne-Black Hills Stage Route.

COLD SPRINGS MONUMENT AND OREGON TRAIL MARKER-3

TITLE: The Oregon Trail
  1841
LEGEND: Cold Springs camping ground. Rifle pits on brow of hill 500 feet north.
  Erected by the Historical Landmark Commission of Wyoming 1943
LOCATION: North side of U.S. Hwy 26 about 1.8 miles west of the turnoff to Guernsey State Park.

The ridge with the rifle pits was used as a defense against the Indian attacks. Just east of the ridge, workers from Fort Laramie quarried lime for use in plaster walls and timber for construction of buildings. Here, too, travelers along the Oregon Trail found water and a suitable camping site.

HISTORIC GUERNSEY SIGN-5

TITLE: Historic Guernsey area
LEGEND: The historic Guernsey area stretches from the chalk rock bluff on the south to the mineral laden hills on the north, with the Oregon Trail indelibly marked along the south side of the river.
REGISTER CLIFF may be found 3 mi. S.E. of this sign; the COVERED WAGON RUTS, worn deep in solid stone 2 mi. S.W., the PONY EXPRESS STATION at Sand Point, 2 mi. S.E.; LUCINDY ROLLINS grave 1 mi. S.W.; WARM SPRINGS 3 mi. S.W.; COLD SPRINGS with rifle pits on knoll north of springs 2 1/2 mi. W. on Highway 26.

Boot Hill Cemetery is one mile south of Hartville, 5 mi. N.E.

One of the largest iron mines in the west is located at Sunrise 6 mi. N.E.
LOCATION: Intersection of East Whalen and South Dakota Avenue at the north end of the city park in Guernsey, Wyoming.

JACQUES LARAMIE MONUMENT-6

TITLE: In honor of Jacques La Ramie
LEGEND: Free trapper, who came to this region around 1815 and met an unknown fate, probably at the hands of Indians, about 1820, on one of the rivers bearing his name between which this monument stands. Tradition says he was an honest, just, and courageous leader and trader. His name is perpetuated by three Laramie Rivers, Ft. Laramie, the Laramie Plains, Laramie Peak, Laramie City, and Laramie County.
  Erected by the Historical Landmark Commission of Wyoming 1941
LOCATION: On the west side of State Route 320 about 4.6 miles north of the junction of State Route 320 and old U.S. Hwy 87 at the north end of Wheatland, Wyoming.

OLINGER'S OVERLOOK—NORTH PLATTE VALLEY-6.1

Introduction Plaque:
TITLE: Olinger's Overlook—North Platte Valley
LEGEND: The valley of the North Platte River offers the most advantageous approach to the easiest crossing of North America's continental backbone—the Rocky Mountain Cordillera. This is a geographic fact understood by pre-historic and historic man since time immemorial.

The route was first trekked by migratory foragers of western arid lands, themselves burdened and aided by packed and travois-trailing dogs. Later, from agrarian regions to the eastward, came Stone Age

PLATTE COUNTY

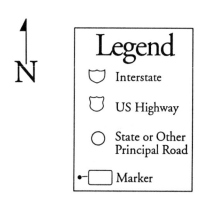

Legend

⬡ Interstate

⬠ US Highway

◯ State or Other Principal Road

•—▢ Marker

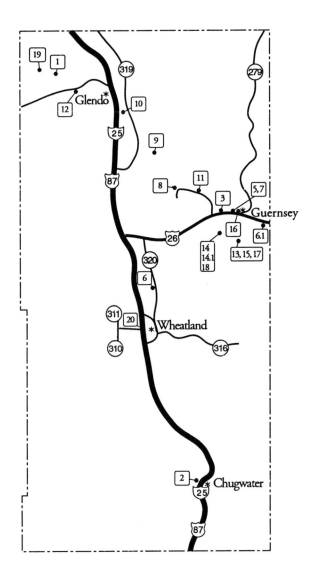

1   Barrel Hoops Site
2   Chugwater Division Stage Station
3   Cold Springs Monument and Oregon Trail Marker
5   Historic Guernsey Sign
6   Jacques LaRamie Monument
6.1 Olinger's Overlook—North Platte Valley
7   Oregon Trail Marker
8   Oregon Trail Marker
9   Oregon Trail Marker
10   Oregon Trail Marker
11   Oregon Trail Marker
12   Oregon Trail Marker
13   Oregon Trail Memorial
14   Oregon Trail Ruts Monument Plaque
14.1 Oregon Trail Informative Sign
15   Pony Express Monument
16   Register Cliff Sign
17   Register Cliff Sign
18   Lucindy Rollins Grave
19   Transcontinental Telegraph Marker
20   The Irrigator Monument

1.

2.

3.

4.

5.

6.

1. The Jacques LaRamie Marker north of Wheatland memorialized an early-day trapper and mountain man.

2. Several markers along the Oregon Trail in Platte County had relics of the pioneering days embedded in them. Memorial plaques of the Oregon Trail Memorial Association and the Pony Express Centennial Association, like the circular plaques on this marker, were placed on markers in 1930-1932.

3. Emigrants along the Oregon Trail in the 1800s placed their names on Register Cliff south of Guernsey as a symbol of their passage. In 1932 the bronze informative and Oregon Trail Memorial Association plaques were erected by visitors of a different era.

4. This large and beautiful bronze plaque designating Oregon Trail Ruts as a Registered National Historic Landmark was placed south of Guernsey in 1966.

5. This new cast-aluminum sign found at the Oregon Trail Ruts replaced an old weathered wooden sign.

6. The Sand Point Pony Express Station near Register Cliff was marked in 1932. Several markers across Wyoming were erected with Pony Express Memorial plaques embedded in them.

artisans to mine hematite (for paint colors) and quarry flint (for implements) in the famous "Spanish Diggings" of the Hartville Uplift, which here forms the valley's northern flank.

At the dawn of historic times and attributable to acquisition of the horse, here developed and flourished migratory tribes whose common culture has been designated Plains Indian. Then, fully recorded by history, came civilized man: first, like the foragers, weary pedestrians; second, like Plains Indians, mounted; and third, a new scene for the Platte, riding in wagons. Later, they drove cattle, laid rails, dug pipelines and built super highways.

To the right and left, signs and siting devices point out landmarks relating to man's activities in the valley.

D. J. Olinger, Wyoming Highway Department engineer and amateur historian.

Plaque #1:
TITLE: Fort Laramie
LEGEND: This sighting device points to the crest of a ridge separating the North Platte and Laramie Rivers. Directly down the opposite slope, on the banks of the Laramie about a mile above the confluence of the streams, stands Fort Laramie. It is about eight miles from here as the crow flies, but twelve miles by road.

Founded in 1834 by fur traders William Sublette and Robert Campbell, who named their log structure Fort William, the post was acquired by the American Fur Company in 1841. That company built an adobe-walled complex nearby which they named Fort John, but the mountain men called it Fort Laramie. This latter name stemmed from the river on which it was located and which, in its own turn, got its name from the trapper Jacques LaRamie, who is believed to have trapped and died in the area in the early 1800's.

The government purchased Fort Laramie in 1849. In the next forty years it became the most famous military post protecting the Oregon Trail and served as a forward base for many campaigns of the Indian Wars. The fort was deactivated in 1890, the land sold into private ownership and the buildings sold at auction or abandoned and allowed to fall into ruins. In 1937 the State of Wyoming purchased the property—land and building ruins—from private owners and gave it back to the federal government. By presidential proclamation in 1938 Fort Laramie National Historic Site became a unit of the National Park System.

Plaque #2
TITLE: Mexican Hill
LEGEND: Spotted through the right-hand sight is Mexican Hill. At Mexican Hill the covered wagon emigrants, having turned into the fort on the Laramie River for information, supplies or repairs, cut over the intervening ridge to regain the Platte River route. There, wagon ruts worn into bedded rock attest to the volume of westward traffic traversing the Oregon Trail during the years 1840 to 1870.

Coming down Mexican Hill's steep slope, drivers roughlocked wheels to keep wagons from running into their own backward-hold-ing though forward-moving teams. Here, besides the animals iron-shod hooves, it was their singular stiff-legged, sliding step—adapted to hold against the forward thrust of heavily loaded wagons—which, together with the locked and sliding, steel-rimmed wheels, contributed to the extraordinary depth of the ruts.

In 1841 Mexican artisans were engaged by the American Fur Company to build the adobe trading post later known as Fort Laramie. This hill took its name from the craftsmen who settled permanently in the vicinity and constructed an irrigation system at the foot of the hill to water their extensive gardens. They sold the produce to fur traders, soldiers and passing emigrants for whom it was a welcome supplement to diets otherwise lacking any fresh foods other than meat.

Plaque #3:
TITLE: North Platte River
LEGEND: In 1739 the brothers Pierre and Paul Mallet, earliest explorers along this river's lower course, named it after the French word for flat. Although the sighting tube aims at a wide, strong flowing current, the North Platte is not navigable.

It is unlikely that prehistoric foragers, habituated to arid environs, would have attempted a journey on water. But flint quarriers and hematite miners, accustomed to cruising midwestern rivers and burdened with the products of their labors, might have tried the Platte. In 1812 Robert Stuart's party of eastbound Astorians, recorded discoverers of this ancient, transmontane route of aborigines, wintered a short distance downstream. They fashioned dugout canoes and embarked on the spring floods of 1813, but their craft soon stranded on sandbars and they finished their journey on foot. Eleven years later Tom Fitzpatrick and other trappers again put a boat in the Platte. They encountered wild waters between canyon walls and, though experienced voyageurs, lost a part of Ashley's valuable furs. Thereafter, mountain men stuck to their horses.

The Platte's chief historical significance, other than as a natural route for transcontinental travel and commerce, relates to the "arid-lands culture theory" of John Wesley Powell, 19th century explorer, ethnologist, engineer and statesman. An agency created through his instigation, the U.S. Bureau of Reclamation, constructed along the Platte one of the west's first great irrigation systems. The prosperity resulting from the regulated spreading of North Platte waters over formerly arid lands is visible for hundreds of miles along the river's course.

Plaque #4
TITLE: The Burlington-Northern Railroad
LEGEND: Pointed out by the sight, Burlington-Northern tracks are in close view. That railroad's forerunner, the Burlington and Missouri, laid rails up the North Platte Valley in 1900. With a view to eventually reaching the Pacific, the company surveyed beyond immediate construction goals—on through South Pass.

Primarily laid down as a supplement to existing feeder lines in Iowa and Nebraska, this branch line was intended for moving Wyoming range livestock to midwestern feedlots and, following fattening, on to metropolitan packing plants. Further considerations were developing possibilities for transporting Platte Valley iron ore, petroleum products and irrigated field crops to established centers of processing and distribution.

Subsequent consolidations have made the Burlington and Missouri part of a vast railroad network. Therein, one of the most profitable sectors connects Gulf Coast ports—via the Platte Valley here and the Yellowstone Valley in Montana—with the Pacific Northwest. Thus the Burlington finally reached the western ocean, but not through the easy grades via South Pass as originally projected.

Though gradual grades were as important to railroad engineer as to wagon train master the more abundant timber for ties and coal for fuel found south and north of the famous pass met the railroader's needs better than the wildlife, grass and water which were essential to the emigrant wagoners following the Oregon Trail through central Wyoming.

Plaque #5
TITLE: Guernsey Pipeline Station
LEGEND: This site points to the Guernsey Pipeline Station, jointly owned by the Platte Pipeline Company, the American Oil Company and the Continental Oil Company. Most of the structures under view were built in 1952 although, owing to the river's favorable grade and southeasterly course, the first pipeline through this vicinity was delivering Platte Valley petroleum wealth to mid-western urban centers

as early as 1918. Technologically, this station is capable of interchanging crude oil among several carrier lines and moving it south to Cheyenne and Denver or east to mid-continent refineries.

Aborigines, from the early foraging societies through the heyday of the Plains Tribes, exploited the North Platte Valley both as a route of travel and commerce and for its own natural wealth. But fur traders, conducting most of their operations further west in the mountains, were chiefly interested in the North Platte as a route of commerce; for covered wagon emigrants, the North Platte was only a necessarily traveled route lying between their past and their future; for Pony Express, stage and telegraph enterprises it was a pathway between the inhabited regions wherein they provided a connecting link; livestock men did exploit the valley's riches but preferred that someone else provide transportational services; railroaders found some local business but that was incidental to their basic operation—the transcontinental haul.

Petroleum concerns, however, like the aborigines before them, have existed on both the valley's natural wealth and its transportational potentials. They have exploited its availability as a route for commerce to increase the value of its products through delivery to areas of maximum demand.

Plaque #6
TITLE: Register Cliff
LEGEND: Register Cliff stands in plain view after it is singled out by the sighting device. This natural landmark, enrolled in the National Register of Historic Places, is a developed area with parking and rest facilities, foot trails and informative signs. A fence protects the earliest names registered on the cliff face. Also fenced is a little cemetery originated by covered wagon emigrants.

The Cliff's historic significance stems from the large number of emigrant names and dates carved in the sandstone-limestone formation. However, it also bears names of early fur traders, Indian Wars participants and names and dates of pioneer ranchers. Some early names have been obliterated by more recent carving, and this made it necessary to fence the portion of the cliff where signatures are most concentrated.

Register Cliff can be reached by a paved and well-marked country road extending three miles southeast from Guernsey.

Plaque #7
TITLE: Sand Point
LEGEND: A monument marking Sand Point appears as a white dot in the center of the sight. Sand deposits caused by currents at a bend in the river evidently gave the site its name. The surrounding meadows have been favorite campsites since prehistoric time.

Seth Ward and William Guerrier established an Indian trade post at Sand Point in 1852. It was an ideal location for trading in hides and furs as well as for supplying Oregon Trail travelers who camped nearby. In 1852 a lady diarist wrote, "We are now encamped directly on the bank of the river, under two fine trees. The station, about a mile below, is in a handsome bend of the stream and consists of two or three log buildings, with a large one of stone, about half erected."

In 1855, Ward and Guerrier moved to Fort Laramie, where Ward soon became post sutler—a position leading to accumulation of a great fortune. Until his death in 1858, Guerrier handled the Fort's Indian trade. Thereafter, B. B. Mills and Antoine Janis managed that trade, moving its headquarters back to Sand Point. Later, under Jules Ecoffey, the post became a stage station and, in 1860 and 1861, it was a Pony Express Station. By 1822, Sand Point was a ranch homestead, and Charles Guernsey acquired the property in 1891.

The country road from Guernsey to Register Cliff passes by Sand Point.

Plaque #8:
TITLE: Guernsey-Frederick Ranch
LEGEND: The sight centers on the headquarters buildings of the Guernsey-Frederick Ranch. That these buildings stand almost in the shadow of Register Cliff is symbolic of the valley's heritage. Here, history emphasizes the Oregon Trail; such other epochs as the storied Cattleman's Frontier are subordinated by memories and the visual landmarks of that nationally famous emigrant road.

Since the days of "open range" and "free grass" the Guernsey-Frederick Ranch has been representative of Wyoming's always important livestock industry. The place is, however, also significant in its own right. It brings together two pioneer ranching family names which also relate to such other facets of state history as frontier military life, political activity, governmental organization and the development of railroads, mines, irrigated lands, schools, churches and banks.

Favorably located and progressively operated, the ranch is as significant in modern times as ever it was in the past.

Plaque #9
TITLE: Oregon Trail Ruts
LEGEND: Although the sight aims at the general location, the Oregon Trail Ruts National Historic Landmark cannot be seen from here. Like Register Cliff, it is a developed historic site, accessible by a good country road.

The terrain here forced travelers to follow a single set of tracks across a relatively soft sandrock formation. Over the years, the volume of emigrant wagon traffic cut ruts so deep as to leave marks of turning wheel-hubs which extend over a length of several hundred feet.

The Ruts are reached by a country road out of Guernsey. It is the same road leading to Register Cliff but, just beyond a bridge over the North Platte, a sign directs the visitor to a side road which brings him, at the end of half a mile, to the parking area. From there, a short foot trail leads to the Ruts.

Plaque #10
TITLE: Laramie Peak
LEGEND: The sight points to Laramie Peak, altitude 10,247 feet, the highest elevation in the Laramie Range. These mountains were originally called the Black Hills, a name deriving from the dark appearance of their evergreen forests as noted from far to the eastward by westward-journeying mountain men. Only the northern end of the range, in northeastern Wyoming and western South Dakota, is now known as the Black Hills.

Although the name of that more legendary than historic figure, Jacques LaRamie, has been given to numerous features of Wyoming geography, apparently this mountain was the first to be so designated. Looming on a distant horizon, that major natural landmark won historic significance through being cited time and again—in the journals, diaries and letters of Oregon Trail travelers—as first evidence of a successful high plains crossing and impending entry into the Rocky Mountains.

One who so recorded a sighting of Laramie Peak, and whose transit triangulations would later make the mountain an important cartographic reference point, was famed Dr. Francis V. Hayden of the U.S. Geological Survey. He wrote, in 1869: "From our camp on the Laramie we enjoyed one of the beautiful sunsets which are not uncommon in this western country. But this was a rare occasion, for the sun passed directly behind the summit of Laramie Peak. The whole range was gilded with golden light, and the haziness of the atmosphere gave to the whole a deeper beauty. Such a scene as this could occur but once in a lifetime."

LOCATION: At a rest area on the south side of U.S. Hwy 26 about 2.5 miles east of Guernsey, Wyoming.

Donald J. Olinger, district engineer for the Southeast District of the Wyoming Highway Department in 1968, first proposed the idea of historical signing at a rest stop that was to be built in the late 1960s along U.S. Hwy 26 east of Guernsey, Wyoming. He collaborated with Paul Westedt, director of the Wyoming Recreation Commission, and together they erected the sighting devices and permaloy plaques that have such a panorama of the North Platte Valley and the Oregon Trail country.

OREGON TRAIL MARKER-7

TITLE: Oregon Trail Memorial
LEGEND: To all pioneers who passed this way to win and hold the west. Trail and Register Cliff one mile south. Erected by people of Guernsey in 1932.
LOCATION: In Guernsey, Wyoming, at the northeast corner of West Whalen Street and South Wyoming Avenue. One block west of City Park.

This marker was dedicated August 5, 1931, in the wake of the Covered Wagon Centennial organized by the Oregon Trail Memorial Association in 1930. An Oregon Trail Memorial metal plaque with a covered wagon in relief identified the marker as part of the movement sponsored by the Association. A Pony Express medallion also identified this site as part of the Pony Express route.

OREGON TRAIL MARKER-8

TITLE: None
LEGEND: At this point the Oregon Trail crossed. Erected by Robt. Rice, V.P. & G.M. C. & S. RY. Jan. l, 1921.
LOCATION: About 6.4 miles northwest of U.S. Hwy 26 on the Wendover Road, just south of the Burlington Northern Railroad tracks. The turnoff to the Wendover Road is about 2.5 miles west of Guernsey, Wyoming.

Robert Rice was the vice president and general manager of the Colorado and Southern Railroad. Another marker, Oregon Trail Marker (Platte County #11) was also erected on the Wendover Road, about 3.7 miles from U.S. Hwy 26.

OREGON TRAIL MARKER-9

TITLE: Oregon Trail
LEGEND: Marked by State of Wyoming 1913
LOCATION: On the divide between Little Cottonwood Creek and Bear Creek. On private land owned by Doug Curtis; permission required to visit.

This was one of the earliest of the Oregon Trail markers, sent to Platte County by the Oregon Trail Commission of Wyoming in October, 1913.
Trail pioneers must have been paradoxically impressed with this divide between the Little Cottonwood Creek and Bear Creek. Laramie Peak loomed to the west in its beauty and magnificence. However, the descent into the North Platte River bottom was steep and rocky, and must have been especially difficult for the covered wagons.

OREGON TRAIL MARKER-10

TITLE: None
LEGEND: 530 yards southeast of this monument on the Oregon Trail was the site of Horseshoe Creek Pony Express and U.S. Military Telegraph and Stage Station built in 1860.
Erected by the Historical Landmark Commission of Wyoming 1937
LOCATION: On the west side of old U.S. Hwy 26/87, about 2.2 miles south of Glendo, Wyoming.

OREGON TRAIL MARKER-11

TITLE: Oregon Trail
LEGEND: Marked by the State of Wyoming 1913
LOCATION: About 3.7 miles northwest of U.S. Hwy 26 on the east side of Wendover Road. The Wendover Road turnoff is about 2.5 miles west of Guernsey, Wyoming.

This marker, provided by the Oregon Trail Commission of Wyoming, was sent to Platte County in October, 1913. Another Oregon Trail marker (Platte County #8) is located 2.7 miles farther on the Wendover Road.

OREGON TRAIL MARKER-12

TITLE: Oregon Trail
LEGEND: Marked by the State of Wyoming 1913
LOCATION: On the south side of the Esterbrook Road, about 7.3 miles west of I-25 at Glendo, Wyoming.

This marker was given to Platte County by the Oregon Trail Commission of Wyoming in October, 1913. The Barrel Hoops Site (Platte County #1) is located on private land several miles northwest of this site.

OREGON TRAIL MEMORIAL-13

TITLE: Oregon Trail Memorial
LEGEND: Dedicated to pioneers of Wyoming. Register Cliff acquired by the State of Wyoming through gift of the Henry Frederick family 1932.
LOCATION: Next to Register Cliff, about 150 yards east of the parking area. About 2.5 miles southeast of Guernsey, Wyoming.

In 1930 the Oregon Trail Memorial Association organized the Covered Wagon Centennial, a national celebration of the Oregon Trail. After the celebration, many markers like this one were erected.

OREGON TRAIL RUTS MONUMENT PLAQUE-14

TITLE: Oregon Trail Ruts
LEGEND: Has been designated a Registered National Historic Landmark.
   Under the provisions of the Historic Sites Act of August 21, 1935 this site possesses exceptional value in commemorating or illustrating the history of the United States.
   U.S. Department of the Interior
   National Park Service
   1966
LOCATION: At the Oregon Trail Ruts Site on the south side of Guernsey, Wyoming. Follow local signing and marking.

OREGON TRAIL INFORMATIVE SIGN-14.1

TITLE: Oregon Trail Ruts—Registered National Historic Landmark
LEGEND: Wagon wheels cut solid rock, carving a memorial to Empire Builders. What manner of men and beasts impelled conveyances weighing on those grinding wheels? Look! A line of shadows crossing boundless wilderness.
Foremost, nimble mules drawing their carts, come poised Mountain Men carrying trade goods to a fur fair—the Rendezvous. So, in 1830, Bill Sublette turns the first wheels from St. Louis to the Rocky Mountains! Following his faint trail, a decade later and on through the 1860's, appear straining, twisting teams of oxen, mules and heavy draft horses drawing Conestoga wagons for Oregon pioneers. Trailing the Oregon-bound *avant garde* but otherwise mingling with those emigrants, inspired by religious fervor, loom footsore and trail worn companies—Mormons dragging or pushing handcarts as they follow Brigham Young to the Valley of Salt Lake. And, after 1849, reacting to

a different stimulus but sharing the same trail, urging draft animals to extremity, straining resources and often failing, hurry gold rushers California bound.

A different breed, no emigrants but enterprisers and adventurers, capture the 1860's scene. They appear, multi-teamed units in draft—heavy wagons in tandem, jerkline operators and bullwhackers delivering freight to Indian War outposts and agencies. Now the apparition fades in a changing environment. Dimly seen, this last commerce serves a new, pastoral society; the era of the cattle baron and the advent of settlement blot the Oregon Trail.

LOCATION: At the Oregon Trail Ruts Site on the south side of Guernsey, Wyoming. Follow local signing and marking.

PONY EXPRESS MONUMENT-15

TITLE: None
LEGEND: Pony Express Station 1860-1861.
LOCATION: On the north side of the graveled Register Cliff Road. About 2.5 miles southeast of Guernsey, Wyoming.

Seth Ward and William Guerrier established a small trading post at Sand Point just west of Register Cliff in the mid-1800s. In 1860-61 it became a Pony Express station known as the Sand Point, or Star Ranch Pony Express Station. See Sand Point (plaque #7) at Olinger's Overlook—North Platte Valley (Platte County #6.1).

REGISTER CLIFF SIGN-16

TITLE: Register Cliff
LEGEND: Emigrants participating in the great continental migrations of the mid-nineteenth century left enduring traces of their arduous passage along trails. On soft rock faces they inscribed their names and dates of passing. These etchings not only confirm their presence on the frontier, they are evidence of the pioneers' realization that they were participants in a dramatic process: the settlement of the trans-Mississippi west. After the first day out of Fort Laramie emigrants paused to mark their passing at Register Cliff, a sandstone bluff 1.5 miles southeast of here.

Register Cliff can be observed more closely by traveling 2.5 miles south-east of downtown Guernsey.

LOCATION: North side of U.S. Hwy 26, about 0.5 miles east of Guernsey, Wyoming.

REGISTER CLIFF SIGN-17

TITLE: Register Cliff
LEGEND: The wayfarer's penchant for inscribing names and dates on prominent landmarks excites the interest of his descendants. Regrettably, marks of historic value are often effaced by later opportunists.

Along the Oregon Trail, famed transcontinental route of the 19th century, pertinent dates are from the 1820's through the 1860's. Three outstanding recording areas exist within Wyoming. Register Cliff here; Independence Rock 180 miles west; and Names Hill a further 175 miles along the Trail's wandering course. Register Cliff and Names Hill are self-evident titles; Independence Rock derives from a July 4th, 1825 observance which, according to some authorities, was staged by Mountain Men of Fur Trade fame.

Register Cliff invited emigrants because broad river bottoms offered pleasing campsites and excellent pasture. Hardship and illness were inevitable to Trail travel; of 55,000 emigrants during a peak year, some 5,000 died enroute. Cliffside graves attest to the high mortality. This being their lot, travelers eagerly sought and singularly valued recuperative layovers. Here, rest offered the opportunity to register.

But not all who registered were worn and grieving emigrants. Early

inscriptions were by Mountain Men inured to wilderness life—many descendants of two centuries of French Fur Trade. One reads: "1829 this July 14". Does it denote an observance? If the American Independence Day was celebrated in 1825 at Independence Rock, could the French trappers have noted Bastille Day at Register Cliff in 1829?

LOCATION: At the beginning of the foot path at Register Cliff, about 2.5 miles southeast of Guernsey, Wyoming.

LUCINDY ROLLINS GRAVE-18

TITLE: Grave of Lucindy Rollins 1849-1934.
LEGEND: Dedicated to the pioneer women of Wyoming
Erected by the Historical Landmark Commission of Wyoming 1934
LOCATION: South of Guernsey, Wyoming, on the Oregon Trail Ruts road, south side of Guernsey, Wyoming, a few hundred yards north of the ruts and near the south bank of the North Platte River.

Lucindy Rollins was a 24-year-old woman from Ohio who succumbed to the hardships of the Oregon Trail. She was buried on this site June 11, 1849.

TRANSCONTINENTAL TELEGRAPH MARKER-19

TITLE: First Transcontinental Telegraph Line 1861
LEGEND: None
LOCATION: The telegraph marker is about 1.25 miles west of the Barrel Hoops Site (Platte County #1). Private land; permission required to visit.

THE IRRIGATOR MONUMENT-20

Irrigator Plaque
TITLE: "The Irrigator"
        Carl Jensen, Sculptor
LEGEND: Dedicated to those whose livelihood has depended, does depend and will depend upon Wyoming's land and water.

Made possible by the Grand Marnier Foundation, the Missouri Basin Power Project, the Wheatland Town Council and clubs, organizations and individuals in and around the Wheatland area.

Commissioned by the Wyoming Centennial Committee of Wheatland and dedicated on June 23, 1990 as a Wyoming Centennial Lasting Legacy.

Centennial Committee Plaque
TITLE: Wyoming Centennial Committee for Wheatland
LEGEND: Mary I. (Polly) White, Chairman
        Gloria Sanford   A.Z. Parr-Stebar
        Secretary   Treasurer

Standing Committee
Eric Alden, Arlene Birkle, Kathleen Brighton, Elvira Call, Charles and Jean Coleman, Charles and Ruth Duncan, Kay Gore, Helen Hay, Carl and Janel Jensen, A. Edward Kendig, Glyda May, Alice Ockinga, Jerry G. Orr, Ruby Preuit, Marge Scholten.

LOCATION: Courthouse yard in Wheatland, Wyoming.

WARM SPRINGS OCTA MARKER-21

TITLE: Warm Springs
LEGEND: Wagon trains heading west found these springs a convenient one-day's travel twelve miles beyond Fort Laramie. There were two main routes from the fort and emigrants travelling either could utilize this campground. Though well known to early mountaineers trapping local streams, Warm Springs was first described by John C. Fremont

who stopped here on July 21, 1842.

Sometimes called the "Big Springs" by emigrants, Warm Springs is best known in Wyoming folklore as "the Emigrant's Laundry Tub". This later term can be confirmed by at least one account, that of Pusey Graves who camped nearby on June 24, 1850. He wrote, "After I finished my letter to send back to the Ft. I proceeded to the spring a distance of 1 1/2 miles with my bucket of dirty clothes".

Early settlers found this area littered with wagon train debris and many graves. Of the graves, only one remains to be seen today. It is located across the draw southwest of here.

Research, Signing and Funding by
Oregon-California Trails Association
August 1988

This is a part of your American heritage. Honor it, protect it, preserve it for your children.

LOCATION: Along the Oregon Trail on private land in Platte County.

ELVA INGRAM OCTA MARKER-22

TITLE: Elva Ingram

LEGEND: On April 15, 1852, James and Ritta Ann Ingram with their nine children left Salem, Henry County, Iowa, for Pleasant Valley, Oregon. The wagon train, consisting of forty people in four families, reached the Fort Laramie area June 21, 1852.

Here on the North Bank (Childs') Road, on Wednesday, June 23, 1852, their daughter, four-year-old Elva Ingram, died. The cause of her death is unknown. On that day eighteen-year-old James Akin, Jr., wrote: "Travel 12 miles very hilly bad roads pine and cedar bluffs— cloudy rainy weather, Elva Ingram died. Camp in good place. Plenty wood no water."

There were seven more deaths in the Richey-Ingram-Akin wagon train, which reached the Willamette Valley late in October 1852.

Research and Signing by
Oregon-California Trails Association
Funding by
Dr. Jack Ingram and Family
Medford Oregon
1987

This is a part of your American heritage. Honor it, protect it, preserve it for your children.

LOCATION: Private land along the Childs Cutoff of the Oregon Trail in Platte County.

SHERIDAN COUNTY

BOZEMAN TRAIL MARKER-1

TITLE: Bozeman Trail
LEGEND: Marked by the State of Wyoming 1914
LOCATION: North side of U.S. Hwy 14, about 2 miles east of the bridge over the Tongue River at Dayton, Wyoming.

See Bozeman Trail Informative Sign and Bozeman Trail Marker (Campbell County #2.1 and 2.2) and Bozeman Trail Marker (Converse County #3.1) for more historical information about the trail.

The Sheridan County Chapter of the Daughters of the American Revolution assisted in locating this site and the three other Bozeman Trail markers in Sheridan County.

BOZEMAN TRAIL MONUMENT-2

TITLE: Bozeman Trail
LEGEND: Marked by the State of Wyoming 1914
LOCATION: On the east side of State Route 331 (Sheridan County Road 1701) just south of the bridge over Goose Creek. About 0.4 miles south of the country school at Beckton, Wyoming.

See Bozeman Trail Marker (Sheridan County #1) for more information.

BOZEMAN TRAIL MARKER-3

TITLE: Bozeman Trail
LEGEND: Marked by the State of Wyoming 1914
LOCATION: On State Route 335, just south of the business area of Big Horn, Wyoming.

See Bozeman Trail Marker (Sheridan County #1) for more information.

BOZEMAN TRAIL BLACKSMITH SHOP-3.1

TITLE: Bozeman Trail Blacksmith Shop
LEGEND: Near here emigrants traversed the Bozeman Trail, 1864-68 to Virginia City, Montana gold mines. Confronted with hostile Indians unwilling to share their hunting grounds, the trail became known as the "Bloody Bozeman" and was discontinued.

Crossing Little Goose Creek to the south and Jackson Creek to the west, the trail was later used from 1879-94 by Patrick Bros. Stage Line from Rock Creek near Laramie, Wyoming to Fort Custer on the Big Horn River in Montana.

This building was a blacksmith shop in the early 1880's to serve the stage line and ranchers of the valley.

Big Horn Wyoming Bicentennial Committee 1976
LOCATION: In Big Horn, Wyoming, about one-half block east of Bozeman Trail Marker (Sheridan County #3).

BOZEMAN TRAIL MONUMENT-4

TITLE: Bozeman Trail
LEGEND: Marked by the State of Wyoming 1914
LOCATION: North side of Pass Creek Road (Sheridan County Road 144), about 1 mile west of its intersection with State Route 345.

See Bozeman Trail Marker (Sheridan County #1) for more information.

BATTLE OF TONGUE RIVER SIGN-5

TITLE: The Battle of Tongue River
LEGEND: On this site during the early morning hours of August 29, 1865, General Patrick Edward Connor led over 200 troops in an attack on Chief Black Bear's Arapaho village. Connor had departed from Fort Laramie on July 30th with 184 wagons, a contingent of Pawnee scouts,

nearly 500 cavalrymen and the aging Jim Bridger as guide. His column was one of three comprising the Powder River Indian Expedition sent to secure the Bozeman and other emigrant trails leading to the Montana mining fields.

During the Battle of Tongue River, Connor was able to inflict serious damage on the Arapahos, but an aggressive counter attack forced him to retreat back to the newly established Fort Connor (later renamed Reno) on the banks of the Powder River. There he received word that he had been reassigned to his old command in the District of Utah.

The Powder River Expedition, one of the most comprehensive campaigns against the Plains Indians, never completely succeeded. Connor had planned a complex operation only to be defeated by bad weather, inhospitable terrain and hostile Indians. Long term effects of the Expedition proved detrimental to the interests of the Powder River tribes. The Army, with the establishment of Fort Connor (Reno), increased public awareness of this area which in turn caused more emigrants to use the Bozeman Trail. This led to public demand for government protection of travelers on their way to Montana gold fields.

LOCATION: Connor Battlefield State Historic Site, at the city park in Ranchester, Wyoming.

CONNOR BATTLEFIELD INFORMATIVE SIGN-6

TITLE: Connor Battlefield State Hist. Site
LEGEND: In 1865 General Patrick E. Connor led the "Powder River Expedition" into this area. This expedition was a part of a broad military program to bring the Indians north of the Platte River under control and halt their depredations along the Western Trails.

At this site Connor's command located and attacked a large party of Arapaho under Black Bear and Old David, destroying 250 lodges. Much of the fighting was hand-to-hand combat and many women and children were killed and captured.

Later events proved the campaign of 1865 to be undecisive.
LOCATION: Southeast corner of intersection of Dayton and Gillette Streets in Dayton, Wyoming.

See Battle of Tongue River Sign (Sheridan County #5) for more information.

CONNOR BATTLEFIELD MONUMENT-7

TITLE: Connor Battlefield State Park
LEGEND: Here Aug. 29, 1865, troops and Indian scouts commanded by Gen. P. E. Connor destroyed an Arapahoe Indian village.

Erected by the Historical Landmark Commission of Wyoming 1936
LOCATION: Connor Battlefield State Historic Site, at the city park in Ranchester, Wyoming. Located on a pyramid of granite rocks 12 feet high and 8 feet square at the base.

CROOK'S CAMPAIGN INFORMATIVE SIGN-8

TITLE: Crook's Campaign, 1876
LEGEND: On this site, the junction of the Big and Little Goose Creeks, General George Crook, with 15 troops of cavalry, 5 companies of infantry, 1325 men and 1900 head of transport animals, headquartered. Joined by Indian allies, the Crows under chiefs Old Crow, Medicine Crow and Plenty Coups and Shoshoni under Washakie, he battled 2500 Sioux 40 miles northeast, on the Rosebud, June 17. Defeated, Crook returned here, occupying these valleys, awaiting reinforcements which arrived in August. He then united General Alfred Terry's army, which included remnants of Custer's 7th Cavalry, to campaign in Montana. Buffalo Bill, Calamity Jane, Frank Grouard, noted western characters, were with this expedition.

SHERIDAN COUNTY

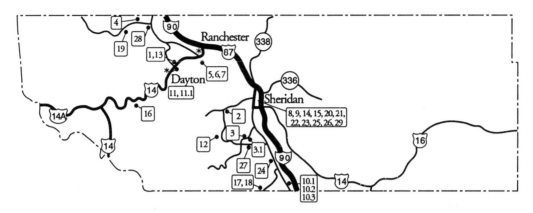

N

Legend

⛉ Interstate

⛊ US Highway

◯ State or Other
   Principal Road

•▭ Marker

1	Bozeman Trail Marker
2	Bozeman Trail Monument
3	Bozeman Trail Marker
3.1	Bozeman Trail Blacksmith Shop
4	Bozeman Trail Monument
5	Battle of Tongue River Sign
6	Connor Battlefield Informative Sign
7	Connor Battlefield Monument
8	Crook's Campaign Informative Sign
9	Crook's Monument
10.1	Fetterman Massacre Informative Sign
10.2	Fetterman Massacre Monument
10.3	Fetterman Interpretive Plaques
11	First Woman Mayor In Wyoming Sign
11.1	Susan Wissler
12	O. P. Hanna Cabin Marker
13	Sawyer Expedition Sign
14	Sheridan's First Cabin
15	Sheridan Inn National Historic Landmark
16	Sibley Monument
17	Wagon Box Fight Marker
18	Wagon Box Monument
19	Slack, Wyoming, Marker
20	Trail End State Historic Site
21	Kendrick Monument
22	Original Sheridan Streetcar
23	Sheridan Steam Locomotive
24	Terrill Marker
25	Coal Miners Memorial
26	Carneyville Marker
27	Bradford Brinton Memorial
28	Ohlman Post Office and Stage Station
29	Peacepipe Memorial

Erected 1964 by Wyoming State Archives and Historical Department and Wyoming State Historical Society.
LOCATION: Triangular park at the intersection of West Dow and Alger Streets in Sheridan, Wyoming.

The Fort Laramie Treaty of 1868 gave the Sioux and Cheyenne Indians control over a large territory that included parts of Montana, Wyoming, Nebraska, and the Dakotas. When the lure of Black Hills gold brought white men into the territory in 1874, the government decided to buy the Black Hills. In 1875, a commission was organized to settle the problem, and when it failed, the Bureau of Indian Affairs directed all Indians to live on reservations. From that point Indians battled white men to keep them out of the territory given them by the 1868 treaty.

The army was to find the Indians and force them to live on the reservations. After a dismal failure on his first expedition into the Powder River country to find Crazy Horse, Crook led a large force north into Montana. On June 17, 1876, Crook's forces were attacked by Sioux and Cheyenne Indians on Rosebud Creek. The day-long battle has been generally considered a draw. Crook returned to his base camp on the junction of the Big and Little Goose Creeks.

Eight days later, the defeat of General George Custer and the 7th Cavalry made it even more clear that the Indians were not going to give up their beloved lands easily.

CROOK'S MONUMENT-9

TITLE: None
LEGEND: Dedicated to the memory of General George Crook, his gallant soldiers and scouts who, in June, 1876, camped in the valley of the Goose Creeks on the present site of Sheridan, while waiting for their Crow and Shoshoni allies.

Sheridan Chapter Daughters of the American Revolution 1939
LOCATION: At Kendrick City Park in Sheridan, Wyoming.

See Crook's Campaign Informative Sign (Sheridan County #8) for more information.

FETTERMAN MASSACRE INFORMATIVE SIGN-10.1

TITLE: Fetterman Massacre
LEGEND: Along this ridge on December 21, 1866, Brevet Lt. Col. William J. Fetterman, 2 officers, 76 enlisted men and 2 civilians were decoyed into ambush and overwhelmed by a superior force of Sioux, Cheyenne and Arapahoe Indians. Fort Phil Kearny, 2 miles south, was built in the summer of 1866 to protect travelers along the Bozeman Trail. The Indians were bent on preventing such encroachment into their last hunting grounds which had been assigned them by the Fort Laramie Treaty of 1851. Sent out to relieve a wagon train that was under attack, Col. Fetterman was ordered not pursue the Indians beyond Lodge Trail Ridge. He disobeyed and led his command to this ridge, where they were engaged in a pitched battle. The final stand was made behind the large boulders at the monument. There were no survivors.

Erected 1965 by the Wyoming State Archives and Historical Department and the Wyoming State Historical Society.
LOCATION: Southwest side of old U.S. Hwy 87, about 17 miles north of Buffalo, Wyoming.

FETTERMAN MASSACRE MONUMENT-10.2

TITLE: None
LEGEND: On this field on the 21st day of December, 1866, three commissioned officers and seventy six privates of the 18th U.S. Infantry, and of the 2nd U.S. Cavalry, and four civilians, under the command of Captain Brevet-Lieutenant Colonel William J. Fetterman were killed by an overwhelming force of Sioux, under the command of Red Cloud. There were no survivors.

LOCATION: Northeast side of old U.S. Hwy 87, about 17 miles north of Buffalo, Wyoming.

Erected in July 1905, the Fetterman Massacre Monument was one of the first markers in Wyoming. Through the efforts of the Fort Phil Kearny Association, Elisha J. Terrill, and Congressman Frank W. Mondell, the federal government appropriated $5,000 for this 20-foot-high monument, constructed by E. C. Williams of Sheridan, Wyoming.

C. G. Coutant, a noted Wyoming historian, suggested in 1905 that the citizens of Sheridan arrange a celebration to dedicate this monument. It was finally dedicated July 4, 1908. General H. B. Carrington, commander of Fort Phil Kearny from 1866 to 1868, gave the main address. According to Grace Raymond Hebard in *Marking The Oregon Trail, The Bozeman Road and Historic Places in Wyoming 1908-1920,* others at the dedication were "Hon. F. W. Mondell, Mr. William Daly, Sr., who had helped to fashion the flag pole for the garrison in July 1866, and Sergeant S. S. Gibson and Mr. William Murphy, who were stationed at Fort Phil Kearny during the troublesome days in the Powder River country."

FETTERMAN INTERPRETIVE PLAQUES-10.3

Plaque #1
TITLE: Attack-Relief-Decoy-Pursuit
LEGEND: By December, 1866, Fort Phil Kearny was in the final phases of construction. Logs for the stockaded post were hauled by wood train from the pinery six miles west of the fort.

On December 21, a heavily escorted wood train left for the pinery. It came under Indian attack about three miles to the west. When pickets on Pilot Hill signaled the train was being attacked, Colonel Henry B. Carrington ordered out a relief party and reluctantly put Captain William J. Fetterman in command. It included two other officers, 76 enlisted men and two civilians. The soldiers in the party were from four companies of the 18th Infantry and one company of the 2nd Cavalry.

The Indians had broken off the attack by the time the relief party was under way but Fetterman pursued them to the crest of Lodge Trail Ridge—so far keeping within range of his orders.

Permaloy plaque #2
TITLE: The Fateful Decision
LEGEND: Fetterman relieved the wood train and chased its attackers to the limit prescribed in orders. His return was all that was necessary to complete a successful mission.

But he continued the chase. He did not return and his decision remains unexplained. The brash young Captain's decision to disobey orders and the resulting annihilation of his command has created a problem for generations of historians. Why did he continue pursuit? What "estimate of the situation" did he make? What thoughts influenced his decision? "None" appears to be a most charitable answer to the questions.

The mixed command of infantry and cavalry had no hope of catching the fleet Indian horseman. Fetterman knew he would be punished for disobeying orders unless he successfully engaged the warriors.

He gave little regard to the broken terrain, laced with pockets, ravines and ridges ideal for concealment. He paid little heed to the warnings given him about the possibility of ambush. He paid no heed to the fact that Indians did not fight according to the "rules of war" he learned in the Civil War. He descended the ridge and his command stretched out—a tantalizing target for the attack. With little thought of the consequences, he charged blindly on, leading his command to its final engagement.
Right sighting device: Shows Fetterman's route over Lodge Trail Ridge.
Left sighting device: Shows Bozeman Road crossing of the Ridge.

1.

2.

3.

4.

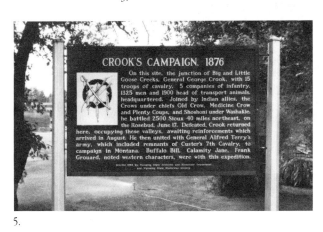

5.

6.

1. Some memorials, like the Sundial Marker in Sheridan County, were uniquely designed.

2. This granite marker erected by the Historical Landmark Commission of Wyoming was placed just below Sibley Lake in the northern Big Horn Mountains.

3. The Daughters of the American Revolution in 1920 erected a red granite marker to commemorate the Wagon Box Fight. Then, in 1936, the Sheridan Chamber of Commerce erected this large Wagon Box Monument adjacent to the first marker.

4. Many early signs degraded Native Americans. This recent sign was written with a more modern sensitivity.

5. Through the cooperation of the Wyoming State Archives and Historical Department and the Wyoming State Historical Society many beautiful informative signs, like this one in Sheridan, were constructed.

6. This early marker, erected in 1936 at the Connor Battlefield near Ranchester, demonstrated the audacity of those responsible for early marking efforts in Wyoming.

Permaloy plaque #3
TITLE: Farthest Pursuit
 Trap Sprung
 Retreat-Defeat-Death
LEGEND: Pickets on Pilot Hill had signaled the fort when the wood train was attacked. They watched Fetterman's command advance to the relief and pursue the attacking Indians who retreated over the crest of Lodge Trail Ridge. They saw Fetterman's men pause on the summit—the boundary that was supposed to be the limit of pursuit. But they only paused, then vanished over the Ridge.

Indian accounts of the subsequent engagement were long in coming and proved fragmentary. The best reconstruction of events was made by relief and recovery parties who found the bodies of their comrades on the field of battle.

Fetterman, chasing decoys beyond the Ridge, met an overwhelming force of Indians. He turned about only to meet others who laid in ambush while he hotly pressed his pursuit.

Retreat along the Bozeman Road was impossible and within an hour, the fate of Fetterman's entire command was sealed.
Sighting device: Shows Fetterman's route of advance and retreat.

Permaloy plaque #4
TITLE: Recovery of the Dead
LEGEND: Two separate parties went forth from Fort Phil Kearny to recover the dead.

The first party was sent while there was still hope that some of Fetterman's men might be alive. Captain Tenodor Ten Eyck and 76 men reached an observation point on Lodge Trail Ridge before the Indians left the battleground. Though seen and challenged by the exuberant victors, he refused to commit his command against such overwhelming odds. When the Indians withdrew, he ventured down the slope and recovered 49 bodies found in one group where the fight climaxed.

Next morning Colonel Carrington led a second party which found the remaining 32 bodies scattered along more than a mile of the Bozeman Road. Most of the bodies had been stripped, scalped and mutilated. The corpses of Captains Fetterman and Brown had powder burns at their temples suggesting suicide. Three pools of blood—within ten feet of the body of Lieutenant George Grummond—evidence of Indian casualties—gave moot testimony to the frenzied fighting. James S. Wheatley and Isaac Fisher, two civilian volunteers, had wanted to test their new Henry repeating rifles. The hundred or more expended cartridges near their mutilated bodies showed how dearly they sold their lives.

The recovery parties found more than 60 separate pools of blood, suggesting removed Indian casualties. Indian spokesmen later acknowledged the loss of thirteen warriors.

LOCATION: Not yet erected.

In the past there had been discussion about placing an interpretive display near the Fetterman Massacre Monument. The project was never completed, but the interpretive plaques were found in storage at the Markers and Monuments maintenance shop at Guernsey State Park. Because of their complete depiction of the historical event, they were included in this book.

FIRST WOMAN MAYOR IN WYOMING SIGN-11

TITLE: First Woman Mayor in Wyoming.
LEGEND: Mrs. Susan Wissler, on May 9, 1911, was elected mayor of Dayton, Wyoming, then a community of about 175 people. She served two terms of two years each. Her administration was marked by civic improvement and community betterment as her campaign promise to curb gambling and regulate the operation of saloons was, in a measure, fulfilled.

The Fetterman Massacre Monument erected in 1905 was one of the very earliest monuments in Wyoming.

Mrs. Wissler was truly a pioneer. She taught in the public schools of this area for several years and actively encouraged her students to go on for further study. As a practical nurse she is remembered for her ministrations in time of trouble. She also owned and operated a millinery and drygoods store for a number of years. Dayton became her home in 1890. She died in 1938.

Erected 1965 by the Wyoming State Archives and Historical Department and the Wyoming State Historical Society.
LOCATION: In Dayton, Wyoming, on the southeast corner of Bridge Street and West 3rd Avenue.

SUSAN WISSLER-11.1

TITLE: Susan Wissler
 1853-1938
LEGEND: Mrs. Susan Wissler owned and operated a millinery shop at this location while serving as mayor of Dayton from 1911 to 1913. Mrs. Wissler was the first woman mayor in Wyoming and the first woman to serve consecutive terms as mayor in the United States. Mrs. Wissler was an excellent teacher and a successful business woman. It is appropriate that she was elected in the first state to grant equal suffrage to woman.
LOCATION: 406 Main Street, Dayton, Wyoming.

O. P. HANNA CABIN MARKER-12

Rock and mortar bench
TITLE: None
LEGEND: Site of first cabin in Northern Wyoming
 O. P. Hanna 1878.

Sundial
TITLE: None
LEGEND: Site of first cabin in what is now Sheridan County.
 Built by O. P. Hanna   August 11, 1878.

LOCATION: About 7 miles southwest of Big Horn, Wyoming. Private property; inquire locally.

SAWYER EXPEDITION SIGN-13

TITLE: Sawyer Expedition fight.
LEGEND: Where the Bozeman Trail crosses Tongue River Valley at this point, Colonel J. A. Sawyer's wagon train and road building expedition of 82 wagons fought the Arapahoe Indians for 13 day, August 31 through September 12, 1865. Captain Cole of the military escort was killed on the ridge across the valley, E. G. Merrill and James Dilleland, drovers, were killed in the wagon circle located between here and the

river. All three are buried in an unknown common grave. From 1879 to 1894 the Patrick Brothers Stage Line used this road from Fort Custer to Rock Creek Station. Bingham Post Office and Stage Station was located here at Tongue River Crossing.

Wyoming Recreation Comm.

LOCATION: On the north side of U.S. Hwy 14, about 2 miles east of the bridge over the Tongue River at Dayton, Wyoming. Adjacent to Bozeman Trail Marker (Sheridan County #1).

Colonel J. A. Sawyer was in charge of improving the Bozeman Trail to the gold fields of southwestern Montana. The Arapahoe Indian attack lasted until a relief party arrived from General P. E. Connor. With Connor's assistance, the road crew completed the improvements to Virginia City, Montana.

SHERIDAN'S FIRST CABIN-14

TITLE: None
LEGEND: Site of the first cabin built in Sheridan 1878-1914
Erected by the D.A.R.
LOCATION: Northwest corner of Smith and Brooks Streets in Sheridan, Wyoming.

In 1914 the Sheridan County Chapter of the Daughters of the American Revolution placed a large granite monument at this site.

The cabin, originally erected by Mr. Mandell in 1878 and known as the Mandell Post Office, was purchased by John Loucks, the founder of Sheridan, in 1882. The cabin was moved five times by various owners. In 1976, the Wyoming chapter of the Colonial Dames of America restored the old log building behind the Trail End Historical Center as part of a Bicentennial project.

SHERIDAN INN NATIONAL HISTORIC LANDMARK-15

TITLE: Sheridan Inn
LEGEND: Sheridan Inn has been designated a Registered National Historic Landmark under the provisions of the Historic Sites Act of August 21, 1935. This site possesses excellent value in commemorating and illustrating the history of the United States.
U.S. Department of the Interior
National Park Service
1964
LOCATION: 856 Broadway Avenue, Sheridan, Wyoming.

The Sheridan Inn was the first building of any size and importance in this part of northern Wyoming. It was built as part of a development program by the Burlington and Missouri Railroad and the Sheridan Land Co. at a cost of $25,000. George Holdrege, general manager for the railroad, conceived the idea and gave to Thomas R. Kimball, an architect from Omaha, Nebraska, the task of designing the structure. Kimball's model was a Scottish inn that he had visited and liked.

The grand opening was July 1, 1893. Many called it the finest hotel between Chicago and San Francisco. In 1894, while under the management of the W. F. Cody Hotel Co., Buffalo Bill frequented the Inn. Other notable visitors were Captain John J. Pershing, Charles M. Russell, William Jennings Bryan, William Howard Taft, and, perhaps, Calamity Jane.

It ceased to operate as a hotel in 1965. Condemned in 1967, it was saved when Mrs. Netje Kings purchased the Inn and set about restoring it. It was designated as a National Historic Landmark in January, 1964.

SIBLEY MONUMENT-16

TITLE: None
LEGEND: Through this vicinity, a scouting party of the 2nd Cavalry, led by Lt. Frederick W. Sibley was attacked by Sioux and Cheyenne Indians on July 7, 1876. In the fight Chief White Antelope was killed. The party abandoned its horses, took to the rugged terrain, and scouts Frank Gruard and Baptiste Poirier guided the 26 soldiers and *Chicago Times* reporter John F. Finerty over the mountains without food, back to their main camp.

Sibley Lake was named by the Sheridan Chapter, D.A.R.
Erected by the Historical Landmark Commission of Wyoming 1954
LOCATION: South side of U.S. Hwy 14 at the Sibley Lake Recreation Area, about 26 miles west of Ranchester, Wyoming.

The Sibley incident attained notoriety partly because of Finerty's writings of the event in *Warpath and Bivouac*, written in 1890. The incident is re-told in the history book of Sheridan County, *Sheridan County Heritage*.

WAGON BOX FIGHT MARKER-17

TITLE: Site of Wagon Box Fight
LEGEND: August 2, 1867
Marked by the State of Wyoming
LOCATION: About 50 feet to the northeast of the Wagon Box Monument (Sheridan County #18). About 5 miles from Fort Phil Kearny.

The Oregon Trail Commission placed this red granite marker in September 1920. The site was located August 2, 1919, by Sergeant S. S. Gibson, who took part in the fight. See Wagon Box Monument (Sheridan County #18) for more historical information.

WAGON BOX MONUMENT-18

TITLE: Wagon Box Fight August 2, 1867.
LEGEND: This monument is erected to perpetuate the memory of one of the famous battles of history. It is dedicated to the courage and bravery of twenty-eight soldiers in Company C. 27th United States Infantry, and four civilians, who held their improvised fort made of fourteen ordinary wagon-boxes, against 3000 Sioux warriors, under the leadership of Red Cloud for a period of six or seven hours under continuous fire. The number of Indians killed has been variously estimated from three hundred to eleven hundred.

The following participated in this engagement:

Capt. Jas. Powell		1st Lt. John C. Jenness*
1st Sgt. John M. Hoover		Corp. Max Littman
1st. Sgt. John H. McQuiery		Corp. Francis Robertson

PRIVATES

Wm. A. Baker	John Condon	Mark Haller
Ashton P. Barton	Thomas Doyle*	Phillip C. Jones
Wm. Black Nolan	V. Deming	Freeland Phillips
Chas. Brooks	John Grady	John L. Somers
Alexander Brown	John M. Garrett	Chas. A. Stevens
Dennis Brown	Henry Gross	Julius Strache
John Buzzard	Samuel Gibson	4 Unknown Civilians
Frederick Claus	Henry Haggerty*	*Killed

Erected April, 1936 by the U. S. Civil Conservation Corps. Under the direction of the Sheridan Chamber of Commerce.
LOCATION: Near Story, Wyoming, and Fort Phil Kearny. Directional signs are easy to follow from either place.

Following the Fetterman fight in December 1866, the U.S. Army was cautious of Indian skirmishes and had lost confidence in protecting the Bozeman Trail. The Indians felt the overwhelming success and were confident of controlling the Bozeman Trail country.

Colonel Jonathan Eugene Smith became the Mountain District's new commander and arrived at Fort Phil Kearny in July 1867. He brought with him a new Model 1866 Springfield rifle, caliber .50-70-450, a much more accurate rifle that could fire up to twenty rounds per minute compared to the three rounds per minute from the older .58 Springfield rifle musket.

Under the command of Captain James Powell, the army had noted increasing Indian signs and formed an oval barricade of wooden wagon boxes at their camp. With a good supply of ammunition for their new breech-loading .50-70 Springfield rifles, the army was on alert for Indian raids.

The Sioux Indians decided to try the decoy and ambush trick that had worked so well at the Fetterman fight. At about 9:00 a.m. on

August 2, 1867, a large band of Indians attacked the army camp. The force of thirty-two soldiers and civilians stayed in their fortification and held them off. Early in the afternoon a relief party from Fort Phil Kearny under Major Benjamin F. Smith drove the Indians to the hills north of the site.

Three white men were killed and two were wounded. Captain James Powell estimated that at as many as sixty of the at least 800 Indians engaged in the fight might have been killed. The estimates of Indians killed have varied from a low of six to sixty up to a high of 300 or even 1500.

The army's morale was greatly boosted by the victory, and confidence in protecting the Bozeman Trail country was restored.

SLACK, WYOMING, MARKER-19

TITLE: Slack, Wyoming
LEGEND: Site of Slack, Wyoming
  Town, Church, Post Office 1890-1911
  Erected by Pass Creek Community July 23, 1978
LOCATION: West of Parkman at the Nicholson Ranch. About 6 miles west of State Route 345 on Sheridan County Road 144 (Pass Creek Road)

Slack, Wyoming, was the hub of a community of Pass Creek homesteaders from the 1880s until about 1911. *Sheridan County Heritage* has further details and information about the town. The drive to Slack passes through some of the nicest scenery in Sheridan County. Bozeman Trail Monument (Sheridan County #4) was erected about one mile west of State Route 345 on the Pass Creek Road.

TRAIL END STATE HISTORIC SITE-20

TITLE: Trail End
LEGEND: The National Register of Historic Places-Wyoming Place No.33
LOCATION: 400 Clarendon Avenue, Sheridan, Wyoming.

Trail End State Historic Site was the home of John B. Kendrick, former Governor and U.S. Senator born in Cherokee County, Texas, on September 6, 1857. Orphaned at an early age, Kendrick was raised by relatives until he went on his own at fifteen. He hired out as a ranch hand to Charles Wulfjen, a Texan who had been ranching in Wyoming for years. In 1879, young Kendrick trailed a herd of cattle from Texas to Wyoming. Fascinated by the new territory, Kendrick continued to work for Wulfjen as foreman of his ranch in eastern Wyoming.

In 1891, Kendrick married Eula Wulfjen, the boss's daughter, and they settled near Sheridan. His "OW" ranch, purchased in 1897, developed into a 200,000-acre spread, and Kendrick became an expert on livestock, cattle diseases, water supply, and marketing.

Kendrick had selected the mansion site years earlier, after being impressed with the beautiful vistas from the hill above Big Goose Creek. The site became his "trail end." Construction began in 1908, and was completed five years later at a cost of $165,000, including furnishings.

When completed, Trail End included eighteen rooms and eight full bathrooms, along with eight porches and balconies, an elevator, telephone, central vacuum cleaning system, and the latest in electrical wiring. Bedrooms and bathrooms occupy most of the second floor. On the third floor is a formal ballroom, complete with musician's loft.

Samples of nearly every tree indigenous to Wyoming were planted on the grounds, including cedar trees brought in from the "OW" ranch.

The Sheridan County Historical Society acquired Trail End from the Kendrick heirs in 1968. It was officially transferred to the State of Wyoming on July 23, 1982. It is operated and maintained as an historic house museum by the State Parks and Historic Sites section of the Wyoming Department of Commerce.

KENDRICK MONUMENT-21

TITLE: John B. Kendrick
LEGEND: 1857-Pioneer-Cattleman-Statesman-Friend-1933
  Erected by his friends
LOCATION: At Kendrick Park in Sheridan, Wyoming.

John B. Kendrick and his wife donated land along Big Goose Creek for a park, originally designated Pioneer Park. They planned "that one day the people of all this part of the state would make Pioneer Park a place in which they could forgather amidst surroundings conducive to the peace and contentment of both mind and spirit." After his death in 1933, the Kendrick Memorial Fund was established under the leadership of R. H. Walsh. Plans were made in 1936 to build a monument in his honor.

In June 1936, this white granite column was dedicated and the park he had donated was renamed Kendrick Park in his honor. Governor Leslie A. Miller delivered the dedicatory address, and John B. Kendrick II, grandson of Kendrick, unveiled the memorial. Eulogies were given by many friends, but the dedication was best portrayed by Governor Miller:

> In the history of nations, few indeed are the men who occupy in the affections of a people the place which was Senator Kendrick's. He carved for himself a niche in the hall of Wyoming's fame which will endure throughout all future generations. We knew him as a neighbor, we loved him as a friend, and Wyoming honored him as a statesman.

See Trail End Historic Center (Sheridan County #20) for more information about John B. Kendrick.

ORIGINAL SHERIDAN STREETCAR-22

TITLE: Original Sheridan Streetcar
LEGEND: 1910 to 1926
  Sheridan County Bicentennial Committee
  J. Ralph Hylton-Chairman

  Streetcar Committee
  Jerry Buckley-Chairman
  Joe Dricar-Conductor
  Louis Poulos
  Nov. 3, 1976
LOCATION: Corner of North Main and Dow Streets in Sheridan, Wyoming.

Interest in an electric streetcar to provide transportation both within Sheridan and out to the nearby coal mining towns developed in the early 1900s. In 1910, Albert Emanuel and William R. Sullivan of Dayton, Ohio Electric Street Railway proposed to build such a system. The first car left the railway barn August 11, 1911. When the coal mines ceased operations the electric railway business diminished. The Sheridan Railway Company suspended operations on April 20, 1926, when the last trip to the mines was made.

Louis Poulos raised the question of restoring one of the old streetcars. The Sheridan County Bicentennial Committee, many individuals, and many businesses restored the car and dedicated it November 3, 1976.

SHERIDAN STEAM LOCOMOTIVE-23

Plaque
TITLE: None
LEGEND: This monument to the development of the west is established by the City of Sheridan and citizens of the Sheridan Community 1962
  N. A. Nelson, Sr., Mayor
  Dr. O. R. Docekal, Chairman
  Contributors (a list of 84 contributors follows)
Sign
TITLE: None
LEGEND: Presented by Chicago, Burlington & Quincy Railroad Co. June 10, 1962.
  Class 0-5-A-Mohawk 4-84-Type, Highspeed combination passenger or freight built in 1940 by C.B. & Q. R.R.Co. shop
  Length of locomotive and tender 106 ft., 5 inches.
  Light weight of locomotive and tender-290 tons
  Starting tractive effort 87,500 lbs.
  Stoker coal type

LOCATION: In Sheridan, Wyoming, just east and across the street from the Sheridan Inn.

The coming of the railroad brought people and prosperity to Sheridan. The Burlington and Missouri Railroad's first passenger train arrived at the Sheridan depot at 10:00 a.m. on November 18, 1892. The last passenger train came to Sheridan on August 24, 1969.

TERRILL MARKER-24
TITLE: E. S. Terrill
LEGEND: Pioneer
  1810-1897
LOCATION: Just north of Banner, Wyoming.

Elisha J. Terrill came west to the Montana gold country in the late 1860s, settling down to ranch near Banner, Wyoming, in 1879. In 1893, Terrill and his neighbors formed the first Fort Phil Kearny Association, dedicated to putting monuments at Fort Phil Kearny and at the Fetterman Battlefield. Terrill worked with Congressman Frank Mondell in erecting the Fetterman Monument dedicated at the Fetterman Battlefield on July 4, 1908.

COAL MINERS MEMORIAL-25
TITLE: Coal Miners Memorial—1973
LEGEND: This statue of an underground coal miner depicts a typical underground coal miner who helped create part or the history of development in Sheridan County. Underground coal mining played an important role in the development of Sheridan County from the late 1800's to 1950. Since 1950 strip mining has taken the place of underground mining.

In 1970 former underground coal miners and relatives of former miners started a memorial in memory of all underground coal miners from which this statue developed.

Even though strip mining has replaced the underground coal miner in this area, the memory still remains.
LOCATION: In the Visitor's Center at the Fifth Street exit on the east side of Sheridan, Wyoming.

Underground coal mining in Sheridan County flourished from 1891 to 1951. Foreign immigrants came to live with the English-speaking ranchers that had preceded them, and names like Piekarczk, Sieczkowski, Lupiezowietz, and Podczerwienski filled the many small coal towns north of Sheridan. Stanley A. Kuzara wrote an excellent book, *Black Diamonds of Sheridan, A Facet of Wyoming History,* that gave a good historical account of early coal mining in Sheridan County.

This monument was dedicated June 24, 1973, at the Chamber of Commerce's Visitor's Information Center in Sheridan. Stanley Kuzara gave a brief history of mining and the men who died in the mines. The memorial statue was made by John Kuchera who was born in 1917 in the coal mining town of Carneyville, Wyoming. Kuchera, now from Sheridan, worked in the coal mines for seventeen years; his father had mined for thirty years. Mike Patz, the oldest miner present at the dedication, worked in the underground mines for forty-nine years and was recognized with the honor of unveiling Kuchera's statue.

CARNEYVILLE MARKER-26
TITLE: Carneyville (Kleenburn)
  1904-1924
LEGEND: This mine was located 9 miles North of Sheridan. Traveling North along Interstate 90, as you approach the 2nd exit after leaving Sheridan, you will turn right. You will notice a great deal of subsidence in the hillside. This is where the Carneyville mining shafts were. This mine employed 450 miners and had two tipple loadouts. In the valley to the right of the shafts lay the mining community of Carneyville (Kleenburn). This community had 150 to 200 houses and approximately 2000 people residing there.

This display coordinated by Tom Smith.
LOCATION: In the Visitor's Center at the Fifth Street exit on the east side of Sheridan, Wyoming.

See Coal Miners Memorial (Sheridan County #25) for more information.

BRADFORD BRINTON MEMORIAL-27
TITLE: Quarter Circle A Ranch
LEGEND: The National Register of Historic Places—Wyoming Place #96
LOCATION: Bradford Brinton Memorial Museum and Ranch at Big Horn, Wyoming.

William Moncreiffe came to Wyoming in 1885 from Scotland. He built the two-story ranch house in 1892. William and his brother, Malcolm, operated the Moncreiffe Ranch until 1923 when it was purchased by Bradford Brinton from Illinois.

When Brinton died in 1936, his sister, Helen Brinton, became owner until her death in 1960. In 1961 the Bradford Brinton Memorial Ranch was opened to public viewing and was administered by the Northern Trust Company of Chicago as trustee as stated in Helen Brinton's will.

OHLMAN POST OFFICE AND STAGE STATION-28
TITLE: Ohlman Post Office and Stage Station
LEGEND: Site of Ohlman Post Office and Stage Station
  1882-1896
  Erected by Parkman Community 1980
LOCATION: On the Sheeley Ranch near Parkman, Wyoming.

PEACEPIPE MEMORIAL-29
TITLE: None
LEGEND: The warfare and enmity which has existed for generations between the Cheyenne and Absaroka nations was solemnly terminated here June 20, 1932 when the chiefs of both nations smoked the pipe of peace together and took each other's hands in friendship. May this friendship endure forever.

Erected by the Sheridan Wyo. Rodeo Inc. in commemoration of this historical event.
LOCATION: Sheridan County fairgrounds at the base of the flagpole.

SUBLETTE COUNTY

ASTORIAN INCIDENT SIGN-1

TITLE: Astorian Incident

LEGEND: Historical Sublette County

On this site, Oct. 18, 1811, sixty one Astorians of the American Fur Company, the squaw of Pierre Dorian and her two children, with one hundred and eighteen horses camped for 5 days. They were on their way to the Pacific Ocean from Montreal via St. Louis. Here they met, traded and powwowed with the Snake Indians, killed buffalo and cured meat. Continuing their journey, they crossed the divide one mile north of here on to the waters of the Columbia River. These were the first white men in what is now Sublette County.

Sublette County Historical Board

LOCATION: North side of U.S. Hwy 189/191, about 35 miles south of Hoback Junction. About 1 mile east of Hoback Rim Station.

Seven other markers relate the history of the Astorian treks across Wyoming. See Astorian Overland Expedition Informative Sign (Campbell County #1), South Pass Interpretive Site and Union Pass Interpretive Plaques-Plaque #3 (Fremont County #28.1 & 35.1), Stuart Campsite Sign (Goshen County #16), Astorians Monument (Lincoln County #1), and First White Man's Cabin Informative Sign and Bessemer Bend Interpretive Site-Plaque #4 (Natrona County #3 & 33) for more information.

BUCKSKIN CROSSING SIGN-2

TITLE: Buckskin Crossing—a landmark.

LEGEND: This part of the Big Sandy River has been known as the Buckskin Crossing since the 1860's. Legend is that a trapper and hunter named Buckskin Joe lived here with his wife and daughter. The daughter died here. This marker is near his cabin site. This crossing was used by the fur companies and trappers, Captain Bonneville, Captain Wm. D. Stewart, and later by John C. Fremont. Captain Stewart's artist—the noted Alfred Jacob Miller—made the first painting of this area in 1837. This ford of the Lander Cutoff of the Oregon Trail, campsite and burial ground was heavily used by the emmigrants, their hundreds of wagons and thousands of mules, cattle and horses. This was the mail route from the east to the west side of the Wind River Mountains in the early 1900's. Big Sandy Creek was named by William Ashley on his trapping expedition in 1825. Of the thousands of people who passed this way only the wagon tracks and graves remain.

Sublette County Historical Society
United States Department of the Interior
Bureau of Land Management

This trail has been marked at all accessible points with brass caps.

LOCATION: East side of Sublette County Road 1804 where the road crosses Big Sandy Creek. About 26.4 miles from U.S. Hwy 191.

CATTLE AND MEN INFORMATIVE SIGN-3

TITLE: Historic Sublette County
Of cattle and men.

LEGEND: Thousands of people, cattle and horses passed this way to the Northwest when the Sublette Cut-off of the Oregon Trail was opened in 1857. None settled in this county. At the close of the Indian Wars in 1877, cattle herds from Oregon came this way to meet the railroad and to stock Wyoming ranges. The first Sublette County herds were started with other western cattle. In 1878-79 Ed Swan's PL, Otto Leifer's O Circle, D.B. Bud's 6 quarter circle, Hugh McKay's 67 and A. W. Smith's Muleshoe outfits settled on nearby Piney Creek. Their cattle were not Longhorns. The county's first barbed wire was unrolled in 1881 on the Circle outfit.

Sublette County Historical Board.

LOCATION: West side of U.S. Hwy 189, about 3 miles north of Big Piney, Wyoming. Alongside Lander Cutoff and Pioneer Monument (Sublette County #10).

The Lander Cutoff of the Oregon Trail, opened to emigrant travel in 1859, actually passes this point. The Sublette Cutoff was south of this point, and crossed the Green River at Names Hill south of LaBarge, Wyoming, in Lincoln County. The Sublette Cutoff was first used in 1832 by William Sublette, and emigrant travel began in 1844.

DESMET MONUMENT-4.1

Metal Plaque

TITLE: None

LEGEND: Commemorating hundredth anniversary of the first mass by Father P. J. DeSmet July 5, 1840.
Dedicated by the Most Reverend P. A. McGovern D. D. July 4, 1940.

Granite Cross

TITLE: None

LEGEND: Holy Mass was offered here for the first time in Wyoming by Father DeSmet July 5, 1840.

LOCATION: About 3 miles east of U.S. 189, near the cemetery at Daniel, Wyoming.

The site of the first Roman Catholic mass in what was to become Wyoming was on a bluff overlooking the Green River where the fur trappers' rendezvous was taking place.

A chapel fourteen feet by fourteen feet, shaped like a half moon, was built of native rock; a granite cross five to six feet high was set within the chapel.

The monument's dedication was reportedly attended by five to six thousand people. Twenty priests from Wyoming parishes assisted Bishop P. A. McGovern.

FIRST DUDE RANCH SIGN-4.2

TITLE: Gros Ventre Lodge

LEGEND: This Lodge, one of the earliest dude ranches in Wyoming, was built on the hill beyond in 1897 by William (Billy) Wells and operated until 1906. It was named for the little Gros Ventre (now Tosi Creek) and was known locally as "Dog Ranch" because of the foxhounds Wells kept for hunting. While Wells guided guests on summer trips through the Green River Valley and Bridger National Forest, the Gros Ventre was most notable as a hunting lodge that served prominent American and British big game sportsmen. The ranch included a central lodge, guest cabins and one of the first wooden bathtubs in western Wyoming.

By 1906 the Gros Ventre was no longer profitable, in part due to the stricter game laws and a shorter hunting season. It was dismantled that year and the main lodge moved across the Green River and converted into a ranch house.

LOCATION: On the east side of the Cora Road (State Route 352), about 27 miles north of its junction with U.S. Hwy 191.

FORT BONNEVILLE INFORMATIVE SIGN-5.1

TITLE: Fort Bonneville
Sisk-ke-dee Agie (Green River) Oregon 1832.

LEGEND: Here, in July, 1832, Captain Benjamin Bonneville erected a fort, two block houses and stockade, for protection from the Blackfoot Indians. He was on leave from the U.S. Army, with his trapping and exploring group of 110 men and 20 wagons. These were the first wagons to cross Southpass. The party scattered and trapped for several years, doing valuable exploring as far as California and the Columbia. In the party were the famed Joe Walker, Joe Meeks and many Delaware Indians. The Fort, a strategic site, was not used in winter. Bonneville and most of his party returned to Missouri August 22, 1835.

SUBLETTE COUNTY

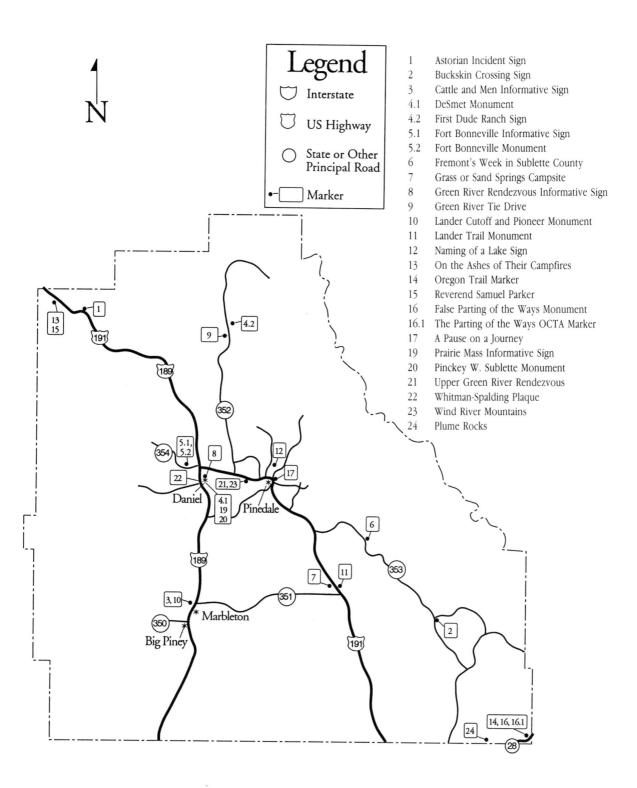

Legend

- ⬡ Interstate
- ⬔ US Highway
- ◯ State or Other Principal Road
- •⬚ Marker

1   Astorian Incident Sign
2   Buckskin Crossing Sign
3   Cattle and Men Informative Sign
4.1   DeSmet Monument
4.2   First Dude Ranch Sign
5.1   Fort Bonneville Informative Sign
5.2   Fort Bonneville Monument
6   Fremont's Week in Sublette County
7   Grass or Sand Springs Campsite
8   Green River Rendezvous Informative Sign
9   Green River Tie Drive
10   Lander Cutoff and Pioneer Monument
11   Lander Trail Monument
12   Naming of a Lake Sign
13   On the Ashes of Their Campfires
14   Oregon Trail Marker
15   Reverend Samuel Parker
16   False Parting of the Ways Monument
16.1   The Parting of the Ways OCTA Marker
17   A Pause on a Journey
19   Prairie Mass Informative Sign
20   Pinckey W. Sublette Monument
21   Upper Green River Rendezvous
22   Whitman-Spalding Plaque
23   Wind River Mountains
24   Plume Rocks

LOCATION: North side of State Route 354, about 3.1 miles west of Daniel Junction (junction of U.S. Hwys 189 and 191).

FORT BONNEVILLE MONUMENT-5.2

TITLE: None
LEGEND: Site of Fort Bonneville
       1832.
       1915.
LOCATION: North side of State Route 354, about 3.1 miles west of Daniel Junction (junction of U.S. Ilwys 189 and 191).

The Oregon Trail Commission inscribed and commemorated this marker on August 9, 1915. Captain H. G. Nickerson and Grace Hebard, president and secretary of the Commission respectively, gave addresses at the ceremonies.

From the writings of Grace Hebard in *Marking The Oregon Trail, The Bozeman Road, and Historic Places in Wyoming 1908-1920*, came the following words:

Bonneville journeyed across the Green River to Horse Creek, where he built, in the heart of the Indian country, a fur post... Although much time and labor were expended on the construction of the post, an early snow made Bonneville move to the West out of the present boundaries of Wyoming, establishing a new fort on the Snake (Idaho). The building of Fort Bonneville, called Fort Nonsense and Bonneville's Folly, in 1832, gives Bonneville the distinction of erecting the first fur fort within the boundaries of Wyoming.

On August 9, 1915, eighty-three years to a day after the fort was built, President H. G. Nickerson and Secretary Grace R. Hebard of the Oregon Trail Commission visited the old site of Bonneville's folly...On hands and knees in the sun, dust and gravel, with mallets and chisels, the members of the commission carved the letters on the stone, which was finally rolled into place with the aid of an automobile, log chains and crowbars.

As the audience sang 'America' it seemed strange to hear the words that stir to national patriotism, out in a locality where before had only been heard the nightly songs of the coyote, the war cry of the Indians and the occasional 'whoop' of the cowboy since the day when the trader and trapper trailed over that part of the country.

FREMONT'S WEEK IN SUBLETTE COUNTY-6

TITLE: Lieutenant J. C. Fremont's week in Sublette County.
LEGEND: On June 10, 1842, J. C. Fremont left St. Louis to explore the Wind River Mountains, with Kit Carson as guide, Charles Preuss, topographer, L. Maxwell, hunter, and 20 Canadian voyageurs, including Basil LaJeunesse. Eight two-wheeled mule-drawn carts were used as far as the Platte River. The party crossed South Pass August 8 and camped here at "Two Buttes" August 9. Leaving 10 men at Boulder Lake, the lieutenant ascended Fremont Peak August 15, stayed here again August 17, and on the 19th re-crossed South Pass. So ended Fremont's exploration of the Wind River Mountains and his stay in Sublette County.
LOCATION: East of Boulder, Wyoming, on State Route 353; about 6.8 miles east of U.S. Hwy 191.

GRASS OR SAND SPRINGS CAMPSITE-7

TITLE: Grass or Sand Springs—and Oregon Trail Campsite.
LEGEND: Here crosses the Lander Cutoff—the northern fork of the Oregon Trail following a route of the fur traders. It was suggested as an emmigrant road by mountain man, John Hockaday in order to avoid the alkali plains of the desert, shorten the trip to the Pacific by five days, and provide more water, grass and wood. In 1857 it was improved as a wagon road by the government under the supervision of F. W. Lander and termed the Fort Kearny, South Pass, Honey Lake Rd. As many as three hundred wagons and thousands of cattle, horses, and mules passed here each day. An expanding nation moved with hope and high courage. The trail—cut deep into the dirt of the plains

and the mountains—remains as a reminder of a great epoch.
Sublette County Historical Society, United States Department of the Interior Bureau of Land Management.
This trail has been marked at all accessible points with brass caps.
LOCATION: On the west side of U.S. Hwy 191, about 38 miles north of Farson, Wyoming. Across the highway from Lander Trail Monument (Sublette County #11).

GREEN RIVER RENDEZVOUS INFORMATIVE SIGN-8

TITLE: 1824   Green River Rendezvous   1840.
LEGEND: A market place of fur trade, from the Mississippi to the Pacific, from Canada to Mexico, where trappers, traders and indians came to barter for the the first great resource of the west. Six rendezvous were held here, gathering not only furs but information of geographic importance to weld the final link in exploration of the new world. It is a tribute to the brave men, both red and white, who blazed the trails for culture and progress, and the lowly beaver who gave it impetus.
Commemorated—each year, the second Sunday in July.
Sublette County Historical Society, Inc.
LOCATION: East side of U.S. Hwy 189 just north of Daniel, Wyoming.

GREEN RIVER TIE DRIVE-9

TITLE: First tie drive on Green River.
LEGEND: Because timber was scarce in neighboring states along the first transcontinental railroad line, the tie business flourished here and in other Wyoming mountain locations. Ties were cut in winter, stored on the river bank until spring, and floated downstream during high water.

Charles DeLoney was a youthful Michigan Civil War veteran who came to Wyoming after the war. An experienced timberman, he contracted with the Union Pacific Railroad in 1867 to supply ties. A crew of 30 men hauled equipment and supplies upriver and constructed a combined office-bunkhouse-cookshack-commissary building between this marker and the river. Cabins were built high in the timber, forcing the men to snowshoe for meals. DeLoney's was the first drive down the river, a trip of 130 miles. Ties were skidded down nearby mountains and held by a boom across the river until the drive. Another boom at Green River City caught the ties near the railhead. The operation continued successfully for two years, and newspaper advertisements as late as fall, 1868 solicited tie hacks to work at the head of the Green River.

Charles DeLoney was a versatile person. He was a rancher, a pioneer merchant in Jackson and helped found the town of Evanston. He was the states first forest supervisor and served in Wyoming territorial and state legislatures.
State of Wyoming
LOCATION: West side of State Route 352 about 20 miles north of Cora, Wyoming. Located just past where the pavement ends.

LANDER CUTOFF AND PIONEER MONUMENT-10

TITLE: None
LEGEND: To all pioneers who passed this way to win and hold the West.
Route of Lander cut-off, first government financed road in Wyoming. Officially called Ft. Kearney, South Pass and Honey Lake Road. Built in 1858 from Rocky Ridge to Ft. Hall to provide shorter route for emigrants.
Erected by Wyoming Historical Landmark Commission 1947
LOCATION: At the junction of U.S. Hwy 189 and State Route 351 just north of Big Piney, Wyoming. Alongside Cattle and Men Informative Sign (Sublette County #3).

1.

2.

3.

1. The Sublette County Historical Society erected markers that were unique. The markers, like this one at Buckskin Crossing on the Lander Cutoff of the Oregon Trail, were not so much different in design, but were massive and supported by huge posts and beams.

2. Constructed in August 1962, A Pause on a Journey Sign was one of several other markers across Wyoming depicting the eastward and westward expeditions of the Astorians.

3. The Wyoming Historical Landmark Commission erected the Pinckey W. Sublette Monument at Daniel Cemetery in 1936.

LANDER TRAIL MONUMENT-11

TITLE: None

LEGEND: To all pioneers who passed this way to win and hold the West.

Route of Lander cut-off, first government financed road in Wyoming. Officially called Ft. Kearney, South Pass and Honey Lake Road built in 1858 from Rocky Ridge to Ft. Hall to provide shorter route for emigrants.

Erected by Wyoming Historical Landmark Commission 1947

LOCATION: On the east side of U.S. Hwy 191 about 38 miles north of Farson, Wyoming. Across the highway from Grass or Sand Springs Campsite (Sublette County #7).

Emigrants called this trail the Lander Trail or the Lander Cutoff. It was a shorter route from South Pass to Fort Hall (in Idaho) than the original Oregon Trail, which trailed south to Fort Bridger then onto Fort Hall. The trail was surveyed in 1857, built in 1858, and records indicate that over 13,000 emigrants traveled it in 1859, its first year of use.

Frederick West Lander, a pioneer engineer for the U.S. Department of Interior, was responsible for the survey and construction parties that established the road.

Other monuments marking the Lander Trail include Fremont County #20, Lincoln County #9 and 18.2, and Sublette County #2, 7, 10, and 11.

NAMING OF A LAKE SIGN-12

TITLE: Green River—Oregon
1833-1844
Historic Sublette County
The Naming of the Lake

LEGEND: On the edge of this magnificent sheet of water, from 1833 to 1844, Capt. William Drummond Stewart of Scotland camped many times with Jim Bridger, other Mountain Men, and Indians. In 1837, his artist, Alfred Jacob Miller, painted the first pictures of this area. On Stewart's last trip in August 1844, eight men in a rubber boat, first boat on the lake, honored their leader by christening these waters as Stewart's Lake, in a joyous ceremony near the Narrows, with six jugs of whiskey. Years later, this glacier-formed lake with its shoreline of twenty-two miles and over six hundred foot depth was named after Gen. John C. Fremont—the map makers knew not that it had been named long before.

Sublette County Historical Board.

LOCATION: South end of Fremont Lake, about 3 miles north of U.S. Hwy 191 at Pinedale, Wyoming.

ON THE ASHES OF THEIR CAMPFIRES-13

TITLE: On the ashes of their campfires
LEGEND: This nearby canyon was a way through the mountains. Its game and Indian trails were followed by the white men. On September 26, 1811, the Astor party, with William Price Hunt, 61 people and 118 horses entered the canyon here, making their way westward to the Pacific Ocean.

The three legendary trappers, Hoback, Reznor, and Robinson, guided the party. These were the first white men to pass this way. From this time on, the stream and canyon became known as the Hoback.

On October 10, 1812, Robert Stuart of the Astor Firm and his 6 companions camped here on their way to St. Louis from Fort Astoria with the message of the failure of Fort Astoria.

On Sunday, August 23, 1835, Jim Bridger's and Kit Carson's brigade of trappers and Indians, and the Reverend Samuel Parker bound northward from the rendezvous on the Green River camped in this area. This basin was known then as Jackson's Little Hole. The Reverend Parker was delivering a sermon to the motley group when buffalo appeared. The congregation left for the hunt without staying for the benediction. This was the first protestant service held in the Rocky Mountains.

Sublette County Historical Society
U.S.F.S. Teton National Forest.
LOCATION: South side of U.S. Hwy 189/191, about 15.5 miles south of Hoback Junction. Adjacent to Reverend Samuel Parker plaque (Sublette County #15).

OREGON TRAIL MARKER-14

TITLE: The Oregon Trail
LEGEND: In memory of those who passed this way to win and hold the West.

Plaque placed by the Historical Landmark Commission of Wyoming 1950
LOCATION: On State Route 28, about 22 miles east of Farson, Wyoming. Adjacent to False Parting of the Ways Monument (Sublette County #16).

REVEREND SAMUEL PARKER-15

TITLE: In tribute to Reverend Samuel Parker.
LEGEND: Who delivered the first Protestant sermon to trappers, hunters, and Indians on Sunday, August 23, 1835, at this point.

Dedicated by the Historical Landmark Commission August 23, 1935
LOCATION: South side of U.S. Hwy 189/191, about 15.5 miles south of Hoback Junction. Adjacent to On the Ashes of their Campfires (Sublette County #13).

FALSE PARTING OF THE WAYS MONUMENT-16

TITLE: "Parting of the Ways"
LEGEND: This marks a fork in the trail, right to Oregon, left to Utah and California.

1812, Robert Stuart and eastbound Astorians used South Pass gateway.
1824, Eleven westbound Ashley-Henry men led by Jedediah Smith and Thomas Fitzpatrick.
1832, N. Wyeth and Capt. B. L. E. Bonneville parties.
1836, Missionaries M. Whitman and H. H. Spalding and Wives.
1841, Bartleson-Bidwell party.
1852, Peak year, estimated 40,000 emigrants.
Erected by The Historical Landmark Commission of Wyoming 1956
LOCATION: On State Route 28, about 22 miles east of Farson,
Wyoming. Adjacent to Oregon Trail Marker (Sublette County #14).

The actual site of the Parting of the Ways is marked by a post and BLM information panel about 9.5 miles southwest from here. See The Parting of the Ways (Sublette County #16.1).

THE PARTING OF THE WAYS OCTA MARKER-16.1

TITLE: The Parting of the Ways
LEGEND: In July 1844 the California bound Stevens-Townsend-Murphy wagon train, guided by Isaac Hitchcock and 81-year old Caleb Greenwood, passed this point and continued nine and one half miles west southwest from here, to a place destined to become prominent in Oregon Trail history—the starting point of the Sublette Cut-off.

There, instead of following the regular Oregon Trail route southwest to Fort Bridger, then northwest to reach the Bear river below present day Cokeville, Wyoming, this wagon train pioneered a new route. Either Hitchcock or Greenwood, it is uncertain which, made the decision to lead the wagons due west, in effect along one side of a triangle.

The route was hazardous, entailing crossing some 50 miles of semi-arid desert in the heat of summer and surmounting mountain ridges, but it saved approximately 85 miles from the Fort Bridger route and 5 or 6 days travel. The route was first known as the Greenwood Cut-off.

It was the Gold Rush year of 1849 that brought this "Parting of the Ways" into prominence. Of the estimated 30,000 Forty-niners probably 20,000 travelled the Greenwood Cut-off which, due to an error in the 1849 Joseph E. Ware guide book, became known as the Sublette Cut-off.

In the ensuing years further refinements of the Trail route were made. In 1852 the Kinney and Slate Creek Cut-offs diverted trains from portions of the Sublette Cut-off, but until the covered wagon period ended, the Sublette Cut-off remained a popular direct route, and this "Parting of the Ways" was the place for crucial decisions.

A quartzite post inscribed—Fort Bridger S. Cut-off—and a Bureau of Land Management information panel now mark the historic "Parting of the Ways" Site.

Research and signing by the:
Oregon-California Trails Association
1988
This is a part of your American heritage. Honor it, protect it, preserve it for your children.
LOCATION: North side of State Route 28, about 22 miles east of Farson, Wyoming. Adjacent to Oregon Trail Marker and False Parting of the Ways Monument (Sublette County #14 & 16).

A PAUSE ON A JOURNEY-17

TITLE: Historical Sublette County
A Pause on a Journey.
LEGEND: On Oct. 16, 1812, the Astorians: Robert Stuart, Ramsey Crooks, Robert McClellan, Joseph Miller, Benjamin Jones, Francis LeClair and Andy Vallee, traveling from Astoria to St. Louis, all their horses having been stolen by Indians, passed this way on foot and forded Pine Creek near here, the first white men known to have seen it.

From Stuart's Journal: "We forded another stream whose banks were adorned with many pines—near which we found an Indian encampment—deserted about a month ago, with immense numbers of buffalo bones strewed everywhere—in center of camp a great lodge of pines and willows—at west end—three persons lay interred with feet to east—at head of each a large buffalo skull painted black—from lodge were suspended numerous ornaments and moccasins."

Six days later, on Oct. 22, 1812, they made the memorable discovery of the South Pass.

Sublette County Historical Board
LOCATION: North side of U.S. Hwy 191 in Pinedale, Wyoming.

PRAIRIE MASS INFORMATIVE SIGN-19

TITLE: The Prairie of the Mass
LEGEND: Rev. Pierre De Smet (1802-73) was born in Belgium but came to America in 1821, joined the Jesuit Society and began his work with the Indians. In his work he established sixteen treaties, crossed the ocean nineteen times and traveled 180 thousand miles on his errands of charity for the Indians who knew him as the "The Sincerest Friend."

On July 5, 1840, in the presence of two thousand Indians, trappers and traders, he offered the first Holy Mass in what is now Wyoming on an altar of native stone decorated with wild flowers. In Father De Smet's own words, "It was a spectical truly moving to the heart of a missionary that this immense family, composed of so many different tribes should prostrate themselves in equal humility before the 'Divine Host.'" The monument at the site was erected in 1925 and a commemorative mass is offered there annually in July. On July 4, 1940, the one hundredth anniversary of the first Mass, a Pontifical High Mass was offered by the Most Rev. Bishop McGovern assisted by more than thirty priests and attended by about two thousand people.

Wyoming State Council of the Knights of Columbus and the Wyoming State Highway Department.
LOCATION: East side of U.S. Hwy 189, about 1.8 miles south of Daniel, Wyoming.

See also DeSmet Monument (Sublette County #4.1).

PINCKEY W. SUBLETTE MONUMENT-20

TITLE: Pinckey W. Sublette
Died 1865
LEGEND: Buried on Fontenelle Creek. Exhumed 1897, taken to the U.S. Circuit Court in St. Louis, Mo., returned by a court order to Sublette County, Wyoming to be buried here July 27, 1935.

Placed July 4, 1936 by the Historical Landmark commission of Wyoming
LOCATION: About 3 miles east of U.S. Hwy 189 near the cemetery at Daniel, Wyoming.

UPPER GREEN RIVER RENDEZVOUS-21

Wooden Sign:
TITLE: Rendezvous—birth of an empire
LEGEND: The river below is the Green. The mountains to the west are the Wyomings (Bear Rivers). Those to the east, the Windrivers. Along the river banks below are the Rendezvous sites of 1833, 1835 (New Fork), 1836, 1837 (Cottonwood), 1839, 1840 and Fort Bonneville. Trappers, traders and Indians from throughout the west here met the trade wagons from the east to barter, trade for furs, gamble, drink, frolic, pray and scheme. The Indians, Delaware and Iroquois brought in by the Hudson Bay Company, Snakes, Bannocks, Gros Ventre, Flatheads, Nez Perce, Crows and Chinooks here made their first contact with the white man. The warring Blackfeet did not participate. The Rocky Mountain Fur Company, Hudson Bay Company, Captain Bonneville, Wyeth and free trappers controlled the trade. The people of God, Marcus and Marcissa Whitman, Mr. and Mrs. Spalding, Samuel Parker, Father Desmet, Jason Lee, and W.H. Gray tempered the hilarity. Jim Bridger, Milton and Bill Sublette, Tom Fitzpatrick, Joe Walker, Joe Meeks, Kit Carson, Baptiste Gervais, Bob Jackson, Moses (Black) Harris, Lucien Fontenelle, Etinne Provot, Henry Fraeb, Andy Dripps, Robert Campbell, Henry Vandenbury, Sir W. D. Stewart and the artist A.J.

Miller all were part of this and left their names imbedded in the annals of the west. Scattering for the value of a beaver plew and to see what was beyond the horizon, their trails became the highways of an empire at the cost of many a violent death.

U.S. National Parks Service and Sublette County Museum Board and Historical Society.
Metal Plaque:
TITLE: Upper Green River Rendezvous
LEGEND: Has been designated a Registered National Historic Landmark
Under the prosvisions of the Historic Sites Act of August 21, 1935 this site possesses exceptional value in commemorating and illustrating the history of the United States.
United States Department of the Interior, National Park Service 1963.

LOCATION: At Trappers Point National Historic Landmark just south of U.S. Hwy 191, about 6 miles west of Pinedale, Wyoming.

WHITMAN-SPALDING PLAQUE- 22

TITLE: To Narcissa Prentiss Whitman and Eliza Hart Spalding, Missionaries.
LEGEND: First white women in Wyoming and first women over Oregon Trail 1836
July 6 to July 18 was spent at "Green River Rendezvous." These pilgrim women took an active part in religious services held here.
Placed here by Wyoming Federation of Woman's Clubs, The Historical Landmark Commission of Wyoming and Sublette County Historica Association.
LOCATION: On the east side of U.S. Hwy 189 at the north end of Daniel, Wyoming.

WIND RIVER MOUNTAINS-23

TITLE: Wind River Mountains
Bridger National Forest
LEGEND: You are looking into the Wind River Mountain Range. So named by Indians and translated into English. These mountains are still in the ice age. The seven largest glaciers in the Rocky Mountains are here. Numerous smaller glaciers also remain.

This side of the mountains comprises the Bridger Wilderness. These 383,000 acres can be traversed only by foot or by horseback. The renewable resources of these national forest lands are managed in the combination that best meets the needs of the American people. The Wind River Mountain country provides some of the best fishing in the United States. There is also good hunting for elk, deer, moose, bighorn sheep and bear.

Six major lakes just outside of the wilderness are being developed by the Forest Service to provide picnic and camp sites. Tourist accommodations are available in the Pinedale area. Additional information on this area may be obtained from the Chamber of Commerce or the Forest Ranger in Pinedale.
LOCATION: At Trappers Point National Historic Landmark just south of U.S. Hwy 191, about 6 miles west of Pinedale, Wyoming.

PLUME ROCKS-24

TITLE: Plume Rocks
LEGEND: In the days before man-made landmarks dominated the landscape, natural features such as Plume Rocks served as travelers signposts. J. Goldsborough Bruff noted in his journal on August 3, 1849, "...on right about 300 yards distant, some low clay bluffs, of a dark dingy red hue, and singularily plume-formed projections on top, from the effects of the elements."

While topographical features like Oregon Buttes served as

navigational points on the horizon, minor features such as Plume Rocks served to keep emigrant travelers more precisely on course. They were especially critical in situations where it was not possible to sight between two navigational points on the horizon both ahead of and behind the travelers.

LOCATION: Adjacent to the Oregon-Mormon Trail, about 2.5 miles west of False Parting of the Ways Monument (Sublette County #16).

This sign was placed by the Bureau of Land Management of Wyoming in its efforts to mark and interpret the Oregon Mormon Trail.

SWEETWATER COUNTY

POINT OF ROCKS MONUMENT-1

TITLE: None
LEGEND: Ruins of Almond Overland Stage Station, 1862-8. Located beyond railroad tracks, 1640 feet to southward of this marker.

Erected by Wyoming Historical Landmark Commission 1947
LOCATION: North side of I-80 at Point of Rocks, on the north side of service road.

This relay station on the Overland Stage Line was also the beginning of the stage line to South Pass City and the Sweetwater mining area. Even though the Union Pacific Railroad replaced the stage for overland travel east to west, the station continued to be busy until 1877 when the mining activity declined near South Pass City.

BRYAN INFORMATIVE SIGN-2

TITLE: Bryan
LEGEND: One mile north of this spot stood the boom town of Bryan. Founded in 1868 as a division point of the Union Pacific Railroad, it grew rapidly and had, at one time, as many as five thousand inhabitants. A twelve-stall roundhouse and huge freight warehouses were constructed and from the latter canvas-topped wagons piled high with goods of all types, departed daily for the South Pass gold mines, eighty miles northeast. The water supply soon proved inadequate and when the South Pass gold mining bubble had burst, the railroad moved its division headquarters to Green River and Bryan became a ghost town.
LOCATION: On the north side of I-80, about 3 miles west of its junction with State Route 372. Access to this marker is from the west-bound lane only.

CONTINENTAL DIVIDE INFORMATIVE SIGN-3

TITLE: Continental Divide
"The Backbone of the Nation"
Elevation 7,178 feet above sea level
LEGEND: The three principal river systems of the U.S. west of the Ohio have their source in Wyoming. The Mississippi thru the Missouri and its branches, the Madison, Gallatin and Yellowstone; the Columbia flowing into the North Pacific, by its longest branch, the Snake; the Colorado by its longest branch, the Green.

Precipitation falling west of this point finds it way into the Green and Colorado and eventually to the Gulf of California, and that falling east of this point finds its way to the Gulf of Mexico by way of the Mississippi drainage basin.
LOCATION: South side of I-80 at the Continental Divide exit northwest of Creston Junction. Just east of Continental Divide Monument (Sweetwater County #4).

CONTINENTAL DIVIDE MONUMENT-4

TITLE: None
LEGEND: "That there should be a Lincoln Highway across the country is the important thing"

In memory of Henry B. Joy, the first president of the Lincoln Highway Association who saw realized the dream of a continuous improved highway from the Atlantic to the Pacific. 1938
LOCATION: South side of I-80 at the Continental Divide exit northwest of Creston Junction. Just west of Continental Divide Informative Sign (Sweetwater County #3).

Engraved between the two paragraphs on this fine granite monument are a statesman and scenes of agricultural, industrial, and historical expansion. A steel picket fence surrounds the monument, with four Lincoln Highway posts about five and one-half feet high at its corners. They originally carried a three-inch circular brass plaque of the Lincoln Head and the wording, "This highway dedicated to Abraham Lincoln." The plaques have disappeared, and have been replaced by concrete inlays of Lincoln.

The idea of a highway across the United States began with Carl Fisher, who established the Lincoln Highway Association. Henry B. Joy was installed as the head of the association, and became a leader in establishing the transcontinental highway.

FIRST COAL MINE MONUMENT-4.1

TITLE: None
LEGEND: Beneath this monument coal was first mined in this district. Site of Union Pacific No. 1 mine. A. D. 1868. Erected September 17, 1938.
LOCATION: About 50 yards southwest of the Union Pacific depot at Rock Springs, Wyoming.

The discovery of coal at the Wyoming towns of Rock Springs, Almy, and Carbon led to the development of the Union Pacific Railroad in southern Wyoming. However, the Union Pacific and the coal industry had periods of instability. Workers went on strike in 1871 against the Wyoming Coal and Mining Company, which did most of the early mining. In the fall of 1875, miners walked out in protest of cut wages, only to be fired and replaced by Chinese. Finding the Chinese easier to deal with, the Union Pacific thereafter brought in more of them until they outnumbered whites in the Wyoming mines. Racial prejudice soon worsened, and on September 2, 1885, twenty-eight Chinese were killed and fifteen others wounded in what we now know as the Rock Springs Massacre.

OLD SOUTH BEND STAGE STATION MONUMENT-5

East face:
TITLE: None
LEGEND: The Old South Bend Stage Station built 1850.

Gift of E. J. Brandly and family to the State of Wyoming in memory of Mrs. E. J. Brandly.

On the Oregon Trail and Pony Express.
South face:
TITLE: None
LEGEND: Pony Express
North face:
TITLE: None
LEGEND: Oregon Trail Memorial Association

LOCATION: About 0.1 miles northwest of the bridge over Black's Fork River in Granger, Wyoming.

Oregon Trail travel began in 1841, and one of its river crossings was over the Ham's Fork just before it joined the Black's Fork. The crossing became a place of rest for livestock and emigrants. Ham's Fork stage station was established at this site around 1856, which also served as a stop on the Pony Express route in 1860 and 1861.

In 1862 the Overland Trail began to see more travel and joined the Oregon Trail at Ham's Fork. However, Ham's Fork lost its identity and became known as South Bend Station. In 1868 when the Union Pacific Railroad came, the town of Granger began.

The deed for the land on which the stage station sat was given to the Historical Landmark Commission of Wyoming on August 21, 1930. The marker was part of the Oregon Trail Memorial Association effort to mark the trail. Association member Mr. William H. Jackson, noted artist of scenes along the Oregon Trail and himself a Trail pioneer, made the marker possible. He had spent nearly three weeks in the area around South Bend Station in the 1860s and had very fond memories of his stay.

SWEETWATER COUNTY

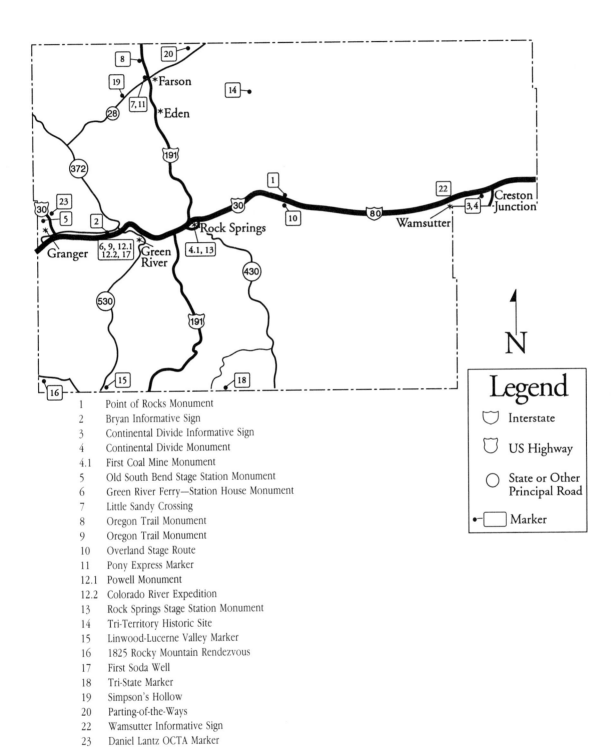

1	Point of Rocks Monument
2	Bryan Informative Sign
3	Continental Divide Informative Sign
4	Continental Divide Monument
4.1	First Coal Mine Monument
5	Old South Bend Stage Station Monument
6	Green River Ferry—Station House Monument
7	Little Sandy Crossing
8	Oregon Trail Monument
9	Oregon Trail Monument
10	Overland Stage Route
11	Pony Express Marker
12.1	Powell Monument
12.2	Colorado River Expedition
13	Rock Springs Stage Station Monument
14	Tri-Territory Historic Site
15	Linwood-Lucerne Valley Marker
16	1825 Rocky Mountain Rendezvous
17	First Soda Well
18	Tri-State Marker
19	Simpson's Hollow
20	Parting-of-the-Ways
22	Wamsutter Informative Sign
23	Daniel Lantz OCTA Marker

1.

1. One of the more magnificent markers was dedicated in July 1939 by the Wyoming Historical Landmark Commission. In spite of vandalism to the marker and the surrounding fence, the Henry B. Joy Monument has remained a symbol of the Lincoln Highway, old U.S. Hwy 30.

2. The Old South Bend Stage Station sign was erected in the era of the Covered-Wagon Centennial. William H. Jackson, noted artist of the Oregon Trail, gave to the State of Wyoming the large Oregon Trail Memorial Association plaque placed on the side of the marker.

3. This large granite monument was erected on Expedition Island, the departure point for John Wesley Powell's Colorado River Expedition.

2.

3.

GREEN RIVER FERRY—STATION HOUSE MONUMENT-6

TITLE: None
LEGEND: The Overland Stage Station route operated 1861-1868.
Green River Division station site 350 yards east.
Erected by the Historical Landmark Commission of Wyoming 1952
LOCATION: In Green River, Wyoming, on the east side of Uinta Drive at the northeast corner of its intersection with Riverview Drive.

The Green River Ferry was the only means of crossing the Green River when it was in full flow. Other crossings and ferries operated upstream, but the Green River Ferry was the only one on the Overland Trail.

LITTLE SANDY CROSSING-7

TITLE: Official Marker Utah Pioneer Trails and Landmarks Association
Little Sandy Crossing
No. 26
Erected June 24, 1933
LEGEND: On Monday evening, June 28, 1847, Brigham Young and Mormon pioneers met James Bridger and party near this place. Both companies encamped here over night and conferred at length regarding the route and the possibility of establishing and sustaining a large population in the valley of the Great Salt Lake. Bridger tried to discourage the undertaking. In this conference he is reported to have

said that he would give one thousand dollars for the first bushel of corn grown in the Salt Lake Valley.
Utah Pioneer Trails & Landmarks Association & Members of Lyman Stake
LOCATION: West side of U.S. Hwy 191, about 50 yards north of its intersection with State Route 28 at Farson, Wyoming. Adjacent to Pony Express Marker (Sweetwater County #11).

The Little Sandy Crossing provided good water for Oregon Trail travelers. However, in August 1860 the creek was dry, noted Sir Richard Burton, who was traveling on the Oregon Trail in this area. "We found nothing but sand, caked clay, sage, thistles and the scattered fragments of campfires, with large ravens picking at the bleaching skeletons."

OREGON TRAIL MONUMENT-8

TITLE: None
LEGEND: To all pioneers who passed this way to win and hold the West. Route of Sublette cut-off from Big Sandy to Bear River traversed after 1843 by emigrants to Oregon and California.
Erected by Wyoming Historical Landmark Commission 1947
LOCATION: West side of U.S. Hwy 191, about 9 miles north of Farson, Wyoming.

See also False Parting of the Ways Monument and The Parting of the Ways (Sublette County #16 & 16.1).

OREGON TRAIL MONUMENT-9

TITLE: None
LEGEND: To all pioneers who passed this way to win and hold the West. Trail crossed 30 miles north this point.
   Erected by people of Green River 1931
LOCATION: In Green River, Wyoming, on the southeast corner of the Sweetwater County Courthouse yard.

   This marker resulted from the efforts of the Oregon Trail Memorial Association, the Historical Landmark Commission of Wyoming, and the people of Green River, Wyoming. It was dedicated August 5, 1931, nearly a year after the national celebration of the Covered-Wagon Centennial.

OVERLAND STAGE ROUTE-10

TITLE: Overland Stage Route
LEGEND: At the beginning of the Civil War military strength in the West declined and often it was impossible to safeguard stages carrying the United States mail along the Oregon/California/Mormon Trail. Early in 1862 "Stagecoach King" Ben Holladay acquired the transcontinental stage business and the United States mail subsidy contract. He named his new company the Overland Stage Line and soon abandoned the central trail.

   Holladay determined that a route further south was better because it would be safer, shorter and closer to Denver where economic growth was taking place due to the 1859 gold rush. The new route, established by trapper and explorers, became known as the Overland Trail.

   The Overland split off from the older Oregon Trail near North Platte, Nebraska. From that point, coaches paralleled the South Platte, rolling west through Colorado before turning north to begin a steep and rocky climb into southern Wyoming where the trail flanked the Medicine Bow Range before turning westward again. After crossing plains, rivers and streams and winding through mountain passes, the trail entered the Green River Basin. Traffic passed through this valley, following Bitter Creek to its confluence with the Green River. It then branched north to join the Oregon Trail near the junction of the Blacks Fork and Hams Fork Rivers. From there the trail continued west and south toward Salt Lake City and eventually Placerville, California.

   The short, but exciting period of Overland Trail transportation lasted for seven years until 1869 when the Union Pacific Railroad replaced the transcontinental Overland stage as the major, east-west transportation system. Nevertheless, the emigrants and settlers continued to use the trail until after the turn of the century.
LOCATION: South side of I-80, at the Point of Rocks interchange.

   A large map atop this sign indicates the path of the Overland Trail from Independence, Missouri through Boise, Idaho, and Salt Lake City, Utah.
   On the north side of Point of Rocks interchange is Point of Rocks Monument (Sweetwater County #1).

PONY EXPRESS MARKER-11

TITLE: None
LEGEND: To the brave men who rode the Pony Express 1860-1861. The site of Big Sandy Station. Gift of Andrew Arnott to the State of Wyoming.
LOCATION: West side of U.S. Hwy 191, about 40 yards north of its intersection with State Route 28 at Farson, Wyoming. Adjacent to Little Sandy Crossing (Sweetwater County #7).

   The Oregon Trail passed several historic sites in this area. The Dry Sandy Crossing was the site of the Dry Sandy Stage and Pony Express Station. Plume Rocks to the east of the Dry Sandy Crossing was a minor trail landmark in this area. The Little Sandy Crossing further west was a common emigrant campsite. Brigham Young and Mormon pioneers met with Jim Bridger at this site on June 28, 1847. The next river crossing was the Big

Sandy Crossing, site of the Big Sandy Stage and Pony Express Station. The Oregon Trail then followed the Big Sandy River on to the Green River.

POWELL MONUMENT-12.1

TITLE: Major Wesley Powell and party
LEGEND: Marking the spot from which Major Wesley Powell and party departed May 24, 1869, to make the first exploration of Green and Colorado Rivers, arriving mouth of Grand Canyon Aug. 29, 1869.
   Plaque placed by Historical Landmark Commission of Wyoming 1949
LOCATION: In Green River, Wyoming, in the center of Green River Island Park (also known as Expedition Island).

COLORADO RIVER EXPEDITION-12.2

East face
TITLE: Powell-Colorado River Expedition
LEGEND: On May 24, 1869, the Powell-Colorado River Expedition, ten men and four boats strong, embarked from these environs on a voyage of adventure resulting in civilization's first definite knowledge of this continent's last unexplored major river drainage. Out of the still shaded but no longer unknown depths of that river's Grand Canyon came, 98 days later, six tattered river veterans to triumphantly beach two water-torn and rock-mauled hulks.

   This adventure, no odyssey if measured by elapsed time alone, easily qualifies by the other standards of suspense, danger and action. Its successful completion captured and held the admiration of a nation.

   John Wesley Powell himself—cast in the hero's role and endowed with rare executive and scientific talents—rode the crest of national acclaim into public service and the highest councils of the republic. Over the years his ever-sharpening executive ability resulted in the creation and productiveness of important federal agencies, while his scientific genius contributed to the advancement of such divergent disciplines as ethnology, geology and agronomy. Perhaps his greatest gift to the nation, conceived during Colorado River explorations, was the theory of arid-land culture. As developed, through his success in fathering the Bureau of Reclamation, this theory has changed the face of western landscapes and caused extensive geographic regions to blossom and thrive.
West face
TITLE: Powell Colorado River Expedition 1869
LEGEND: None

Bronze plaque
TITLE: Expedition Island
LEGEND: Has been designated a Registered National Historic Landmark
   Under the provisions of the Historic Sites Act of August 21, 1935 this site possesses exceptional value in commemorating or illustrating the history of the United States.
   U.S. Department of the Interior, National Park Service
   1969

LOCATION: In Green River, Wyoming, at the west end of Green River Island Park (also known as Expedition Island).

   On the west face of the monument is an engraved map of Wyoming, Colorado, Utah, and Arizona, showing the routes of the Grand Canyon expedition.
   Also located in the center of this very nice park is Powell Monument (Sweetwater County #12.1).

ROCK SPRINGS STAGE STATION MONUMENT-13

TITLE: Rock Springs Stage Station Site
      Also the Springs
LEGEND: Erected to the memory of those brave pioneers who passed

this way to win and hold the west.

LOCATION: In Rock Springs, Wyoming, on the east side of Springs Drive, about 0.5 miles north of its intersection with Elk Road.

This monument was dedicated November 11, 1934. The site was given to the Historical Landmark Commission by the Union Pacific Coal Company.

TRI-TERRITORY HISTORIC SITE-14

Bronze plaque

TITLE: Tri-Territory Historic Site

LEGEND: Marking the common boundary of the Louisiana Purchase (1803) the Northwest Territory (1846) and Mexico (1848). The site is located where the Continental Divide crosses the 42 parallel North Latitude.

Dedicated September 24, 1967 by the Kiwanis Clubs of Lander, Rawlins, Riverton, and Rock Springs, Wyoming.

Permaloy plaque

TITLE: Tri-Territory Historic Site

LEGEND: This site, where the Continental Divide crosses the 42° parallel, North Latitude, was first claimed by Spain through the presumptive right of early discoveries and explorations. The area was also a part of Acadia, granted in 1603 by Henry IV of France, and part of New England as granted to the Plymouth Colony by James I, transferred to the Massachusetts Bay Colony in 1629. In 1682, LaSalle claimed for France the whole basin of the Mississippi River (thus including the northeastern portion of this site).

France ceded its claim to Spain in 1762 but regained them in 1800 and sold the region of "Louisiana" to the United States in 1803.

Great Britain claimed the western portion of the site in 1792 and the United States laid formal claims in 1818 until the 42° parallel was accepted as the boundary between United States and Spain in 1819. Mexico, after gaining independence from Spain in 1821, reconfirmed the boundary lines. In 1824, Great Britain relinquished her claim to the area of the Columbia River basin, reaffirming this action by the Treaty of 1846 establishing the right of the United States to the "Oregon Country." On July 4, 1848, the cession of territory by Mexico was proclaimed giving to the United States the undisputed right to all of Wyoming.

The monument on this site was constructed by the Kiwanis Clubs of Lander, Rawlins, Riverton and Rock Springs, Wyoming, in cooperation with the Bureau of Land Management of the U.S. Department of the Interior. The site was dedicated on September 24, 1967. Elevation is 7,775 feet above sea level.

LOCATION: This marker is a long distance from anywhere and should be visited only in good weather. From Farson, Wyoming, travel 12.5 miles northeast on State Route 28; then turn to the east onto a dirt road with Bureau of Land Management markers directing the remaining 31 miles to the monument.

It can also be reached by a similarly well-marked dirt road north of the Jim Bridger Power Plant.

This marker requires patience and time to find. A half-day trip should be planned, and the road should be traveled in good weather. The marker, scenery, and wildlife make this site truly enjoyable.

LINWOOD-LUCERNE VALLEY MARKER-15

Center plaque

TITLE: Linwood Bay

SUBTITLE #1: Linwood—The Town that Drowned

LEGEND: From this point you can see Linwood Bay of the Flaming Gorge Reservoir. Beneath the surface of the reservoir at the far western end, lies the site of the town of Linwood. When Flaming Gorge Dam was built in the early 1960's, the rising waters of the reservoir covered the small town. It was laid out in 1900 by George Solomon who carefully planted many rows of cottonwood trees, giving the town its name "Linwood."

This area is a reminder of the colorful and exciting days of Indians, trappers, explorers, settlers, cowboys and outlaws. Although Linwood itself has vanished, the memory of one of the last towns of the "Old West" lingers on.

SUBTITLE #2: The Green River

LEGEND: In front of the vista point is the original bed of the mighty Green River, the major source of water for Flaming Gorge Reservoir.

SUBTITLE #3: The 41st Parallel

LEGEND: The Utah-Wyoming border, located on the 41st parallel, ran directly through the middle of Linwood making it an interesting community since it was in two different states.

SUBTITLE #4: Henry's Fork

LEGEND: Named for Maj. Andrew Henry, the fork was an early camping and gathering place for trappers, traders and explorers. Gen. William H. Ashley originated the "rendezvous" system for fur trade here. Early in July, 1825, 120 trappers and mountain men arrived at the first rendezvous site, approximately 15 miles up Henry's Fork, to trade furs and supplies.

SUBTITLE #5: Uncle Jack Robinson's Cabin

LEGEND: The first permanent settler in the area was John Robinson, known as "Uncle Jack Robinson," who built a cabin on Lower Henry's Fork in 1834-35. The cabin was moved to a location near Flaming Gorge Recreation Area.

SUBTITLE #6: Other Points

LEGEND: Also located in the area was Jim Baker's Trading Post, established in 1839. Soon after, the famous explorer, Jim Bridger, built a fort at Bridger Bottom. The famous Colorado River expedition led by John Wesley Powell camped below this point in 1869.

SUBTITLE #7: Two Canals

LEGEND: The Lucerne Valley Land and Water Company Canal and the People's Canal were completed near the turn of the century. The canals brought irrigation to the settlers in the dry valleys.

SUBTITLE #8: Bob Swift's Bucket O' Blood Saloon

LEGEND: Located a few hundred yards from Uncle Jack's cabin, the "wild and wooly" saloon was frequented by such outlaws as Butch Cassidy and the Sundance Kid, the McCarty boys, and the Curry gang.

SUBTITLE #9: The Linwood School or "Stateline School"

LEGEND: The school, which was constructed in the fall of 1904, has the distinction of being the only school in the country to be run by two different state school boards—the north half of the school was in Wyoming and the south half was in Utah. The school is now used as a grainary one mile north of its original location.

SUBTITLE #10: Octagonal Dancehall

LEGEND: The dance hall was a beautiful and magnificent structure and had the first real hardwood floor in the region.

East plaque

TITLE: Nearby Points of Interest

SUBTITLE #1: The Uinta Mountains

LEGEND: The only major mountain range in the Western Hemisphere to run east and west, the Uinta Mountains form the southern boundary of this area.

SUBTITLE #2: Flaming Gorge

LEGEND: Named by John Wesley Powell in 1869, Flaming Gorge is probably the most interesting and dramatic geological feature in the area. It is located in front of you to the left at the end of the range of mountains.

SUBTITLE #3: Different Geological Formations

LEGEND: It's interesting to note the different geological formations of the area. The rocks generally lie flat and are light colored and soft. In

Utah, the rocks are more colorful and have been bent and forced upward by tremendous earth pressure.

Dedication and Memorial Plaque
TITLE: None
LEGEND: Erected by U.S. Forest Service, Daggett County Historical Society, Natural History Association, and Daggett County Lions Club.

In memory of Tim and Bertha Potter, Keith Smith, Paul Williams, and George and Minnie Rasmussen.

LOCATION: On a turnoff from State Route 530, about 42 miles south of Green River, Wyoming.

1825 ROCKY MOUNTAIN RENDEZVOUS-16

TITLE: 1825 Rocky Mountain Rendezvous
LEGEND: "When all had come in, he (Ashley) opened his goods, and there was a general jubilee...We constituted quite a little town, numbering at least eight hundred souls,...half were women and children. There were some...who had not seen any groceries, such as coffee, sugar, etc. for several months. The whiskey went off as freely as water, even at the exorbitant price he sold it for. All kinds of sports were indulged in with a heartiness that would astonish more civilized societies."

Taken from *The Life and Adventures of James P. Beckwourth*, as told to Thomas D. Bonner, this passage describes a raucus social event; the rendezvous. Here, mountain men swapped stories, tested their skills, and shared news of friends. The annual event was actually begun as a time saving measure whereby trappers could replenish supplies and trade furs, without traveling to St. Louis each summer. North of this point on Henrys Fork of the Green River, between Birch and Burnt Fork Creeks, the first Rocky Mountain Rendezvous was held during June and July, 1825. Held under the direction of William Ashley the gathering was planned for the Green River, but was moved up Henrys Fork because that site provided better forage for animals. One-hundred twenty trappers gathered to barter their furs at Burnt Fork. Among those assembled were some of the industry's most colorful characters; General Ashley, Jedediah Smith, Bill Sublette, Davey Jackson, Tom Fitzpatrick, Etienne Provost, James Beckwourth and a still green Jim Bridger. On July 2, 1825, Ashley and his men headed for St. Louis with a load of furs worth $50,000.

Held annually throughout the region until 1840, when the demand for beaver pelts decreased, the rendezvous is remembered as one of the western frontiers most colorful traditions. Modern day mountain men still reenact these 19th century "fur fairs".
LOCATION: On the south side of State Route 414 between the small Wyoming towns of Burntfork and McKinnon. This marker is about 60-65 miles southwest of Green River, Wyoming, or about 30-35 miles southeast of Lyman, Wyoming.

This monument was dedicated May 13, 1989, with Henry F. Chadey as master of ceremonies. Although Adrian Reynolds and Ned Frost, early promoters of this historic event, had died, Henry Chadey continued to work with others to erect this monument.

FIRST SODA WELL-17

TITLE: Sodium Carbonate Brine
LEGEND: Where sodium carbonate brine was discovered in 1896, which was the forerunner of the present sodium chemical industry in this area.
LOCATION: On the grounds of the Sweetwater County garage in Green River, Wyoming. Not easily accesible.

Green River, Wyoming, is known as the "Trona Capital of the World." Trona, a natural ore known as sodium sesquicarbonate, was laid down fifty million years ago in southwestern Wyoming when all the water evaporated

from salty lakes. Although trona was discovered in 1939, mining and refining began in 1952. Trona is refined into soda ash (sodium carbonate) which is used in the production of glass, detergents, and baking soda.

TRI-STATE MARKER-18

TITLE: Public Land Survey Monument
Tri-State Corner of the States of Wyoming, Utah & Colorado (Lat. 41° 00' 42.616" N., Long. 109° 02' 42.158" W.; Elevation 8402')
LEGEND: This point was monumented by U.S. surveyor, Rollin J. Reeves, on July 19, 1879 while completing the survey of the west boundary of the State of Colorado and the east boundary of Utah Territory. The boundary line separating Wyoming Territory from Colorado and Utah Territories was surveyed by U.S. surveyor, A.V. Richards, in 1873.

The original monument was found to be disturbed in 1931 and was remarked by U.S. Cadastral Engineer, E.V. Kimmel, with a brass tablet seated in a concrete monument.

This monument is one of the corners of The National Rectangular Cadastral Survey System, inaugurated in 1785, that has aided the development and orderly settlement of the public lands in the western states. From these monuments, state and local governments and private citizens are provided with easily identifiable boundaries. Such monuments serve as a base for the work of private surveyors in making accurate land subdivisions and descriptions.

U.S. Department of the Interior Bureau of Land Management

This Tri-State Historical Monument was erected by the Kiwanis Clubs of Rock Springs, Wyoming and Craig, Colorado and the Lions Club of Daggett County, Utah, in cooperation with the Bureau of Land Management, and dedicated on August 21, 1966. Imbedded in the concrete base of this monument are some of the original stones which marked the location in 1879.
LOCATION: This marker is a long way from anywhere and should be visited only in good weather during the summer. Follow U.S. Hwy 191 for 31 miles south of I-80. Then travel easterly 11 miles on a dirt road, where directional signs to the monument are found. It is another 10 miles to the site.

This site provides a beautiful half-day drive beginning in the arid country on the east side of Flaming Gorge Reservoir and ending on a high aspen-covered mountain ridge.

SIMPSON'S HOLLOW-19

TITLE: Simpson's Hollow
LEGEND: Here on Oct. 6, 1857, U.S. Army supply wagons led by a Capt. Simpson were burned by Major Lot Smith and 43 Utah militiamen. They were under orders from Brigham Young, Utah Territorial Governor, to delay the army's advance on Utah. This delay of the army helped effect a peaceful settlement of difficulties.

The day earlier a similar burning of 52 army supply wagons took place near here at Smith's Bluff
LOCATION: On the north side of State Route 28, about 10 miles southwest of Farson, Wyoming.

The information below was taken from *Fort Bridger: A Brief History* by R. S. Ellison:

After arriving in the Great Salt Lake Valley in July 1847, the Mormons staked out their independent state. It was no secret that the Mormons under the leadership of Brigham Young disliked being a part of the United States.

In September 1850, Congress created the territory of Utah. Various events led to worsening relationships between the federal government and the new territory. Soon after James Buchanan became President of the United States in 1857, he appointed new territorial officers and ordered an army of 2,500 men, led by Colonel Albert Sydney

Johnston, to accompany the new governor, Alfred Cumming, to Salt Lake City.

The Mormons were determined not to let the government interfere with their lives and business. Small groups of Mormon militiamen harassed the wagon trains between the Green River and the Ham's Fork. One of those incidents was the conflict at Simpson's Hollow. On October 5, 1857, Lot Smith and a band of Mormon raiders captured and burned twenty-three wagons with supplies destined for Johnston's army. This and several other raids on supply wagons kept the government's military and the new territorial governor from reaching Utah until the next year.

PARTING-OF-THE-WAYS-20

TITLE: Parting-of-the-Ways

LEGEND: This point on the trail is called The Parting-of-the-Ways. The trail to the right is the Sublette or Greenwood Cutoff and to the left is the main route of the Oregon, Mormon, and California Trails. The Sublette Cutoff was opened in 1844 because it saved 46 miles over the main route. It did require a 50 mile waterless crossing of the desert and therefore was not popular until the gold rush period. The name tells the story, people who had traveled a thousand miles together separated at this point. They did not know if they would ever see each other again. It was a place of great sorrow. It was also a place of great decision—to cross the desert and save miles or to favor their livestock. About two-thirds of the emigrants chose the main route through Fort Bridger instead of the Sublette Cutoff.

LOCATION: On the Oregon-Mormon Trail about 12 miles west of the False Parting of the Ways Monument (Sublette County #16).

This marker was placed by the Bureau of Land Management of Wyoming in its efforts to interpret the Oregon-Mormon Trail.

JOHNNY WILLIAMS OCTA MARKER-21

TITLE: Johnny Williams

LEGEND: This is the probable gravesite of ten-year-old Johnny Williams, who died on or about June 20, 1851.

Johnny was riding in the rear of the baggage wagon when the oxen took fright and ran. Johnny went to the front of the wagon and clung to the driver but was thrown out; the wheels of the wagon ran over his head.

His mother wrote this in a letter to Johnny's grandmother: "We buried him there by the roadside, by the right side of the road, about one-half mile before we crossed the Fononelle. We had his grave covered with stones to protect it from wild animals and a board with his name and age and if any of our friends come through I wish they would find his grave and if it needs, repair it."

Research and Signing by
Oregon-California Trails Association
Funding by
Chester E. Buck Memorial Fund
1987

This a part of your American heritage. Honor it, protect it, preserve it for your children.

LOCATION: Private land along the Oregon Trail in Sweetwater County.

WAMSUTTER INFORMATIVE SIGN-22

TITLE: Wamsutter

LEGEND: "On summer nights, this lonely place is merely a small group of lights set in blackness and silence. Over the immense darkness, stars shine brilliantly, neither dimmed by other lights nor hidden by smoke and dust in the air. A meteor flames against the sinking stars; an aeroplane, winging toward Cheyenne or Salt Lake City, seems trying to imitate it. Wamsutter is on the edge of the Red Desert, where colors change hourly, according to the brilliance and direction of the sunlight." (from *Wyoming: A Guide to Its History, Highways, and People*, 1941.) This is the Great Divide Basin. To the south and west the waters flow to the Pacific Ocean. To the east and north they flow to the Atlantic. But here, atop the nation's Continental Divide, the waters drain inward, with no outlet to the sea. Ute and Shoshoni Indians once roamed this semiarid desert but were eventually forced out after the 1850s by increasing numbers of whites traveling along a transcontinental corridor containing the Overland Trail (15 miles south). Stage stations served as the first settlements until 1868 when the Transcontinental Railroad was built. Wamsutter emerged as a section town on the mainline of the Union Pacific, and later developed as a railhead for shipping cattle and sheep with stockgrowers from Wyoming and Colorado using the stock yards. In the early 1900s, as new lines were built, Wamsutter's importance began to decline. However, the Lincoln Highway—which became U.S. 30 and then Interstate 80—brought many travelers and Wamsutter hung on as a service community. Eventually, oil, natural gas, and uranium were discovered, securing the town's existence. Wamsutter, the oldest continually occupied town within the basin, like many Wyoming communities expanded and contracted to accommodate economic realities and a microcosm of Wyoming history.

LOCATION: 243 McCormick Street (old U.S. Hwy 30) in Wamsutter, Wyoming.

DANIEL LANTZ OCTA MARKER-23

TITLE: Daniel Lantz

LEGEND: On April 2, 1850, a California-bound company of gold seekers left their homes in the Wayne County, Indiana, towns of Richmond, Boston, and Centerville. Daniel Lantz, age 45, a wagon maker from Centerville, was a member of this party.

The company arrived here at Black's Fork on July 9. Daniel Lantz had been ill for several days, but on July 10 his condition was so much worse that the company agreed to stop "until there was change in him for better or worse." They camped all that day and the next. The dying man was tended by the company's doctor, Dr. David S. Evans of Boston, who did not believe that Lantz could live another morning.

James Seaton of Centerville recorded the death of Daniel Lantz in his diary entry for July 12, 1850: "Mr. Lantz is still alive but insensible. He lived until 9 1/2 o'clock A.M. When he was no more he was buried at sunset near the road in a very decent manner. His grave was marked by a neat stone. His disease was the bloddy flux. There are 10 more get the same disease but none serious."

Daniel Lantz left a wife, Mary, and five children behind in Indiana to mourn their loss. The Centerville company reached Johnson's Ranch near Hangtown in the California goldfields on September 15.

Research, Signing and Funding by the:
Oregon-California Trails Association
1989

This is a part of your American heritage. Honor it, protect it, preserve it for your children.

LOCATION: On the Oregon Trail about 1.5 miles northeast of Granger, Wyoming.

TETON COUNTY

JOHN COLTER MONUMENT-1

TITLE: John Colter

LEGEND: This Bay is named for John Colter, discoverer of the Teton Mountains and scenic wonders of the Upper Yellowstone. Experienced as a hunter for the 1804-1806 Lewis and Clark Expedition, he explored this region in winter of 1807-1808 in the employ of fur trader Manuel Lisa.

Dedicated on the 150th anniversary of Colter's historic passage 1957

Wyoming Historical Society participating

LOCATION: Edge of Jackson Lake at the end of Main Street, Jackson, Wyoming, in the Colter Bay area.

See three other markers regarding John Colter: Colter Monument (Teton County #2), Colter's Hell Sign (Park County #5), and Mountain Man Memorials (Park County #17).

COLTER MONUMENT-2

West side

TITLE: John Colter

LEGEND: First white man in Wyoming, passed this way in 1807 and discovered Yellowstone Park.

Dedicated by the Historical Landmark Commission of Wyoming, July 4, 1939

South side

TITLE: George Washington Memorial Park

LEGEND: Two hundredth anniversary

Dedicated 1932

Rededicated 1975

LOCATION: In the city park in Jackson, Wyoming.

JOHN HOBACK-3

TITLE: John Hoback, Guide of Astorians.

LEGEND: "John Hoback, Jacob Reznor and Edward Robinson, trappers from Kentucky, in 1811 guided the Astorian land expedition under William Price Hunt across the northern part of present Wyoming to the Snake River. From this junction of the Snake and Hoback Rivers the Hunt group passed through Jackson Hole, over Teton Pass and on to Henry's Fort in Idaho. In this area, Hoback and his companions were detached from the expedition to trap beaver. The following summer the eastbound Astorians led by Robert Stuart, met them in the wilderness, starving and destitute, having been robbed by the Indians. They were given clothing and equipment and continued hunting and trapping until the winter of 1813 when they were killed by the Indians. The River here was named by Wilson Price Hunt for his guide."

Teton County Historical Society, Bridger-Teton National Forest.

LOCATION: South side of U.S. Hwy 191/189, about 1 mile southeast from Hoback Junction.

Although the native rock and mortar were added in 1979, the original marker was dedicated September 15, 1968.

JACKSON HOLE INFORMATIVE SIGN-4

TITLE: This is Jackson Hole.

LEGEND: The entire valley between the Teton and Gros Ventre Mountains was named Jackson's Hole in 1829 by William Sublette, after his partner, David E. Jackson, who loved to trap there. The early fur hunters called any mountain-encircled valley a "hole". It was changed to Jackson Hole in the 1920's for the sake of brevity.

LOCATION: East side of U.S. Hwy 26/89/191, about 3 miles north of Jackson, Wyoming. This is the south entrance to Grand Teton National Park.

MORMON MONUMENT-5

TITLE: Jackson Hole

LEGEND: Daughters of Utah Pioneers
No. 123
Erected Sept. 1948.

In 1889, five Mormon families pioneered Jackson Hole making the trip of 28 miles in 14 days over Teton Pass. Their leader was Elijah N. Wilson, known among the people as "Uncle Nick"—famous Indian Scout and Pony Express Rider. They found 18 single men living in the valley. These families established homes and later built a fort for protection against the Indians. The first L.D.S. services were held on Easter Sunday 1890. Sylvester Wilson was the first presiding elder.

Teton County Company, Wyoming.

LOCATION: Northeast side of the junction of U.S. Hwy 191 and State Route 22, about 1 mile west of Jackson, Wyoming.

Originally a Pony Express plaque was also embedded in the north face of this granite marker; it was vandalized and was not replaced.

TOGWOTEE PASS SIGN-6

Main sign

TITLE: Togwotee Pass
Continental Divide

LEGEND: Named in 1873 by Captain W. A. Jones honoring his Shoshone Indian guide, Togwotee.

Elevation 9,658 feet

Shoshone and Teton National Forests

Plaque #1

TITLE: Togwotee Pass

LEGEND: Blackfoot, Crow and Shoshone Indian hunting parties, following the trail of elk, deer and buffalo, made the first human trail through this pass. Next came such courageous mountainmen as John Colter, Jim Bridger, Joe Meeker and Kit Carson, who courted death in the search for prime beaver pelts.

Capt. Jones, Corps of Engineers, U.S. Army was on reconnaissance for a wagon road across these mountains when he was guided by Togwotee. In 1898, the army built the first wagon road over Togwotee to assist troop movements protecting the westward flow of pioneers. The first auto road was constructed in 1922.

TOGWOTEE (pronounced toe-go-tee) means Lance Thrower in Shoshone.

Plaque #2

TITLE: Parting of the waters

LEGEND: Here, on the Continental Divide, the course of mighty rivers is decided. Moisture from melting snow and summer showers filters into the soil, later emerging as small streams which form the rivers. The Wind and Missouri Rivers to the East, the Snake and Columbia to the West.

Two Ocean Creek, not far from here, was so named because its waters cascade both east and west from the top of the Divide watershed to finally reach both Atlantic and Pacific Oceans.

TETON COUNTY

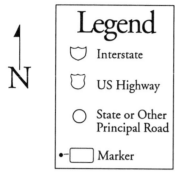

Legend

⬡ Interstate

⬡ US Highway

◯ State or Other
Principal Road

•–⬚ Marker

1   John Colter Monument
2   Colter Monument
3   John Hoback
4   Jackson Hole Informative Sign
5   Mormon Monument
6   Togwotee Pass Sign
7   Trappers Monument
8   Dick Turpin Monument
9   Blackrock Station Sign
10 Miller House Sign
11 Gros Ventre Slide Sign
12 Jackson Lake Dam
13 "Uncle Nick" Wilson Plaque

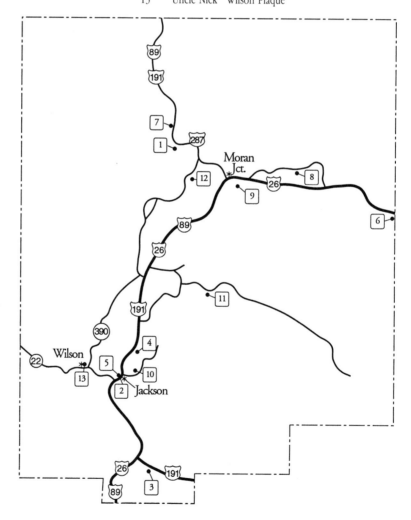

Plaque #3
TITLE: Moving Mountains
LEGEND: Natural forces sculptured the scene before you over 15,000 years ago. Glaciers gouged out the huge valleys from massive layers of lava. The Breccia (bretch-yuh) cliffs are composed of angular pieces of rock cemented together with finer materials.

The ground you stand on constantly changes as nature continues to shape it. Wind tears at the thin soil. Rains attacks and erodes the bare ground. In such ways "mountains are moved."

Where possible man seeks to slow this process slowing the force of water with dams, and maintaining a protective cover of vegetation in the form of grass or timber.

LOCATION: On the west side of U.S. Hwy 26/287 at Togwotee Pass, between Moran Junction and Dubois, Wyoming.

TRAPPERS MONUMENT-7

TITLE: None
LEGEND: In memory of the bold trappers who passed this way to win and hold the west.
Placed by the Historical Landmark Commission of Wyoming 1940
LOCATION: About 0.5 mile west of U.S. Hwy 89/191/287 at the Leek's Marina turnoff.

Leek's lodge was built between the years 1925 and 1927, before Grand Teton National Park was formed. Stephen N. Leek was a conservationist, naturalist, photographer, lecturer, and writer. He became interested in the elk migration through Jackson Hole as the valley became more populated and civilized, and became a leader in efforts to form an elk refuge. In 1912 the National Elk Refuge was formed from two thousand acres belonging to Robert Miller. See Miller House Sign (Teton County #10).

DICK TURPIN MONUMENT-8

TITLE: Dick Turpin
LEGEND: In memory of Dick Turpin, soldier, scout and pioneer, settled here 1887. Erected by the Trustees Robert E. Miller, F. Buchenroth, C. R. Van Vleck and Wm. L. Simpson.
Dedicated by the Historical Landmark Commission 1940
LOCATION: On old U.S. Hwy 287/26 at the entrance to Turpin Meadow Ranch, about 19 miles east of Moran Junction.

BLACKROCK STATION SIGN-9

TITLE: The Old Blackrock Station
LEGEND: In days gone-by, this log cabin served as the Ranger's Office for the Buffalo District of the Teton National Forest, located 35 miles north of the town of Jackson. The building brings back some of the historic flavor of the Jackson Hole Country. The furnishings are typical of a District Forest Ranger's Office in the early days.

This small rustic cabin was sufficient to meet the needs of the hardy Forest Rangers of that era. Their primary duties of forest protection and law enforcement kept them in the woods most of the time. Simple as it was the cabin was a welcome sight to the Ranger, especially during the long cold winter months.
Please look inside for a brief glimpse into the past.
Teton National Forest
LOCATION: South side of U.S. Hwy 26/287 at the Teton National Forest Ranger Station east of Moran Junction.

MILLER HOUSE SIGN-10

TITLE: The Miller House
LEGEND: This house & cabin were built at the turn of the century by Robert E. Miller, first supervisor of Teton National Forest. In 1915 the

Fish and Wildlife Service purchased the building and 1240 acres as the nucleus for the National Elk Refuge in an effort to preserve elk winter range in Jackson Hole.

Through the Teton County Historical Society the house was placed on the National Register of Historic Places in 1969.
LOCATION: Just north and east of Jackson, Wyoming, about 0.7 miles south of the National Elk Refuge.

GROS VENTRE SLIDE SIGN-11

TITLE: The Gros Ventre Slide
LEGEND: Before you lie the remnants of one of the largest earth movements in the world.

On June 23, 1925, earth, rock and debris moved rapidly from an altitude of 9000 feet, across the valley bottom and up the slope of the red bluffs behind you. The action lasted only minutes but a river was damned and the landscape changed.
Gros Ventre Slide Geological Area
U.S. Department of Agriculture
LOCATION: About 5 miles east of Kelly, Wyoming, along paved road which follows the Gros Ventre River.

JACKSON LAKE DAM-12

Main sign
TITLE: Jackson Lake Dam
LEGEND: Jackson Lake Dam, a vital link in the development of the water and land resources of the Upper Snake River Basin, was built and is operated by the Bureau of Reclamation, U.S. Dept. of the Interior. It was originally authorized for irrigation—some 1,100,000 acres of the fertile Snake River Valley—and for flood control along the Snake and lower Columbia Rivers. Outdoor recreation and fish and wildlife conservation have become important project benefits.

History sign
TITLE: History
LEGEND: The Reclamation Service first surveyed Jackson Lake in 1902-03, leading to construction in 1905-07 of a temporary pole-crib dam to store 200,000 acre-feet of water. It rotted and failed in July of 1910, and in 1911 a new concrete structure was begun to restore the vital water supply for the farmers on the Minidoka Project. An unending string of freight wagons hauled cement from the railhead at Ashton, Idaho, over 90 miles away, often through deep snow and at temperatures down to 50° below zero. The 70-foot high structure, completed in 1916, raised the maximum lake elevation 17 feet, and increased the storage capacity to 847,000 acre-feet.

LOCATION: Jackson Lake Dam in Grand Teton National Park.

"UNCLE NICK" WILSON PLAQUE-13

TITLE: Elijah Nicholas "Uncle Nick" Wilson
April 8, 1843-December 27, 1915
LEGEND: In 1889, Uncle Nick led the first Mormon settlers over Teton Pass into Jackson Hole. It took 14 days to travel from Victor, Idaho, to Wilson, Wyoming, the town that bears his name.

As a child, Uncle Nick lived with Chief Washakie's band of Shoshone Indians. He later was a Pony Express rider, a scout for General Albert S. Johnston, and an Overland Stage driver. In Wilson, Uncle Nick was the first Presiding Elder for the Mormon Church and had the first hotel, general store, and post office.

This monument is dedicated summer, 1989, on the 100th anniversary of the pioneer crossing of Teton Pass.
LOCATION: Next to Post Office in Wilson, Wyoming.

1.

2.

3.

4.

1. Colter Monument was dedicated in Jackson City Park, July 4, 1939, by the Wyoming Historical Landmark Commission.

2. The Daughters of the Utah Pioneers erected this sign in 1948 as a memorial to the five Mormon families who pioneered Jackson Hole in 1889.

3. The Dick Turpin Monument at the Turpin Meadow Ranch was dedicated in 1940 by the Wyoming Historical Landmark Commission.

4. This historical marker was dedicated in Hoback Canyon on September 15, 1968, by the Teton County Historical Society.

FIRST ASCENT OF THE GRAND TETON-14

TITLE: Commemorating
    First Ascent of the Grand Teton,
    August 11, 1898
LEGEND: By the pioneers Hon. William O. Owen, Engineer and Surveyor, Rev. Franklin S. Spalding, Frank L. Petersen and John Shive, Ranchers

This tablet placed here during the Convention of the National Editorial Association held in Jackson Hole in connection with the Dedication of the Grand Teton National Park July 29, 1929

By direction of the State Legislature of Wyoming (S.J.R., No.3, 1929) by F. M. Fryxell, Phil Smith, William Gilman.

The tablet is the gift of Emma Matilda Owen.

LOCATION: Originally placed on the summit of the Grand Teton. The bronze tablet was vandalized and its whereabouts is not known.

The following information came from the text of an address delivered by William O. Owen on July 28, 1929, on the occasion of the dedication of the Grand Teton National Park:

William O. Owen first saw the Tetons in 1883 and first attempted an ascent of the Grand Teton in 1891. After several unsuccessful attempts, he succeeded August 11, 1898. The four men who climbed the peak chiseled their names on the summit and placed a steel rod and the Rocky Mountain Club's metal banner in one of the granite crevices.

The first recorded attempt to scale the Grand Teton was that of M. Michaud, a French trapper, in 1843. Several other summit attempts failed until the Owen party success in 1898; no one else reached the summit for another twenty-five years. In honor of the feat, the U.S. Geographic Board gave Owen's name to the second highest peak in the Teton Range.

On July 30, 1929, Prof. F. M. Fryxell of Augustana College, Illinois, and Phil Smith and Wm. Gilman, of Jackson Hole, Wyoming, carried a 22 X 11-1/2 inch bronze tablet to the summit, fastening it to the rock with cement and bolts. The tablet was later vandalized, and its whereabouts is not known.

UINTA COUNTY

BEAR RIVER CITY SIGN-1

TITLE: Bear River City.

LEGEND: Nothing remains today as a reminder that Bear River City was one of the notorious "end-of-track" towns along the original Union Pacific Transcontinental Railroad line. Initially called Gilmer, the town was first settled by lumberjacks, who arrived in 1867 and supplied ties to the approaching railroad. The population of the settlement swelled to nearly 2,000 as construction of the Echo Tunnel in Utah and the onset of winter held up track laying.

This railroad boom town, its name changed to Bear River City, developed a reputation for unparalleled rowdiness. The town consisted of a few stores and boarding houses standing alongside numerous saloons and gambling parlors. These liquor and gaming establishments catered to a nefarious crowd, causing the *Frontier Index* to report Bear River City as "the liveliest city, if not the wickedest in America."

The *Frontier Index*, a traveling newspaper printed at various points along the Union Pacific route, outraged Bear River City's lawless element by endorsing vigilante activity as a means of eliminating undesireables. Whipped to a frenzy, on November 20, 1868 an unruly mob burned down the Index office. The town's law-abiding citizens retaliated against the mob and the ensuing battle lasted well into the night. Order had been restored by the time troops arrived from Fort Bridger the next morning.

The railroad, not riotous mobs, caused the town's demise when the Union Pacific refused to construct a siding connecting Bear River City to the main line. The populace hurriedly packed their belongings and moved on to Evanston, a town which offered better prospects. The hoopla, which marked the short history of Bear River City became only a memory.

LOCATION: North side of State Route 150, about 9.3 miles southeast of Evanston, Wyoming. About 1.1 miles southeast of Mormon Monument (Uinta County #8).

BEEHIVE MONUMENT-2

TITLE: None

LEGEND: Erected by the members of the Woodruff Stake in honor of the Mormon Pioneers who passed this point, Wednesday July 7, 1847 and in subsequent years.

LOCATION: South side of the rest area off of I-80 at Lyman, Wyoming.

The Mormons were forced to move from New York in 1831 and from Ohio in 1838. Less than nine months later, they were forced to move from Missouri and established their own town of Nauvoo, Illinois. By 1844 the Mormons were facing religious pressures and started a move westward in 1846. In the spring of 1847, Brigham Young led a party of 148 Mormon pioneers along the Oregon Trail to Fort Bridger and later into the Salt Lake Valley.

CHARCOAL KILNS MONUMENT-3

TITLE: Charcoal Kilns

LEGEND: Charcoal kilns were built by Moses Byrne, 1869, to supply the pioneer smelters in the Utah valley.

Erected by the Historical Landmark Commission of Wyoming 1956

LOCATION: About 15 miles southwest of Fort Bridger, about 5 miles from the Leroy Road exit off of I-80.

Moses Byrne came to Wyoming in 1867. In 1869 he built five charcoal kilns near Piedmont, Wyoming, located on the Mormon-California Emigrant Trail and along the original route of the Union Pacific in 1868. Each kiln was "thirty feet high and thirty feet in circumference with an entrance eight feet high and walls two feet thick." Wood was transformed into charcoal to be used in the iron smelters in the Salt Lake Valley.

The ghost town of Piedmont, the three remaining kilns, and the Byrne Cemetery are all that remain in the desolate valley that once was the center of activity for the Byrne family. The remains of the houses and cemetery are marked with small plaques: Joseph Byrne Home 1885-1935; Thomas Hinshaw Home 1878-1935; Moses Byrne Home 1869-1931; and Byrne Cemetery 1870-1931. A principal monument in the cemetery remembers Moses and Catherine Byrne. Moses— Jan. 2, 1820 to Mar. 22, 1904. Catherine, Wife of M. Byrne—Sep. 12, 1829 to Nov. 15, 1902.

CHURCH BUTTE—MORMON MONUMENT-4

TITLE: Church Butte

LEGEND: Erected July 24, 1930 in honor of the Mormon pioneers who passed this point, early in July, 1847 and in subsequent years.

LOCATION: Although the monument no longer exists, the natural phenomenon Church Butte still marks the site about 10 miles southwest of Granger, Wyoming.

This marker was similar to the Beehive Monument (Uinta County #2) in that they both memorialized the pioneers of the early Mormon migration. This landmark along the Oregon Trail, Church Butte, was also known as "Solomon's Temple" and formed the backdrop for Mormon religious services.

EVANSTON INFORMATIVE SIGN-5

TITLE: Evanston

LEGEND: Evanston was established by the Union Pacific Railroad Company late in 1868. In the first county election, September 6, 1870, Evanston was chosen county seat. Union Pacific Railroad shops moved here in the fall of 1871. Timber and sawmill operations were the leading business. Cattle and sheep ranching became the basic industry of Unita county. In the '70s and early '80s, a Chinese Joss House, one of the three in the United States, attracted thousands of Chinese for Chinese New Year's Day ceremonies. About four hundred Chinese normally lived in "China Town" and worked in the Almy coal mines. The Joss House burned on January 26, 1922.

LOCATION: North side of Bear River Drive just east of the fairgrounds in Evanston, Wyoming.

Like other towns across southern Wyoming, Evanston grew up as an end-of-the-track settlement. Many such towns quickly disappeared as the railroad moved on. Evanston survived, but the town was not assured permanency until the railroad located its roundhouse and machine shops there July 4, 1871. Evanston was named for James A. Evans, a railroad surveyor who plotted the city.

FORT BRIDGER SIGNS-6.0 to 6.18

ENTRANCE MONUMENT-6.0

TITLE: Fort Bridger.

LEGEND: Established as a trading post in 1834. U.S. Military Post on the Overland Trail June 10, 1858 to October 6, 1890.

This monument is erected by a few interested residents of the Community in the year 1914.

INFORMATIVE SIGN-6.1

TITLE: Old Fort Bridger
        Pioneer trading post

LEGEND: The Fort was established about 1842 by Jim Bridger, discoverer of Great Salt Lake; notable pioneer, trapper, fur trader, scout and guide. Bridger was born at Richmond, Virginia, March 17, 1804, and died at Westport, Missouri, July 17, 1884. His unerring judgement regarding problems of trappers, traders, soldiers, emigrants and gold seekers, bordered on the miraculous, and his advice was

UINTA COUNTY

N

Legend

Interstate

US Highway

State or Other
Principal Road

Marker

1	Bear River City Sign
2	Beehive Monument
3	Charcoal Kilns Monument
5	Evanston Informative Sign
6.0-6.18	Fort Bridger Signs
7	Fort Supply Monument
8	Mormon Monument
11	First Brick Church Marker
12	Almy Centennial Historical Marker

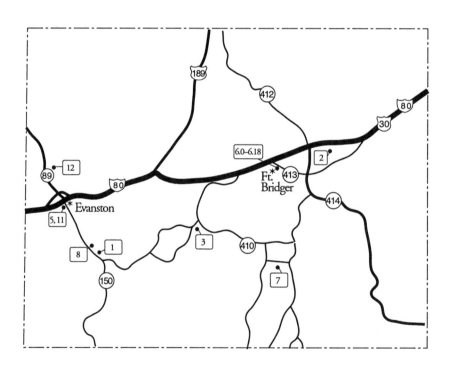

universally in demand in the early history of this state.

Bridger has been prominently recognized as America's greatest frontiersman and the west's most gifted scout.

GATEWAY MONUMENT-6.2

TITLE: The Pony Express

LEGEND: 120 celebrated riders rode 650,000 miles with only one rider killed by Indians, one schedule not completed and one mail lost.

National Pony Express Centennial Association.

Dwight D. Eisenhower—Chairman	Waddell F. Smith—President
Lola M. Homsher—Vice President	L.C. Bishop—Director at Large
1860-1861	1960-1961

SUTLER'S STORE-6.3

TITLE: Sutler's Store

LEGEND: The Post Trader's or Sutler's Store, shown as it appeared about 1871, was owned and operated by Judge W. A. Carter, a prominent citizen in Territorial Wyoming. The east-west wing on the left was removed sometime after the Fort was abandoned by the Army in 1890. The Carter family is buried in the cemetery on Officer's Row.

PONY EXPRESS—OREGON TRAIL-6.4

TITLE: Fort Bridger.

LEGEND: Established 1858 as a military post
also Pony Express station and on the Oregon Trail.

POST SUTLER'S COMPLEX-6.5

Plaque #1

TITLE: The Post Trader

LEGEND: The buildings in this area are virtually all that remain of the once thriving commercial empire of Judge William Alexander Carter and his wife Mary, Fort Bridger's only two Post Traders. Carter arrived at Fort Bridger with Colonel Albert S. Johnston's Army in 1857 and soon received the appointment as Post Trader. Selling to soldiers, emigrants, railroad builders, cattlemen, settlers, and Indians, William Carter amassed a fortune and became one of Wyoming Territory's most influential citizens. His interests extended into lumbering, agriculture, livestock, mining, and politics. Carter's "Bug" brand was known on the cattle ranges of four states. Carter County, Dakota Territory (antedating Wyoming Territory) was named for him as was Carter Mountain in northern Wyoming. The Carters entertained such notables as President Chester A. Arthur, James Bridger, Chief Washakie, Mark Twain, Jay Gould, Sidney Dillon, Generals Sherman, Harney, Crook, Augur and Bisbee.

After William's death on November 7, 1881, Mary E. Carter assumed her husband's position and carried on the empire he began in 1857. With Fort Bridger's abandonment in 1890, Mary became the caretaker until the government auctioned off the buildings in 1895. The Carter family maintained the family business through the early Twentieth Century. Judge and Mrs. Carter's contributions to the Rocky Mountain West, though of different nature, compare with those of James Bridger.

Plaque #2

TITLE: The Post Trader's Store

LEGEND: Although Judge Carter dabbled in many areas, his main responsibility revolved around his activities as the post trader at Fort Bridger. In this store he sold various items not supplied by the Army to the garrison, including limited amounts of liquor. A post council of administrators set a ceiling on prices to make sure that the military received a fair deal. In addition to food, dry goods and other items regularly found in a general store of the period, Carter also provided a post office, as well as telegraph and even telephone service in the store's many years of operation. When Judge Carter died in 1881, his wife, Mary, continued in her husband's footsteps. She operated the store and its many facets, and when the government abandoned the fort in 1890, she became the custodian of the grounds until they were sold.

The building itself was an "L" shape with one wing of white-washed wood running to the east and west for the store and a stone section which stood to the northeast for a tavern. The remains of this last section measures 25 feet 5 inches by 53 feet 4 inches. The walls rise 10 1/4 feet and the peak of the roof is 16 feet.

Plaque #3

TITLE: House, Warehouse and Mess Hall

LEGEND: At the northeast corner of Judge Carter's complex rose the log chinked ice house. Three doors at the southern side appeared one over the other, allowing this tall building of 18 feet 7 inches by 14 1/4 feet to be entered at all levels as the ice stock began to grow lower with the coming of warmer weather. Ice could be taken to the stone building next door, the two story contained the beef and included a type of walk-in freezer while the upper portion of this large 24 feet by 60 feet facility could hold stock such as dry goods. An "L" off the southeast corner provided space for Carter's employees to take their meals. Two windows and a center door faced to the east to provide light and some additional warmth from the morning sun. This side measured 32 feet while the shorter ends were 18 feet.

Plaque #4

TITLE: School House, Milk House & Wash House

LEGEND: As an indication of his wealth and influence William Carter provided three buildings not commonly available to the average person on the American frontier. The first frame building served the family as a private school. It measured a mere 11 feet 3 inches by 14 feet 3 inches. Here the six children of Judge Carter received their rudiments of education. The adjacent stone structure was the milk house, an 11 feet by 16 1/2 feet processing and storage facility for luxury dairy products. The third building, the wash house, a 20 feet 2 inches by 11 feet 5 inches frame affair, made it possible for the Carters to bathe in relative comfort and also to have the servants do the wash. Inside this small edifice is a "washing machine," a new invention of the frontier. The walls of all these buildings rose less than 10 feet.

Plaque #5

TITLE: Carriage House, Stables and Chicken Coop

LEGEND: This set of buildings completed the holdings of the Post Trader. The first board and batten building with the large double doors served as the carriage house. Judge Carter owned several animal drawn vehicles which lent an air of wealth to the isolated frontier outpost. He also constructed a stable next to the carriage house for his teams, as well as for use by the Pony Express for the little more than a year that this service kept a station at Fort Bridger. A tack room connected to the stables, as did a crude low wooden shelter for such stock as milk and beef cows. Adjacent to this shelter is the frame chicken coop. The Carriage House is the largest of these buildings at 21 feet by 16 feet 3 inches while the enclosed stable measures 12 feet 9 inches by nearly 16 feet. None of these structures stand more than 10 feet high.

Plaque #6

TITLE: Post Trader's House

LEGEND: Judge Carter began building his home in 1858 and continually added onto it as his family grew and his status improved. The house was a frame structure with board and batten siding. Two

1.

2.

3.

4.

5

6.

1. The Wyoming Historical Landmark Commission dedicated the Charcoal Kilns Monument at Piedmont in 1956.

2. In June 1933 the Utah Pioneer Trails and Landmarks Association placed this plaque on the remnant of the Mormon Wall at Fort Bridger.

3. Mormons were early leaders in marking historic sites. Their monuments frequently displayed a beehive, like the Beehive monument at the Lyman Rest Stop.

4. This marker and its memorial plaques from the Pony Express Centennial Association and the Oregon Trail Memorial Association were placed near the entrance of Fort Bridger in the early 1930s.

5. In September 1924, the Mormon Monument southeast of Evanston was dedicated by the Woodruff Stake of the Church of Jesus Christ of Latter Day Saints.

6. Informative signs, like The Post Sutler's Complex, were used in place of bronze and granite markers in the 1960s and provided more space for historical interpretation.

Several historical markers were built at the entrance to Fort Bridger. The plaque on the right was dedicated in 1914 by "a few interested residents of the community." The wooden informative sign was erected by the Wyoming State Archives and Historical Department and the Wyoming State Historical Society about 1960. The Pony Express sign on the left was dedicated in 1961.

bay windows flanked the front porch. The Carters boasted one of the largest libraries in the region, and enjoyed several conveniences found in fine Eastern residences of the period. For this reason noted scientists, generals, railroad executives and other distinguished travelers welcomed an invitation to the house. A President of the United States and Mark Twain even visited the residence in its hayday. Unfortunately, a fire destroyed the historic structure in the 1930's.

THORNBURGH-6.6

TITLE: "Thornburgh" was a dog...
LEGEND: Named after Major T. T. Thornburgh who was killed in a fight with the Ute Indians near the White River Agency, September 29, 1879. The dog was a survivor of a wagon train burned during the battle and grew up as a military camp follower. Eventually he ended up at Fort Bridger.

On several occasions Thornburgh distinguished himself by his heroic deeds including catching a commissary thief, warning a sentinel of marauding Indians, saving the life of a soldier in a knife fight and rescuing a small boy from drowning.

At Fort Bridger, Thornburgh became the devoted companion of a freighter, "Buck" Buchanan, and the favorite of many who frequented the Post. Thornburgh died September 27, 1888 as the result of being kicked by one of Buchanan's mules.

It is said that Thornburgh's master lies in an unmarked grave in the city cemetery at Salt Lake City.

THORNBURGH GRAVE-6.7

TITLE: None
LEGEND: Thornburgh died September 27, 1888. Man never had a better, truer, braver friend. Sleep on old fellow. We'll meet "Across the Range".

This is actually a dog's grave. The dog belonged to Major Thornburgh who was killed. The dog was given to another party, who buried him here.

This poem from Elizabeth Arnold Stone appeared in the *Wyoming Churchman*, February, 1925, with an article about the grave:

There is a burial ground that lies
Beneath the fair Wyoming skies;
It stretches out austere and vast
And holds the records of a past
Where men may read from nature's page
The secrets of a bygone age.
And in the valley far below,
Close to the water's murmuring flow,
A little mound lies all alone,
Marked by a simple marble stone—
A dog's grave, with this legend strange:
We too shall meet beyond the range.
It is the record of a love
More lasting than the peaks above;
Mountains may crumble, earth decay,
But love and faith pass not away.
Then pause beside this grave that lies
Beneath the fair Wyoming skies!

FORT BRIDGER IN 1889-6.8

TITLE: Fort Bridger in 1889
LEGEND: Above is a copy of a watercolor of Fort Bridger done by Merritt D. Houghton (1845-1918), known for his historic illustrations of Wyoming towns, ranches and mines. The view is toward the south and the Uinta Mountains.

In 1889, the date of this painting, the fort had but one year remaining in its existence as a United States military post. The following year, as a result of the vanishing frontier and the lack of a need for forts such as this one, the army abandoned Fort Bridger.

A number and name description is listed locating all of the sites at Fort Bridger.

MORMON OCCUPATION-6.9

TITLE: Title unknown.
LEGEND: The involvement of the Mormons in the affairs of Fort Bridger constituted a short, but eventful period. A few remnants of their industry may still be found.

After the establishment of Fort Supply, twelve miles to the south, in 1853, Lewis Robison acquired Bridger's trading post in 1855, supported in his endeavor by Brigham Young. Under Robison's proprietorship, trade with the emigrants, trappers, and Indians continued much as usual around the post for the next two years.

Early in 1857, Brigham Young instructed Robison to fortify his property for protection from the Indians. Brigham was probably also apprehensive about the clouds of discontent gathering between the Mormons in Utah and the United States Government. Throughout the summer, as a punitive force of federal troops marched westward across the plains toward Utah, Robison worked hard with cobblestone and mortar to construct a walled enclosure. The main Fort, was 100 feet square with walls 16 feet in height and 5 feet at the base. Attached was a horse corral, 80 feet by 100 feet, with walls 8 feet in height and 2 1/2 feet wide at the base.

Robison completed the walls in August of 1857. Just before "Johnston's Army" reached Fort Bridger in November, the Mormons instituted a "scorched earth" policy and deserted and burned both Fort Bridger and Fort Supply. The fire-gutted stone walls then became a quartermaster storage facility. Subsequent military construction resulted in most of Robison's fort being leveled to the ground.

This marker was absent during site visits in 1986 and 1989. However, because the content of this marker portrayed the Mormon involvement in Fort Bridger, its legend was included here for history's sake.

MORMON WALL-6.10

TITLE: The Mormon Wall
LEGEND: Official Marker
Utah Pioneer Trails and Landmarks Association
No. 25.
Erected June 25, 1933.

On August 3, 1855 the Church of Jesus Christ of Latter-Day Saints concluded arrangements for the purchase of Fort Bridger from Luis Vasquez, partner of James Bridger, for $8,000.00. Final payment was made October 18, 1858. A cobblestone wall was erected in the fall of 1855, replacing Bridger's stockade. A few additional log houses were built within the Fort. The place was evacuated and burned on the approach of Johnston's Army September 27, 1857. A portion of the wall is here preserved. In 1855, Fort Supply was established by Brigham Young six miles south where crops were raised for the emigrants.

Utah Pioneer Trails and Landmarks Association.

MUSEUM-6.11

TITLE: Fort Bridger Museum
LEGEND: This building was originally the main barracks when the fort was abandoned.

Rehabilitated and dedicated in 1951 by the Historical Landmark Commission of Wyoming.

FORT BRIDGER BANDSTAND-6.12

TITLE: Fort Bridger Bandstand
LEGEND: This reconstruction of the original Fort Bandstand was undertaken to honor Lulu Goodrick, long-time friend and supporter of historic Fort Bridger.
Lulu Goodrick May 10, 1913-November 24, 1982
Dedication July 2, 1983

POST SUN DIAL-6.13

TITLE: Post Sun Dial
LEGEND: Made under direction of Major E. R. S. Canby 10th Infantry Post Commander 1852-1860. Killed by Modoc Indians.

OFFICERS' QUARTERS AND ENLISTED MEN'S BARRACKS-6.14

TITLE: Officers' Quarters and Enlisted Men's Barracks
LEGEND: This sketch of Fort Bridger appeared in the June 16, 1873 issue of *New York's Daily Graphic*. Shown are six log officers' quarters on the left; the hospital in the background; and the enlisted men's barracks on the right.

COMMANDING OFFICER'S QUARTERS-6.15

TITLE: Commanding Officer's Quarters
1884-1890
LEGEND: This structure was of frame construction and completed in 1884 during a period of extensive improvement at the Post. It supplanted the old log Commanding Officers Quarters which had been in use since 1858.

After the abandonment of Fort Bridger in 1890, the building was sold and moved to a new location a short distance to the northeast.

The structure subsequently served as a hotel for several years.

THE CARTER CEMETERY-6.16

TITLE: The Carter Cemetery.
LEGEND: The decedents re-interred here in 1933 represent a very significant cross section of those individuals whose names and contributions will ever be associated with Fort Bridger's early history. Of particular interest are...

"UNCLE JACK" (JOHN) ROBERTSON—an early mountain trapper who came to the vicinity in the 1830's and remained until his death. A colorful local character, it is said he was instrumental in convincing Jim Bridger of the wisdom of establishing a trading post on the Black's Fork.

VIRGINIA BRIDGER HAHN—born at Fort Bridger on July 4, 1849, daughter of the intrepid Jim Bridger by his second wife, a Ute Indian.

"JUDGE" WILLIAM ALEXANDER CARTER who came to Fort Bridger with the United States Army in 1857; stayed to become a merchant-sutler; and with his family and associates went on to establish one of the most extensive business enterprises in Wyoming Territory.

This cemetery was established on Fort grounds through the efforts of William A. Carter, Jr. and the Historical Landmark Commission of Wyoming.

1ST COMMANDING OFFICER'S QUARTERS-6.17

TITLE: 1st Commanding Officer's Quarters
LEGEND: From 1858 to 1890 the area in the foreground was occupied by the log and frame structure shown in the photograph. The building was the fourth log Officers' Quarters in a row of six constructed shortly after Fort Bridger was declared a military post in 1857. For sixteen years it served as the Commanding Officer's residence with frame extensions added in 1868 and 1873 to provide a kitchen, servants room, parlor and two bedrooms. A new frame Commanding Officer's Quarters was completed in 1884 after which this building was divided into an Officers' Quarters and into Court Martial and Military Board rooms.

FIRST SCHOOLHOUSE PLAQUE-6.18

TITLE: The First School House in Wyoming
LEGEND: Daughters of Utah Pioneers
No. 52
Erected Aug. 25, 1939

In 1860, Judge Wm. A. Carter erected this school house for the education of his four daughters, two sons and other children of the fort. Competent instructors from the East were employed and the students of this school were permitted to enter eastern colleges without further preparation. Thus, the way was paved for future education in Wyoming.

Uinta County Company.

LOCATION: These signs are located at the entrance to Fort Bridger State Historic Site or on its grounds.

Much of the following information came from the National Register of Historic Places Inventory-Nomination Form prepared in 1969 by Bill Barnhart, Assistant Historian of the Wyoming Recreation Commission. Information was also found in Robert S. Ellison's *A Brief History of Fort Bridger*:

Fort Bridger's long and varied history spans every major phase of Western frontier development except the fur trade. Its establishment, early operation, and namesake relates to one of the most famous of all the early trappers and explorers, James Bridger.

The decline of the Rocky Mountain fur trade in the late 1830s forced the "mountain men" who remained on the frontier to seek new occupations. Jim Bridger established a small trading post in the valley of the Black's Fork of the Green River and formed a partnership with Louis Vasquez. Erected in

1842, the post was open for business early in 1843.

Bridger's proposed intention was to establish trade with the friendly neighborhood Indians and with the emigrants who passed the fort on their way west. Due to its convenient location on the Overland Route, Fort Bridger became second in importance only to Fort Laramie as a resupply and outfitting point for travelers between the Missouri River and the Pacific Coast. In the decade after establishment, the fort was visited by numerous parties of Indians, emigrants, gold seekers, adventurers, explorers, and the militarily significant Stansbury Expedition when it passed through in 1849. A majority of the "plains travelers" during this period sooner or later stopped at Fort Bridger.

A dispute over the fort's ownership developed in 1853. The Mormons, who had settled the valley of the Salt Lake in 1847, claimed they had purchased it for $8,000 from Jim Bridger, who denied such a transaction had ever occurred. In the fall of 1853, two parties of Mormons sent from Salt Lake City came to the vicinity, established Fort Supply, and took over Fort Bridger. They used the forts to aid converts to the church as they traveled the trail to Salt Lake City, to establish trade with the other emigrants, and to check the threat of Indian hostilities the Mormons claimed Bridger was promoting.

Friction developed between the Mormons and the federal government in the late 1850s. President Buchanan dispatched U.S. troops to the area in 1857 precipitating the so-called "Mormon War." Upon the approach of "Johnston's Army," the Mormons deserted and burned both Fort Bridger and Fort Supply. Colonel A. S. Johnston, later famous as a Confederate General, immediately took over the sites and declared Fort Bridger to be a military reservation. In 1858 it was officially made a military post and a building program started.

The early 1860s were eventful years at Fort Bridger. In addition to military activities, the fort served as a major station for the Pony Express, the Overland Stage Line, and the transcontinental telegraph. Troops from the fort patrolled the trails and frequently provided escort and protection when constant Indian depredations made travel hazardous. Regular Union troops, who arrived at Fort Bridger after the Civil War, found it in a state of poor repair, and a renewed building program was soon begun.

Two events created new excitement around Fort Bridger in 1867. Northeast of the fort, around the South Pass and Sweetwater region, "gold fever" had precipitated a lively "boom." At about the same time, Union Pacific Railroad construction proceeded along a route just to the north. The fort became an important supply point, and troops again provided travelers and workers protection from hostile Indian harassment.

Indian peace treaties signed at Fort Bridger proved quite successful. A treaty signed on July 2, 1863, attained the Shoshone's promise not to molest whites traveling along the trails in return for $10,000 in trade goods each year for twenty years. Five years and one day later, another treaty was signed here with Washakie's Shoshone Indians. The tribe, in treaty with General C. C. Augur representing the Indian Peace Commissioner, was given a large reservation east of the Wind River Mountains. With Chief Washakie's leadership and Jim Bridger's advice, the Shoshone subsequently acquired a reputation as trustworthy friends of the white man.

A period of relative peace existed in the Black's Fork River valley during the 1870s, despite the "Indian Wars" sweeping through the northern Plains. Though strategically located, Fort Bridger never served as the base for any of the major military expeditions, although a number of troops stationed at the fort were re-assigned for fighting purposes.

The post was abandoned in 1878 but reactivated in 1880. Through the 1880s, the military erected additional buildings and barracks and made many general improvements. With the Indians on reservations and the passing of the frontier, however, posts like Fort Bridger were no longer needed. On October 1, 1890, Fort Bridger was permanently abandoned.

Although the military departed, many early residents made the fort and the valley their home. Most prominent was the family of Judge W. A. Carter, who first arrived with the army during the "Mormon War" and received an appointment as Fort Bridger's first post trader. Upon his death in 1881, he had amassed a considerable fortune through a variety of business enterprises. His livestock operation was one of the largest of its time in Wyoming—so large, in fact, that his cattle ranged as far as the Montana line.

In the 1920s, sentiment developed among many Wyoming citizens to preserve Fort Bridger in light of its significant role in the development of the Rocky Mountain West. As a result, the State of Wyoming acquired the site along with the few remaining buildings in 1928. The final acquisition was completed February 1, 1929, through the efforts of the Historical Landmark Commission of Wyoming and other interested parties. Robert S. Ellison, chairman of the Commission, Warren Richardson, treasurer of the

Commission, and Roy A. Mason of Kemmerer and the citizens of Lincoln County played important roles in the original acquisition. It was the Commission of 1947-1949 that planned and accomplished the rehabilitation of the Big Barracks at Fort Bridger into a new museum.

Today Fort Bridger is a State Historic Site under the jurisdiction of the Wyoming State Parks & Historic Sites.

FORT SUPPLY MONUMENT-7

TITLE: Site of Fort Supply

LEGEND: Established in November, 1853, by Captain John Nebeker and Captain Isaac Bullock who located here with a number of Latter Day Saints. This was the first place in Wyoming where land was irrigated.

Abandoned in 1857.

The site was given to Wyoming by Hinton Hansen.

Erected by the Historical Landmark Commission 1937

LOCATION: South side of Uinta County Road 274, about 3 miles southwest of Robertson, Wyoming.

Fort Supply was built in 1853 as a supply station for Mormon emigrants traveling over the Mormon-California Trail. The stockade was finished in 1855, and it supplied travelers with oats and wheat and fresh produce. Trouble developed between the federal government and the new territory in Utah, and President James Buchanan sent a large contingent of the U.S. Army, under the leadership of Col. Albert Sidney Johnston, to enforce the laws of the United States in the new territory. As Johnston's army approached southwest Wyoming, the Mormons began their retreat into Utah. The Mormons burned Fort Supply and Fort Bridger in 1857. The so-called "Mormon War" began with the approach of Johnston's army and ended six months later without a direct confrontation between the U.S. Army and the Mormon militia.

MORMON MONUMENT-8

TITLE: None

LEGEND: Erected by the members of the Woodruff Stake of the Church of Jesus Christ of Latter Day Saints in honor of the Pioneers who passed this spot July 12, 1847 under the leadership of Brigham Young.

Dedicated September 28, 1924.

LOCATION: North side of State Route 150, about 8.2 miles southeast of Evanston, Wyoming. About 1.1 miles northwest of Bear River City Sign (Uinta County #1).

The Mormon-California Trail crossed State Route 150 at this site.

PONY EXPRESS—OVERLAND STAGE MONUMENT-10

TITLE: None

LEGEND: The Pony Express route operated through here April 3, 1860 to October 24, 1861.

The Overland Stage Station route in operation 1861 to 1868.

In memory of the pioneers who passed this way to win and hold the west.

Erected by the Historical Landmark Commission of Wyoming 1953

LOCATION: It was originally located on U.S. Hwy 30 in Evanston, Wyoming. Having been knocked over and fractured, it was not replaced.

Typical of the Historical Landmark Commission of Wyoming, this monument was a tall granite marker with a Pony Express rider engraved on the top and a stagecoach engraved in the middle. Ernest Dahlquist, a member of the Commission, acted as chairman of the dedication held in September 1954. Although the monument no longer stands, it was included out of historical interest for the monument and the site.

FIRST BRICK CHURCH MARKER-11

TITLE: First Brick Church

LEGEND: Daughters of Utah Pioneers
    No. 78
    Erected Nov. 1, 1941

In February, 1873, a branch of the Church of Jesus Christ of Latter-day Saints was organized in Evanston by President William Budge of Bear Lake Valley, Idaho. On May 23, 1873, William G. Burton was ordained Bishop. On June 24, 1890, this ward was incorporated under the laws of the State of Wyoming and named Evanston. The Board of Trustees were James Brown, Thomas Parkinson, John Whittle, Frank Mills and Arthur W. Sims. In 1890 this group, with James Brown as Bishop, built the first brick church in Wyoming.

Camp Meedles and Camp Wyutana

LOCATION: Just south of the junction of Main Street and 7th Street in Evanston, Wyoming.

ALMY CENTENNIAL HISTORICAL MARKER-12

TITLE: Almy

LEGEND: Nineteenth Century railroads were dependent upon coal for fuel. The vast coal reserves of southern Wyoming helped determine the route of the transcontinental Union Pacific Railroad and were the basis for Wyoming's first energy boom. Communities sprang up along the line and several with coal deposits or rail facilities survived. Coal mines were opened in the surrounding Bear River Valley in 1868. Dreams of prosperity lured miners from England, Scandinavia, China, and from throughout the United States to settle in "Wyoming Camp", which later became Almy. Named for James T. Almy, a clerk for the Rocky Mountain Coal Company and located three miles northwest of Evanston, Almy was strung out along the Bear River for 5 miles. This particular "string-town" owed its existence solely to coal mining. Her 4,000 residents suffered more than their share of mining tragedies. On March 4, 1881, the first mine explosion west of the Mississippi to claim lives, killed 38 men in just one of many serious disasters to strike Almy. In January of 1886, 13 more died and on March 20, 1895, the third worst mine explosion in Wyoming history, claimed the lives of 61 men. The State Coal Mine Inspector determined the Almy mines "among the most dangerous in the state". Finally, in 1900 the mines were closed by the Union Pacific due to labor troubles and explosions. Almy lost its principal industry, the population dwindled and the town suffered the fate of many railroad coal towns throughout Wyoming.

LOCATION: On State Route 89, about 1 mile northwest of Evanston, Wyoming.

WASHAKIE COUNTY

LEIGH MONUMENT-1

TITLE: None
LEGEND: In Memory of Gilbert Leigh
       September 14, 1884
       Erected by a Ranchman
LOCATION: At the point of the ridge dividing Leigh Creek and Ten Sleep Creek. Not easily accessible. Inquire locally.

See Leigh Creek Monument Informative Sign (Washakie County #2).

LEIGH CREEK MONUMENT INFORMATIVE SIGN-2

TITLE: Leigh Creek Monument
LEGEND: Across the canyon, on the point, the Leigh Creek Monument topped with the cross was erected in 1889 in memory of an English nobleman who fell 200 feet to his death over the canyon wall, while in pursuit of mountain sheep. The monument was laid up of native stone in dry mortar and is approximately ten feet square at the base. It contains a marble slab facing west with the inscription. Gilbert E. Leigh died October 23rd, 1884.

He was the guest of the Bar X Bar Cattle Company a remittance man, and had spent most of his adult life as a big game hunter.
LOCATION: On the south side of U.S. Hwy 16, about 8.9 miles east of Ten Sleep, Wyoming.

Some information about markers can be misleading. According to *Wyoming: A Guide to Historic Sites*, prepared by the Wyoming Recreation Commission in 1976, the monument's story is slightly different from the informative sign above. From the book:

> On a rock rim high above the base of Ten Sleep Canyon is a massive native stone monument erected in 1885 by Robert Stewart, well-known Sheridan area guide. It is a memorial to Gilbert Leigh, an English nobleman and big game hunter who was killed in a fall from the canyon wall. Although his body was buried in a Stoneleigh, England, churchyard, a year after his death Robert Stewart spent many hours building a monument to Leigh on the canyon rim above the place where the accident occurred. On a marble slab is engraved:
> In Memory of Gilbert Leigh
> September 14, 1884
> Erected by a Ranchman

SHEEPMEN BURIAL SITE-3

TITLE: Historical marker
LEGEND: Burial site of the sheepmen killed in Apr. 1909 during the Spring Creek raid, an incident of the cattlemen sheepmen range war.
    Joe Allemand, Joe Lazier, and Joe Emge.
    Memorial installed by the Jolly Neighbors Club 1961.
LOCATION: Marker is located about 13 miles from Ten Sleep, Wyoming, on private land of the Rome Hill Ranch. Can be reached following State Route 474 and then the Spring Creek Road. Inquire locally.

It is generally agreed that Wyoming ranges were first grazed by cattle. With the introduction of sheep to the free public grazing lands during Wyoming's territorial days, conflict ensued. Cattlemen claimed that sheep ate the grass too short, that their hooves destroyed the roots of the grasses, and that they polluted streams. Confrontations between cattlemen and sheepmen began at the turn of the century, and according to *Wyoming: A Guide to Historic Sites*, "fifteen men and a boy and perhaps ten thousand sheep were killed."

The conflicts continued for years, climaxing in April 1909 with the Spring Creek Raid. Fifteen men attacked a sheep camp on Spring Creek near Ten Sleep, Wyoming, killing two wealthy sheepmen, Joe Allemand and Joe Emge, and one of their herders, Joe Lazier. Seventy-five sheep were also killed. Seven men were arrested in May of that year: George Sabin, M. A.

Alexander, Thomas Dixon, Herbert Brink, Charles Faris, Albert F. Keys, and Ed F. Eaton. Two of the men plea bargained, and the five others received penitentiary sentences varying from three years to life. Leadership by the Wyoming Wool Growers Association and public sentiment against the conflict deterred further raids and murdering of sheepmen and herders.
See Spring Creek Raid Monument (Washakie County #7).

"DAD" WORLAND MONUMENT-5

TITLE: None
LEGEND: To all pioneers and in memory of C. H. "Dad" Worland for whom the town was named. He erected the stage station on the old Bridger Trail about 100 yards north of here. That spot was the original town site established in 1904. The town moved across the river in 1906.
Erected by the Historical Landmark Commission of Wyoming 1954
LOCATION: On the northwest side of U.S. Hwy 16, about 0.5 miles west of the bridge over the Big Horn River.

Charles H. Worland, an early pioneer of the southern Big Horn Basin, best known as a sheepman, established the first townsite of Worland on the western side of the Big Horn River. In 1906 and 1907 when the Chicago, Burlington & Quincy Railroad built its line from Frannie, Wyoming, to Worland, the tracks were laid on the opposite side of the river from Worland. During that winter when the river was frozen, the early settlers moved across to the east side of the river, to be near the railroad.

W. A. RICHARDS MONUMENT-6

TITLE: W. A. Richards.
LEGEND: In memory of W. A. Richards first man to attempt to divert water from the Big Horn river to be used for irrigation. 1884
    Sponsored by South Flat Women's Club.
    Erected by Paul Frison 1969.
LOCATION: South of Worland, Wyoming, about 0.2 miles south of the bridge over No Water Creek. The marker is on private land west of State Route 432.

William A. Richards was a leader in reclaiming land for farming in the Big Horn Basin. In 1895 he told the legislature of "this vast wealth of land and water lying idle, side by side, awaiting only the magic touch of labor and capital, intelligently combined, to be coined into wealth."

Richards was Wyoming's governor from 1895 to 1899. He served as Assistant Commissioner of the General Land Office from 1899 to 1903 and as Commissioner from 1903 to 1907.

SPRING CREEK RAID MONUMENT-7

Informative sign
TITLE: Spring Creek Raid
    April 2nd, 1909
LEGEND: Cattlemen of the Big Horn Basin dominated the range for many years and set up boundaries or "deadlines" where sheep were forbidden. Fierce animosity grew between the opposing sheep and cattle ranchers as several sheep camps were raided during the late 1800s and early 1900s.

In late March, 1909, Joe Allemand, a Basque sheepman, and Joe Emge, a cattleman turned sheepman, left Worland headed for Spring Creek with 5000 head of sheep. They were accompanied by Allemand's nephew, Jules Lazier, and two sheepherders, Bounce Helmer and Pete Cafferall. Talk spread like wildfire across the western slope of the Big Horn Mountains as the deadline was crossed and plans were soon made to head off this intrusion.

On the moonlit night of April 2, 1909, seven masked riders approached the sheep camp's two wagons where the herders slept. Gunfire lit the night as rifles blazed. Emge and Lazier were killed in their wagon and both wagons were set afire. Allemand emerged from the flames, but was quickly shot down.

WASHAKIE COUNTY

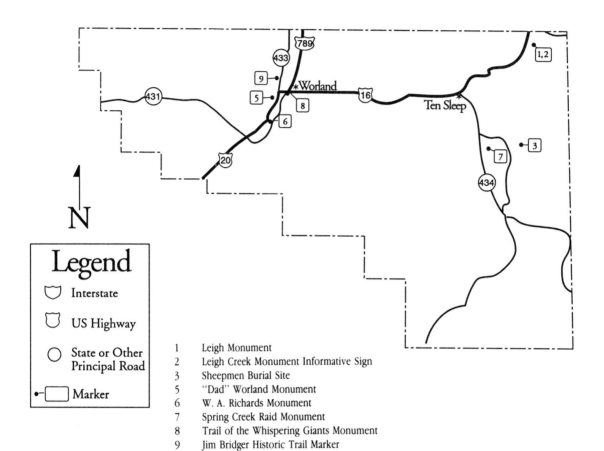

N

Legend

⬡ Interstate

⬡ US Highway

◯ State or Other
    Principal Road

•⬭ Marker

1   Leigh Monument
2   Leigh Creek Monument Informative Sign
3   Sheepmen Burial Site
5   "Dad" Worland Monument
6   W. A. Richards Monument
7   Spring Creek Raid Monument
8   Trail of the Whispering Giants Monument
9   Jim Bridger Historic Trail Marker

1. In about 1960, the Leigh Creek Monument was erected in Tensleep Canyon by the Wyoming State Archives and Historical Department, the Wyoming State Historical Society, and the Washakie County Historical Society.

2. Three sheepmen killed at the end of the cattlemen-sheepmen range wars in 1909 were memorialized by this stone marker placed on the Rome Hill Ranch.

The monument on this side of the road is situated at the site of the south wagon. The monument on the north side of Spring Creek is near the location of the wagon where the sheepmen were killed. Five of the perpetrators were convicted and sent to prison. Public reaction against this brutal and tragic act left no doubt that violence on Wyoming's open range would no longer be tolerated.

South site
TITLE: None
LEGEND: Site of south wagon where Bounce Helmer and Pete Cafferall were captured by masked raiders and their wagons burned on the night of April 2nd 1909.

North site
TITLE: Not available
LEGEND: Not available

LOCATION: On the east side of State Route 434, about 6.5 miles south of Ten Sleep, Wyoming.

Clay Gibbons of Worland, Wyoming, became keenly aware of the Spring Creek Raid after seeing a painting by Larry Edgar entitled "Night Riders of the Nowood." Gibbons was the force behind the research and the development of this monument, dedicated eighty years after the raid. Over 900 people attended the ceremonies April 2, 1989.

TRAIL OF THE WHISPERING GIANTS MONUMENT-8

TITLE: None
LEGEND: To the American Indian
        One monument in each state
        Peter Toth Sculptor
        September 28, 1980
LOCATION: Southwest corner of the Washakie County Courthouse lawn in Worland, Wyoming.

JIM BRIDGER HISTORIC TRAIL MARKER-9

TITLE: Jim Bridger Historic Trail
LEGEND: In 1864 an alternate route to the goldfields of western Montana was needed due to frequent hostile actions along the Bozeman Trail. Though the Civil War raged on, the Nation continued its westward expansion through the efforts of men like Jim Bridger. A trapper, explorer, trader, hunter, scout and guide, Jim Bridger led

miners north from the area we now call Fort Caspar. From there the trail led northwesterly through the southern Big Horn Mountains, across the Big Horn Basin, crossing the Shoshone River, into Montana through what was known as Pryor Gap, and finally rejoining the Bozeman Trail. The Bridger Trail reduced the threat of hostile actions against emigrants heading north and proved an important route in the settlement of the Northwest.

The Bridger Trail crossed the Big Horn River approximately 12 miles southwest of here, near where the community of Neiber stands today. The original Bridger Trail passed very close to this location as it paralleled the Big Horn River on its way north.

This commemorative site was developed jointly by the Wyoming Highway Department, the Wyoming Centennial Wagon Train, Inc. and the Department of the Interior Bureau of Land Management, for your use and enjoyment.
LOCATION: On State Route 433 about 2.5 miles north of Worland, Wyoming.

WESTON COUNTY

CAMBRIA MINING CAMP SIGN-1

TITLE: Cambria mining camp.

LEGEND: About 5 miles west is the site of the once picturesque Cambria Mining Camp—now a vacant ghostly place. In 1887 Frank Mondell, sent by the construction firm, Kilpatrick Brothers and Collins, discovered coal at Cambria. This was the first coal found along a proposed rail route suitable for use in the locomotives of the day.

It made possible the extension of the Burlington through previously isolated northeastern Wyoming, and the founding of Newcastle in 1889.

Cambria was a prideful community of three churches and nary a saloon. Fifteen hundred people of 23 nationalities lived harmoniously there; 13,000,000 tons of coal were mined before seams played out in 1928.

Reminiscing old-timers sigh, "there was never a place like it".

LOCATION: On the west side of U.S. Hwy 85, about 5.3 miles north of the intersection of U.S. Hwys 16 and 85 in Newcastle, Wyoming.

CAMP JENNEY STOCKADE—OREGON TRAIL MARKER-2

TITLE: Tributary to Oregon Trail

LEGEND: None

LOCATION: Adjacent to Camp Jenney Stockade cabin and across the street from the National Guard Armory in Newcastle, Wyoming.

The Twentieth Century Club, a women's club in Newcastle, initiated the idea of preserving the Jenney Stockade cabin in 1929. Faced with demolition at its original location on the LAK ranch east of Newcastle, the structure was dismantled piece by piece, the logs were "numbered and carefully laid in their original position on a new location on the Weston County Library block." In 1982 when additions were planned to the library, the Twentieth Century Club "again spearheaded a drive to save the building." The cabin was relocated to the Anna Miller Museum complex adjacent to the Greenwood Cemetery and across the street from the National Guard Armory.

During the Covered-Wagon Centennial in 1930, many Oregon Trail Memorial plaques were placed by the Oregon Trail Memorial Association. This specific marker was the only one in Wyoming that was placed off the Oregon Trail. No record of its dedication or placement could be found.

CAMP JENNEY INFORMATIVE SIGN-3.1

TITLE: Camp Jenney

LEGEND: Campsite of the first authorized military expedition into the Black Hills. On September 12, 1857 Lt. G. K. Warren of the U.S. Topographical Engineers and his party, camped here and erected a log corral, 17 years before the famous Custer Expedition. On June 3, 1875 the expedition headed by Prof. Walter P. Jenney, under military escort commanded by Col. R. I. Dodge of Ft. Laramie, camped on the location of Lt. Warren's camp and corral. A stockade was erected and became known as Camp Jenney. The stockade was a stopover for gold seekers during the winter 75-76 and later became a stage station. The Stockade is now located by the Anna Miller Museum.

LOCATION: On the south side of U.S. Hwy 16, about 4 miles east of Newcastle, Wyoming. Adjacent to Jenney Stockade Monument (Weston County #3.2).

JENNEY STOCKADE MONUMENT-3.2

TITLE: The Jenney Stockade

LEGEND: One-half mile east of this spot was a supply depot for Army units convoying the Professor W. P. Jenney Party, which, in 1875,

surveyed mineral and other resources of the Black Hills for the United States. In 1876 it was a station of the Cheyenne-Deadwood Stage Line.

Dedicated by the Historical Landmark Commission of Wyoming, August 31, 1940

LOCATION: South side of U.S. Hwy 16, about 4 miles east of Newcastle, Wyoming. Adjacent to Camp Jenney Informative Sign (Weston County #3.1).

CANYON SPRINGS STAGE STATION SIGN-4

TITLE: Canyon Springs Stage Station

LEGEND: The scene of the only successful raid on a Deadwood treasure coach. On September 26, 1878, the treasure coach, carrying between 20,000 and 140,000—reports vary—was held up at this place. Hugh Cambell, a passenger, was killed and the driver, Gale Hill, was badly wounded. Scott Davis, the shotgun messenger, killed one of the outlaws and fatally wounded another, the others escaped.

Part of the treasure was recovered. Legend has it that some of the gold was buried near here. The little log station was torn down a few years ago.

Wyoming Recreation Commission

LOCATION: On the east side of U.S. Hwy 85 at Four Corners, Wyoming. Adjacent to Blue Star Memorial Highway Sign (Weston County #4.1).

The site of this robbery was along the Cheyenne-Deadwood Stage Route on upper Beaver Creek, about three miles east of Four Corners, Wyoming. Canyon Springs was about thirty-seven miles south of Deadwood, South Dakota, and twenty miles north of Jenney Stockade near present day Newcastle. It was a stage route relay station, but is best remembered as the site of the daring stage coach robbery.

BLUE STAR MEMORIAL HIGHWAY SIGN-4.1

TITLE: Blue Star Memorial Highway

LEGEND: A tribute to the Armed Forces that have defended the United States of America.

Sponsored by Wyoming Federation of Garden Clubs in cooperation with State Highway Department

LOCATION: On the east side of U.S. Hwy 85 at Four Corners, Wyoming. Adjacent to Canyon Springs Stage Station Sign (Weston County #4).

CHEYENNE-DEADWOOD TRAIL SIGN-5

TITLE: Cheyenne-Deadwood Trail and Beaver Creek Station

LEGEND: The Cheyenne-Deadwood Trail, a heritage precious to state and nation, was used by gold seekers and Black Hills emigrants from 1876 to 1887. Crossing U.S. Highway 16 at this point, it followed Stockade Beaver Creek, passing Beaver Creek Stage Station and winding on to Deadwood via Canyon Springs Stage Station near present Camp Mallo. From the Beaver Creek Stage Station, 13 miles north of here, searchers hunted for the treasure coach robbed at Canyon Springs in 1878. This robbery was the only successful raid on a Black Hills treasure coach.

Between Beaver Creek and Canyon Springs Station, in a deep canyon, lies the grave of an old buffalo hunter. The head stone reads "Hank Mason killed by a bear 1893."

LOCATION: North side of U.S. Hwy 16, about 4.8 miles east of Newcastle, Wyoming.

SITE OF FIELD CITY SIGN-6

TITLE: Site of Field City

LEGEND: The deserted site of Field City or Tubb Town offers silent

WESTON COUNTY

N

Legend

⬡ Interstate

⬡ US Highway

◯ State or Other
Principal Road

•─▢ Marker

1   Cambria Mining Camp Sign
2   Camp Jenney Stockade—Oregon Trail Marker
3.1 Camp Jenney Informative Sign
3.2 Jenney Stockade Monument
4   Canyon Springs Stage Station Sign
4.1 Blue Star Memorial Highway Sign
5   Cheyenne-Deadwood Trail Sign
6   Site of Field City Sign
7   Hanging of Diamond Slim Sign
8   Christ Church Sign
9   Flying V Cambria Inn

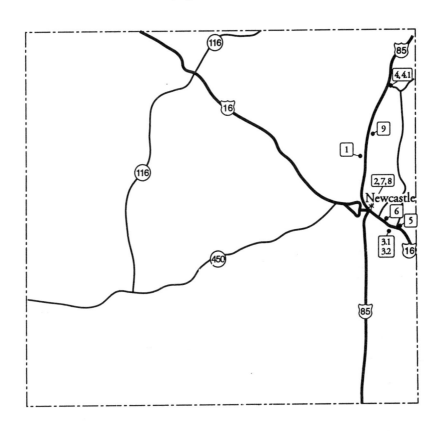

1.

2.

3.

1. This cast aluminum sign marks the site of Field City.

2. In 1940, the Historical Landmark Commission of Wyoming dedicated a bronze marker at the Jenney Stockade Site, and in the early 1960s the Wyoming State Archives and Historical Department erected the informative sign.

3. Directional markers such as this one near the Jenney Stockade Site aid travelers in locating markers along Wyoming highways.

testimony to the boom and bust fate of many western towns.

In the spring of 1889 Deloss Tubbs, a businessman from Custer, Dakota Territory, laid out Field City around his store on the east bank of Salt Creek. Tubbs, together with saloon keeper F. R. Curran, foresaw the economic advantages of locating a townsite along the anticipated route of the Burlington and Missouri River Railroad. Idled at Alliance, Nebraska, for want of suitable locomotive coal to continue its northwest course, the B & M sought a connection with the transcontinental Northern Pacific at Billings, Montana. Recently discovered coal deposits at Cambria, nine miles northwest of Tubb Town, made the railroad extension possible.

Within a few months Tubb Town could boast of a milk ranch, newspaper and Chinese laundry. However, the town's saloons, dance halls, and sporting houses fostered a "hell raising" notoriety. The first ordinance passed by the new residents reportedly stated that "no one shall pass through without paying sufficient toll to set 'em up to the bunch."

The eagerly awaited connection with the Burlington and Missouri upon which Tubb Town staked its future failed to materialize. Land price disagreements resulted in a reroute two miles west. In November, 1889, the railway reached the fledgling community of Newcastle.

Residents of Tubb Town, accepting the inevitable, packed up their businesses and belongings and moved en masse to Newcastle. Thus, Field City died unceremoniously in the year of its birth, leaving only memories and occasional symptoms of "Tubb Town hangover" to

perplex Newcastle citizens.

LOCATION: North side of U.S. Hwy 16, about 3 miles east of Newcastle, Wyoming.

Elizabeth Thorpe Griffith recorded the history of Field City in a section of the book entitled *And Then There Was One*. Cambria, Field City, and Newcastle grew up in response to the forthcoming railroad to northeastern Wyoming. The book tells the interesting histories of each of the communities.

HANGING OF DIAMOND SLIM SIGN-7

TITLE: The Hanging of Diamond L. Slim Clifton

LEGEND: Beyond this sign, this side of the bridge on the main track, there was once a bridge on the spur that ran up the canyon to the Cambria Mining Camp. In imagination you might see the ghost of "Diamond L. Slim" Clifton hanging from this phantom bridge.

Slim was hung in 1903 for the murder of a young couple, Louella and John Church, Slim's neighbors and friends. People throughout northeastern Wyoming, angered by the grisly deed, stormed the jail, took the prisoner from Sheriff Billy Miller at gunpoint and dragged Slim to the bridge. Masked men slipped the noose around Slim's neck and dropped him from the bridge, neatly decapitating him. Such was vigilante justice.

LOCATION: North side of Main Street just east of the railroad tracks in Newcastle, Wyoming.

CHRIST CHURCH SIGN-8

TITLE: None
LEGEND: Oldest Church in Weston County
LOCATION: Corner of Wentworth and Seneca Streets in Newcastle, Wyoming.

Construction of Christ Church Episcopal was started in 1889 and finished in 1890. The cornerstone was laid on October 11, 1890. According to *The Newcastle News,* one of three local newspapers at the time:

> The name of any person found in the pages of this week's News will "go thundering down the ages." As a copy of this week's issue will be kindly deposited under the corner stone of the new Episcopal church to be laid on Saturday, October 11th, by Rev. J. E. Sulger. It will be read some where in the great future, between the two eternal peaks.

> The establishment of the Episcopal church here is due to M. T. Glover of Washington, whose interests were enlisted last winter by some remarks of Bishop Talbot, in relation to the growth and thrift of our city. He manifested his interest by offering to donate $500 toward the erection of a church, and this was the nucleus from which will be built one of the handsomest churches in the northwestern country. The citizens of Newcastle responding to the appeal of Bishop Talbot, have shown their generosity in a most marked manner, illustrative of the largeness of heart, which is the badge of western people. Rev. Mr. Sulger has been most cordially received wherever he presented the subscription list, and the townspeople have given most liberally with the result that the church is now under process of construction, the foundation walls being almost completed. The church will be erected on two lots beautifully situated on the rising ground of Summit street, generously donated by the Lincoln Land company.

> The contract for a $1,500 church was originally let to Mr. Miller, but owing to a recent visit of Capt. R. O. Philips, and in conversation with Rev. Mr. Sulger, means were taken to erect a larger and handsomer church, which will cost somewhere about $2,500. This is due entirely to the kindness of Capt. Philips and the Lincoln Land Company.

> The Bishop visited Newcastle on July 15th, and having secured the support of the people he sent Rev. Mr. Sulger here who arrived on July 27th, and who has since been successfully pushing the subscription list.

> The Episcopal services are now held in the masonic hall and are well attended. The corner stone of the new edifice will be laid Saturday, Oct. 11, 1890.

The History of CHRIST CHURCH (Episcopal) written by Dorothy J. Johnson, Barbara Johnson, and Mary Capps in 1976 detailed the beginnings and growth of the church. The original cornerstone was re-dedicated on October 7, 1990, and a new time capsule was dedicated for the next one hundred years.

FLYING V CAMBRIA INN-9

TITLE: Cambria Flying V Casino
LEGEND: The National Register of Historic Places—Wyoming Place No. 149.
LOCATION: On the east side of U.S. Hwy 85, about 8 miles north of Newcastle, Wyoming.

The town of Cambria, Wyoming, was founded in 1888 when coal was discovered in the deep canyon north of present-day Newcastle, Wyoming. The coal seams played out in 1928, and the people slowly moved out of the canyon. Before the mines closed, Ellwood Rabenold and other owners of the Cambria Fuel Company built a memorial building and recreation park in the Salt Creek Valley. Miners contributed hours of labor in building the two-story sandstone building. The beams used were timbers from the mines, and bricks above the windows were from the coke ovens. Stained glass windows were donated by Cambria residents, and a museum once housed memorabilia from the town. Adequate funds were never available to maintain Cambria Park Memorial and Museum, and the structure passed into private ownership.

Photograph Credits

All photos by Richard Collier, State Historic Preservation Office, except those identified below:

Page 2　　1. Ezra Meeker Historical Society
　　　　　2. Frances Seely Webb Collection, Casper College Library
　　　　　3. Ezra Meeker Historical Society

Page 3　　1. Irene Weppner Collection
　　　　　2. Mike Jording

Page 5　　*Covered-Wagon Centennial and Ox-team Days,* Oregon Trail Memorial Edition published for Oregon Trail Memorial Association

Page 6　　1. Wyoming State Archives, Museums, and Historical Department
　　　　　2. Wyoming State Archives
　　　　　3. Wyoming State Archives

Page 8　　1. *Marking the Oregon Trail, The Bozeman Road and Historic Places in Wyoming, 1908-1920*
　　　　　2. Wyoming State Archives
　　　　　3. Wyoming State Archives
　　　　　4. Wyoming State Archives

Page 9　　1. Jim Snyder, *The Lingle Guide/Guernsey Gazette*
　　　　　2. Wyoming State Archives

Page 10　 1. National Park Service, Fort Laramie National Historic Site
　　　　　2. Wyoming State Archives
　　　　　3. Wyoming State Archives

Page 14　 1. Wyoming State Archives
　　　　　2. *First Biennial Report of the Historical Landmark Commission of Wyoming, 1927-1928*
　　　　　3. Wyoming State Archives
　　　　　4. National Park Service, Grand Teton National Park

Page 16　 1. Wyoming State Archives
　　　　　2. Irene Weppner Collection
　　　　　3. Wyoming State Archives
　　　　　4. Wyoming State Archives
　　　　　5. Irene Weppner Collection

Page 19　 1. Wyoming State Archives
　　　　　2. Wyoming State Archives
　　　　　3. Irene Weppner Collection

Page 20　 Wyoming State Archives

Page 22　 All photos from Wyoming State Archives

Page 25　 1. Wyoming State Archives
　　　　　2. Mark Junge, SHPO
　　　　　3. Mark Junge, SHPO

Page 28　 2. Mike Jording
　　　　　3. Dan Dockstader, *Star Valley Independent*
　　　　　4. Dan Davis, Davis Photography

Page 30　 All photos from Wyoming State Archives

Page 202　2. David Miles, Newcastle
　　　　　3. David Miles, Newcastlc